The Canadian Writer's Workplace

The Canadian Writer's Workplace

THIRD EDITION

John Roberts | **John Scarry** | **Sandra Scarry**

HARCOURT
BRACE
CANADA

Harcourt Brace & Company, Canada

Toronto Montreal Fort Worth New York Orlando
Philadelphia San Diego London Sydney Tokyo

Requests for permission to make copies of any part of the work should be mailed to: Permissions, College Division, Harcourt Brace & Company, Canada, 55 Horner Avenue, Toronto, Ontario M8Z 4X6.

Every reasonable effort has been made to acquire permission for copyright material used in this text, and to acknowledge all such indebtedness accurately. Any errors and omissions called to the publisher's attention will be corrected in future printings.

Canadian Cataloguing in Publication Data

Roberts, John A., 1944–
    The Canadian writer's workplace

3rd ed.
Includes index.
ISBN 0-7747-3564-3

1. English language — Rhetoric.   2. English language — Rhetoric — Problems, exercises, etc.   3. English language — Grammar — Problems, exercises, etc.   I. Scarry, John. II. Scarry, Sandra, 1946–   .   III. Title

PE1413.R62 1997   808'.042   C97-93045908

Acquisitions Editor: Kelly V. Cochrane
Developmental Editor: Su Mei Ku
Editorial Co-ordinator: Jeannine Maxfield
Production Editor: Laurel Parsons/Stacey Roderick
Production Co-ordinator: Sheila Barry

Copy Editor: Margaret Allen
Cover and Interior Design: Kevin Connolly
Typesetting and Assembly: Bookman Typesetting Co.
Printing and Binding: Webcom Limited

Cover Art: Reprinted by permission of Pierre-Paul Pariseau.
This book was printed in Canada.

2 3 4 5   02 01 00 99

Preface

The Canadian Writer's Workplace, Third Edition, is a complete program of grammar and writing activities for students who need to build their writing skills in order to produce college-level work. This book gives the student the ability to write with control, a crucial skill that is needed not only in English courses, but also in virtually every other course taken in college. *The Canadian Writer's Workplace* can help students get the most out of any college course that calls for the ability to write clearly and effectively.

Many of the important features that were successful for students and teachers who worked with the first two editions of the book have been retained in this third edition.

Completeness

The book begins with a detailed study of sentences, then helps students practise solid paragraph development, and finally shows them how to develop the complete college essay. At each step along the way, numerous practice exercises and writing assignments reinforce what is being learned. The Appendices are largely concerned with word usage, but also contain a section on proofreading and revising. The readings section is new to this edition.

The approach taken in *The Canadian Writer's Workplace* is unusual in that grammar and writing skills are taught in detail within the covers of a single book. When you use *The Canadian Writer's Workplace*, there is no need to look for a supplemental book containing grammar work or a book to teach writing skills; everything you need for teaching grammar skills and writing development is contained in the book you are now holding. You will be pleased to find that the grammar work of the book has been especially selected with one major goal in mind: to meet the needs of the college writer who must understand how sentence parts work together. The thrust of the grammar throughout this book is intended to help the student writer feel comfortable using a variety of sentence structures when composing paragraphs and essays.

Flexibility

The format of *The Canadian Writer's Workplace* allows an instructor to work on different exercises with an entire class, or allows individual students to work with a tutor in a lab, or a group of students to work by themselves. The answers to many of the exercises and practices appear in the Answer Key at the end of the book; the remaining answers are to be found in the Instructor's Manual. As a result, students can do many of the exercises on their own, checking their answers as they work. The book is also flexible in that certain sections can be skipped if the material is not needed for a particular class — or a class might begin with a later section, with the earlier chapters being used as a review.

Part II, "Mastering the Paragraph," can be a useful point of departure for a writing class. An instructor can work backward from this point to concentrate on the sentence if the needs of a class lie in that direction, or can move ahead to Part III if the students' abilities are stronger.

Stimulating Content

The exercises in the book present material that deals with current events or subjects that are of contemporary interest. Not only are many of the exercises based on material from such fields as history or science, but the model paragraphs and essays in Parts II and III are taken from a wide range of novels, essays, short stories, and books of non-fiction, many of them by world-famous authors. *The Canadian Writer's Workplace* contains a number of unique features that will afford the college student in Canada an insight into various aspects of Canadian culture. In addition to works by internationally known authors, this book features excerpts from short stories, essays, and novels by Canadian authors. The readings section includes fiction and non-fiction selections by Canadian authors. *The Canadian Writer's Workplace* is intended to be, then, more than a writing and composition book — it is a tool to explore Canadian culture as well.

Additional Features

An instructor's manual is available for use with this book. It contains answers to at least one exercise from each group of exercises so that instructors can use these exercises for testing, if desired. The manual also contains hints for teaching students of writing skills (including techniques for the use of groups in the classroom), and specific suggestions for activities that can be used with the material in the book.

The Canadian Writer's Workplace is a flexible tool, one that works *for* the instructor and *with* the student. It strengthens grammar skills and places special emphasis on strong paragraph writing, which is the basic building block of the complete essay. It also enables the student to understand and construct a complete college essay, often the goal of the English instructor at this level. The student who carefully uses this book and works consistently with his or her instructor throughout the semester should be able to look forward with confidence to success in college writing.

New to the Third Edition

The students and instructors who have used the first two editions of *The Canadian Writer's Workplace* have appreciated the features found in the major parts of the book. They have also appreciated the in-depth treatment of grammar skills and the step-by-step approach to the writing process offered in the book. The results have been a well-balanced program of integrated grammar and writing skills, a program that addresses the real classroom needs of both the instructor and the student. Among the additional features new to the third edition are the following:

- Each chapter in Part I begins with a "Quick Quiz," designed to assess students' skills in the material in that chapter. Based on the results of this quiz, the instructor can choose either to skip over the material in the chapter, or to spend extra time on the material in question if the students' skills are shown to be weak.

- A valuable new feature, "Working Together," can be found at the end of every chapter in the book. "Working Together" gives the student an additional opportunity to confirm the work that has just been finished. Each "Working Together" section enables the class to break into groups, an approach that provides opportunities for the peer editing and peer review that many teachers use to enhance their classes today. "Working Together" is a versatile resource for the instructor who uses *The Canadian Writer's Workplace*, extending the work of the book into different classroom activities. Each activity is related to the work that the class has just completed.

- An entire chapter is devoted to cause and effect (Chapter 17) — a section that is valuable not only for the writing instruction it contains, but also for the critical thinking skills that it teaches.

- New work on pronouns and case is found in Chapter 6, "Making Sentence Parts Work Together." Chapter 6 has, in fact, been significantly rewritten from earlier editions to make definitions clearer and to eliminate redundancies.

- New concepts are introduced with a clear definition and practice exercises in each chapter.

- Examples, model paragraphs, and exercises have been updated to make them more relevant to today's students.

- Chapters on definition and classification in earlier editions have been combined into one chapter (Chapter 16).

- A selection of ten readings has been added to the end of the book. Each reading is followed by five questions, which call upon students to apply skills taught in the book. In keeping with the practical approach used in the book, this section provides opportunities for students to relate their learning to published models. The readings contain a selection of non-fiction and fiction, and include all of the major genres (description, narration, etc.) studied in *The Canadian Writer's Workplace*.

- The book has been redesigned, making it easier to read through the use of a clearer format, removal of unnecessary exercises, and more judicious use of space.
- Most exercises in the appendices have been eliminated.
- Correction symbols on the inside front cover have been simplified.
- An easy-to-use "Combining Clauses" chart has been included on the inside front cover.
- A chart of transitional words and phrases has been added to the inside back cover.
- The length of the book has been reduced considerably from that of previous editions. We have eliminated unnecessary exercises, combined material in chapters, removed unnecessary model paragraphs, and thoroughly edited material from previous editions.

Acknowledgements

For their significant contribution to the development of this edition, we express our deep gratitude to: Sheree Bloxham (Seneca College), Nicholas Collins (Capilano College), Barbara Danbrook (Humber College), Robert Einarsson (Grant MacEwan College), Enid Gossin (Seneca College), Bettie Holmes (Seneca College), Crystal Hurdle (Capilano College), Don Lake (Cambrian College), Joan Pilz (Humber College), Ann Rostrup (Seneca College), Nadya Schultz (Cambrian College), Josef Stavroff (Seneca College), Jim Streeter (Seneca College), Mariann Sturdy (College of New Caledonia), Karen Thomson (Douglas College), and Lian Zhang (Capilano College).

Finally, a big thank you to the team at Harcourt Brace: Kelly Cochrane, Su Mei Ku, Jeannine Maxfield, and Laurel Parsons. Their hard work and dedication have made this edition possible.

A Note from the Publisher

Thank you for selecting *The Canadian Writer's Workplace*, Third Edition, by John Roberts, John Scarry, and Sandra Scarry. The authors and publisher have devoted considerable time to the careful development of this book. We appreciate your recognition of this effort and accomplishment.

We want to hear what you think about *The Canadian Writer's Workplace*. Please take a few minutes to fill in the stamped reply card at the back of the book. Your comments and suggestions will be valuable to us as we prepare new editions and other books.

Brief Contents

PART III   Structuring the College Essay

PART IV   Readings

PART V   Appendices

Contents

PART II   Mastering the Paragraph

PART III   Structuring the College Essay

PART IV   Readings

P A R T   V   Appendices

PART I

Developing the Complete Sentence

Chapter 1
Finding Subjects and Verbs in Simple Sentences

QUICK QUIZ Test yourself on your knowledge of subjects and verbs. In each of the following sentences, find the subject and verb. Write your answers in the spaces provided. The answers to the questions follow the quiz.

Subject	Verb
COUPLES	END
MARRIAGE	IS
STUDIES	HAVE BEEN DONE
MARRIAGES	ATTENTION
POSITIVE ATTITUDE	TOWARD

1. Nearly 65 000 couples end their marriages every year in Canada.
2. In this country, the average length of a marriage is just over twelve years.
3. Many studies have been done on the reasons for the break-up of marriages.
4. There has not been so much attention given to successful marriages.
5. A positive attitude toward the partner appears to be the most important quality in a successful marriage.

Answers:
1. Subject: couples, Verb: end
2. Subject: length, Verb: is
3. Subject: studies, Verb: have been done
4. Subject: attention, Verb: has been given
5. Subject: attitude, Verb: appears

Why Should We Use Complete Sentences When We Write?

If you walk up to a friend at noon and say, "Lunch?" you are expressing an idea by using a shortened form of a complete thought: you are asking your friend to join you for lunch. Even though we do not always use complete sentences in daily conversation, we usually have complete thoughts in mind. We say and hear words and phrases such as "Lunch?" every day, and these words and phrases seem to be complete thoughts because both the speaker and the listener supply the missing words in their own minds. When your friend hears you say, "Lunch?" he or she is able to quickly understand the meaning: "Would you like to join me for lunch?"

You are free to use language in this way when you speak, but you must use a different approach in more formal speaking and writing situations. In writing down your thoughts, you cannot assume that another person will finish your thoughts for you. Each of your written thoughts must be a complete expression of what is in your mind.

The purpose of writing is to communicate something of value to a reader. Once you understand how the parts of a complete sentence work, you will be able to focus as much attention on *what* you are saying as you devote to *how* you are saying it. Once you understand how the parts of a complete sentence work, you can take control of the sentence. You will have the power to make words work for you.

What Is a Complete Sentence?

Def A **complete sentence** must contain a subject and a verb, as well as express a complete thought.

How Do You Find the Subject of a Sentence?

The subject of a sentence is the person or thing about which the rest of the sentence makes an assertion. Any sentence must be about someone or something, and therefore every sentence must have a subject. To find the subject of any sentence, ask yourself this question: Who or what is the sentence about? When you have answered this question, you have found the subject of the sentence.

 PRACTICE Examine each of the following sentences and ask yourself who or what each sentence is about. Draw a line under the subject in each sentence.

1. The happy child played.
2. The young Nikki Turner played.
3. She played.
4. The park grew chilly.
5. The leaves stirred.
6. A thought suddenly struck her.
7. Her mother and father would be waiting.

Since the subject of a sentence is made up of either one or more nouns (or a word, phrase, or clause that functions like a noun), learning some of the different terms used in traditional grammar to describe these different nouns is helpful.

1. The happy child played.

The sentence is about the *child*. In this case, the subject is a common noun.

> **Def**
>
> **Nouns** name persons, places, and things. Most nouns are common nouns. **Common nouns** are the general names for all the persons, places, and objects around us. They are not capitalized.
>
> *Examples:* man, province, cereal

2. The young Nikki Turner played.

The sentence is about *Nikki Turner*. In this case, the subject *Nikki Turner* is made up of two proper nouns.

> **Def**
>
> **Proper nouns** name particular persons, places, or things. They are always capitalized.
>
> *Examples:* Claudio, Saskatchewan, Shredded Wheat

Notice that words like *young* and *happy* can be put in front of nouns to describe them further. These words are called **adjectives**. *The* along with *a* and *an* are called **articles**.

3. She played.

The sentence is about *she*.

> **Def**
>
> Words that can be used in the places of nouns such as *she*, *he*, *it*, *we*, *I*, *you*, and *they* are called **pronouns**.

4. The park grew chilly.

The sentence is about the *park*, a common noun. Can you replace this noun first with a proper noun and then with a pronoun?

_____ALBERTA_____ grew chilly.

_____SHE_____ grew chilly.

5. The leaves stirred.

The sentence is about *leaves*. Here the common noun is not about a person or place but a thing. What pronoun could take the place of *leaves*?

_____WE_____ stirred.

6. A thought suddenly struck her.

The sentence is about a *thought*.

You cannot see or touch a thought, but it is a noun. Nouns we cannot see or touch are called **abstract nouns**. These abstract nouns can be concepts such as *justice* or *love*, or qualities such as *goodness* or *honesty*. The opposite of an abstract noun is a concrete noun. **Concrete nouns** can be seen and touched. Nouns like *child*, *leaves*, or *park* are examples of concrete nouns.

7. Her mother and father would be waiting.

The sentence is about *mother and father*. The subject is made up of two nouns joined by *and*.

> A **compound subject** is made up of two or more nouns joined together by *and*, *or*, *either/or*, or *neither/nor*.

Not *every* noun or pronoun functions as a subject. Nouns and pronouns can also function as **objects**. Can you find a noun in the following sentence that is not the subject of the sentence?

Nikki drank the water.

Guide to Finding the Subject of a Sentence

Definition: The subject of a sentence is who or what the sentence is about.
How to find the subject: Ask yourself, "Who or what is this sentence about?"

- Subjects usually come early in the sentence.
- Subjects can be modified by adjectives.
- Subjects can be compound.

Look for these two kinds of words as your subjects:

1. **Nouns:** the names of persons, places, or things

Common	or	Proper	Concrete	or	Abstract
aunt		Aunt Mary	face		loneliness
country		Nigeria	people		patriotism
watch		Timex	jewellery		time

2. **Pronouns:** take the place of nouns

Personal	Indefinite	Relative	Demonstrative
I	one	who	this
you	each	that	that
he, she, it	some, someone, somebody, something	what	these
we	any, anyone, anybody, anything	which	those
they	nobody, nothing		
	everyone, everybody, everything		
	all		
	many		
	several		

E X E R C I S E 1   Finding the Subject of a Sentence

Underline the subject in each of the following sentences. An example is done for you.

The <u>loudspeaker</u> blared.

1. The <u>train</u> stopped.
2. <u>Steven Laye</u> had arrived!
3. <u>He</u> was afraid.
4. <u>Everything</u> looked so strange.
5. The fearful <u>man</u> held his bag tightly.
6. The <u>tunnel</u> led up to the street.
7. <u>Buses</u> and <u>cars</u> choked the avenues.

E X E R C I S E 2   Finding the Subject of a Sentence

Underline the subject in each of the following sentences.

1. The <u>road</u> twisted and turned.
2. A young <u>boy</u> hurried along briskly.
3. <u>He</u> carried an important message.
4. A red-winged <u>blackbird</u> flew overhead.
5. Dark <u>clouds</u> and a sudden <u>wind</u> encouraged him to hurry faster.
6. His <u>family</u> would be elated.
7. <u>Someone</u> was working in the yard.

How Do You Find the Subject in Sentences with Prepositional Phrases?

The sentences you worked with in Exercises 1 and 2 were short and basic. If we wrote only such sentences, our writing would sound choppy. Complex ideas would be difficult to express. One way to expand the simple sentence is to add prepositional phrases.

Example: He put his suitcase on the seat.

On is a preposition. *Seat* is a noun used as the object of the preposition. *On the seat* is the prepositional phrase.

A **prepositional phrase** is a group of words containing a preposition and an object of the preposition with its modifiers. Prepositional phrases contain nouns, but these nouns are *never* the subject of the sentence.

In sentences with prepositional phrases, the subject may be difficult to spot. Consider the following sentence:

In the young man's apartment, books covered the walls.

In the sentence above, what is the prepositional phrase? Who or what is the sentence about?

To avoid making the mistake of thinking that a noun in the prepositional phrase could be the subject, it is a good practice to cross out the prepositional phrase.

~~In the young man's apartment,~~ books covered the walls.

With the prepositional phrase crossed out, it now becomes clear that the subject of the sentence is the noun *books*.

 When you are looking for the subject of a sentence, do not look for it within the prepositional phrase.

You can easily recognize a prepositional phrase because it always begins with a preposition. Study the following list so that you will be able to quickly recognize all of the common prepositions.

Common Prepositions			
about	below	in	since
above	beneath	inside	through
across	beside	into	to
after	between	like	toward
against	beyond	near	under
along	by	of	until
among	down	off	up
around	during	on	upon
at	except	outside	with
before	for	over	within
behind	from	past	without

In addition to these common prepositions, English has a number of prepositional combinations that, together with other words, also function as prepositions.

Common Prepositional Combinations		
ahead of	in addition to	in reference to
at the time of	in between	in regard to
because of	in care of	in search of
by means of	in case of	in spite of
except for	in common with	instead of
for fear of	in contrast to	on account of
for the purpose of	in the course of	similar to
for the sake of	in exchange for	

EXERCISE 1   **Creating Sentences with Prepositional Phrases**

Use each of the ten prepositions that follow to write a prepositional phrase. Then write a sentence containing that prepositional phrase. Two examples are done for you.

TIP   Notice that when a prepositional phrase begins a sentence, a comma usually follows the phrase. (Sometimes, if the prepositional phrase is short, the comma is omitted.)

Preposition	Prepositional Phrase	Sentence
before	before breakfast	My cousin called before breakfast.

Preposition	Prepositional Phrase	Sentence
between	between the two barns	Between the two barns, the old Buick lay rusting.

Preposition	Prepositional Phrase	Sentence
1. in	IN THE HOUSE	WE SAT IN THE HOUSE
2. with	WITH MY GIRLFRIEND	I WENT FOR A WALK WITH MY GIRLFREIND
3. of	OF COURSE	OF COURSE, I LIKE YOU!
4. from	FROM YOUR UNCLE	YOU RECIVED A LETTER FROM YOUR UNCLE
5. during	DURING THE MOVIE	DURING THE MOVIE WE DRANK POP
6. by	BY FAR	BY FAR, MY FAVRIT COLVOR IS GREEN
7. for	FOR YOU	THE BOTTLE OF WINE IS FOR YOU

EXERCISE 2   **Finding Subjects in Sentences with Prepositional Phrases**

Remember that you will never find the subject of a sentence within a prepositional phrase. In each of the following sentences, cross out any prepositional phrases. Then underline the subject of each sentence. An example is done for you.

On the circus grounds, <u>Lisa</u> wandered among the elephants, horses, and camels.

1. <u>Young people</u> in the circus search for travel, adventure, danger, and romance.
2. However, after a few weeks of pulling cages and sleeping on hay, m<u>ost of these</u> people get tired of the circus and go back home.
3. The art of <u>clowning</u>, for instance, is very serious work.
4. Today, a <u>circus clown</u> must graduate from Clown College in Venice, Florida.
5. The <u>staff</u> of Clown College looks across the country for applicants.
6. <u>Admission</u> to the college is not easy.
7. Only sixty <u>people</u> out of three thousand applicants are admitted.

What Are the Other Problems in Finding Subjects?

Sentences with a Change in the Normal Subject Position

Some sentences begin with words that indicate that a question is being asked. Such words as *why, where, how*, and *when* give the reader the signal that a question will follow. Such opening words are not the subject. The subject will be found later on in the sentence. The following sentences begin with question words:

Why is *he* going away?
How did *he* find his sister in the city?

Notice that in each sentence the subject is not found in the opening part of the sentence. By answering questions or changing the question into a statement, you can make the subject easier to spot.

He is going away . . .
He found his sister . . .

Using *there*

The word *there* can never be the subject of a sentence.

There is a new teacher in the department.

Who or what is this sentence about? This sentence is about a teacher. *Teacher* is the subject of the sentence.

Commands

Sometimes a sentence contains a verb that gives an order:

Go to Timmins.
Help your sister.

In these sentences the subject *you* is not written, but it is understood. This is the only case where the subject of a sentence may be left out when you write a sentence.

Sentences That Contain Appositive Phrases

An **appositive phrase** is a group of words in a sentence that gives us extra information about a noun in the sentence.

Example: Don Koyama, the retired chemist, sat at his desk.

In this sentence, the words *the retired chemist* make up the appositive phrase because they give you extra information about Don Koyama. Notice that commas separate the appositive phrase from the rest of the sentence. If you leave out the appositive phrase when you read the sentence, the thought will still be complete.

Don Koyama sat at his desk.

Now the subject is clear: *Don Koyama*.

TIP   **When you are looking for the subject of a sentence, you will not find it within an appositive phrase.**

EXERCISE 1   **Finding Hidden Subjects**

Each of the following sentences contains an example of a special problem in finding the subject of a sentence. First, cross out any prepositional phrases or appositive phrases. Then underline the subject of each sentence. An example is done for you.

What can <u>we</u> learn ~~from the study of an ancient civilization~~?

1. ~~Look at a~~ <u>map</u> ~~of South America.~~
2. Where is ~~the ancient city of~~ <u>Chan Chan</u>?
3. Here ~~on the coastal desert of northern Peru~~ stand the <u>remains</u> ~~of this city of the kings.~~
4. <u>Chan Chan</u>, ~~once the fabulously wealthy centre of the Chimor~~, is situated ~~in one of the driest, bleakest regions in the world.~~
5. <u>It</u> was the largest pre-Columbian city in South America.
6. ~~In the ruins of this city~~, scientists have found <u>fragments</u> ~~to piece together the mystery of the past.~~
7. How could this <u>civilization</u> have survived ~~this hostile environment and become so advanced?~~

EXERCISE 2   Finding Hidden Subjects

Each of the following sentences contains an example of a special problem in finding the subject of a sentence. First, cross out any prepositional phrases or appositive phrases. Then underline the subject of each sentence. An example is done for you.

> The <u>*Maid of the Mist*</u>, ~~an exciting boat ride~~, is a favourite stop ~~for many tourists to Niagara Falls.~~

1. How can you tell a stranger from a native?
2. There are sometimes unmistakable signs.
3. However, be careful not to assume too much.
4. A <u>middle-aged man</u> ~~with three cameras around his neck and a family following behind him~~ is nearly always a tourist.
5. ~~On the other hand~~, a strange hairdo or an exotic outfit may just be the sign of a creative individual.
6. In Canada, ~~even a foreign language~~ is not always the sign ~~of a stranger.~~
7. On your next trip, try to separate the strangers from the natives.

How Do You Find the Verb of a Sentence?

Every sentence must have a verb. Verbs can be divided into three classes:

1. Action: An **action verb** tells what the subject is doing.

   Donovan Bailey *ran* in the Olympics.

2. Linking: A **linking verb** indicates a state of being or condition.

   The crowd *seemed* spellbound during his race.

3. Helping: A **helping verb** combines with a main verb to form a verb phrase and gives the main verb a special time or meaning.

   Canadians *can* expect strong performances in the future.

Verbs tell time. Use this fact to test for a verb. If you can put the verb into different tenses in the sentence, that word is a verb.

> *Present:* (Today) he *runs*.
> *Past:* (Yesterday) he *ran*.
> *Future:* (Tomorrow) he *will run*.

Action Verbs

Action verbs tell us what the subject is doing and when the subject does the action.

The woman *studied* ballet.

What was the woman doing?   studying

What is the time of the action?   past (*ed* is the past tense ending)

Action Verbs

Most verbs are action verbs. Here are a few examples:

arrive	learn	open	watch
leave	forget	write	fly
enjoy	help	speak	catch
despise	make	teach	wait

EXERCISE 1   **Finding Action Verbs**

Each of the following sentences contains an action verb. Find the action verb by first crossing out any prepositional or appositive phrases and underlining the subject of the sentence. Then circle the verb (the word that tells what the subject is doing). Note also the time of the action: past, present, or future. An example is done for you.

Many people (begin) hobbies in childhood.

1. Some people (collect) very strange objects.
2. One man (saves) the fortunes from fortune cookies.
3. A group in Alberta often (meets) to discuss their spark plug collections.
4. People in Brandon (gather) many types of barbed wire.
5. Collectors take (pride) in the possession of unusual items.
6. A collection, like odd rocks or unique automobiles, (gives) a person some individuality.
7. Collections (keep) us happy from childhood to old age.

EXERCISE 2   **Finding Action Verbs**

Each of the following sentences contains an action verb. Find the action verb by first crossing out any prepositional or appositive phrases and underlining the subject of the sentence. Then circle the verb (the word that tells what the subject is doing). Note also the time of the action: past, present, or future. An example is done for you.

Attitudes toward medical practices often (change.)

1. Traditional Chinese medicine harnesses ancient (healing) techniques in the practice of "qigong."
2. Masters of this Chinese practice claim the ability to (cure) many diseases.
3. The master (projects) a mysterious force into his students.
4. The hands of the Chinese gigong practitioner (pound) at the air above a patient.
5. Many patients (respond) to this invisible force.

6. Some patients (sway) their bodies with the power of the force.
7. Some doctors conduct research in China in hopes of (finding) the secrets of this ancient art.

Linking Verbs

A **linking verb** is a verb that joins the subject of a sentence to one or more words that describe or identify the subject.

For example:

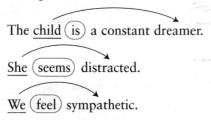

The <u>child</u> (is) a constant dreamer.

<u>She</u> (seems) distracted.

<u>We</u> (feel) sympathetic.

In each of these examples, the verb links the subject to a word that identifies or describes the subject. In the first example, the verb *is* links *child* with *dreamer*. The verb *seems* links the pronoun *she* with *distracted*. Finally, in the third example, the verb *feel* links the pronoun *we* with *sympathetic*.

act	feel
appear	grow
be (am, is, are,	look
was, were, have been)	seem
become	taste

EXERCISE 1   Finding Linking Verbs

Each of the following sentences contains a linking verb. Find the linking verb by first underlining the subject of the sentence. Then draw an arrow to the word or words that identify or describe the subject. Finally, circle the linking verb. An example is done for you.

<u>Dreams</u> are very important to the Native peoples of Canada.

1. My <u>dream</u> last night was wonderful.
2. <u>I</u> had become middle-aged.
3. In a sunlit <u>kitchen</u> with a book in my hand, I appeared <u>relaxed</u> and happy.
4. The <u>house</u> was empty and quiet.
5. In the morning light, the <u>kitchen</u> felt cozy.

6. I seemed to have grown calmer.
7. I felt satisfied with life.

EXERCISE 2   **Finding Linking Verbs**

Each of the following sentences contains a linking verb. Find the linking verb by first underlining the subject of the sentence. Then draw an arrow to the word or words that identify or describe the subject. Finally, circle the linking verb. An example is done for you.

Surprises (can be) fun.

1. We were anxious to make the evening a success.
2. The apartment looked empty.
3. Everyone remained quiet.
4. Martha turned red at the sound of "Surprise!"
5. She seemed surprised.
6. All of her presents were lovely.
7. The birthday party was a complete success.

Helping Verbs (also called auxiliary verbs)

Some verbs can be used to help the main verb express a special time or meaning.

Sentence Using Auxiliary Verb	Time Expressed by Auxiliary Verb
He *is* sleeping.	right now
He *might* sleep.	maybe now or in the future
He *should* sleep.	ought to, now or in the future
He *could have been* sleeping.	maybe in the past

Common Helping Verbs
can, could
may, might, must
shall, should
will, would
forms of the irregular verbs *be*, *do*, and *have*

REMEMBER that *be*, *do*, and *have* are also used as main verbs of sentences. In such cases, *be* is a linking verb while *do* and *have* are action verbs. All other helping verbs are usually used only as helping verbs.

WATCH OUT for adverbs that may come in between the helping verb and the main verb.

Def

Adverbs are words that can modify verbs, adjectives, or other adverbs.

In the following sentence, the word *often* is an adverb coming between the verb phrase *can frighten*. For a list of adverbs, see p. 327.

Dreams (can) often (frighten) young children.

EXERCISE 1 **Finding Helping Verbs**

Each of the following sentences contains a helping verb in addition to the main verb. In each sentence, first underline the subject. Then circle the entire verb phrase. An example is done for you.

In some writing classes, students (must keep) a diary of their work.

1. There could be several advantages to keeping a diary.
2. In a journal, a person can safely express true feelings without fear of criticism by family or friends.
3. You will be able to capture your memories before they fade.
4. Important, too, would be the development of a writing style and the improvement of language skills.
5. A journal might awaken your imagination.
6. It may unexpectedly bring pleasure and satisfaction.
7. You should seriously consider the purchase of one of those lovely fabric-bound notebooks.

Chapter Review Exercises

EXERCISE 1 **Finding Subjects and Verbs in Simple Sentences**

In each of the following sentences, cross out any prepositional phrases or appositive phrases. Then underline the subject and circle the complete verb. An example is done for you.

The modern family (has been disrupted) by many negative outside influences.

1. Mother and Dad always blame me for any trouble with my sister.
2. My sister, the most popular girl in her class, is two years older than I.
3. Yesterday, for instance, she was trying on her new graduation dress.
4. Helpfully, I took out her new shoes and purse for her.
5. Margaret instantly became furious with me.
6. I was only sharing Margaret's excitement about her new clothes.

EXERCISE 2 **Finding Subjects and Verbs in Simple Sentences**

In each of the sentences in the following paragraph, cross out any prepositional or appositive phrases. Then underline the subject and circle the complete verb.

Go West! Western Australia, one of the remaining great boom areas of the world, constitutes one-third of the Australian continent. Why did people by the tens of thousands go to western Australia in the late 1800s? In 1894, Leslie Robert Menzies jumped off his camel and landed in a pile of gold nuggets. In less than two hours, this man gathered over a million dollars in gold. He eventually took 5 t of gold to the bank by wheelbarrow! Kalgoorlie and Boulder, the two boom towns that grew up there, boast the richest golden mile in the world. With all the gold seekers, this surface gold did not last very long. Now the only bands of rich ore lie more than 1200 m down under the ground. There are many ghost towns with their empty iron houses and rundown chicken coops.

Student Writing Exercise

E X E R C I S E 1   **Composing Complete Sentences**

Below are two lists, one of subjects and one of verbs. Using any subject from one list and any verb from the other list, compose complete sentences. Use each subject and each verb only once. Try to vary the position of the subject in the sentence. An example is done for you.

Many dogs chased cars on our street.

1. dogs	is
2. nose	chased
3. she	are
4. dentist	was
5. Saskatchewan	singing
6. fishing	has
7. problems	screams
8. obeying	see
9. mailbox	approaches
10. storm	looks

1. DOGS ARE MY FAVORIT ANIMIAL.
2. YOUR NOSE LOOKS BROKEN!
3. WHEN WE WENT RUNNING, SHE WAS IN FRONT.
4. YOU CAN ALLWAY HEAR SCREAMS WHEN YOU GO TO THE DENTIST.
5. SASKATCHEWAN LOOKS VERY MUCH THE SAME
6. FISHING HAS BECOME MY FAVORIT PASS TIME.
7. I HAVE PROBLEMS SINGING.
8. DID YOU SEE HOW WELL THE DOG WAS OBEYING HIS MASTER?
9. MY MAIL BOX WAS FULL.
10. THE STORM ALLWAYS APROCHES FROM THE WEST

Working Together

Review the names for sentence parts by doing this crossword puzzle. Feel free to look back in the chapter for the answers.

Crossword Puzzle: Reviewing the Terms for Sentence Parts

Across

1. Verbs like *hop*, *sing*, and *play* are called _____ verbs.
4. A helping verb
6. Every sentence has a _____ and a verb.
8. A helping verb
9. Which of the following is a preposition?
   must, upon, they
12. A preposition
14. *Word, witch, wall*, and *willow* are examples of the part of speech called a _____.
15. Most nouns are _____ nouns. They are not capitalized.
18. In the following sentence, which word is an adjective?
   His pet theory was disproved.
21. A preposition
22. In the following sentence, which word is an abstract noun?
   The era was not economically successful.
23. A preposition
24. A word that can take the place of a noun.

Down

1. *Joy, confidence, peace* are examples of this kind of noun; the opposite of a concrete noun.
2. Which word is the subject in the following sentence?
   Here is the tube of glue for Toby.
3. An indefinite pronoun
4. A plural pronoun
5. *Look, appear, feel*, and *seem* are examples of _____ verbs.
7. Which word is the object of the preposition?
   The car must weigh over a ton.
10. The opposite of a common noun.
11. A pronoun
13. A preposition
16. A helping verb
17. Which of the following is a proper noun?
   king, Nero, hero, teen
19. Which of the following is an adjective?
   net, tan, Nan, man
20. Which word is the verb in the following sentence?
   Run down to the car for our bag.
21. A common linking verb.

Chapter 2
Correcting the Fragment in Simple Sentences

QUICK QUIZ Test yourself on your knowledge of fragments. Some of the examples below are complete sentences; some are fragments (only parts of sentences). Write *C* if the example is a complete sentence. Write *F* if the example is a fragment. The answers to the questions follow the quiz.

_____ *C* _____   1. Chocolate was discovered in the New World.

_____ *F* _____   2. By explorers such as Columbus and Cortés.

_____ *F* _____   3. The Natives drinking a beverage never seen before by the Europeans.

_____ *C* _____   4. Spanish conquerors added cane sugar to the drink.

_____ *F* _____   5. To make it more pleasant for European tastes.

Answers:
1. C
2. F
3. F
4. C
5. F

Recognizing Sentence Fragments

Once you have learned that a sentence must have a subject and a verb, and that a sentence must also express a complete thought, you are on your way to correcting one of the most frequent errors in student writing — the fragment. A fragment is an incomplete sentence. Although many of our daily conversations are informal and sometimes contain fragments, standard writing is always more formal and requires complete sentences.

The fragment is a major problem for many student writers. In the writer's mind, a thought may be clear; however, on paper the idea may turn out to be incomplete, missing a subject or a verb. In this section, you will improve your ability to spot incomplete sentences or fragments, and you will learn how to correct them. This practice will prepare you to avoid such fragments in your own writing.

Practise Putting a Conversation into Complete Sentences

The following conversation is one that a couple of students might have at the start of their English class. Rewrite the conversation in complete thoughts or standard sentences. Remember the definition of a sentence:

TIP   A complete sentence has a subject and a verb and expresses a complete thought.

JOHN: Early again.
LESIA: Want to get a front-row seat.
JOHN: Your homework done?
LESIA: Nearly.
JOHN: Think he'll give a quiz today?
LESIA: Hope not.
JOHN: Looks like rain today.
LESIA: Better not; haven't got a bag for these new books.
JOHN: Going to the game Saturday?
LESIA: Probably.

1. YOU ARE EARLY FOR CLASS AGAIN.
2. DID YOU WANT TO GET A FRONT-ROW SEAT?
3. IS ALL OF YOUR HOMEWORK DONE
4. I NEARLY FINISHED ALL OF THE CHAPTERS.
5. DO YOU THINK THE TEACHER WILL GIVE A QUIZ?
6. I HOPE THAT THERE IS NOT A QUIZ!
7. IT LOOK LIKE IT MIGHT RAIN.
8. I HOPE IT DOSENT RAIN B/C I DIDN'T BRING A BAG FOR MY NEW BOOKS.
9. ARE YOU GOING TO THE GAME ON SATURDAY?
10. I WILL PROBABLE GO TO THE GAME.

Remember, when you write in complete sentences, this writing may be somewhat different from the way you would express the same idea in everyday conversation with a friend.

Although you will occasionally spot incomplete sentences in professional writing, you may be sure the writer is using these fragments intentionally. In such cases, the fragment may capture the way a person thinks or speaks, or it may create a special effect. A student developing his or her writing skills should be sure to use only standard sentence form so that thoughts will be communicated effectively. Nearly all the writing you will do in your life — letters to friends, business correspondence, papers in school, or reports in your job — will demand standard sentence form. Fragments will be looked upon as a sign of ignorance rather than creative style!

What Is a Fragment?

Def   A **fragment** is a piece of a sentence.

A fragment is not a sentence for one of the following reasons:

a. The subject is missing.

     delivered the plans to my office

b. The verb is missing.

     the architect to my office

c. Both the subject and verb are missing.

     to my office

d. The subject and verb are present but the words do not express a complete thought.

     when the architect delivered the plans

E X E R C I S E   1   **Understanding Fragments**

Each of the following groups of words is a fragment. In the blank to the right of each fragment, identify what part of the sentence could be added to make the fragment into a sentence.

     a. Add a subject.
     b. Add a verb.
     c. Add a subject and a verb.
     d. The subject and verb are already present, but need to express a complete thought.

An example is done for you.

Fragment	**Add**
the red fox	b. verb
1. returned to the river	_SUBJECT_
2. a bird on the oak branch	_VERB_

How Do You Correct a Fragment?

You can eliminate fragments in one of two ways:

1. Add the missing part or parts to develop the fragment into a complete sentence:

> *Fragment:* across the lake
> *Add:* subject and verb
> *Sentence:* I swam across the lake.

2. Join the fragment to another sentence. In order to do this, you will need to make use of the comma, the colon, or the dash, or you may not need to use punctuation. For example,

a. Using the comma

> *Fragment:* including a stop at the shoe store
> *Other Sentence:* He has to make a number of purchases.
> *Fragment Eliminated:* He has to make a number of purchases, including a stop at the shoe store.

b. Using the colon

> *Fragment:* pie, cake, and pudding
> *Other Sentence:* I have a number of favourite desserts.
> *Fragment Eliminated:* I have a number of favourite desserts: pie, cake, and pudding.

c. Using the dash

> *Fragment:* more often than she should
> *Other Sentence:* She goes to the casino every day.
> *Fragment Eliminated:* She goes to the casino every day — more often than she should.

d. Using no punctuation

> *Fragment:* on top of the mountain
> *Other Sentence:* We planned to plant the flag.
> *Fragment Eliminated:* We planned to plant the flag on top of the mountain.

E X E R C I S E   2   Making Fragments into Sentences

Change the fragments of Exercise 1 into complete sentences by adding the missing part or parts that you have already identified.

1. returned to the river

_____

2. a bird on the oak branch

   A BIRD SAT ON THE OAK BRANCH .

3. between the island and the mainland

   WE SAILED BETWEEN THE ISLAND AND THE MAINLAND

4. the hawk in a soaring motion

   THE HAWK WAS IN A SOARING MOTION.

5. the fishing boats on the lake

   THE FISHING BOAT WAS ON THE LAKE.

6. dropped like a stone into the water

   HE DROPPED LIKED A STONE INTO THE WATER.

7. the fisherman put

   THE FISHERMAN PUT HIS NET INTO THE WATER.

E X E R C I S E 3   Making Fragments into Sentences

Each of the following sentences contains one or more fragments. First read the passage, then locate the fragments in each passage. Correct the fragments by joining them to other sentences, using either a comma, a colon, a dash, or no punctuation.

1. Fishing is one of the oldest sports in the world, and can be one of the most relaxing. A person with a simple wooden pole and line can have as much fun as a sportsman. With expensive equipment. For busy executives, overworked teachers, and even presidents of nations; fishing can be a good way to escape from the stress of demanding jobs.

2. The first electric car was built in 1887. Six years later, it was sold commercially. At the turn of the century, people had great faith in new technology. In fact, 300 electric taxicabs were operating in New York City by 1900. However, electric cars soon lost their popularity. The new gasoline engine became more widely used. With our concern over pollution, perhaps electric cars will become desirable once again.

3. Inuit obtain most of their food from the sea. They eat seals and walruses, whales, fish, and sea birds in abundance. Inuit boil some of their food. They eat other foods uncooked because of the scarcity of fuel. Inuit get important vitamins and minerals, by eating every part of the animal they kill. The heart, the liver, and even the digestive tracts of the animals have great food value for the Inuit.

Don't Confuse Phrases with Sentences

Fragments are usually made up of phrases. These phrases are often mistaken for sentences because they are groups of words. However, they do not fit the definition of a sentence.

What Is a Phrase?

A **phrase** is a group of words that go together but that lack one or more of the elements necessary to be classified as a sentence.

How Many Kinds of Phrases Are There?

In English, there are a number of types of phrases that you should learn to recognize. Some of them you have already studied in the previous chapter. Remember, a phrase is not a complete sentence; it is a sentence fragment, and as such must be either joined to another sentence or made into a complete sentence.

1. **Noun phrase:** a group of words that functions as a noun.

   Noun phrase: large square bricks
   Complete sentence: The garage is built with *large square bricks*.

2. **Prepositional phrase:** a group of words beginning with a preposition.

   Prepositional phrase: on the porch
   Complete sentence: Many of our neighbours are sitting *on the porch*.

3. **Verb phrase:** a group of words that functions as a verb.

   Verb phrase: is walking
   Complete sentence: My best friend *is walking* to my house.

4. **Infinitive phrase:** a group of words beginning with an infinitive.

   Infinitive phrase: to have a good job
   Complete sentence: I think it's important *to have a good job*.

EXERCISE 1   Identifying Phrases

Identify each of the underlined phrases in the following sentences.

1. To visit Montreal is a thrill for most Canadians.   _INFINITIVE_

2. Many people love to see the French culture.   _INFINITIVE_

3. Museums, restaurants, shopping, and the varied
   night life offer endless possibilities for the tourist.   _PREV_

4. On the subways, tourists experience one of the
   cleanest underground transit systems in North
   America.   _PREP_

5. My brother Don rode the subway under the
   St. Lawrence River.   _Noun_

6. A landowner from the country, he enjoyed the continental atmosphere of Quebec's largest city.   *Noun ... l.*

7. Montreal's continual fascination is its rich mix of cultures and lifestyles from all over the world.   *PREP.*

EXERCISE 2   Identifying Phrases

Identify each of the underlined phrases in the following sentences.

1. In Canada,[1] crime seems to be increasing[2] at an alarming rate.[3]

2. Stories about many major crimes[4] can be seen[5] almost daily in the newspapers.[6]

3. To avoid[7] the issue will not solve the problem.

4. Citizens should be concerned[8] and try to make their views known[9] to their elected officials.[10]

1. _PREP._
2. _INFINITIVE_
3. _PREP_
4. _NOUN_
5. _VERB_
6. _PREP_
7. _INFINITIVE_
8. _VERB_
9. _INFINITIVE_
10. _PREP_

How Do You Make a Complete Sentence from a Fragment That Contains a Participle?

Def

Participles are verbals, words that look like verbs but do not function as verbs in a sentence.

Some examples are

running
sitting

Participles are usually found in phrases, and as such can often cause sentence fragments if not used properly. Participles usually end in *-ing*, and need a verb or another group of words to form a phrase.

The man was *running* to the store.
Sitting on the bench, I saw the pigeon.

T I P   **Watch out for *-ing* words. No word ending in *-ing* can be the complete verb of a sentence.**

Fragment: he <u>talking</u> in his sleep

1. Add a helping verb to the participle:

    He <u>is talking</u> in his sleep.

2. Change the participle to a different form of the verb:

    He <u>talks</u> in his sleep.

3. Use the participle as an adjective, being sure to provide a subject and verb for the sentence:

    <u>Talking in his sleep</u>, he muttered something about his boss.

E X E R C I S E   1   **Correcting the Fragment That Contains a Participle**

Make four complete sentences from each of the following fragments. Use this example as your model.

Fragment: using the back stairway

a. He <u>is using</u> the back stairway.
b. He <u>uses</u> the back stairway.
c. <u>Using the back stairway</u>, he got away without being seen.
d. <u>Using the back stairway</u> is not a good idea.

1. moving out of the house

    a. <u>THE PEOPLE LIVEING UP STAIRS WERE MOVING OUT OF THE HOUSE.</u>
    b. <u>ON SATURDAY WE ARE MOVING OUT OF THE HOUSE</u>
    c. <u>THEY ARE MOVING OUT OF THE HOUSE.</u>
    d. <u>MOVENG OUT OF THE HOUSE IS NOT A GOOD IDEA.</u>

2. talking on the telephone

    a. <u>THE GIRLS ARE ALWAYS TALKING ON THE TELEPHONE</u>
    b. <u>SHE TALKS ON THE TELEPHONE</u>
    c. <u>TALKING ON THE TELEPHONE, SHE GOT A SORE EAR</u>
    d. <u>TALKING ON THE TELEPHONE IS YOUR FAVORIT PASS TIME.</u>

3. driving the car down Highway 60

    a. <u>SHE IS DRIVING THE CAR DOWN HIGHWAY 60.</u>
    b. <u>SHE DROVE THE CAR DOWN HIGHWAY 60.</u>

c. _Driving . the car down Highway 60, he got into an accident_

d. _" ___ that is very safe._

EXERCISE 2   Correcting the Fragment That Contains a Participle

The following passage contains four fragments containing participles. Circle the fragments and correct them in one of the four ways shown in Exercise 1.

At last taking the driving test. I felt very nervous. My mother was sitting in the back seat. All my papers sitting on the front seat. The inspector got into the car and sat on my insurance form. He looked rather sour and barely spoke to me. I was Trying not to hit the curb, I parallel parked surprisingly well. I managed to get through all the manoeuvres. Now tensely waiting for the results.

→ At last I was taking the driving test.

→ All my papers sat on the front seat.

→ I felt tense as I waited for the results

Chapter Review Exercises

EXERCISE 1   Correcting the Fragment

Rewrite each fragment so that it is a complete sentence.

1. Early morning is a time of peace in my neighbourhood.

2. the grey mist covering up all but the faint outlines of nearby houses.

3. the shapes of cars in the streets and driveways

    I looked at the shapes of cars parked in street and driveways.

4. to sit and look out the window

    I love to sit and look out the window.

5. holding a steaming cup of coffee, is my morning ritual.

6. the only sound the rumbling of a truck .

[handwritten annotations above line 6: "T", "WAS" (with ^ mark), "E", "THE"]

_____

7. passing on the highway a kilometre away FROM THE STOP SIGN.

[handwritten annotations above line 7: "HE", "ED"]

_____

E X E R C I S E   2   **Recognizing the Fragment**

The paragraph below contains fragments. Read the paragraph. Then write *complete* after each example that is a complete sentence. Write *fragment* after each example that is a phrase or piece of a sentence. Keep in mind that a sentence must have a subject and verb as well as express a complete thought.

> That afternoon the street was full of children. Taking a shower in the rain. Soaping themselves and rushing out into the storm. To wash off the suds. In a few minutes, it was all over. Including the rubdown. The younger children took their showers naked. Teetering on the tips of their toes and squealing to one another. The stately coconut palm in one corner of the patio. Thrashed its branches high over the dripping children bouncing on the cobblestones.

1. That afternoon the street was full of children.   _____Com._____

2. Taking a shower in the rain.   _____f_____

3. Soaping themselves and rushing out into the storm.   _____F_____

4. To wash off the suds.   _____f_____

5. In a few minutes, it was all over.   _____C_____

6. Including the rubdown.   _____F_____

7. The younger children took their showers naked.   _____C_____

8. Teetering on the tips of their toes and squealing to one another.   _____F_____

9. The stately coconut palm in one corner of the patio.   _____F_____

10. Thrashed its branches high over the dripping children bouncing on the cobblestones.   _____F_____

E X E R C I S E   3   **Correcting the Fragment**

Rewrite the paragraph in Exercise 2. Correct the fragments in one of the following three ways:

    a. Join the phrase to the sentence preceding it.
    b. Join the phrase to the sentence that follows it.
    c. Add a subject and/or verb so that the sentence is complete.

THE CHILDREN WERE TAKING SHOWERS
IN THE RAIN. THEY SOAPED THEMSELVES
AND RUSHED OUT INTO THE STORM.
THE USED THE WATER TO WASH
OF THE SUDS. THEY TEETERED ON
THE TIPS OF THERE TOES AND
SQUEALED AT ONE ANOTHER.
T

EXERCISE 4 Correcting the Fragment

Each of the following passages contains a fragment. Underline the fragment, and on the lines beneath each passage, rewrite the passage so that it is composed of complete sentences.

1. The moon rose high in the sky. All of us worked quickly to pitch the tent. Then WE
   making a fire.
   MADE

   Revised passage: _____

   _____

   _____

2. Raising the drinking age to 21 saves the lives of all drivers. The drinkers and non-drinkers. Every province should raise the drinking age to 21.

   Revised passage: _____

   _____

3. Companies do a lot of research before they name a new product. Based on the results of a market research team, The company makes its final selection.

   Revised passage: _____

   _____

   _____

4. The day of my eighteenth birthday, the reservations made at a fine restaurant. My father came home early from work.

[handwritten: or T ... we made]

Revised passage: _____

_____

_____

5. Francie loved to see her mother grind the coffee. Her mother would sit in the kitchen with the coffee mill clutched between her knees. Grinding away with a furious turn of her left wrist. The room filled up with the rich odour of freshly ground coffee.

Revised passage: _____

_____

_____

Working Together

Read the Audi advertisement illustrated below. Notice that this advertisement contains many fragments. The writing we must produce for college or professional purposes is often very different from the kind of writing we find in advertisements and other kinds of popular writing. This kind of writing is short and snappy but grammatically incorrect. Why do you think the advertiser would choose to write in this way? Rewrite the entire advertisement using only complete sentences.

Audi Traction. Like a lot of things in life you take it for granted, then boom. It's taken away. And oh how you want it back. It doesn't take much. Gravel on the offramp. A soft shoulder on a rainy night.

That's why we developed quattro™ all-wheel drive for our luxury cars. Very serious grip. High performance traction. Quattro continuously distributes power between the front and back wheels, whichever has the best hold of the road. It happens instantly. And the extra traction quattro provides could be the difference between being in a collision, or avoiding a collision. So which is better, protection or traction? Get both. In an Audi quattro all-wheel drive. For more information call 1-800-668-AUDI.

Audi 90 quattro

Chapter 3
Combining Sentences Using Co-ordination

QUICK QUIZ Test yourself on your knowledge of combining sentences using co-ordination. Each of the following pairs of sentences could be combined into a single sentence. Among the four choices given, place an *X* in front of the example that is correct. Answers to the questions follow the quiz.

Chocolate became a popular drink throughout Europe.
It was thought to be good for your health.

_____ 1. Chocolate became a popular drink throughout Europe, it was thought to be good for your health.

____X____ 2. Chocolate became a popular drink throughout Europe because it was thought to be good for your health.

_____ 3. Chocolate became a popular drink throughout Europe, but it was thought to be good for your health.

_____ 4. Chocolate became a popular drink throughout Europe and good for your health.

Answers:
2. is correct.

So far you have worked only with the simple sentence. If you go back and read a group of these sentences, such as those on page 7, you will see that writing only simple sentences would result in a choppy style. Also, you would have trouble trying to express more complicated ideas.

You will therefore want to learn how to combine sentences. You can do this by using particular marks of punctuation and special connecting words called **conjunctions**. The two major ways of joining sentences together are called **co-ordination** and **subordination**.

What Is Co-ordination?

Def The pairing of similar elements — words, phrases or clauses — to give equal weight to each is called **co-ordination**. Co-ordination can link two independent clauses to form a compound sentence.

You can use co-ordination whenever you have two sentences that are related and that contain ideas of equal importance. There are three ways to combine such sentences. All three ways result in a new kind of sentence called a **compound sentence**. Before you study these three methods, however, it is important to understand the term *independent clause*. The **independent clause** is a group of words that could be a simple sentence. In a compound sentence we could say we are combining simple sentences, or we could say we are combining *independent clauses*. Don't let the term confuse you. *Independent* means that the words could stand alone as a sentence, and *clause* means that there is a subject and a verb. *IC* will mean *independent clause* in the work that follows.

Use a Comma Plus a Co-ordinating Conjunction

TIP **The first way to combine independent clauses is to use a comma plus a co-ordinating conjunction. A conjunction is a connecting or joining word.**

IC	, and	IC
He spoke forcefully	, and	I felt compelled to listen.

Connectors: Co-ordinating Conjunctions

and	**Used in Pairs**
but	either . . . or
or, nor	neither . . . nor
for (meaning "because")	not only . . . but also
yet	
so	

PRACTICE In each of the following compound sentences, draw a single line under the subject and draw two lines under the verb for each independent clause. Then circle both the co-ordinating conjunction and the comma. An example has been done for you.

The <u>speaker</u> <u><u>rose</u></u> to his feet (, and) the <u>room</u> <u><u>became</u></u> quiet.

1. The <u>audience</u> <u><u>was</u></u> packed, (for) this was a man with an international reputation.
2. <u>He</u> <u><u>could have</u></u> told about all his successes, (but) instead he spoke about his dis-appointments.
3. His <u>words</u> <u><u>were</u></u> electric, (so) the crowd was attentive.
4. <u>I</u> <u><u>should have</u></u> brought a tape recorder, (or) at least I should have taken notes.

Did you find a subject and verb for both independent clauses in each sentence?

Now that you understand the structure of a compound sentence, you need to think about the meanings of the different co-ordinating conjunctions and how they can be used to show the relationship between two ideas, each idea being given equal importance.

Meaning of Co-ordinating Conjunctions	
to add an idea:	and
to add an idea when the first clause is in the negative:	nor
to contrast two opposing ideas:	but, yet
to introduce a reason:	for
to show a choice:	or
to introduce a result:	so

E X E R C I S E 1   **Combining Sentences Using Co-ordinating Conjunctions**

Each of the following examples contains two simple sentences that could be related with a co-ordinating conjunction. Decide what relationship the second sentence has to the first, and then select the conjunction that will make sense. Refer to the previous chart, "Meaning of Co-ordinating Conjunctions," to help you decide on the relationships. An example is done for you.

She broke her arm.
She couldn't play in the finals.

Relationship of second sentence to first: <u>result</u>
Conjunction that introduces this meaning: <u>so</u>
New compound sentence:

She broke her arm, **so** she couldn't play in the finals.

1. Mr. Watson is kind and patient.
   His brother is sharp and nagging.

   Relationship of second sentence to first: _CONTRAST_

   Conjunction that introduces this meaning: _BUT_

   _____

   _____

2. The two men are having great difficulty.
   They are trying to raise a teenager.

   Relationship of second sentence to first: _INTRODUCE A REASON_

   Conjunction that introduces this meaning: _FOR_

_____

_____

3. Young Michael has no family of his own.
   He feels angry and alone.

   Relationship of second sentence to first: _ADD AN IDEA_

   Conjunction that introduces this meaning: _AND_

_____

_____

4. Michael hasn't been doing well in school.
   He isn't involved in any activities outside school.

   Relationship of second sentence to first: _ADD AN IDEA_

   Conjunction that introduces this meaning: _AND_

_____

_____

5. Mr. Watson encouraged Michael to do volunteer work at the hospital.
   This might show Michael the satisfaction of helping other people.

   Relationship of second sentence to first: _INTRO A RESULT_

   Conjunction that introduces this meaning: _So_

_____

_____

6. Mr. Watson's brother wanted Michael to spend more time on his homework.
   He also wanted him to get a job that would bring in some money to help with expenses.

   Relationship of second sentence to first: _Two opposing IDEAS_

   Conjunction that introduces this meaning: _but_

_____

_____

7. Michael liked going to the hospital.
   He was doing something important.

   Relationship of second sentence to first: _ADD AN IDEA_

   Conjunction that introduces this meaning: _AND_

_____

_____

E X E R C I S E   2   **Combining Sentences Using Co-ordinating Conjunctions**

Each of the following examples contains two simple sentences. In each case, join the sentences to form a new compound sentence. Use a comma and one of the seven co-ordinating conjunctions. Be sure the conjunction you choose makes sense in the sentence. For example:

Two simple sentences: Many farmers are desperate. They are going bankrupt.

Compound sentence: Many farmers are desperate, *for* they are going bankrupt.

1. The farmers in Canada want to work.
   They are experiencing severe financial difficulty.

   FOR

2. Some people are losing their farms.
   The banks are refusing to make further loans.

   AND

3. The government programs have not been effective.
   The public cannot do anything.
   (Use *nor.* You will have to change the word order in the second sentence.)

   NOR   CAN   THE   PUBLIC   DO   ANYTHING

4. The farmers feel neglected.
   They are protesting to the government.

   SO

5. There is an increased need for farm products.
   The government pays farmers not to grow food.

   YET

6. Everyone needs what the farmers produce.
   We should be concerned about their problems.

   AND

7. In the future, fewer people will become farmers.
   The problem is likely to become increasingly serious.

   AND _____

   _____

Use a Semicolon, an Adverbial Conjunction, and a Comma

TIP   **A second way to combine independent clauses is to form the compound sentence by using a semicolon, an adverbial conjunction, and a comma.**

IC	; therefore,	IC
I had worked hard	; therefore,	I expected results.

Another set of conjunctions that have meanings similar to the common coordinating conjunctions are called **adverbial conjunctions** (or conjunctive adverbs). These connecting words will give the compound sentence you write more emphasis. They may also sound slightly more formal to you than the shorter conjunctions *and* and *but*. The punctuation for these connectors is somewhat more complex.

Connectors: Frequently Used Adverbial Conjunctions

Addition (and)	**Alternative (or)**	**Result (so)**
in addition	instead	accordingly
also	otherwise	consequently
besides	hence	
furthermore	therefore	
likewise	thus	
moreover		

Contrast (but)	**Emphasis**	**To Show Time**
however	indeed	meanwhile
nevertheless	in fact	
nonetheless		

PRACTICE   In each of the following compound sentences, draw a single line under the subject and draw two lines under the verb for both independent clauses. Then circle the semicolon, adverbial conjunction, and comma. For example:

The jet was the fastest way to get there (; moreover,) it was the most comfortable.

1. The restaurant is always too crowded on Saturdays; nevertheless, it serves the best food in town.
2. The land was not for sale; however, the house could be rented.
3. The lawsuit cost the company several million dollars; consequently, the company went out of business a short time later.
4. The doctor told him to lose weight; furthermore, she insisted he also stop smoking.

E X E R C I S E   1   **Combining Sentences Using Adverbial Conjunctions**

Combine each pair of sentences below to make a compound sentence. Use a semi-colon, an adverbial conjunction, and a comma. Be sure the conjunction you choose makes sense in the sentence. For example:

Two simple sentences: Our family would like to purchase a computer. We must wait until prices come down further.

Compound sentence: Our family would like to purchase a computer; *however,* we must wait until prices come down further.

1. Most people prefer to write with a pen or pencil.
   The computer is quickly becoming another favourite writing tool. (Show contrast.)

   _____ ; HOWEVER , _____

   _____

2. Computers provide a powerful way to create and store pieces of writing.
   They will become even more important in the future. (Add an idea.)

   _____ ; IN ADDITION , _____

   _____

3. Computers have already revolutionized today's offices.
   No modern business can afford to be without them. (Show result.)

   _____ ; CONSEQUENTLY , _____

   _____

4. The prices of many computers are coming down these days.
   More and more people see that owning a computer is a real possibility. (Show result.)

   _____ ; CONSEQUENTLY , _____

   _____

5. Some children know more about computers than many adults.
   Some children are teaching adults how to operate computers. (Add an idea.)

   _____ ; LIKEWISE , _____

   _____

6. Professional writers have become enthusiastic about the use of computers. There are still some writers who will use only a ballpoint pen. (Show contrast.)

_; HOWEVER,_____

_____

7. We have many technological aids to writing. Let us not forget that the source for all our ideas is the human brain. (Show contrast.)

_; HOWEVER,_____

_____

E X E R C I S E 2   Combining Sentences Using Adverbial Conjunctions

For each example, add the suggested adverbial conjunction and another independent clause that will make sense. Remember to punctuate correctly.

1. (however) We were told not to leave the building _; HOWEVER,_____ WE WENT TO THE GROSERY STORE.

2. (therefore) I hadn't done the homework very carefully _; THEREFORE,_ I GOT MANY ANSWERS WRONG ON THE QUIZ.

3. (otherwise) He accepted the job he was offered _; OTHERWISE,_ HE WOULD NOT BE ABLE TO PAY HIS RENT.

4. (instead) Domenic doesn't like office work _; INSTEAD,_____ HE PERFERS TO PLAY GOLF.

5. (in fact) The running shoes are expensive _; IN FACT,_____ THEY COST 3 TIME AS MUCH AS A SIMILER BRAND.

6. (furthermore) The doctor advised my father to stop smoking _; FURTHERMORE,_ HE ADVISED HIM TO START EXERCISEING.

7. (consequently) The hurricane struck last night _; CONSEQUENTLY,_ THE RED CROSS WAS CALLED TO HELP WITH DISASTER RELIEF.

Use a Semicolon

TIP **The third way to combine two independent clauses is to use a semicolon.**

IC	;	IC
He arrived at ten	;	he left at midnight.

This third method of combining sentences is used less often. No connecting word is used. The semicolon takes the place of the conjunction.

Two independent clauses: I used to watch the Toronto Blue Jays play baseball at Exhibition Stadium. Tonight I'm going to see them play in the SkyDome.

Compound sentence: I used to watch the Toronto Blue Jays play baseball at Exhibition Stadium; tonight I'm going to watch them play in the SkyDome.

The semicolon was used in this example to show that the content of the two clauses is closely related and therefore belongs together in one sentence.

When sentences are combined by using a semicolon, the grammatical structure of each sentence is often similar:

The women pitched the tents; the men cooked the dinner.

EXERCISE 1   Combining Sentences Using the Semicolon

For each of the independent clauses below, add your own independent clause that is a related idea with a similar grammatical structure. Join the two clauses with a semicolon. An example is done for you.

Independent clause: He wrote the speech.
Compound sentence: He wrote the speech; she gave it.

1. The apartment was light and airy.

   THE APARTMENT WAS LIGHT AND AIRY; WE RENTED IT RIGHT AWAY

2. Shoppers were pushing grocery carts down the aisles.

   SHOPPERS WERE PUSHING GROCERY CARTS DOWN THE AISLES; THE MALL WAS VERY BUSY

3. I plan to learn two foreign languages.

   I PLAN TO LEARN TWO FOREIGN LANGUAGES; I LIKE SPANISH AND FRENCH

4. I tried to explain.

   I TRIED TO EXPLAIN; I WAS MISUNDERSTOOD

5. Many teenagers spend hours listening to rock music.

   MANY TEENAGERS SPEND HOURS LISTENING TO ROCK MUSIC; ADULTS TEND TO LISTEN TO CLASSICAL

EXERCISE 2 Combining Sentences Using the Semicolon

For each of the independent clauses below, add your own independent clause that is a related idea with a similar grammatical structure. Join the two clauses with a semicolon. An example is done for you.

> *Independent clause:* The guests are putting on their coats.
>
> *Compound sentence:* The guests are putting on their coats; the cab is at the door.

1. The pickup truck was filled with old furniture.

   THE PICKUP TRUCK WAS FILLED WITH OLD FURNITURE; THE FURNITURE WAS OLD AND RICKTY.

2. Children played in the streets.

   CHILDREN PLAYED IN THE STREETS; ADULTS SAT ON THE PORCHES.

3. We expected them to understand.

   WE EXPECTED THEM TO UNDERSTAND; THE CONSEPS WERE VERY COMPLEX.

4. The older men wore ties.

   THE OLDER MEN WORE TIES; THE OLDER WOMEN WERE SKIRTS.

5. She hoped her boyfriend would soon call.

   SHE HOPED HER BOYFRIEND WOULD SOON CALL; HE CALLED SHORTLY AFTER 10:00 PM.

Chapter Review Exercises

EXERCISE 1 Combining Sentences Using Co-ordination

Combine each pair of sentences below to make a compound sentence. Choose from the three methods you have studied in this chapter. If you choose a conjunction, be sure that it clearly shows the relationship between the ideas.

1. For many people, mathematics is a necessary evil.
   To a few, mathematics provides a lifetime of challenge and fun.

   FOR MANY PEOPLE, MATHEMATICS IS A NECESSARY EVIL; HOWEVER, TO A FEW, MATHEMATICS PROVIDES A LIFETIME OF CHALLENGE AND FUN

2. Most Canadians have studied math only to grade twelve.
   This limits their ability to understand new scientific developments.

   Most Canadians have studied math only to grade twelve and this

3. Their knowledge extends to little more than basic arithmetic.
   People in the seventeenth century knew as much about math as most Canadians today.

   ; indeed,

4. Few Canadians study math at the university level.
   Many promising mathematics graduates move to the United States.

   ; consequently furthermore

5. Many schools form math teams to compete in area contests.
   Other schools encourage interest in math with math clubs.

   , and

6. Some schools suffer from a lack of good science and math teachers.
   These people have found better-paying jobs in industry.

   because

7. Our future may depend on finding and adequately paying good teachers.
   Canadian students may continue to trail behind those of many other countries in math and science ability.

   ; meanwhile

EXERCISE 2   Combining Sentences Using Co-ordination

Below are five simple sentences. Using each sentence as an independent clause, construct a compound sentence. Use each of the three possible methods you have studied in this chapter at least once.

1. The beach was crowded. (Add an idea.)

2. The first apartment had no bedroom. (Show a contrast.)

; THE SECOND APARTMENT HAD
2 BEDROOMS.

3. January had been bitterly cold. (Show a result.)

; CONSICENTLY, ARE HEATING BILL
WAS HIGH.

4. The young model wore dark glasses to hide her identity. (Introduce a reason.)

, FOR IF SHE HAD'NT PEOPLE WOULD
NOT LEAVE HER ALONE.

5. The community waited for news. (Show time.)

; MEANWHILE, THEY ALL WORRIED

Working Together

A controversial issue today concerns the wide gap in the amount of wages people in different professions earn. For instance, some sports figures and entertainers earn millions every year. How are wages presently determined in our society? How do you think wages should be determined? Should there be a minimum wage in Canada? Should everybody earn the same salary? Divide into groups and discuss the subject for 15 minutes.

Following the general discussion, practise combining sentences using co-ordination by writing ten sentences about the subject of wage differences. If you like, you may try to summarize the ideas of your group. The goal is to use each of the following co-ordinating conjunctions to combine two independent clauses:

and, but, or, nor, for, yet, so
either/or, neither/nor, not only/but also

After working on these sentences for 15 minutes, exchange papers and answer the following questions about the sentences on the paper you have:

1. In each case, has the writer combined two independent clauses?
2. In each sentence, does the co-ordinating conjunction carry the correct meaning for the sentence?
3. Is the punctuation correct?

Chapter 4
Combining Sentences Using Subordination

Q U I C K   Q U I Z   Test yourself on your knowledge of combining sentences using subordination. Combine each of the following pairs of sentences using either a subordinating conjunction or a relative pronoun. Answers to the questions follow the quiz.

1. I live alone with two cats.
   ~~They~~ with They sleep on the braided rug in my bedroom.

   _____

2. The police stood by the door.
   They blocked our entrance.

   THE POLICE   STOOD BY THE DOOR SO THAT

3. She wore high heels.
   ~~They~~ made marks in the wooden floor.

   THAT

   _____

4. My aunt is my favourite relative.
   Her name is Bharati.

   MY AUNT BHARATI, IS MY FAVOURITE RELIVE

5. His outfit was classy. but
   His hair was dirty and unattractive.

   _____

Answers:
1. I live alone with two cats who sleep on the braided rug in my bedroom.
2. The police stood by the door so that they blocked our entrance.
3. She wore high heels that made marks in the wooden floor.
4. My aunt, whose name is Bharati, is my favourite relative.
5. His outfit was classy although his hair was dirty and unattractive.

What Is Subordination?

When you use co-ordination to combine sentences, the ideas in both the resulting clauses are given equal weight. However, ideas are not always equally important.

 Def

> **Subordination** is the method used to combine sentences whose ideas are not equally important.

Subordination allows you to show which idea is the main idea.

The sentence that results when two sentences are combined using subordination is called a **complex sentence**. We identify the two or more ideas that are contained within this complex sentence by calling them **clauses**. The main idea clause is called the **independent clause**. It could stand alone as a simple sentence. The less important idea is called the **dependent clause** because even though this clause has a subject and a verb, it is dependent on the rest of the sentence for its meaning. Consider the following clauses:

Independent clause: That girl will leave.
Dependent clause: If that girl will leave . . .

Notice that both clauses in the examples above have a subject and a verb. (The subject is *girl* and the verb phrase is *will leave*.) The difference is that the dependent clause has an additional word. *If* is a special kind of connecting word that makes the clause "dependent" on an additional idea. A dependent clause does not make sense by itself. The thought is not complete. Below is the same dependent clause with an independent clause added to it.

If that girl will leave, I can finish my homework.

Now the thought is complete.

In your work with sentences, you will want to be comfortable writing sentences with dependent clauses. For this you will need to practise using two kinds of "connecting" words: subordinating conjunctions and relative pronouns. First, practise using subordinating conjunctions.

Use a Subordinating Conjunction to Create a Complex Sentence

Following is a list of subordinating conjunctions. These connecting words signal the beginning of a dependent clause. Be sure to learn them. It is a good idea to memorize them.

Connectors: Common Subordinating Conjunctions

after	if, even if	unless
although	in order that	until
as, as if	provided that	when, whenever
as long as, as though	rather than	where, wherever
because	since	whether
before	so that	while
even though	though	

Function of Subordinating Conjunctions

To introduce a *condition:* if, even if, as long as, provided that, unless (after a negative independent clause)

> **I will go *as long as* you go with me.**
> **I won't go *unless* you go with me.**

To introduce a *contrast:* although, even though, though

> **I will go *even though* you won't go with me.**

To introduce a *cause:* because, since

> **I will go *because* the meeting is very important.**

To show *time:* after, before, when, whenever, while, until (independent clause is negative)

> **I will go *whenever* you say.**
> **I won't go *until* you say it is time.**

To show *place:* where, wherever

> **I will go *wherever* you send me.**

To show *purpose:* in order that, so that

> **I will go *so that* I can hear the candidate for myself.**

You have two choices of how to write the complex sentence. You can begin with the dependent clause, or you can begin with the independent clause.

First way:	DC	,	IC
Example:	If Barbara leaves	,	we can finish our homework.

Second way:	IC	DC
Example:	We can finish our homework	if Barbara leaves.

TIP   **The comma is used when you begin a sentence with a dependent clause.**

When a sentence begins with an independent clause, a comma may not always be needed. For example, the comma is omitted if the dependent clause is essential to the main idea of the speaker.

PRACTICE

Below are three pairs of sentences. Combine each pair by using a subordinating conjunction. Write the sentence two different ways. First, begin the sentence with the dependent clause and use a comma. Second, begin the sentence with the independent clause and use a comma only if necessary.

1. (Use *since*.) The librarian took constant coffee breaks.
   The boss fired him.

   a. ~~THE BOSS FIRE~~ THE LIBRARIAN TOOK CONSTANT COFFEE BREAKS, THE BOSS FIRED HIM

   b. THE BOSS FIRED HIM SINCE THE LIBRARIAN TOOK CONSTANT COFFEE BREAKS

2. (Use *after*.) He won the wrestling match.
   He went out to celebrate.

   a. ~~AFTER HE W~~ HE WENT OUT TO CELEBRATE AFTER HE WON THE WRESTLING MACT.

   b. HE WON THE WRESTLING MATCH, ~~THEN~~ HE WENT OUT TO CELEBRATE

3. (Use *when*.) Halyna returned from Europe this spring.
   The family was excited.

   a. ~~HALYNA~~ THE FAMILY WAS EXCITED WHEN HALYNA RETURNED FROM EUROPE THIS SPRING

   b. HALYNA RETURNED FROM EUROPE THIS SPRING, THE FAMILY WAS EXCITED.

EXERCISE 1

Recognizing Dependent and Independent Clauses

In the blank to the side of each group of words, write the letters *IC* if the group is an independent clause (a complete thought) or *DC* if the group is a dependent clause (not a complete thought even though it contains a subject and a verb).

DC	1. while the photographer was getting ready
DC	2. before the show began
IC	3. I seldom go to the movies by myself
DC	4. even if it rains
IC	5. the Trivial Pursuit game lasted five hours

_____×_DC_____   6. whenever I see you

_____DC_____   7. since I did not take the medicine

E X E R C I S E 2   **Recognizing Dependent and Independent Clauses**

In the blank to the side of each group of words, write the letters *IC* if the group is an independent clause (a complete thought) or *DC* if the group is a dependent clause (not a complete thought even though it contains a subject and a verb).

_____DC_____   1. when his back was turned

_____IC_____   2. he stared at his watch angrily

_____DC_____   3. even though I offered to walk with him

____×_IC_____   4. this was a new development

_____IC_____   5. I was so astonished

_____DC_____   6. unless I acted at once

_____DC_____   7. after my brother arrived

E X E R C I S E 1   **Using Subordinating Conjunctions**

Use each of the subordinating conjunctions that follow to compose a complex sentence. An example is done for you.

> ***Subordinating conjunction:*** after
>
> > ***Complex sentence:*** After the game was over, we all went out for pizza.

Remember that a complex sentence has one independent clause and at least one dependent clause. Every clause must have a subject and a verb. Check your sentences by underlining the subject and verb in each clause.

• Can you explain why the following sentence is not a complex sentence?

> After the game, we all went out for pizza.

• *After the game* is a prepositional phrase, not a dependent clause. *After,* in this case, is a preposition. It is not used as a subordinating conjunction to combine clauses.

1. as if

_____AS IF WASINT WET ANOUGHS,_____

_____

2. before

_____BEFORE ANYONE COULD EAT, THEA HAD: MINISTER_____

_____TO SAY GRACE_____

3. until

Until the rain has stopped, we aren't going anywhere.

4. how

~~How can they do that~~ ?

5. because (Begin with the independent clause. Traditional English grammar frowns on beginning a sentence with *because*. Ask your instructor for his or her opinion.)

_____

_____

E X E R C I S E   2   **Combining Sentences Using Subordination**

Combine each pair of sentences using subordination. Look back at the list of subordinating conjunctions if you need to.

1. He was eating breakfast. _which_
   The results of the election came over the radio.

   _____

   _____

2. The town council voted against the plan, _because_
   They believed the project was too expensive.

   _____

   _____

3. I will see my teacher tonight, _provided that_
   She is speaking at the university this evening.

   _____

   _____

4. The worker hoped for a promotion. _even though_
   Not one person in the department was promoted last year.

   _____

   _____

5. The worker hoped for a promotion. _since_
   He made sure all his work was done accurately and on time.

   _____

   _____

E X E R C I S E 3   **Combining Sentences Using Subordination**

Rewrite the following paragraph using subordination to combine some of the sentences wherever you feel it would be effective. Be prepared to discuss the reasons for your choices. You might also want to discuss places where co-ordination might be a good choice.

Many Canadian communities collect refuse from its source. Waste is delivered to a waste disposal site. Very little waste is recycled. Very little waste is burned. Many smaller towns and villages cannot afford a waste collection service or a proper waste disposal site. Smaller communities are prevalent in Canada. Improperly operated dumps outnumber the better-operated facilities used by larger communities. Over the next few years, many of our landfills will close. They are getting full. Some places in Ontario already truck their trash to the United States. The garbage continues to pile up. The newspapers print stories about it every week. Trash is not a very glamorous subject. People in every town talk about the problem.

Use a Relative Pronoun to Create a Complex Sentence

Often sentences can be combined with a relative pronoun.

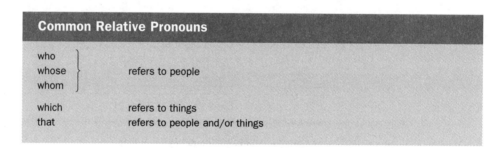

Common Relative Pronouns	
who whose whom	refers to people
which	refers to things
that	refers to people and/or things

Two simple sentences: The researcher had a breakthrough.
He was studying diabetes.

These sentences are short and choppy. To avoid this choppiness, a writer could join these two related ideas with a relative pronoun.

*Combining sentences with
a relative pronoun:* The researcher who was studying diabetes had a breakthrough.

Now join a third idea to the sentence (use *which*).

Third idea: He reported the breakthrough to the press.

 TIP   **Remember to put the relative pronoun directly after the word it relates to.**

> *Incorrect:* The researcher, which he reported to the press, had a
>   breakthrough.

The relative pronoun and its clause *who was studying diabetes* refers to *the researcher*, not to *a breakthrough*. The relative pronoun *which* and its clause *which he reported to the press* does refer to *breakthrough*. This clause will follow the noun *breakthrough*.

> *Correct:* The researcher *who was studying diabetes* had a
>   breakthrough, *which he reported to the press.*

P R A C T I C E   Combine each of the three pairs of sentences into one complex sentence by using a relative pronoun. Do not use commas. An example is done for you.

>   **First sentence:** That woman created the flower arrangement.
> **Second sentence:** She visited us last weekend.
> **Combined sentence:** That woman who visited us last weekend created the
>   flower arrangement.

1. The chemistry lab is two hours long.
   I attend that chemistry lab.

   Combined: THE CHEMISTRY LAB, WHICH I
   ATTENDED WAS TWO HOURS LONG

2. The student assistant is very knowledgeable.
   The student assistant is standing by the door.

   Combined: THE STUDENT HOW IS WHO IS VERY
   KNOWLOEABLE IS STANDING BY THE DOOR

3. The equipment was purchased last year.
   The equipment will make possible some important new research.

   Combined: THE EQUIPMENT PURCHASED LAST
   YEAR WILL ALOUGHT FOR IMPORTANT
   NEW RESEARCH.

How Do You Punctuate a Clause with a Relative Pronoun?

Punctuating relative clauses can be tricky because there are two types of relative clauses.

1. Those that are basic to the meaning of the sentence:

   > Never eat fruit *that isn't washed first.*

   The basic meaning of the sentence is not "never eat fruit." The relative clause is necessary to restrict the meaning. This clause is called a **restrictive clause** and does not use commas to set off the clause. *Note:* Clauses beginning with the pronoun *that* are usually in this category.

2. Those that are not basic to the meaning of the sentence:

> Mother's fruit salad, *which consisted of grapes, apples, and walnuts,* was delicious.

In this sentence, the relative clause is not basic to the main idea. In fact, if the clause were omitted, the main idea would not be changed. This clause is called a **nonrestrictive clause.** Commas are required to indicate that the information is nonessential. *Note:* Clauses beginning with the pronoun *which* are usually in this category.

P R A C T I C E

Choose whether or not to insert commas in the sentences that follow. Use these examples as your models.

The man *who is wearing the Hawaiian shirt* is the bridegroom.

The bridegroom can be identified only by his Hawaiian shirt. Therefore, the relative clause *who is wearing the Hawaiian shirt* is essential to the meaning. No commas are necessary.

Al, *who was wearing a flannel shirt,* arrived late to the wedding.

The main idea is that Al was late. What he was wearing is not essential to that main idea. Therefore, commas are needed to set off this nonessential information.

1. Canada's first census, which was taken in 1667, showed 3215 non-Native inhabitants in 668 families.
2. Most of these families were French Canadians, who lived near the St. Lawrence River.
3. By the time of Confederation, the population of the country had risen to 3 463 000, which was an increase of 1077 percent over 200 years.
4. If the population, which is about 30 000 000 persons in Canada, now, increases by a similar percentage we'll have a population of 280 200 000 by the year 2167.
5. Where do you think will we put everyone who will live in Canada then?

[handwritten: MISTAKE IN BOOK ←]

E X E R C I S E 1   Combining Sentences Using Relative Pronouns

Add a clause that begins with a relative pronoun to each of the following sentences. Use each of the possibilities at least once: who, whose, whom, which, that. Be sure to punctuate correctly. An example has been done for you.

> **Simple sentence:** The leader was barely 1.5 m tall.
> **Complex sentence:** The leader, who was always self-conscious about her height, was barely 1.5 m tall.

1. The prime minister, *who was unsure,* asked his advisers for help.

2. His advisers, *whose objective were the same,* met with him on Parliament Hill.

3. Even the leader of the opposition *that hope for the prime minister to make a mistake,* appeared visibly alarmed.

4. The meeting _THAT WAS SCHDUACED FOR 1_ began at two o'clock.

5. Every idea _WHICH THE INVENTOR HAD_ was examined in great detail.

6. One adviser _WHO WAS AN EXPERLT ARCHTFLX_ was completely opposed to the plan.

7. Finally the group agreed on a plan of action _WHICH THEY IMPLEMENTED_.

E X E R C I S E 2   **Combining Sentences Using Relative Pronouns**

Combine the following pairs of sentences using a relative pronoun.

1. Stress can do a great deal of harm.
   We experience stress every day.

   STRESS, WHICH WE EXPERENCE EVERYDAY,
   CAN CAUSE A GREAT DEAL OF HACM

2. People often use food to help them cope.
   Some people work long hours at demanding jobs.

   PEOPLE WORKING DEMANDING JOBS, THAT
   HAVE LONG HOURS, OFTEN USE FOOD TO HELP THEM COPE.

3. The practice of eating to cope with stress is often automatic.
   The practice of eating to cope often goes back to childhood.

   THE PRACTICE OF EATINGING TO COPE
   THAT OFTEN GOES BACK TO CHILDHOOD IS OFTEN DONE
   TO COPE WITH STRESS.

4. Foods can actually increase tension.
   People turn to foods in times of stress.

   STRESSFUL TIMES, WHICH TURN PEOPLE TO
   FOOD CAN ACTUALLY INKREISE TENSION

5. One of the biggest mistakes people make is to use alcohol as an aid to becoming calm.
   Alcohol is really a depressant.

   ALCOHOL IS A DEPRESSANT, WHICH SOME
   PEOPLE MAKE THE MISTAKE

6. People should eat three light meals a day and two small snacks.
   People want to feel a sense of calm.

   INORDER TO FEEL CALM, PEOPLE SHOULD
   EAT 3 MEALS A DAY AND TWO LIGHT SNACKS

7. Eat a good meal at regular intervals to help avoid stress.
   Binge eating puts on pounds, drains you of energy, and increases your stress level.

   _____

   _____

Chapter Review Exercises

E X E R C I S E   1   **Combining Sentences with a Subordinating Conjunction or a Relative Pronoun**

Combine each of the following pairs of sentences using either a subordinating conjunction or a relative pronoun. Be sure that the word you use makes sense in the sentence.

1. People have been fascinated for centuries by the problem of stuttering; Modern science is only beginning to understand some of the underlying causes of the problem.

   _____

   _____

   _____

   _____

2. For some people stuttering disappears by itself AND
   For others, stuttering continues into adulthood.

   _____

   _____

   _____

3. Stutterers usually keep their affliction UNLESS
   they seek professional help.

   _____

   _____

4. It is true that there is some psychological basis for stuttering.
   It is true that psychologists have not been able to solve the problem.

   THERE IS PSYCHOLOGICAL BASIS FOR STUTTERING
   , YET PSYCHOLOGISTS HAVE BE UNABLE TO SOLVE
   THE PROBLEM

5. All kinds of scientists have looked at the problem from all different angles.
   There is no single answer to stuttering.

   SCIENTIST , WHOM SCIENTIST HAVE
   ABROCHED THE PROBLEM OF STUTERING FROM MANY
   DIFFRENT ANGLES, BUT HAVE YET TO FIND
   A SINGULAR ANSWER

6. Stuttering runs in families.
   Children of such families have greater chances of becoming stutterers.

   _____

   _____

7. You hear someone say he or she knows the causes of stuttering.
   You know that person cannot be speaking scientifically.

_____

_____

Combining Sentences Using Co-ordination and Subordination

To finish this chapter, we'll look at a selection from Himani Bannerji, a writer born in Calcutta, India, who came to Canada in the 1960s. Below are some simple sentences from parts of her short story "In The First Circle." Look over the sentences, and then rewrite the paragraph, combining sentences wherever you think it would improve the meaning and style. The Answer Key will give you a version, although there is certainly more than one way to revise it. Don't be afraid to change the wording slightly to accommodate the changes you want to make.

It is evening. I am afraid. The sun's rays are weak. That red crucible sunk in the clouds is only a dim reflection of itself. It is not a source of light or life. The plains stretch far into the distance behind me. The human dwellings, the villages and cities are far away. They are hidden by the rising mist and fog from the swamps. Only reeds rustle in the wind and waterbirds cry disconsolately there. Beside me, the little grassy glade that I stand in, is a forest — ghana, swapada, shankula. It is dense and full of dangerous beasts of prey. The overhanging foliage has the appearance of clouds. They hold and nourish a damp darkness. The giant trunks of the trees have grown so close together. The forest becomes both a prison and a fort. No footpaths are visible. The undergrowth denies the possibility of making an inroad.

Working Together

This exercise will help you feel more comfortable with using sentences of subordination. First, divide into groups. Then consult the list of subordinating conjunctions on page 44. One student begins a sentence and ends with a subordinating conjunction; then the second student finishes the idea. Work your way through all the subordinating conjunctions. In each case, help each other understand the proper connection between the ideas expressed.

	1st student begins	**2nd student finishes**
Example:	I walked home *after*	I had finished the job.

The group must listen carefully to judge whether each sentence is a correct example of subordination. Are there two independent clauses joined with a subordinating conjunction? Does the sentence make sense?

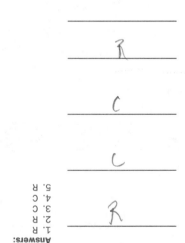

Chapter 5
Correcting the Run-on

Test yourself on your knowledge of run-ons. Some of the examples below are complete sentences; some are run-ons (sentences incorrectly joined together). Write *C* if the example is a complete sentence. Write *R* if the sentence is a run-on. Answers to the questions follow the quiz.

_____ 1. Strong competition exists among chocolate companies, each carefully guards its own recipes.

___*R*___ 2. In 1980, newspapers all over the world carried the story of the great chocolate recipe robbery it sounded like a spy movie.

___*C*___ 3. A young worker for a Swiss chocolate company needed money to buy an automobile so he tried to sell the secret company recipes to Saudi Arabia, Russia, and China.

___*C*___ 4. The worker thought the recipes were safely hidden in a locker in a train station, but the Swiss police caught him and recovered the recipes.

___*R*___ 5. The company decided not to press charges the worker was given a suspended sentence.

Answers:
1. R
2. R
3. C
4. C
5. R

A teenager came home from school with a long face.

DAUGHTER: I had a terrible day.

MOTHER: What happened?

DAUGHTER: Well, to start with my hair looked terrible <u>and then</u> the science teacher called on me to give my oral report <u>and</u> I was counting on having another day at least to get ready for it <u>and</u> when I got to English class I realized I had left my purse in science class <u>and</u> I didn't have time to go back and get it <u>and</u> to top it off Mrs. Edmunds gave us a surprise quiz on our reading assignment.

MOTHER: <u>And</u> I thought my day was bad!

This is probably typical of many conversations you have had at one time or another. In telling about a series of events, we sometimes join the events together as if they were one long thought. A problem arises when you want to write down these events in acceptable writing form. Writing ideas down as if they are all one thought without any punctuation to help the reader is not acceptable. Such a sentence as the one above is called a **run-on**. You cannot combine independent clauses without some kind of punctuation.

How Many Kinds of Run-ons Are There?

The Different Kinds of Run-on Sentences

1. *The fused run-on:* two or more independent clauses that run together without any punctuation

   I met Diana again we were happy to see each other.

2. *The comma splice:* two or more independent clauses that run together with only a comma

   I met Diana again, we were happy to see each other.

3. *The "and" run-on:* two or more independent clauses that run together with a co-ordinating conjunction but no punctuation

   I met Diana again and we were happy to see each other.

How Do You Make a Complete Sentence from a Run-on?

Guide for Correcting Run-ons

1. Make two simple sentences with end punctuation:

   I met Diana again. We were happy to see each other.

2. Make a compound sentence using one of the three methods of co-ordination:

   I met Diana again, and we were happy to see each other.
   I met Diana again; furthermore, we were happy to see each other.
   I met Diana again; we were happy to see each other.

3. Make a complex sentence using subordination:

   When I met Diana again, we were happy to see each other.
   We were happy to see each other when I met Diana again.

EXERCISE 1 Recognizing and Correcting Run-ons

The following story is written as one sentence. Rewrite the story, making sure to correct the run-on sentences. Put a period at the end of each complete thought. You may have to omit some of the words that loosely connect the ideas together, or you may want to use co-ordination and subordination. Remember to start each new sentence with a capital letter.

FURTURMORE,

Well, to start with my hair looked terrible, and then the science teacher called on me to give my oral report, and I was counting on having another day at least IN to get ready for it. and when I got to English class I realized I had left my purse in science class, and I didn't have time to go back and get it. and to top it off Mrs. Edmunds gave us a surprise quiz on our reading assignment.

Recognizing and Correcting Run-ons

The following story is written as one sentence. Rewrite the story, making sure to correct the run-on sentences. Put a period at the end of each complete thought. You may have to omit some of the words that loosely connect the ideas together, or you may want to use co-ordination and subordination. Remember to start each new sentence with a capital letter.

My best friend is accident-prone. If you knew her you'd know that she's always limping, having to write with her left hand, or wearing a bandage on her head or ankle, last week for example she was walking down the street minding her own business when a shingle from someone's roof hit her on the head and THEN she had to go to the emergency ward for stitches, then this week one of her fingers is purple because someone slammed the car door on her hand, sometimes I think it might be better if I didn't spend too much time with her you know her bad luck might be catching!

Revising Run-ons

Each of the following examples is a run-on. Supply four possible ways to revise each run-on. Use the guide on page 56 if you need help.

1. Intelligence tests for children are not always useful they are a basic tool for measurement in most schools.

   Two simple sentences:

   INTELLIGENCE TEST FOR CHILDREN ARE NOT ALWAYS USEFUL, THEY ARE BASIC TOOL FOR MEASUREMENT IN MOST SCHOOLS

   Two kinds of compound sentence:

   a. INTELLIGENCE TEST FOR CHILDREN ARE NOT ALWAYS USEFUL, AND THEY ARE A BASIC TOOL MES. IN MIST SCHOOLS

   b. INTELIGENCE TEST FOR CHILDREN ARE NOT ALWAYS USEFUL ; HOWEVER THEY ARE AR. A BASIC TOOL FOR MEASUREMENT IN MOST SCHOOLS

   Complex sentence:

   WHILE INTELLENCE TESTS FOR CHILDREN ARE NOT ALWAYS USEFUL, THEY ARE A BASIC TOOL FOR MEASUREMENT IN MOST SCHOOLS

2. Many people are opposed to gambling in all its forms they will not even buy a lottery ticket.

Two simple sentences:

MANY PEOPLE ARE OPPOSED TO GAMBLING IN ALL FORMS.

THEY WILL NOT EVEN BUY A LOTTERY TICKET.

Two kinds of compound sentence:

a. MANY PEOPLE ARE OPPOSED TO GAMBLING
IN ALL FORMS. INFACTED, THEY WILL

b. NOT EVEN BUY A LOT. TICKET.

Complex sentence:

MANY PEOPLE ARE OPP. TO GAMBLING IN ALL FORMS,
THEY WILL NOT EVEN BUY A LOT TICKET,

3. Public transportation is the major problem facing many of our cities little is being done to change the situation.

Two simple sentences:

PUBLIC TRANSPORTATION IS THE MAJOR
PROBLEM FACING MANY OF ARE CITYS. LITTLE IS BEING
DONE TO CHANGE THE SITUATION.

Two kinds of compound sentence:

a. PUBLIC TRANSPORTATION IS THE MAJOR PROBLEN
FACING MANY OF ARE CITYS; FURTHERMORE, LITTLE IS
BEING DONE TO CHANGE THE SITUATION,

b. ..... OF ARE CITYS, AND LITTLE IS BEING
DONE ... THE SITUATION.

Complex sentence:

PUBLIC TRANSPORTATION IS THE MAJOR PROBLEM FACING
MANY OF ARE CITYS, YET LITTLE IS BEING DONE TO
CHANGE THE SITUATION.

4. Travel is a great luxury one needs time and money.

Two simple sentences:

TRAVEL IS A GREAT LUXURY.
ONE NEEDS TIME AND MONEY

Two kinds of compound sentence:

a. TRAVEL IS A GREAT LUXURY, WHICH FOR
ONE NEEDS TIME AND MONEY

b. TRAVEL IS A GREAT LUXURY; CONSIKENTLY ONE NEEDS TIME AND MONEY.

Complex sentence:

ONE NEEDS TIME AND MONEY TO TRAVEL SINCE IT IS A GREAT LUXURY.

5. The need for a proper diet is important in any health program all the junk food on the grocery shelves makes it hard to be consistent.

Two simple sentences:

THE NEED FOR A PROPER DIET IS IMPORTANT IN ANY HEALTH

ALL THE JUNK FOOD ON THE GR. SHEL. MAKES IT HARD

Two kinds of compound sentence: of CONSISTENT

a. THE NEED FOR A PROPER DIET IS IMPORTANT IN ANY HEALTH PROGRAM; HOWEVER ALL THE

b. JUNK FOOD ON THE GROCERY SHELVES MAKES IT HARD TO BE CONSISTENT

Complex sentence:

_____

_____

_____

EXERCISE 2 Revising Run-ons

Each of the following examples is a run-on. Supply four possible ways to revise each run-on. Use the guide on page 56 if you need help.

1. The airline has begun its new route to the islands everyone is looking forward to flying there.

Two simple sentences:

_____

_____

Two kinds of compound sentence:

a. _____

_____

b. _____

_____

Complex sentence:

_____

_____

2. The movie begins at nine o'clock let's have dinner before the show.

Two simple sentences:

THE MOVIE BEGINS AT NINE o'clock.
LET'S HAVE DINNER BEFORE THE SHOW.

Two kinds of compound sentence:

a. THE MOVIE BEGINS AT NINE O'CLOCK, AND WE'T HAVE DINNER BEFORE THE SHOW

b. THE MOVIE BEGINS AT NINE O'CLOCK; ALSO, LET HAVE DINER BEFORE THE SHOW

Complex sentence:

THE MOVIE BEGINS AT NINE, SO LET HAVE DINNER BEFORE.

3. The studio audience screamed at the contestant they wanted her to try for the big prize.

Two simple sentences:

THE STUDIO AUDIENCE SCREAMED AT THE CONTESTANT. THEY WANTED HER TO TRY FOR THE BIG PRIZE.

Two kinds of compound sentence:

a. THE STUDIO AUD. SCREAMED AT THE CONT.; CONSEQUENTLY, THEY WANTED HER TO GO FOR THE BIG PRIZE

b. THE STUDIO-AUD. SCREAMED AT THE CONT BECAUSE THEY WANTED HER TO TRY FOR THE BIG PRIZE

Complex sentence:

THE STUDIO AUDIENCE SCREAMED AT THE CONTESTENT, AND THEY WANTED HER TO GO FOR THE BIG PRIZE.

4. The baby covered his eyes he thought he could disappear that way.

Two simple sentences:

THE BABY COVERED HIS EYES. HE THOUGHT HE COULD DISAPPEAR THAT WAY.

Two kinds of compound sentence:

a. *THE BABY COVERED HIS EYES, AND HE THOGH HE COULD DISAPPEAR.*

b. *THE BABY COVERED HIS EYES; IN FACT, HE THOUGH HE COULD DISAPPEAR*

Complex sentence:

THE BABY COVERED HIS EYES, HE THOUGH HE COULD DISAPPEAR.

5. The waitress smiled she told us the specials of the day.

Two simple sentences:

THE WAITRESS SMILED.
SHE TOLD US THE SPECIALS OF THE DAY

Two kinds of compound sentence:

a. *THE WAITRESS SMILED, AND THEN SHE TOLD US THE SPECIALS OF THE DAY*

b. *THE WAITRESS SMILED; MEANWHILE, SHE TOLD US THE SPECIALS OF THE DAY*

Complex sentence:

THE WAITRESS SMILED AS SHE TOLD US THE SPECIALS OF THE DAY

Chapter Review Exercises

E X E R C I S E 1   **Editing for Run-ons**

Rewrite the following paragraph, correcting all run-on sentences.

Commercial farming in Atlantic Canada is concentrated in the dairy, poultry, and horticultural sectors, the most important crop in the region, particularly in New Brunswick and Prince Edward Island, is potatoes. In Ontario and Quebec, farming is highly diversified and includes specialty crops such as soybeans, tobacco, fruit, and vegetables. In the Prairie region, most of the country's wheat, oats, barley, rye, flaxseed, canola, mustard, and sunflowers are grown livestock raising is also very important in Canada with the majority of ranches being located in the three prairie provinces.

E X E R C I S E 2   Editing for Run-ons

Rewrite the following paragraph, correcting all run-on sentences.

> Although the metric system was legalized in Canada in 1871, the British Imperial system of units, based on yards, pounds, gallons, etc., continued to be used until the 1960s, with rapidly expanding technology and worldwide trade, the need for an international measurement system became apparent. Britain decided to convert to the system the United States was studying a similar move. A number of Canadian businesses favoured the metric system in January 1970 the government passed legislation stating that a single, coherent measurement system based on metric units should be used for measurement purposes in this country.

Working Together

In the telling of a story, it is tempting to use run-ons that merge the events of the story in one long sentence. Choose a movie or book you have seen or read recently and retell the plot. In about 20 minutes, write as much of the story as you can remember, being careful to write only on every other line, separating each word, and writing clearly so your classmates can read what you have written. Exchange papers and read the paper you receive in order to check for run-ons. When you have found what you believe to be a run-on, put a mark beside that sentence and be ready to read the sentence or put it on the board for class discussion.

Chapter 6
Making Sentence Parts Work Together

QUICK QUIZ Test yourself on your knowledge of how sentence parts work together. On the line before each sentence below, write the correct form of the verb. Answers to the questions follow the quiz.

goes   1. The history of trading in spices (goes, go) back thousands of years.

HAVE   2. Some writers from ancient Rome (has, have) recorded cinnamon being brought to Italy from Africa in the first century A.D.

WERE   3. In the year 1252, the famous traveller Marco Polo reported that pepper and ginger (was, were) being imported to China from India.

WAS   4. Each group of explorers that went to Asia (was, were) astonished at the number of unusual spices to be found there.

WERE   5. Not only pepper but also cloves (was, were) among the spices that offered great wealth to those who could supply European and North American markets.

Answers:
1. goes
2. have
3. were
4. was
5. were

For your sentences to be logical, all parts of each sentence must agree. Agreement, according to the *Holt Handbook*, is the correspondence between words in number, gender, or person. Subjects and verbs agree in number (singular or plural) and person (first, second, or third); pronouns and their antecedents agree in number, person, and gender (masculine, feminine, and neuter).

Since most students frequently have problems with agreement in their writing, you should work through this chapter carefully so that you will be able to look for these trouble spots in your own writing.

Subject–Verb Agreement within the Sentence

Def

A verb must agree with its subject in **number**.

he			I	
she			you	
it	}	sleep<u>s</u>	we	} sleep
any singular noun			they	
			plural	

Example: The baby *sleeps*.   *Example:* The babies *sleep*.

> **T I P**   Remember that a verb that goes with a singular noun or pronoun (except *I* or *you*) needs a final *s*.

P R A C T I C E 1   Underline the correct verb in the following sentences.

1. The dog (bark, <u>barks</u>).
2. It (wake, <u>wakes</u>) up the neighbourhood.
3. The neighbours (<u>become</u>, becomes) very angry.
4. People (<u>deserve</u>, deserves) a quiet Sunday morning.
5. I (throws, <u>throw</u>) an old shoe at the dog.

Special Problems in Making Verbs Agree with Their Subjects

1. **The subject is not always the noun closest to the verb. Remember, do not look for the subject within a prepositional phrase.**

   In the example that follows, the subject is underlined, the prepositional phrase is crossed out, and the verb is circled.

   The hairline <u>cracks</u> ~~in the engine~~ (present) a serious threat to passengers' lives.

2. **Many indefinite pronouns take a singular verb.**

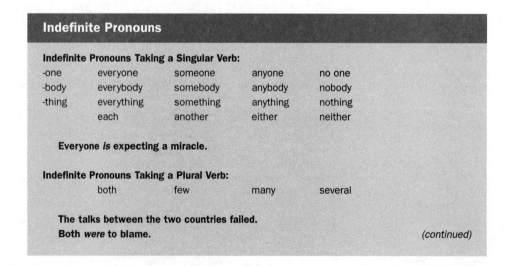

Indefinite Pronouns

Indefinite Pronouns Taking a Singular Verb:

-one	everyone	someone	anyone	no one
-body	everybody	somebody	anybody	nobody
-thing	everything	something	anything	nothing
	each	another	either	neither

Everyone *is* expecting a miracle.

Indefinite Pronouns Taking a Plural Verb:

both	few	many	several

The talks between the two countries failed.
Both *were* to blame.

(continued)

(continued)

Indefinite Pronouns Taking a Singular or Plural Verb Depending on the Meaning in the Sentence:

any	all	more
none	some	most

The books are gone   **All *were* very popular.**
The sugar is gone.   **All of it *was* spilled.**

3. **When a pair of conjunctions is used, the verb agrees with the subject closer to the verb.**

> Neither the textbook nor my lecture *notes explain* the meaning of the term "tidal wave."

Textbook and notes together make up the compound subject. Since *notes* is closer to the verb, the verb agrees with *notes*.

Pairs of Conjunctions
neither . . . nor
either . . . or
not only . . . but also

4. **In some sentences, the subject can come after the verb. In these cases, be sure that the verb agrees with the subject.**

> Here *is* the *surprise* I promised you.
> Who *were* the *people* with you last night?

5. **A group noun in Canadian English usually takes a singular verb if the group acts as a unit. (The test is to substitute the word *it* in place of the group noun.)**

> The town *council is planning* a Canada Day celebration.

In this sentence, the council is acting as a unit. "It" is planning a celebration. Therefore, the verb is singular.

A group noun takes a plural verb if the members of the group act as individuals. (The test is to substitute the word *they* for the group noun and see if it sounds right.)

> The town *council are preparing* their speeches for this event.

In this sentence, the council members are individually preparing speeches. *They* substitutes for the group noun in this sentence. Since the individuals are acting separately, the verb is plural.

Common Group Nouns

audience	family
class	group
committee	jury
council	number
crowd	team

6. The verbs *do* and *be* are often troublesome. Remember that standard English uses *s* for the third person singular.

The Verb to do

I do	we	
you do	you (plural)	do
he	they	
she } does		
it		

The Verb to be (Past Tense)

I was	we	
you were	you	were
he	they	
she } was		
it		

PRACTICE 2   Underline the verb that agrees with the subject.

1. He (doesn't, don't) study in the library anymore.
2. We (was, were) hoping to find him there.
3. The library (doesn't, don't) close until eleven o'clock.
4. (Was, Were) you late tonight?
5. Ann (doesn't, don't) care if you stay until closing time.

EXERCISE 1   **Making the Subject and Verb Agree**

In the blanks next to each sentence, write the subject of the sentence and the correct form of the verb. An example is done for you.

	Subject	Verb
The eleven proposals for the development of a new building at Laurier Circle (has, have) been submitted to the city.	proposals	have

1. The price of airline tickets to England (has, have) remained fairly reasonable.   England
2. His decision (requires, require) a lot of thought.   DECISION
3. She (doesn't, don't) know the answer to any of the test questions.   SHE
4. Either the elevator operator or the security guard (see, sees) every visitor.   VISITOR
5. The committee (agree, agrees) to the fund-raising projects for this year.   COMMITTEE
6. Potato chips and soda (is, are) most of her diet.   DIET
7. One of the people in the audience (is, are) my brother.   BROTHER

E X E R C I S E 2   Making the Subject and Verb Agree

In the blanks next to each sentence, write the subject of the sentence and the correct form of the verb.

	Subject	Verb

1. Included in the price of the trip (<u>was</u>, were) five nights in a lovely hotel and all meals. — TRIP _____

2. Nobody in the family (<u>knows</u>, know) how to swim. — FAMILY _____

3. Jerry and Aldo (works, <u>work</u>) well together. — JERRY AND ALDO _____

4. The number of essay questions on the apprenticeship exam (<u>seems</u>, seem) to be increasing. — EXAM _____

5. Where (<u>is</u>, are) the wrapping paper for these packages? — WRAPPINGPAPPEL _____

6. In the entire building there (is, <u>are</u>) only two windows. — BUILDING _____

7. Either the fruit pie or that chocolate cake (<u>looks</u>, look) like the best choice for your picnic. — PIE _____

Pronouns and Case

The case of a personal pronoun is determined by the function it serves in a sentence. Pronouns can function as subjects or subject complements (subjective case); as direct objects, indirect objects, or objects of prepositions (objective case); or as indicators of ownership (possessive case).

Guide to Pronoun Case

Pronouns Used as Subjects	Pronouns Used as Objects	Pronouns Used as Possessives
I	me	my (mine)
you (sing.)	you (sing.)	your (yours)
he	him	his (his)
she	her	her (hers)
it	it	its (its)
who	whom	whose
whoever	whomever	
we	us	our (ours)
you (pl.)	you (pl.)	your (yours)
they	them	their (theirs)

Use the guide above to choose the correct answers in the following examples:

1. (She, Her) is singing at the concert tonight.
2. Today, you and (I, me) have to buy the tickets.
   Hint: When you have a compound subject or object, it is easier to pick the correct pronoun if you read the sentence without one of the subjects:

   Today, (I, me) have to buy the tickets.

3. He sold (us, we) the best seats in the house.
4. To (who, whom) should I address the letter?
5. Her voice is much stronger than (he, him, his).
   Hint: In a comparison, it is easier to pick the correct pronoun if you complete the comparison.

   Her voice is much stronger than (he, him, his) voice is.

6. (Who, Whom, Whose) music was left on the piano?

E X E R C I S E 1   Choosing Correct Pronoun Forms

Circle the correct pronoun in each of the sentences below.

1. Matthew and (she, her) presented the project today.
2. Between you and (I, me), I think it was outstanding.
3. Their visual materials will help (whoever, whomever) will study the project later.
4. He is usually a better speaker than (she, her).
5. (Whoever, Whomever) heard them agreed that it was an impressive presentation.
6. (Who, Whom) do you think made the best points?
7. I am not as deeply involved in my project as (they, them).
8. Their research was much more detailed than (us, our, ours).
9. The professor gave both Carolyn and (he, him) A's.
10. My partner and (I, me) will have to work harder to reach this standard.

E X E R C I S E 2   Choosing Correct Pronoun Forms

Circle the correct pronouns in the following paragraph.

When my mother and (I, me) decided to care for my very ill father at home, some of our friends objected. My sister and (they, them) said we would be exhausted and unable to handle the stress. To (who, whom) could we go for help in the middle of the night? My father, (who, whom) we believed would be happier at home, had been our first consideration. Of course, we would have benefited if my mother or (I, me) had been a nurse. However, we did have a visiting nurse available at times. We were more confident than (they, them) that we could handle the situation.

Pronoun–Antecedent Agreement

1. **A pronoun must agree in number (singular or plural) with any other word to which it refers.** That word to which the pronoun refers is known as the pronoun's **antecedent**.

All the *students* worked on *their* final drafts.

The antecedent of the pronoun *their* is the noun *students*, and since *students* is plural, the pronoun *their* is also plural.

The following sentence contains a pronoun–antecedent disagreement in **number**:

Everyone worked on *their* final draft.

The problem in this sentence is that *everyone* is a singular word, but *their* is a plural pronoun. You may often have heard people use the plural pronoun *their* to refer to a singular subject. In fact, the above sentence may sound correct, but it is still a mistake in formal writing. Here are two approaches a writer might take to correct this sentence:

Everyone worked on *his* final draft.

Although you may encounter this approach in current writing, it is unpopular because it is widely considered a sexist construction.

Everyone worked on *his/her* final draft.

This form is technically correct, but if it is used several times, it sounds awkward and repetitious.

The best solution is to revise such a construction so that the antecedent is plural, as we indicated in our original example above:

All the students worked on *their* final drafts.

Another problem with pronoun–antecedent agreement in number occurs when a demonstrative pronoun (*this, that, these, those*) is used with a noun. That pronoun must agree with the noun it modifies:

Singular: this kind, that type

> ***Incorrect:*** *These kind* of shoes hurt my feet.
> ***Correct:*** *This kind* of shoe hurts my feet.

Plural: these kinds, those types

> ***Incorrect:*** *Those type* of cars always need oil.
> ***Correct:*** *Those types* of cars always need oil.

P R A C T I C E   1   Rewrite each of the following sentences so that the pronoun agrees with its antecedent in *number*.

ALL THE PEOPLE

1. ~~Everyone~~ should bring their suggestions to the meeting.

A _____

2. ~~This~~ sorts of clothes are popular now.
THESE

_____

WASN'T
3. There ~~was not~~ anyone who knew what they were doing.

_____

THEY
4. If ~~the~~ bird-watchers hope to see anything, ~~one~~ must get up early.

_____

5. ~~These~~ type of book appeals to me.
THIS

_____

2. **Pronouns must also agree with their antecedents in person.**

The following incorrect sentence contains a pronoun–antecedent disagreement in **person**:

When mountain climbing, *one* must maintain *your* concentration at all times.

The sentence could be correctly rewritten as follows:

When mountain climbing, *one* must maintain *one's* concentration at all times.
When mountain climbing, *you* must maintain *your* concentration at all times.
When mountain climbing, *I* must maintain *my* concentration at all times.
When mountain climbing, *we* must maintain *our* concentration at all times.

PRACTICE 2 Rewrite each of the following sentences so that the pronoun agrees with its antecedent in *person*.

your KNOWLEDGE.
1. I enjoy math exams because ~~you~~ can show what ~~you~~ know.

_____

I
2. When I took geometry, ~~we~~ discovered that frequent review of past assignments helped make the course seem easy.

_____

THEIR
3. People always need to practise ~~your~~ skills in order not to forget them.

_____

ONE has
4. Math games can be fun for one if ~~you have~~ a spirit of curiosity.

_____

you
5. When studying math, you must remember that ~~we~~ have to "use it or lose it."

_____

3. **The antecedent of a pronoun should not be missing, ambiguous, or repetitious.** Following is a sentence with a missing antecedent:

> *Missing antecedent:* In Florida, *they* have many beautifully developed retirement areas.
>
> *Possible revision:* Florida has many beautifully developed retirement areas.

In the first sentence, who is meant by *they*? If the context has not told us that *they* refers to the government or to the developers, then the antecedent is missing. The sentence should be rewritten in order to avoid *they*.

In the next sentence, the antecedent is ambiguous.

> *Ambiguous antecedent:* Margaret told Lin that *she* needed to earn $1000 during the summer.
>
> *Possible revision:* Margaret said that Lin needed to earn $1000 during the summer.

In the first example, *she* could refer to either Margaret or Lin. The sentence should be revised in a way that will avoid this confusion.

The last example illustrates a repetitious antecedent.

> *Repetitious pronoun and antecedent:* The newspaper article, *it* said that Earth Day, 1993, re-established humankind's commitment to the earth.
>
> *Possible revision:* The newspaper article said that Earth Day, 1993, re-established humankind's commitment to the earth.

The subject should be either *article* or, if there is already an antecedent, *it*. Using both the noun and the pronoun results in needless repetition.

PRACTICE 3 Rewrite each of the following sentences so that the antecedents are not missing, ambiguous, or repetitious.

1. The biologist asked the director to bring back his microscope.

_____

_____

2. In the report, it says that the number of science and engineering students seeking doctoral degrees has fallen 50 percent since the mid-sixties.

_____

_____

3. At the laboratory, they said the research had run into serious difficulties.

_____

_____

4. The testing equipment was accidentally dropped into the aquarium and it was badly damaged.

_____

_____

5. I don't watch the ten o'clock news anymore because they have become too slick.

THE TEN O'CLOCK NEWS HAS BECOME

TOO SLICK FOR ME TO WATCH.

E X E R C I S E   1   **Making Pronouns and Antecedents Agree**

Each of the following sentences contains errors with pronouns. Revise each sentence so that pronouns agree with their antecedents and so that there are no missing or ambiguous antecedents.

1. His father mailed him his high school yearbook.

   HIS FATHER MAILE HIS SON HIGH SCHOOL YEARBOOK
   TO HIM

2. No one wants their income reduced.

   NONE OF THE EMPLOYES WANTS THEIR INCOME
   REDUCED

3. When a company fails to update its equipment, they often pay a price in the long run.

   WHEN A COMPANY FAILS TO UPDATE IT'S EQUIPMENT
   IT OFTEN PAY THE PRICE IN THE LONG RUN

4. The woman today has many more options open to them than ever before.

   THE WOMEN TODAY HAVE MANY MORE
   OPTIONS OPEN TO THE EVER BEFORE.

5. Everybody knows their own strengths best.

   PEOPLE TEND TO KNOW THERE OWN STENGHS
   BEST

6. Each of the workers anticipates their summer vacation.

   _____

7. If the campers want to eat quickly, each one should help themselves.

   INORDER FOR THE CAMPER TO EAT QUICKYLY
   THEY MUST HELP THEMSEIVES

E X E R C I S E   2   **Making Pronouns and Antecedents Agree**

Each of the following sentences may contain an error with pronouns. Revise each sentence so that pronouns agree with their antecedents and so that there are no missing or ambiguous antecedents. If a sentence is correct, mark a *C* on the lines provided.

1. The teacher suggested to the parent that he might have been too busy to have noticed the child's unhappiness.

   THE PARENTS LISEWED, AS THE
   TEACHER EXPLAINED THAT HE MAY
   HAVE BEEN TO BUSY TO HAVE NOTICED
   THE CHILDS UNHAPPINESS

2. The county submitted their [~~or~~] proposal for the bridge repairs.

_____

_____

3. We all rushed away from all the trees to our cars because you had to wait for the thunderstorm to stop.

   THE GROUP RUSHED AWAY FROM THE TREES

   TOWARDS THE CARS, TO WAIT FOR THE TUNDERSTORM TO STOP [~~THERE~~]

4. A young person does not [~~Do not~~] receive enough advice on how they should choose their career. CHOSSES

   _____

   _____

5. These types of watches are very popular.

   _____

6. People were taken forcibly from our homes. THEIR

   _____

7. No one brought their books today.

   NONE OF THE STUDENTS BROUGHT THEIR

   BOOKS TODAY

Parallel Structure: Making a Series of Words, Phrases, or Clauses Balance within the Sentence

Which of the following sentences achieves a better sense of balance?

> His favourite hobbies are playing the trumpet, listening to jazz, and to go to concerts.
> His favourite hobbies are playing the trumpet, listening to jazz, and going to concerts.

If you selected the second sentence, you would have made the better choice. The second sentence uses parallel structure to balance the three phrases in the series (playing, listening, and going). By matching each of the items in the series with the same *-ing* structure, the sentence becomes easier to understand and more pleasant to read. You can make words, phrases, and even sentences in a series parallel:

1. **Words in a series should be the same parts of speech.**

   > *Incorrect:* The town was small quiet and the atmosphere was peaceful.
   > (The series is composed of two adjectives and one clause.)
   > *Correct:* The town was small quiet and peaceful.
   > (*Small, quiet,* and *peaceful* are adjectives.)

2. **Phrases in a series should be the same kind of phrase (infinitive phrases, prepositional phrases, verb phrases, noun phrases, participial phrases).**

> *Incorrect:* Her lost assignment is in her closet, on the floor, and the clothes are hiding it.
> (Two prepositional phrases and one clause.)
> *Correct:* Her lost assignment is in her closet, on the floor, and under a pile of clothes.
> (Three prepositional phrases beginning with *in, on,* and *under.*)

3. **Clauses in a series should be parallel.**

> *Incorrect:* One clerk polished the antique spoons; they were placed into the display case by the other clerk.
> *Correct:* One clerk polished the antique spoons; the other clerk placed them in the display case.

P R A C T I C E

Each of the following sentences has an underlined word, phrase, or clause that is not parallel. Make the underlined section parallel.

1. My favourite armchair is lumpy, worn out, and <u>has dirt spots everywhere.</u>

   _____ IS COVERED WITH DIRTY SPOTS _____

2. She enjoys reading novels, studying the flute, and <u>also sews her own clothes.</u>

   _____ AND SEWING HER OWN CLOTHS _____

3. He admires teachers who make the classroom an exciting place and <u>willingly explaining material more than once.</u>

   _____

E X E R C I S E 1   Revising Sentences for Parallel Structure

Each of the following sentences needs parallel structure. Underline the word, phrase, or clause that is not parallel and revise it so that its structure will balance with the other items in the pair or series. An example is done for you.

> *Incorrect:* The best leather comes from Italy, from Spain, and <u>is imported from Brazil.</u>
> *Correct:* The best leather comes from Italy, from Spain, and <u>from Brazil.</u>

1. Winter in Edmonton is very windy and has many <u>bitterly cold days.</u>

   WINTER DAYS IN EDMONTON ARE VERY WINDY AND BITTERLY COLD

2. I would prefer to <u>fix an old car</u> than watching television.

   I WOULD PREFFER FIXING AN OLD CAR TO WATCHING TELEVISION

3. George is a helpful neighbour, a loyal friend, and <u>dedicated to his children.</u>

   DEDICATED FATHER

4. The apartment is crowded and without light.

_____DARK_____

5. The dancer is slender and moves gracefully.

____GRACEFUL____

6. The nursery was cheerful and had a lot of sun.

____SUNNY____

7. My friend loves to play chess, to read science fiction, and working out at the gym.

_____

_____

EXERCISE 2 **Revising Sentences for Parallel Structure**

Each of the following sentences needs parallel structure. Underline the word, phrase, or clause that is not parallel and revise it so that its structure will balance with the other items in the pair or series.

1. The dog had to choose between jumping over the fence, or he could have dug a hole underneath it.

____OR DIGGING A HOLE UNDER IT.____

_____

2. She disliked going to the beach, hiking in the woods, and she didn't care for picnics, either.

____AND PICNICS____

_____

3. As I looked down the city street, I could see the soft lights from restaurant windows, I could hear the mellow sounds of a nightclub band, and carefree moods of people walking by.

____AND SENCE THE CAREFREE MOODS OF THE____

____PEOPLE WALKING BY____

4. The singers have been on several road tours, have recorded for two record companies, and they would also like to make a movie someday.

____AND HAVE EXPRESSED AN ENTRESSED IN____

____MAKEING A MOVIE.____

5. They would rather order a pizza than eating their sister's cooking.

____THAN EAT THERE SISTERS COOKING____

_____

6. I explained to the teacher that my car had broken down, my books had been stolen, <u>and I left my assignment pad at home.</u>

    AND MY ASSIGMENT PAD WAS AT HOME

7. That night the prisoner was sick, discouraged, <u>and she was filled with loneliness.</u>

    AND LONELY

Misplaced and Dangling Modifiers

 Modifiers are words or groups of words that function as adjectives or adverbs.

That is, they describe or modify other words in the sentence. If a modifier is put in the wrong place or in an ambiguous or awkward place in the sentence, the meaning will be unclear. If the modifier has no word at all to modify, the result might be confusing or even unintentionally humorous.

TIP **A modifier must be placed close to the word, phrase, or clause it modifies so that the reader can understand the intended meaning.**

Below are examples of how several problems with modifiers can be revised to make the meanings clear. Study these examples carefully. After you are able to recognize them in the exercises that follow, you will begin to recognize them in your own writing as well.

 Misplaced Modifiers — modifiers that have been placed in wrong, ambiguous, or awkward positions

1. **The modifier in the wrong place**

> *Wrong:* The salesperson sold the used car to the customer that needed extensive body work.

Who or what needs body work — the car or the customer?

> *Revised:* The salesperson sold the customer the used car that needed extensive body work.

Be especially careful to put each of the following words closest to the word, phrase, or clause it modifies.

| almost | exactly | just | nearly | scarcely |
| even | hardly | merely | only | simply |

Notice how the meaning in each of the following sentences changes depending on where the modifier is placed.

Only Charlene telephoned my brother yesterday.
Charlene only telephoned my brother yesterday.
Charlene telephoned only my brother yesterday.
Charlene telephoned my only brother yesterday.
Charlene telephoned my brother only yesterday.

2. **The awkward modifier that interrupts the flow of the sentence**
   The adverb *only* could be better placed so it would not split the infinitive *to call.*

   Awkward: Cheryl planned to only call my sister.
   Revised: Cheryl planned to call only my sister.

3. **The "squinting modifier" — an ambiguous modifier that could describe a word or words on either side of it**

   Squinting: Cheryl having telephoned secretly appeared at the scene of the crime.

   Did Cheryl telephone secretly or appear secretly?

   Revised: Having secretly telephoned, Cheryl appeared at the scene of the crime.

Def

Dangling Modifier — a modifier in a sentence that has no word, phrase, or clause that the modifier can describe

   Dangling: Working on the car's engine, the dog barked all afternoon.

   Who worked on the engine? Was it the dog?

   Revised: Working on the car's engine, I heard the dog barking all afternoon.

   or

   The dog barked all afternoon while I was working on the car's engine.

E X E R C I S E 1   Revising Misplaced or Dangling Modifiers

Revise each sentence so there is no misplaced or dangling modifier.

1. Victor fed the dog wearing his tuxedo.

   <u>Victor was wearing his tuxedo when he fed the dog</u>

2. Visiting the Vancouver Aquarium, the killer whales entertained us.

WHEN WE VISITED THE VAN. AQUARIM WE WERE ENTENED BY THE KILLER WHALES.

3. Hoping to see the news, the television set was turned on and all ready by seven o'clock.

IN ORDER TO WATCH THE NEW, WE TURN ON THE TV. AT 7 o'clock.

4. A woodpecker was found in Cuba that had been considered extinct.

A WOODPECKER THAT WAS CONSIDER TO BE EXTINCT WAS FOUND IN CUBA.

5. After running over the hill, the farm was visible in the valley below.

AFTER RUNNING OVER THE HILL, I SAW THE FARM IN THE VALLY BELOW.

6. The truck caused a traffic jam, which was broken down on the highway, for kilometres.

THE TRUCK WHICH WAS BROCKEN DOWN CAUSED A TRAFIC JAM A KK LONG.

7. Hanging from the ceiling in my bedroom, I saw three spiders.

THERE WERE 3 SPIDERS HANGING FROM THE CEICING IN MY BEDROOM.

EXERCISE 2   Revising Misplaced or Dangling Modifiers

Revise each sentence so there is no misplaced or dangling modifier.

1. Leaping upstream, we fished most of the day for salmon.

WE FISHED FOR MOST OF THE DAY AND COULD SEE THE SAMON LEAPING UP STREAM

2. At the age of ten, my family took a trip to Fredericton.

AT THE AGE OF TEN, I TOOK A TRIP WITH MY FAMILY TO FREDRICTON

3. Skimming every chapter, my biology textbook suddenly made more sense.

I FOUND THAT MY BIO TEXTBOUK MADE MORE SENCE AFTER I SKMED THROUGH EVER CHAPTER.

4. Running up the stairs, the train left for Montreal.

WELL I WAS RUNNING UP THE STAIRS, THE TRAIN LEFT FOR MONTREAL.

5. Working extra hours last week, my salary increased dramatically.

LAST WEEK

MY SALARY INCREASED DRAMATICLY ^B/C I WORK EXTRA HOURS.

6. We watched a movie in the theatre for which we had paid five dollars.

WE PAID 5 DOLLARS TO WATCH A MOVIE IN THE THEATER.

7. Dressed in a Dracula costume, I thought my son looked perfect for Halloween.

MY SON DRESSED AS DRACULA FOR HALLOWEEN.

Chapter Review Exercises

EXERCISE 1   Making Sentence Parts Work Together

Each of the sentences below has a part that does not work with the rest of the sentence. Find the error and correct it.

1. A new medical study of thousands of Chinese show new connections between diet and health.

A NEW MEDICAL STUDY OF THOUSANDS OF CHINESE PEOPLE SHOWED CONNECTIONS BETWEEN DIET & HEALTH.

2. Eating a lot of animal protein, the researchers found Western people have many health problems.

RESEARCHERS FOUND THAT WESTERN PEOPLE THAT EAT LOTS OF ANIMAL PROTEIN MAY HAVE HEALTH PROBLEMS

3. A person who lives in one place for a long time and who eats the same food all the time makes perfect subjects for a study on diet.

THE PERFECT SUBJECT FOR A STUDY ON DIET IS SOMEONE WHO EATS THE SAME THINGS ALL THE TIME.

4. A Chinese person eats very few calcium products, but they get calcium in other ways.

CHINESE PEOPLE TEND TO EAT FEW DAIRY PRODUCTS

5. They believe we should eat mostly vegetables.

VEGITARIANS BELIVE PEOPLE SHOULD EAT MOSTLY VEGETABLES

6. One of the many results of the study are an awareness of better eating habits.

ONE OF THE MANY RESULTS OF THE STUDY WAS THAT PARTICIPANTS[?] BECAME MORE AWARE OF BETTER EATING HABITS

7. The Chinese who eat the most protein also have the highest rate of serious illness like heart disease, diabetes, and suffering from cancer.

CHINESE PEOPLE WHO HAVE DIET WHICH CONSIST OF HIGH LEVELS OF PROTEIN ARE PRIME CANDIDATES FOR HEART DESIK DIBETES AND CANCER

EXERCISE 2   Making Sentence Parts Work Together

Read the following paragraph. Look for errors in agreement, parallel structure, and misplaced or dangling modifiers, and then rewrite your corrected version.

Cowboys became important in the United States after the American Civil War who lived on large ranches in Texas, Montana, and other western states. One of the traditional names for cowboys are "cowpokes" although they prefer to be called "cowhands." The equipment for cowboys came into use because of his many practical needs. The wide-brimmed cowboy hat served as a bucket to hold water, as a sort of whip to drive cattle, and waving to other cowboys a few hills away. Cowboys began to wear tight trousers because they did not want loose pants to catch in bushes as they chased cattle. The rope is a cowboy's most important tool since they use it to catch cattle, pull wagons, tie up equipment, and even killing snakes. The famous roundup, which takes place twice a year, are important because cattle are separated, classified, and selected for market. When cowboys get together for such a roundup, they often hold a rodeo as a celebration. Rodeos give cowboys opportunities to compete in riding bareback, wrestling steer, and to rope calves.

Working Together

The photograph shows a family portrait from the 1930s. What is the earliest photograph you have of one or more members of your own family? From stories you have been told by other members of the family, what do you know about these relatives? What do you believe you can tell about them from their photographs?

Use the next 20 minutes to write freely on this subject. When you have finished your work, review what you have written. Look for the kinds of errors you have studied in this chapter. These errors include lack of subject–verb agreement, lack of pronoun–antecedent agreement, lack of parallelism, and misplaced and dangling modifiers. Then exchange your paper with another member of the class and proofread that classmate's paper. Are you able to spot any of your classmate's errors?

Chapter 7
Solving More Problems with Verbs

**QUICK QUIZ** Test yourself on your knowledge of verb forms. In each of the following sentences, choose the correct verb tense for the verb in the dependent clause. Answers to the questions follow the quiz.

1. The program will continue only after the coughing and fidgeting _have stopped_. (to stop)

2. Since he was poor and unappreciated by the music world when he died in 1791, Mozart did not realize the importance that his music _would have_ (to have) in the twentieth century.

3. Dad will tell us tonight if he _will buy_ (to buy) a new car next month.

4. Einstein studied only subjects that he _enjoyed_. (to like)

5. We know that science _is_ (to be) now close to finding a cure for leukemia.

Answers:
1. have stopped, stop
2. would have
3. will buy
4. liked
5. is

Since every sentence contains at least one verb, and this verb can take one of many forms, it is worth a good deal of your time and effort to understand these many forms and their uses. So far in this book, you have learned to recognize verbs (Chapter 1) and to make them agree with their subjects (Chapter 6). In this chapter, you will study several other areas that often cause difficulty for writers:

> Irregular Verbs
> Verb Tense Consistency
> Sequence of Verb Tenses
> Present Perfect and Past Perfect Tenses
> Active and Passive Voice
> The Subjunctive

What Are the Principal Parts of the Irregular Verbs?

The English language has more than 100 verbs that do not form the past tense or past participle with the usual *-ed* ending. Their forms are irregular. When you listen to young children, you often hear them utter expressions such as "Yesterday

I *cutted* myself." Later on, they will learn that the verb *cut* is unusual, and they will change to the irregular form, "Yesterday I *cut* myself." The best way to learn these verbs is to listen to how they sound. Pronounce them out loud over and over until you have learned them. If you find that you don't know a particular verb's meaning, or you cannot pronounce a verb and its forms, ask your instructor for help. Most irregular verbs are very common words that you will be using often in your writing and speaking. You will want to know them well.

Practising Fifty Irregular Verbs

These are the three principal parts of irregular verbs:

Simple Form (also called Infinitive Form)	Past Form	Past Participle (used with perfect tenses after *has, have,* or *will have,* or with passive voice after the verb *to be*)

I. Eight verbs that do not change their forms
    (Notice they all end in *-t* or *-d*)

Simple Form	Past Form	Past Participle
bet	bet	bet
cost	cost	cost
cut	cut	cut
fit	fit	fit
hit	hit	hit
hurt	hurt	hurt
quit	quit	quit
spread	spread	spread

II. Two verbs that have the same simple present form and past participle

Simple Form	Past Form	Past Participle
come	came	come
become	became	become

PRACTICE 1 Fill in the correct form of the verb in the following sentences.

(cost) 1. Last year the tuition for my education ____cost____ 7 percent more than the year before.

(quit) 2. I have ____quit____ trying to guess my expenses for next year.

(spread) 3. The message has ____spread____ that college costs continue to spiral.

(hit)   4. Most parents have been ___HIT___ with large tax increases.

(become)   5. Financing a child's higher education has ___BECOME___ a difficult task.

III. Twenty verbs that have the same simple past form and past participle

Simple Form	Past Form	Past Participle
bend	bent	bent
lend	lent	lent
send	sent	sent
spend	spent	spent
creep	crept	crept
keep	kept	kept
sleep	slept	slept
sweep	swept	swept
weep	wept	wept
teach	taught	taught
catch	caught	caught
bleed	bled	bled
feed	fed	fed
lead	led	led
speed	sped	sped
bring	brought	brought
buy	bought	bought
fight	fought	fought
think	thought	thought
seek	sought	sought

PRACTICE 2 Fill in the correct form of the verb in the following sentences.

(buy)   1. Last year the school district ___BOUGHT___ new chemistry texts.

(spend)   2. Some parents felt they had ___SPENT___ too much money on these new books.

(bleed)   3. They claimed the taxpayers were being ___BLED___ dry.

(keep)   4. These parents argued that the school should have ___KEEPED___ the old books.

(think)   5. The teachers ___THOUGHT___ the old books were worn out.

IV. Twenty verbs that have all different forms

Simple Form	Past Form	Past Participle
blow	blew	blown
fly	flew	flown
grow	grew	grown
know	knew	known
throw	threw	thrown
begin	began	begun
drink	drank	drunk
ring	rang	rung
shrink	shrank	shrunk
sink	sank	sunk
sing	sang	sung
spring	sprang	sprung
swim	swam	swum
bite	bit	bitten (or bit)
hide	hid	hidden (or hid)
drive	drove	driven
ride	rode	ridden
stride	strode	stridden
rise	rose	risen
write	wrote	written

PRACTICE 3   Fill in the correct form of the verb in the following sentences.

(sing)   1. Last night, the tenor ___SANG___ "The Flower Song" from *Carmen.*

(grow)   2. Over the past few performances, his audiences have ___grown___.

(begin)   3. I first ___BEGAN___ to enjoy his singing when I heard his voice on the radio last spring.

(hide)   4. I have never ___HIDDEN___ my admiration for the tenor voice.

(know)   5. Famous tenors like Enrico Caruso, John McCormack, and Luciano Pavarotti are ___Known___ all over the world.

EXERCISE 1   **Knowing the Irregular Verb Forms**

Supply the past form or the past participle for each verb in parentheses.

Ever since people ___BEGAN___ to write, they have ___WRITTEN___
                                 (begin)   (write)

about the great mysteries in nature. For instance, no one ___KNEW___
                                                                     (know)

why the dinosaurs disappeared. Scientists now have _____ ~~CAN~~ BET _____ on
(bet)

one strong possibility. That possibility is that 65 million years ago, a 10-km-wide

chunk of rock _____ HIT _____ the earth and _____ THROW _____ up a thick
(hit)   (throw)

cloud of dust. The dust _____ KEPT _____ the sunlight from the earth; there-
(keep)

fore, certain life forms disappeared. Some scientists have _____ THOUGHT _____
(think)

that this could also have _____ SHRUNK _____ the earth's animal population by
(shrink)

as much as 70 percent. Other scientists are not so sure that this is the answer.

They believe time has _____ HIDDEN _____ the real reason for the disappear-
(hide)

ance of the dinosaurs.

EXERCISE 2 Knowing the Irregular Verb Forms

Supply the past form or the past participle for each verb in parentheses.

Medical researchers have _____ SOUGHT _____ a cure for the common cold,
(seek)

but so far they have _____ FOUGHT _____ without success. The cold virus has
(fight)

_____ SPREAD _____ throughout the world, and the number of cold victims has
(spread)

_____ RISEN _____ every year. Past experience has _____ TAUGHT _____ us
(rise)   (teach)

that people who drink plenty of liquids and take aspirin get over colds more

quickly than those who do not, but this is not a good enough remedy. People

~~have~~ HAD also believed that you _____ FEED _____ a fever and starved a cold, but
(feed)

recent research has _____ LED _____ to a disclaimer of this belief. It has
(lead)

_____ COST _____ a lot of time and effort to search for a vaccine, but so far
(cost)

the new knowledge has not _____ BROUGHT _____ a cure.
(bring)

Avoid Unnecessary Shifts in Verb Tense

Do not shift verb tenses as you write unless you intend to change the time of the action.

> *Shifted tense:* The customer *asked* (past tense) for the prescription, but the pharmacist *says* (present tense) that the ingredients *are being ordered* (present tense).

Revised: The customer *asked* (past tense) for the prescription, but the pharmacist *said* (past tense) that the ingredients *were being ordered* (past tense).

EXERCISE 1   Correcting Unnecessary Shifts in Verb Tense

Each sentence below has an unnecessary shift in verb tense. Revise each sentence so that the tense remains consistent.

1. After I complete that writing course, I took the required history course.

   COMPLETED

2. In the beginning of the movie, the action was slow; by the end, I am sitting on the edge of my seat.
   WAS

3. The textbook gives the rules for writing a bibliography, but it didn't explain how to do footnotes.   *doesn't*

   GAVE

4. While working on her report in the library, my best friend lost her note cards and comes to me for help.

   CAME

5. The encyclopedia gave several pages of information about astronomy, but it doesn't give anything about black holes.

   HAVE ANY INFORMATION

6. The invitation requested that Juan be at the ceremony and that he will attend the banquet as well.

   ALSO

7. This is an exciting book, but it had too many characters.

   THE BOOK WAS EXCITING

EXERCISE 2   Correcting Unnecessary Shifts in Verb Tense

The following paragraph contains unnecessary shifts in verb tense. Change each incorrect verb to past tense.

Doctor Norman Bethune grows up in Gravenhurst, Ontario. He was educated in Toronto and serves as a stretcher bearer in World War I. He contracted tuberculosis and thereafter devotes himself to helping other victims of the disease when he practises surgery in Montreal. He also invents or redesigned twelve medical and surgical instruments. Bethune travelled to Russia in 1935, joined the Communist party, and goes to Spain in 1936, where he organized the first mobile blood transfusion service during the Spanish Civil War. After returning to Canada, he shortly left for overseas again, this time to China, where he helped the Chinese Communists in their fight against Japan. "Spain and China," he writes, "are part of the same battle." While there, he contracted an infection and died. Mao's essay "In Memory of Norman Bethune," prescribed reading during China's Cultural Revolution, urges all Communists to follow Bethune's example of selfless dedication to others. Bethune is the best-known Canadian to the Chinese, and many Chinese visit his Canadian birthplace.

What Is the Sequence of Tenses?

The term **sequence of tenses** refers to the proper use of verb tenses in complex sentences (sentences that have an independent clause and a dependent clause).

The guide that follows shows the relationship between the verb in the independent clause (IC) and the verb in the dependent clause (DC).

Independent Clause	Dependent Clause	Time of the DC in Relation to the IC
If the tense of the independent clause is in the **present** (he *knows*), here are the possibilities for the dependent clause:		
He knows	that she *is* right.	same time
	that she *was* right.	earlier
	that she *will be* right.	later
If the tense of the independent clause is in the **past** (he *knew*), here are the possibilities for the dependent clause:		
He knew	that she *was* right.	same time
	that she *had been* right.	earlier
	that she *would be* right.	later
If the independent clause is in the **future** (he *will tell*), here are the possibilities for the dependent clause:		
He will tell us	if she *goes*.	same time
	if she *has gone*.	earlier
	if she *will go*.	later

PRACTICE   In each of the following sentences, choose the correct tense for the verb in the dependent clause. Use the guide above if you need help.

1. The golf tournament <u>will continue only</u> after the thunder and lightning _HAS STOPPED_

(to stop)

2. Since he thought that he was buying a well-maintained car, Enzo <u>did not realize</u> the problems that this car _WOULD HAVE_ in the months to come.

(to have)

3. I <u>will know</u> when I get my next paycheque whether or not I _CAN BUY_ a stereo next week.

(to buy)

4. Albert Einstein <u>failed</u> the entrance exam at the Swiss Federal Institute of Technology because he _WAS NEVER_ a very disciplined student.

(to be) + never

5. Jacob <u>ate</u> only those foods that he _LIKED_ .

(to like)

6. Cancer researchers <u>think</u> it's likely that a cure for most cancers _WILL SOON_ _BE_ found.

(to be) + soon

7. I <u>know</u> that my best course of action _IS_ to tell the truth.

(to be)

How Do You Use the Present Perfect and the Past Perfect Tenses?

Forming the Perfect Tenses

> *Present perfect tense:* *has* or *have* + past participle of the main verb
> has worked
> have worked
> *Past perfect tense:* *had* + past participle of the main verb
> had worked

What Do These Tenses Mean?

Def   The **present perfect tense** describes an action that started in the past and continues to the present time.

Jennifer *has worked* at the hospital for ten years.

This sentence indicates that Jennifer began to work at the hospital ten years ago and is still working there now.

Examine the following time line. What does it tell you about the present perfect tense?

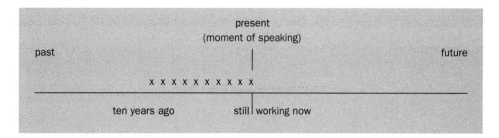

Other example sentences of the present perfect tense:

She *has studied* violin since 1980.
I *have* always *appreciated* his generosity.

 The **present perfect tense** can also describe an action that has just taken place, or where the exact time of the action in the past is indefinite.

Has Jennifer *found* a job yet?
Jennifer *has* (just) *found* a new job in Moncton.
Have you ever *been* to Kapuskasing?
Yes, I *have been* there three times.

If the time were definite, you would use the simple past:

Jennifer *found* a new job yesterday.
Yes, I *was* there last week.

 The **past perfect tense** describes an action that occurred before another activity or another point of time in the past.

Jennifer *had worked* at the hospital for ten years *before* she *moved* away.

In this sentence, there are two past actions: Jennifer *worked*, and Jennifer *moved*. The action that took place first is in the past perfect (*had worked*). The action that took place later, and was also completed in the past, is in the simple past (*moved*).

Other examples using the **past perfect tense:**

I *had* just *finished* when the bell *rang.*
He *said* that Randall *had told* the class about the experiment.
He *had provided* the information *long before* last week's meeting.

P R A C T I C E

Complete the following sentence by filling in each blank with either the present perfect tense or the past perfect tense of the verb given.

1. Yolanda told us that she ___LIVED___ in Athabaska before she moved
   (live)
   to Mexico City.

2. Mexico City ___HAS FASCINATED___ visitors for many years.
   (fascinate)

3. This city ___BECAME___ the largest city in the world, and people
   (become)
   ___WATCH___ it grow larger every year.
   (watch)

4. The suburbs of the city ___HAVE overwhelmed___ old villages that ___HAVE EXISTED___
   (overwhelm)   (exist)
   peacefully since the days of the Aztecs.

5. Today, Mexico City ___HAS BUILT___ a computer-controlled subway system
   (build)
   to deal with its huge transportation problem.

What Is the Difference between Active and Passive Voice?

Active and Passive Voice

In the **active voice**, the subject does the acting:

The committee made the decision.

Choose the active voice generally in order to achieve direct, economical, and forceful writing. Most writing, therefore, should be in the active voice.

In the **passive voice**, the subject is acted upon:

The decision was made by the committee.
or
The decision was made.

Notice in these passive sentences, the actor is not only de-emphasized by being moved out of the subject place but may be omitted entirely from the sentence.

Choose the passive voice to de-emphasize the actor or to avoid naming the actor altogether.

Study the two sentences below. The first is in the active voice and the second is in the passive. In what situations would a writer want to use the active voice, and in what situations might the writer need to use the passive?

Roberta Bondar orbited the earth in 1992.
The earth was orbited by Roberta Bondar in 1992.

How might the passive voice be used in historical accounts? What are the disadvantages of the passive voice?

How Do You Form the Passive Voice?

Subject Acted Upon	+ Verb *To Be*	+ Past Participle	+ *by* Phrase (Optional)
The race	was	won	(by the runner)
The fish	was	cooked	(by the chef)
The books	are	illustrated	(by the artists)

PRACTICE

Fill in the following chart by making all sentences on the left active voice and all sentences on the right passive voice. Then discuss with your classmates and instructor why you might choose the active voice or the passive voice in each case.

Active Voice

1. THE CHILD DIALED THE WRONG NUMBER

2. MY GRANDMOTHER CROCHETED THE SWEATER VERY CAREFULLY

3. The tornado struck Cherry Creek last spring.

4. The wind blew the leaves across the yard.

5. PLATFORM SHOES WERE FASHIONABLE IN THE 60'S

Passive Voice

1. The wrong number was dialled by the child by mistake.

2. The sweater was crocheted very carefully by my grandmother.

3. LAST SPRING CHERRY CREEK WAS STRUCK BY A TORASSO

4. THE LEAVES WERE BLOWN ACROSS THE YARD BY THE WIND

5. In the sixties, platform shoes were worn by many fashionable young men and women.

What Is the Subjunctive?

Def

The **subjunctive** is an as yet unrealized situation.

Use the subjunctive in *that* clauses expressing demands, resolutions, or requests, and in sentences that express a condition contrary to a fact or a wish. With *that* clauses, use the base form of the verb (*see, think, be*) whether the subject is singular or plural. Use *were* in clauses that express a wish and in contrary-to-fact clauses beginning with *if*.

Recognize the three instances that call for the subjunctive:

1. Unreal conditions using *if* or *wish*

    If <u>he were</u> my teacher, I would be pleased.
    I *wish* <u>he were</u> my teacher.

2. Clauses starting with *that* after verbs such as *ask, request, demand, suggest, order, insist,* or *command*

    I *demand* that <u>she work</u> harder.
    Sullivan *insisted* that <u>Jones report</u> on Tuesday.

3. Clauses starting with *that* after adjectives expressing urgency, as in *it is necessary, it is imperative, it is urgent, it is important,* and *it is essential*

    It is necessary that <u>she wear</u> a net covering her hair.
    It is essential that <u>Robert understand</u> the concept.

Other Problems with Verbs

Do not use more than one **modal auxiliary** (*can, may, might, must, should, ought*) with the main verb.

> *Incorrect:* Matt *shouldn't ought* to sell his car.
> *Correct:* Matt *ought not* to sell his car.
> or
> Matt *shouldn't* sell his car.

Do not use *should of, would of,* or *could of* to mean *should have, would have,* or *could have.*

> *Incorrect:* Elana *would of* helped you if she *could of.*
> *Correct:* Elana *would have* helped you if she *could have.*

Chapter Review Exercises

E X E R C I S E   1   Solving Problems with Verbs

Revise each of the following sentences to avoid problems with verbs.

1. He ~~hadn't~~ ought NOT to drive so fast.

_____

2. It is essential that Krista goes to class tonight.

_____

3. I wish I was a senior. ~~were~~

_____

4. She sung for a huge crowd Saturday night. ~~sang~~

_____

5. I was shook up by the accident.

THE ACCIDENT SHOOK ME UP.

6. The books were studied by the students.

THE STUDENTS STUDIED THE BOOKS.

7. My father ask me last night to help him build a deck.

C

E X E R C I S E 2   Solving Problems with Verbs

Some of the verbs in the following paragraph are incorrect. Find the errors and correct them.

I knowed I was in big trouble in chemistry when I took a look at the midterm exam. My semester should of been a lot better. The first day I had my new textbook, I put it on the back shelf of a taxi and forgot it when I got out. Then I catched a cold and miss the next two classes. When I finally start off for class, I missed the bus and walked into the classroom half an hour late. The teacher scowls at me and ask to speak to me after class. I use to always sit in the front row so I could see the board and hear the lectures, but now that I am late I have to take a seat in the last row. I wish I was able to start this class over again the right way. No one had ought to have such an unlucky start in any class.

Working Together

Student Profile: On a separate piece of paper, answer the following five questions about yourself. Write on every other line to make your writing more readable. Write freely for 20 minutes. Then exchange papers with another student. Using a pencil, circle each verb in the student's writing. Are any of the verbs incorrect in their form or in their tense? Be prepared to share examples with the class.

1. Tell about the first book you remember ever looking at or reading.
2. Who was your most memorable teacher in elementary school? What is it about this teacher that you remember?
3. Who was the person outside of school who taught you the most?
4. What are the magazines you subscribe to or would like to subscribe to and why?
5. When you have a day or half day to yourself, how do you spend that time?

Chapter 8
Punctuating Sentences Correctly

 **QUICK QUIZ** Test yourself on your knowledge of commas. In each of the following sentences, place commas wherever they are needed. Answers to the questions follow the quiz.

1. White-collar criminals, dishonest company executives, are being exposed in growing numbers.
2. White-collar criminals are found in industrial plants, government offices and banks.
3. For example, manufacturers have been caught cheating the government, and well-known banks have been caught laundering money.
4. In the past, white-collar criminals have not been prosecuted very vigorously by the law.
5. However, some executives are now being given jail sentences for their white-collar crimes.

Answers:
1. criminals, executives,
2. plants, offices,
3. example, government,
4. past,
5. However,

The Eight Basic Uses of the Comma

Many students feel very uncertain about when to use the comma. The starting point is to concentrate on a few basic rules. These rules will cover most of your needs.

The tendency now in English is to use fewer commas than in the past. There is no one perfect set of rules on which everyone agrees. However, if you learn the eight basic rules explained in this chapter, your common sense will help you figure out what to do in other cases. Remember that a comma usually signifies a pause in a sentence. As you read a sentence out loud, listen to where you pause. This is often your clue that a comma is needed. Notice that in each of the examples for the following eight uses, you can pause where the comma is placed.

I. **Use a comma to separate items in a series.**

> I was angry, fretful, and impatient.
> I was dreaming of running in the race, finishing among the top ten, and collapsing happily on the ground.

- A series means more than two items.
- Some writers omit the comma before the *and* that introduces the last item.

I was angry, fretful and impatient.

- When an address or date occurs in a sentence, each part is treated like an item in a series. A comma follows each item even if there are only two items:

  I lived at 14 Tartan Avenue, Halifax, Nova Scotia, for many years.
  I was born on October 15, 1954, in the middle of Hurricane Hazel.

- A comma does not follow the last item in a series unless that last item is part of an address or a date.
- A group of adjectives may not be regarded as a series if some of the words "go together." You can test this by putting *and* between each item. If it doesn't work, then don't use commas.

  I carried my *old, dark green* coat.
  I took the *four black spotted* puppies home.
  I rode in his *new red sports* car.

PRACTICE 1   In each of the following sentences, insert commas wherever they are needed.

1. Problems with the water supply of Canada the United States Europe and other parts of the world are growing.
2. Water is colourless tasteless odourless and free of calories.
3. You will use on an average day 90 L of water for flushing 120 L for bathing and washing clothes and 95 L for other uses.
4. It took 450 L of water to create the eggs you ate for breakfast 13 250 L for the steak you might eat for dinner and over 200 000 L to produce the steel used to make your car.
5. By 1970 the English–Wabigoon river system which runs through Grassy Narrows Ontario had become polluted with mercury.

II. **Use a comma along with a co-ordinating conjunction (to join sentences of equal rank or value) to combine two simple sentences (also called independent clauses) into a single compound sentence. (See Chapter 3 on co-ordination.)**

  The house was on fire, but I was determined not to leave my place of safety.

Be careful that you use the comma with the conjunction only when you are combining sentences. If you are combining only words or phrases, no comma is used.

  I was safe but not happy.
  My mother and father were searching for me.
  I was neither in class nor at work.

PRACTICE 2   In each of the following sentences, insert commas wherever they are needed.

1. The most overused bodies of water are our rivers but they continue to serve us daily.

2. Canadian cities often developed next to rivers and industries followed soon after in the same locations.

3. The people of the industrial age can try to clean the water they use or they can watch pollution take over.

4. The Great Lakes are showing signs of renewal yet the struggle against pollution there must continue.

5. Most people have not been educated about the dangerous state of our water supply nor are all our members of Parliament fully aware of the problem.

III. **Use a comma to follow introductory words, expressions, phrases, or clauses.**

A. Introductory words (such as *yes, no, oh, well*)

Oh, I never thought he would do it.

B. Introductory expressions (transitions such as *as a matter of fact, finally, secondly, furthermore, consequently*). See the transition chart on the inside back cover.

Therefore, I will give you a second chance.

C. Introductory phrases

Long prepositional phrase: In the beginning of the course, I thought I would never be able to do the work.
Participial phrase: Walking on tiptoe, the young mother quietly peeked into the nursery.
Infinitive phrase: To be quite honest, I don't believe he's feeling well.

D. Introductory dependent clauses beginning with a subordinating conjunction (see Chapter 4)

When the food arrived, we all grabbed for it.

PRACTICE 3   In each of the following sentences, insert commas wherever they are needed.

1. To many people from Canada the plans to supply more water to the United States seem unnecessary.

2. However people in the western United States know that they have no future without a good water supply.

3. In 1935 the federal government initiated irrigation schemes on the Canadian prairies.

4. Of the total 1.4 percent of Canadian farmland was irrigated by 1981.

5. Learning from the past modern farmers are trying to co-operate with nature.

IV. **Use commas surrounding a word, phrase, or clause when the word or group of words interrupts the main idea.**

A. Interrupting word

We will, however, take an X-ray.

   B. Interrupting phrase

      Prepositional phrase: I wanted, of course, to stay.
        Appositive phrase: Ann, the girl with the red hair, has a wonderful
                    sense of humour.

   C. Interrupting clause

      He won't, I think, try that again.
      Ann, who has red hair, has a wonderful sense of humour.

TIP   **Sometimes the same word can function differently.**

She came to the dance; however, she didn't stay long.

In this sentence, *however* is used to combine independent clauses.

She did, however, have a good time.

In this sentence, *however* interrupts the main idea.

TIP   **Sometimes the same clause can be used differently.**

Ann, who has red hair, has a wonderful sense of humour.

In this sentence, *who has red hair* interrupts the main idea of the sentence, and so commas are used.

The girl who has red hair is my sister Ann.

The clause *who has red hair* is part of the identity of "the girl." This clause does not interrupt the main idea but is necessary to and part of the main idea. Therefore, no commas are used.

PRACTICE 4   In each of the following sentences, insert commas wherever they are needed.

   1. Natural disasters, I believe, have not been historically significant.
   2. They have, however, significantly affected the lives of many Canadians.
   3. Canada's worst coal-mine disaster, at Hillcrest, Alberta, occurred on June 19, 1914.
   4. In Springhill, Nova Scotia, furthermore, 424 persons were killed in the mines between 1881 and 1969.
   5. Avalanches, storms, and floods which are natural disasters, have also made their marks on the face of our country.

  V. **Use a comma around nouns in direct address.**

     I thought, Maria, that I saw your picture in the paper.

PRACTICE 5   In each of the following sentences, insert commas wherever they are needed.

1. Dear, your tea is ready now.
2. I wonder, Samir, if the game has been cancelled.
3. Dad, could I borrow $5?
4. I insist, sir, on speaking with the manager.
5. Ayesha, is that you?

VI. **Use a comma in numbers of 1000 or larger.**

1,999
1,999,999,999

> **TIP**   **In the metric system of measurement, _spaces_ — not commas — are used in numbers of 1000 or larger. (However, numbers of four digits need not be separated.) This practice is becoming more widespread in Canada.**
>
> **4000 _or_ 4 000**
> **38 622**

PRACTICE 6   In each of the following numbers, insert commas or spaces wherever they are needed.

1. 4876454
2. 87602
3. 156439600
4. 187000
5. 10000000000000

VII. **Use a comma to set off exact words spoken in dialogue.**

"Let them," she said, "eat cake."

> **TIP**   **The comma as well as the period is always placed inside the closing quotation marks.**

PRACTICE 7   In each of the following sentences, insert commas wherever they are necessary.

1. "I won't," he insisted, "be a part of your scheme."
2. He mumbled, "I won't incriminate myself."
3. "I was told," the defendant explained, "to answer every question."
4. "This court," the judge announced, "will be adjourned."
5. "The jury," said Al Tarvin of _The Star_, "was hand-picked."

VIII. **Use a comma where it is necessary to prevent a misunderstanding.**

Before eating, the cat prowled through the barn.

P R A C T I C E   8   In each of the following sentences, insert commas wherever they are needed.

1. Kicking the child was carried off to bed.
2. To John Ben Wicks is the funniest cartoonist.
3. When you can come and visit us.
4. Whoever that is is going to be surprised.
5. Skin cancer seldom kills doctors say.

E X E R C I S E   1   **Using the Comma Correctly**

In each of the following sentences, insert commas wherever they are needed.

1. The penguins that live in an area of South Africa near the coast are an endangered species.
2. One breeding ground for these penguins tiny Dassen Island is northwest of Cape Town.
3. Today fewer than 60 000 penguins can be found breeding on this island.
4. At one time seabirds that stole the penguins' eggs were the only threat to the funny-looking birds.
5. Human egg collectors not to mention animals that simply take the eggs have constantly reduced the penguin population.
6. However the worst threat to the penguins is oil pollution.
7. If a passing tanker spills oil many penguins can die.

E X E R C I S E   2   **Using the Comma Correctly**

In each of the following sentences, insert commas wherever they are needed.

1. The Commonwealth Games were first held in Hamilton Ontario in 1930.
2. The first games known as the British Empire Games attracted 400 competitors from eleven countries.
3. By 1978 during the Commonwealth Games in Edmonton nearly 1500 athletes from 41 countries competed.
4. Canada has been a leading supporter of these games which are held every four years.
5. Memorable performances feats by both Canadian and non-Canadian athletes have become a benchmark of the games.
6. In Edmonton Canadian athletes won 45 gold 31 silver and 33 bronze medals in 1978.
7. Next to the Olympics the Commonwealth Games are one of the world's best international competitions.

Other Marks of Punctuation

The Apostrophe

Use the apostrophe as follows:

I. **To form the possessive, add *'s* or an apostrophe:**

A. Add *'s* to singular nouns:

> the pen of the teacher = the teacher*'s* pen
> the strategy of the boss = the boss*'s* strategy
> the work of the week = the week*'s* work

> **Watch out that you choose the right noun to make possessive. Always ask yourself *who* or *what* possesses something. In the sentence above, the teacher possesses the pen, the boss possesses the strategy, and the week possesses the work.**

Note these unusual possessives:

> *Hyphenated words:* mother-in-law*'s* advice
> *Joint possession:* Lucy and Desi*'s* children
> *Individual possession:* John*'s* and Steve*'s* ideas

B. Add *'s* to irregular plural nouns that do not end in *-s.*

> the hats of the children = the children*'s* hats
> the harness for the oxen = the oxen*'s* harness

C. Add *'s* to indefinite pronouns:

> everyone*'s* responsibility
> somebody*'s* wallet

Indefinite Pronouns			
anyone	everyone	no one	someone
anybody	everybody	nobody	somebody
anything	everything	nothing	something

> **Possessive pronouns in English (*his, hers, its, ours, yours, theirs, whose*) do *not* use an apostrophe.**

Whose key is this?
The key is *his*.
The car is *theirs*.

D. Add only an apostrophe to regular plural nouns ending in *-s*.

the coats of the ladies = the ladies' coats
the store of the brothers = the brothers' store

TIP   A few singular nouns ending in the *s* or *z* sound are awkward-sounding if another *s* sound is added. You may in these cases drop the final *s*. Let your ear help you make the decision.

Jones' car or Jones's car

II. To form certain plurals in order to prevent confusion, use *'s*.

Numbers: 100's
Letters: a's and b's
Years: 1800's or 1800s
Abbreviations: Ph.D.'s
Words referred to in text: He uses too many *and's* in his writing.

TIP   Be sure *not* to use the apostrophe to form a plural in any case other than these.

III. To show where letters have been omitted in contractions, use an apostrophe.

cannot = can't
should not = shouldn't
will not = won't (the only contraction that changes its spelling)
I am = I'm
she will = she'll

E X E R C I S E   1   **Using the Apostrophe**

Fill in each of the blanks below using the rules you have just studied for uses of the apostrophe.

1. rays of the sun   the ___Sun's___ rays

2. sleeve of the dress   the ___Dress'___ sleeve

3. width of the feet   the ___feets___ width

4. the house of Antony and Maria   ___Antony's___ house
   (joint possession)   ___and___
                                       ___Maria's___

5. the idea of nobody   NoBoDY'S idea

6. The book belongs to him.   The book is His _____.

7. in the century of 1700   in the 1700's

8. That is her opinion.   THAT'S _____ her opinion.

9. shirts for boys   Boys' _____ shirts

10. the cover of the book   the Book's _____ cover

EXERCISE 2   **Using the Apostrophe**

Fill in each of the blanks below using the rules you have just studied for uses of the apostrophe.

1. clarity of the ice   the ICE'S _____ clarity

2. the flight of the geese   the GEESE'S flight

3. the work of Ann and Chris
   (individual possession)   Ann's & Chris's work

4. the plan of someone   SOMEONE'S plan

5. The drums belong to her.   The drums are hers.

6. the terrible year of two   the terrible TWO'S

7. We cannot leave yet.   We CAN'T _____ leave yet.

EXERCISE 3   **Using the Apostrophe**

Fill in each of the blanks below using the rules you have just studied for uses of the apostrophe.

1. the engine of the train   the TRAIN'S _____ engine

2. the spirit of the class   the CLASS'S _____ spirit

3. the centre for women   the WOMEN'S centre

4. the wish of everybody   EVERYBODY'S wish

5. The toys belong to them.   The toys are THERE'S.

6. The child mixes up *b* and *d*. The child mixes up his
                                    b's & d's.

7. I will not leave this house.   I CAN'T _____ leave this house.

8. the grain of the wood   the WOOD'S _____ grain

9. the story of the owners   the ___*owners'*___ story

10. the policies of Ridge School
    and Orchard School
    (individual possession)   ___*Ridge and*___ policies
                                                Orchard school's

Quotation Marks

Use quotation marks as follows:

I. **For a direct quotation:**

    "Please," I begged, "don't go away."

    Not for an indirect quotation:

    I begged her not to go away.

II. **For material copied word for word from a source:**

    According to Statistics Canada, "Families or individuals spending 58.5 percent or more of their pre-tax income on food, clothing, and shelter are in financial difficulty."

III. **For titles of shorter works such as short stories, one-act plays, poems, articles in magazines and newspapers, songs, essays, and chapters of books:**

    "A Modest Proposal," an essay by Jonathan Swift, is a masterpiece of satire.
    "The Woodcutter's Third Son," a short story by Hugh Hood, deals with both sacred scripture and mystical folklore.

TIP Titles of longer works such as novels, full-length plays, and names of magazines or newspapers are underlined when typed or handwritten. In a printed book, these titles appear in italics: for example, *Maclean's* magazine and *Country Living*.

IV. **For words used in a special way:**

    "Duckie" is a term of affection used by the British, the way we would use the word "honey."

PRACTICE 1   In each of the following sentences, insert quotation marks wherever they are needed.

1. The Hot House is one of the stories contained in Rosemary Sullivan's *More Stories by Canadian Women*.
2. Nellie McClung said I'll never believe I'm dead until I see it in the papers.
3. The prime minister told his caucus that they would have to settle the problem in the next few days.

4. "Punk is a particular form of rock music.

5. She read the article "Whiz Kids" in *The Review*.

If these five sentences were handwritten or typed, which words would have to be underlined?

The Semicolon

Use the semicolon as follows.:

I.   **To join two independent clauses whose ideas and sentence structure are related:**

He decided to consult the map; she decided to ask the next pedestrian she saw.

II. **To combine two sentences using an adverbial conjunction:**

He decided to consult the map; however, she decided to ask the next pedestrian she saw.

III. **To separate items in a series when the items themselves contain commas:**

I had lunch with Linda, my best friend; Mrs. Zhangi, my English teacher; and Jan, my sister-in-law.

Notice in the last example that if only commas had been used, the reader might think six people had gone to lunch.

PRACTICE 2   In each of the following sentences, insert a semicolon wherever one is needed.

1. One of the best ways to remember a vacation is to take numerous photos; one of the best ways to recall the contents of a book is to take notes.

2. The problem of street crime must be solved; otherwise, the number of vigilantes will increase.

3. The committee was made up of Kevin Corey, a writer; Anita Lightburn, a professor; and T.P. O'Connor, a politician.

4. The bank president was very cordial; however, he would not approve the loan.

5. Robots are being used in the factories of Japan; eventually, they will be common in this country as well.

The Colon

Use the colon as follows:

I.   **After a *complete* sentence when the material that follows is a list, an illustration, or an explanation:**

A. A list:

Please order the following items: five dozen pencils, twenty rulers, and five rolls of tape.

Notice that no colon is used when there is not a complete sentence before the colon.

The courses I am taking this semester are Freshman Composition, Introduction to Psychology, Art Appreciation, and Survey of Canadian Literature.

B. An illustration or explanation:

She was an exceptional child: at seven she was performing on the concert stage.

II. **Following the salutation of a business letter:**

To whom it may concern:
Dear Madam President:

III. **In telling time:**

We will eat at 5:15.

IV. **Between the title and subtitle of a book:**

Plain English Please: A Rhetoric

 P R A C T I C E 3 In each of the following sentences, insert colons wherever they are needed.

1. Three Canadian-born comedians have become well known in the United States; John Candy, Dan Aykroyd, and Catherine O'Hara.
2. The official has one major flaw in his personality:greed.
3. The restaurant has lovely homemade desserts such as German chocolate layer cake and Baked Alaska.
4. The college offers four courses in English literature:Romantic Poetry, Shakespeare's Plays, The British Short Story, and The Modern Novel.
5. Arriving at 6:15 in the morning, Marlene brought me a sausage-and-cheese pizza, soda, and a litre of ice cream.

The Dash and Parentheses

Like the comma, the dash and parentheses can also be used to show an interruption of the main idea. The particular form you choose depends on the degree of interruption.

T I P **Use the dash for a less formal and more emphatic interruption of the main idea.**

He came — I thought — by car.

She arrived — and I know this for a fact — in a pink Cadillac.

 TIP   **Use parentheses to insert extra information that some of your readers might want to know but that is not essential for the main idea. Such information is not emphasized.**

Gabrielle Roy (1909–83) wrote *The Tin Flute.*

Plea bargaining (see page 28) was developed to speed court verdicts.

PRACTICE 4   In each of the following sentences, insert dashes or parentheses wherever they are needed.

1. Herbert Simon is—and I don't think this is an exaggeration—a genius.
2. George Eliot—her real name was Mary Ann Evans—wrote *Silas Marner.*
3. You should—in fact I insist—see a doctor.
4. Unemployment brings with it a number of other problems (see the study by Brody, 1982).
5. Mass media television, radio, movies, magazines, and newspapers are able to transmit information over a wide range and to a large number of people.

EXERCISE 1   **Other Marks of Punctuation**

In each of the following sentences, insert marks of punctuation wherever they are needed.

1. To measure crime, sociologists have used three different techniques: official statistics, victimization surveys, and self-report studies.
2. "David" is one of the best-loved poems of Earle Birney.
3. The lake this summer has one major disadvantage for swimmers: weeds.
4. Farley Mowat has written numerous books for adults; however, he also writes very popular books for children.
5. Tuberculosis (also known as consumption) has been nearly eliminated by medical science.
6. The Victorian Period (1837–1901) saw a rapid expansion in industry.
7. He promised me—I know he promised that he would come—to my graduation.

EXERCISE 2   **Other Marks of Punctuation**

In each of the following sentences, insert marks of punctuation wherever they are needed.

1. Many young people have two feelings about science and technology: awe and fear.
2. Mr. Doyle, the realtor; Mrs. Tong, the bank officer; and Ivan Petroff, the lawyer, are the three people to help work out the real estate transaction.
3. The book was entitled *English Literature: The Victorian Age.*

4. "I decided to walk to school," she said, "because the bus fare has been raised again."
5. She brought a bathing suit, towel, sunglasses, and several books to the beach.
6. The conference—I believe it is scheduled for sometime in January—will focus on the development of a new curriculum.
7. The complex lab experiment has these two major problems: too many difficult calculations and too many variables.

Chapter Review Exercises

E X E R C I S E   1   **Editing for Correct Punctuation**

Read the following paragraph and insert the following marks of punctuation wherever they are needed:

   a. commas to separate items in a series
   b. comma with co-ordinating conjunction to combine sentences
   c. comma after introductory words, phrases, or clauses
   d. commas around words that interrupt main idea
   e. comma to set off spoken words
   f. parentheses
   g. quotation marks
   h. lines under titles of full-length works of art
   i. semicolon
   j. apostrophe

   Tom Thomson (1877–1917) is often remembered as the artist "of Canada's North." He was born on August 4, 1877 near Leith Ontario. During the twenties, Thomson apprenticed as a machinist enrolled in business college, and then spent a few years in Seattle working as an engraver. In 1906, he took art lessons and first used oil paint. His first important painting, done in 1917 and titled "A Northern Lake" was sold for $250, a great deal of money in those days. Thomson led the vanguard of a new movement in Canadian art. One reviewer said "Thomson paints a world of phenomena of colour and of form which will not be touched by another artist." Thomson drowned at Canoe Lake, Algonquin Park, July 8, 1917. Among his many works are: Ottawa by Moonlight, Autumn's Garland and Jackpine.

E X E R C I S E   2   **Editing for Correct Punctuation**

Read the following paragraph and insert the following marks of punctuation wherever they are needed:

   a. commas to separate items in a series
   b. comma with co-ordinating conjunction to combine sentences
   c. comma after introductory words, phrases, or clauses
   d. commas around words that interrupt main idea

e. comma in numbers of 1000 or larger
f. parentheses
g. quotation marks
h. lines under titles of full-length works of art
i. semicolon
j. colon
k. apostrophe

Albert Schweitzer was a brilliant German philosopher physician musician clergyman missionary and writer on theology. Early in his career he based his philosophy on what he called reverence for life. He felt a deep sense of obligation to serve humanity. His accomplishments as a humanitarian were great consequently he was awarded the Nobel Peace Prize in 1952. Before Schweitzer was 30 he had won an international reputation as a writer on theology as an organist and authority on organ building as an interpreter of the works of Johann Sebastian Bach and as an authority on Bachs life. When he became inspired to become a medical missionary he studied medicine at the university in Strasbourg Germany. He began his work in French Equatorial Africa now called Gabon in 1913 where his first consulting room was a chicken coop. Over the years he built a large hospital where thousands of Africans were treated yearly. He used his $33 000 Nobel prize money to expand the hospital and set up a leper colony in fact he even designed all the buildings. One of Schweitzers many famous books which you might like to find in the library is entitled Out of My Life and Thought. His accomplishments were so many music medicine scholarship theology and service to humanity.

Working Together

Work with a group of your classmates. Each group in the class will make up an exam to test the other students' knowledge of punctuation. From any book, choose a paragraph that uses a variety of punctuation. Have one person from the group carefully write out or type the paragraph without its punctuation. Then make enough copies so a group or the entire class can take the test. Is your test a fair one? Is it too easy or too hard? Does it cover the material studied in this chapter?

Chapter 9
Part I Review:
Using All You Have Learned

Editing Sentences for Errors

In the following exercises, you will find all the types of sentence problems that you have studied thus far.

Major Sentence Errors: Fragments
Run-ons
Incorrect punctuation
Sentence parts that do not work together

E X E R C I S E   1   **Editing Sentences for Errors**

The following examples contain sentence errors studied in Part I. If you think the example is a complete and correct sentence, mark it with a *C*. If the example has an error, correct it. An example is done for you.

Incorrect: A group of Gypsies who now live in Ireland.
Correct: A group of Gypsies now live in Ireland.

or

A group of Gypsies, who now live in Ireland, make their living by repairing pots and pans.

1. Gypsies now living in many countries of the world.

GYPSIES NOW LIVE IN MANY COUNTRIES
OF THE WORLD

2. The international community of scientists agrees that these Gypsies originally came from India thousands of years ago.

_____

_____

3. After the original Gypsies left India they went to Persia there they divided into groups.

   AFTER THE ORIGINAL GYPSIES LEFT INDIA, THEY WENT TO PERSIA; THERE, THEY DIVIDED INTO GROUPS

4. One branch of Gypsies went west to Europe the other group decided to go east.

   ONE BRANCH OF GYPSIES WENT WEST TO EUROPE, WHILE THE OTHER GROUP DECIDED TO GO EAST

5. In the Middle Ages (476–1453), some Gypsies lived in a fertile area of Greece called Little Egypt.

   C

6. Gypsies often found it hard to gain acceptance in many countries because of their wandering lifestyle.

   C

7. Today Gypsy families may be found from Canada to Chile living much as his ancestors did thousands of years ago.

   TODAY, GYPSY FAMILIES MAY BE FOUND FROM CANADA TO CHILE, LIVING MUCH AS THEIR ANCESTORS DID THOUSANDS OF YEARS AGO.

EXERCISE 2   Editing Sentences for Errors

The following examples contain sentence errors studied in Part I. If you think an example is a complete and correct sentence, mark it with a *C*. If the example has an error, correct it. An example is done for you.

Incorrect: The Supreme Court of Canada the highest court for all legal issues of federal and provincial jurisdiction was created in 1949.

Correct: The Supreme Court of Canada, the highest court for all legal issues of federal and provincial jurisdiction, was created in 1949.

1. Before that time all appeals were addressed to a high court in the United Kingdom.

   BEFORE 1949, ALL APPEALS WERE ADDRESSED TO THE HIGH COURT IN THE UNITED KINGDOM

2. A chief justice heads the Supreme Court there are also eight junior justices.

   _A CHIEF JUSTICE HEADS THE SUPREME
   COURT; THERE ARE ALSO EIGHT JUNIOR JUSTICE_

3. Since at least three of the judges must be appointed from Quebec.

   _NATIONALY, AT LEAST 3 JUDGES MUST
   BE APPOINTED FROM QUEBEC._

4. Three other judges are traditionally appointed from Ontario as well one is from
   the Maritimes and two from Western Canada.

   _THREE OTHER JUDGES ARE TRADITIONALY
   APPOINTED FROM ONTARIO; ONE FROM THE MARITIMES,
   AND TWO FROM WESTERN CANADA_

5. The Supreme Court is also a general court of appeal for criminal cases.

   _C_

6. If a guilty verdict has been reached in a first-degree murder trial in a lower court,
   The Supreme Court automatically reviews the case.

7. Bertha Wilson, the first woman to sit on the Supreme Court, was appointed in
   1982.

E X E R C I S E   3   Editing Sentences for Errors

The following examples contain sentence errors studied in Part I. If you think an
example is a complete and correct sentence, mark it with a *C*. If the example has an
error, correct it. An example is done for you.

> ***Incorrect:*** Science fiction writers have created magic rays that can
> destroy entire cities, but in recent years a magic ray in
> the form of laser beams have become scientific fact.
>
> ***Correct:*** Science fiction writers have created magic rays that can
> destroy entire cities, but in recent years a magic ray in
> the form of laser beams has become scientific fact.

1. The laser beam, a miracle of modern science, already has many practical uses in
   today's world.

2. Laser beams are narrow, highly concentrated beams of light that burns brighter than the light of the sun.

_____

_____

3. Scientists have found many possible military uses for the laser, but they are hoping it can be converted into constructive uses.

_____

_____

4. John Polanyi, Canadian winner of the 1986 Nobel Prize for chemistry, conducted early experiments on the use of lasers.

_____

_____

5. The possibility of making a laser was first described in 1958, and two years later in California the first laser beam was created.

_____

_____

6. Since they are so precise, laser beams are used in medicine to help make a specific diagnosis and to perform operations, such as repairing delicate retinas and the removal of cancerous tumours.

_____

_____

_____

7. The future uses of the laser seems endless, and it is up to us whether we want to use this invention for war or for peaceful purposes.

_____

_____

Editing Paragraphs for Errors

E X E R C I S E   1   Editing Paragraphs for Errors

Correct all of the punctuation and grammatical errors in the following paragraph.

Once upon a time whenever I tried to make my writing interesting and imaginative with all sorts of similes, and metaphors and colourful language, I forgot about my grammar and spelling. My essays were full of sentence fragments, comma splices and run-ons. Moreover, my syntax was always scrambled. Even I had trouble figuring out what I had intended to say originally, although I could tell

 131.00 XX

that I had started with brilliant ideas. Help has finally arrived however since I have done all the exercises in my grammar book I now have perfect command of English grammar whereas one time I bit my nails when I handed in an assignment I worry no more no longer do I need to worry about essays being handed back bleeding to death after being savaged by some sadistic English teacher wielding his or her red pen no longer will my sleep be curtailed by hours of tedious rewrites moreover from now on I'm expecting straight As all the way.

EXERCISE 2   Editing Paragraphs for Errors

Correct all of the punctuation and grammatical errors in the following paragraphs.

The first difficulty to overcome in coming to grips with the Canadian North is to decide where it begins, And to determine its extent. We in Canada avoid the issue by sectioning the North into segments. Like an orange, SO we can deal with each section separately. If you ask him to define the North, the geographer will dazzle you with technical terms like permafrost, tree line, boreal and tundra, he understands this kind of language, Although nobody else does. But there is no real boundary defining the North. The situation resembles the attainment of maturity; nobody agrees on a definition of what it is, but everybody recognizes it when it appears.

There is a second problem preventing study of the Canadian North: The incredible cold. It is so cold at times, That a pail of water thrown into the air would freeze, Before reaching the ground! Motorized vehicles, which modern explorers depend on for their excursions, Are rendered all but useless on these coldest days, the grease in the gearboxes becomes as thick as cement, Even though block heaters permit the engines to be started, The drive train becomes so encumbered by this frozen grease, The vehicle, although having power, is unable to translate this power into motion. The snowmobile, with its simplified drive mechanism, has revolutionized northern winter travel, Because it does not suffer from the drive train problem facing conventional vehicles.

Working Together

Below are several sentences on the topic of body language. Use this information to write a paragraph of at least ten sentences on the topic. Using the skills of co-ordination and subordination, be sure to use a variety in your sentence combining examples. Try various combinations before you begin to write.

1. Judy folds both arms across her chest defensively.
   Her boss may help Judy relax by folding her own arms in the same position and then relaxing them.

2. The speaker pauses.
   He intends to continue with an additional statement.

His head remains straight.
His eyes do not change.

3. Several prime ministers are aware of body language.
   They use it to manipulate their listeners.
   Comedians imitate these prime ministers.
   They can use this body language to give an unmistakable imitation of each national leader.

4. In a fashion show, a model may look stiff and unnatural.
   This reveals the model's lack of personal connection to the audience.

5. Sometimes strangers find themselves very close to each other.
   This invasion of one's personal space is uncomfortable.
   This occurs in an elevator or a crowded subway.
   People do not look at each other.
   They may stare straight ahead, or up at a lighted floor indicator.
   In many large cities, speaking to someone in this close situation would not be considered appropriate.

6. All members sitting at a round table are equal.
   At a rectangular table, the dominant person tends to take the position at one end of the table.
   In many families, the father has the position at the head of the table.

PART II

Mastering the Paragraph

Chapter 10
Working with Topic Sentences and Controlling Ideas

What Is a Paragraph?

Def

> A **paragraph** is a group of sentences that develops one main idea. A paragraph may stand by itself as a complete piece of writing, or it may be a section of a longer piece of writing, such as an essay.

No single rule will tell you how long a paragraph should be, but if a paragraph is too short, the reader will feel that basic information is missing. If the paragraph is too long, the reader will be bored or confused. An effective paragraph is always long enough to develop the main idea that is being presented. A healthy paragraph usually consists of at least six sentences and no more than ten or twelve sentences. You have undoubtedly read paragraphs in newspapers that are only one sentence long, but in fully developed writing one sentence is usually not an acceptable paragraph.

What Does a Paragraph Look Like?

Some students come to college unaccustomed to using margins, indentation, and complete sentences, which are essential parts of paragraph form. Study the following paragraph from Elizabeth Pollet's "A Cold-Water Flat," to observe the standard form.

> I got the job. I worked in the bank's city collection department. For weeks I was like a mouse in a maze: my feet scurried. Every seventh day I received thirteen dollar bills. It wasn't much. But, standing beside the pneumatic tube, unloading the bundles of mail that pelted down and distributing them according to their texture, size, and color to my superiors at their desks, I felt humble and useful.

Notice how the first word is indented. A consistent margin is used on each side of the text (for a manuscript page, this margin should be one inch), and there is a blank space after the final word.

E X E R C I S E   **Standard Paragraph Form**

Write the following six sentences in standard paragraph form. As you write, use margins, indentation, and complete sentences. Each sentence must begin with a capital letter and end with a period, question mark, or exclamation point.

1. In the large basement of the school, thirty families huddled in little groups of four or five.
2. Volunteer workers were busy carrying in boxes of clothing and blankets.
3. Two Red Cross women stood at a long table sorting through boxes to find sweaters and blankets for the shivering flood victims.
4. One heavyset man in a red woollen hunting jacket stirred a huge pot of soup.
5. Men and women with tired faces sipped their steaming coffee and wondered if they would ever see their homes again.
6. Outside the downpour continued.

What Is a Topic Sentence?

Def

A **topic sentence** is the sentence in a paragraph that states the main idea of that paragraph. It is the most general sentence of the paragraph. All the other sentences of the paragraph serve to explain, describe, extend, or support this main-idea sentence.

Most paragraphs you read will begin with the topic sentence. However, some topic sentences come in the middle of the paragraph; others come at the end. Some paragraphs have no stated topic sentence at all; in these cases, the main idea is implied. College students are usually advised to use topic sentences in all college work in order to be certain that the writing has a focus and develops a single idea at a time. Whether you are taking an essay exam in a history course, doing a research paper for a sociology course, or writing an essay in a composition course, thoughtful use of the topic sentence will always bring better results. Good topic sentences help both the writer and the reader to think clearly about the main points.

Following are two paragraphs. Each paragraph makes a separate point, which is stated in its topic sentence. In the first paragraph, the topic sentence is first; in the second, last. Read the paragraphs and notice how the topic sentence is the most general sentence; it is the main idea of each paragraph. The other sentences explain, describe, extend, or support the topic sentence.

Model Paragraph 1

"Turn down the volume and turn down the danger." That's the theme of a campaign by the Canadian Hearing Society, warning that personal stereos can be harmful to your health. The non-profit group, which has distributed

thousands of fact sheets to high school students, hopes to make them aware that permanent hearing loss can result from prolonged exposure to any intense noise — whether pleasant or unpleasant.

Model Paragraph 2

Mountains of disposable diapers are thrown into garbage cans every day. Tonnes of yogurt containers, pop cans, and plastic items are discarded without so much as a stomp to flatten them out. If the old Chevy is not worth fixing, tow it off to sit with thousands of others on acres of fenced-in junkyards. Radios, televisions, and toasters get the same treatment, because it is easier and often less expensive to buy a new product than to fix the old one. Who wants a comfortable old sweater if a new one can be bought on sale? No thought is given to the fact that the new one will look like the old one after two or three washings. *We are the great "Let's junk it" society!*

EXERCISE 1   Finding the Topic Sentence of a Paragraph

Each of the following paragraphs contains a topic sentence that states the main idea of the paragraph. Find this sentence and underline it.

1. The air shaft was a horrible invention. Even with the windows tightly sealed, it served as a sounding box so you could hear everybody's business. Rats scurried around the bottom. There was always the danger of fire. A match absently tossed into the air shaft by a drunk under the impression that it was falling into the yard or street would set the house afire in a moment. There were vile things cluttering up the bottom. Since this bottom couldn't be reached (the windows being too small to admit the passage of a body), it served as a fearful repository for things that people wanted to put out of their lives. Rusted razor blades and bloody cloths were the most innocent items.

2. Anything can happen at a county agricultural fair. It is the perfect human occasion — the harvest of the fields and of the emotions. To the fair come the man and his cow, the boy and his girl, the woman and her green tomato pickle, each anticipating victory and the excitement of being separated from his or her money by familiar devices. It is at a fair that a person can be drunk forever on liquor, love, or fights; at a fair that your front pocket can be picked by a trotting horse looking for sugar, and your hind pocket by a thief looking for a fortune.

EXERCISE 2   Finding the Topic Sentence of a Paragraph

Each of the following paragraphs contains a topic sentence that states the main idea of the paragraph. Find this sentence and underline it. The topic sentence will not always be the first sentence of the paragraph.

1. The Canadian game of hockey was born during long northern winters uncluttered by things to do. It grew up on ponds and rivers, in big open spaces, unorganized, often solitary, only occasionally moving into arenas for practices or games. In recent generations, that has changed. Canadians have moved from farms and

towns to cities and suburbs; they've discovered skis, snowmobiles, and southern vacations; they've civilized winter and brought it indoors. A game we once played on rivers and ponds, later on streets and driveways and in backyards, we now play in arenas, in full team uniforms, with coaches and referees; or, to an ever-increasing extent, we don't play at all.

2. When you remember something, your brain uses more than one method to store the information. You have short-term memory, which helps you recall recent events; you have long-term memory, which brings back items that are further in the past; and you have deep retrieval, which gives you access to long-buried information that is sometimes difficult to recall. Whether these processes are chemical or electrical, we do not yet know, and much research remains to be done before we can say which with any certainty. The brain is one of the most remarkable organs, a part of the body that we have only begun to investigate. It will be years before we even begin to understand all its complex processes.

How Do You Find the Topic in a Topic Sentence?

To find the topic in a topic sentence, ask yourself this question: What is the topic the writer is going to discuss? Below are two topic sentences. The first topic is underlined. Underline the topic in the second example.

Backpacking in the mountains last year was an exciting experience.
College registration can be stressful.

E X E R C I S E   1   Finding the Topic in the Topic Sentence

Find the topic in each of the following topic sentences. For each example, ask yourself this question: What is the topic the writer is going to discuss? Then underline the topic.

1. Remodelling an old house can be frustrating.
2. College work demands more independence than high school work.
3. A well-made suit has three easily identified characteristics.
4. Growing up near a museum had a profound influence on my life.
5. My favourite room in the house would seem ugly to most people.
6. A student who goes to school full-time and also works part-time has to make careful use of every hour.
7. One of the disadvantages of skiing is the expense.

E X E R C I S E   2   Finding the Topic in the Topic Sentence

Find the topic in each of the following topic sentences. For each example, ask yourself this question: What is the topic the writer is going to discuss? Then underline the topic.

1. To my surprise, the basement had now been converted into a small studio apartment.

2. Of all the prime ministers, Pierre Trudeau probably enjoyed the greatest popularity.

3. Scientists cannot yet explain how an identical twin often has an uncanny knowledge of what the other twin is doing or feeling.

4. If you don't have a car in Canada, you have undoubtedly discovered that rail transportation is in a state of decay.

5. When we met for dinner that night, I was shocked at the change that had come over my friend.

6. According to the report, current tax laws greatly benefit those who own real estate.

7. *Reader's Digest,* the Canadian English edition, is the leading paid-circulation magazine in the country.

What Is a Controlling Idea?

Every topic sentence contains not only the topic but also a controlling idea.

Def   This **controlling idea** tells us the position the writer has taken on the topic.

For example, in the topic sentence "Backpacking in the mountains last year was an exciting experience," the topic is "backpacking" and the controlling idea is that this backpacking trip was "exciting." Another person on the same trip might have had another attitude toward the trip. The person might have found the trip exhausting or boring. A single topic can therefore have any number of possibilities for development since the writer can choose from a limitless number of controlling ideas, depending on his or her attitude.

How Do You Find the Controlling Idea of a Topic Sentence?

When you look for the controlling idea in a topic sentence, ask yourself this question: What is the writer's attitude toward the topic?

In each of the following examples, the topic is underlined and the controlling idea is circled.

Sealfon's Department Store is my (favourite) store in town.

Sealfon's Department Store is (too expensive) for my budget.

EXERCISE 1   **Finding the Controlling Idea**

Below are ten topic sentences. For each sentence, underline the topic and circle the controlling idea.

1. Vigorous exercise is a good way to reduce the effect of stress on the body.
2. St. John's and Corner Brook differ in four major ways.
3. Television violence causes aggressive behaviour in children.

4. Athletic scholarships available to women are increasing.
5. Caffeine has several adverse effects on the body.
6. Madame Benoit, a famous gourmet cook, had an amusing personality.
7. Training a parakeet to talk takes great patience.

EXERCISE 2 **Finding the Controlling Idea**

Below are ten topic sentences. For each sentence, underline the topic and circle the controlling idea.

1. Piano lessons turned out to be a disaster.
2. The training of Japanese police is quite different from Canadian police training.
3. An Olympic champion has five distinctive characteristics.
4. The candidate's unethical financial dealings will have a negative impact in this campaign.
5. A bicycle ride along the coast is a breathtaking trip.
6. The grocery store is another place where people waste a significant amount of money every week.
7. Being an only child is not as bad as people think.

Choosing Your Own Controlling Idea

Teachers often assign one general topic on which all students must write. Likewise, when writing contests are announced, the topic is generally the same for all contestants. Since very few people have exactly the same view of or attitude toward a topic, it is likely that no two papers would have the same controlling idea. There could be as many controlling ideas as there are people to write them. The secret of writing a good topic sentence is to find the controlling idea that is right for you.

EXERCISE **Choosing Controlling Ideas for Topic Sentences**

Below are two topics. For each topic, think of three different possible controlling ideas, and then write a different topic sentence for each of these controlling ideas. An example is done for you.

Topic: My mother

Three possible controlling ideas:
1. Unusual childhood
2. Silent woman
3. Definite ideas about alcohol

Three different topic sentences:
1. My mother had a most unusual childhood.
2. My mother is a very silent woman.
3. My mother has definite ideas about alcohol.

1. **Topic:** My father

   First controlling idea: _____

   First topic sentence: _____

   _____

   Second controlling idea: _____

   Second topic sentence: _____

   _____

   Third controlling idea: _____

   Third topic sentence: _____

   _____

2. **Topic:** The Northwest Territories

   First controlling idea: _____

   First topic sentence: _____

   _____

   Second controlling idea: _____

   Second topic sentence: _____

   _____

   Third controlling idea: _____

   Third topic sentence: _____

   _____

Chapter Review Exercises

EXERCISE

Further Practice Writing the Topic Sentence

Develop each of the following topics into a topic sentence. In each case, the controlling idea is missing. First, decide on an attitude you might take toward the topic. Then use the attitude you have chosen to write your topic sentence. When you are finished, underline your topic and circle your controlling idea. Be sure your topic sentence is a complete sentence and not a fragment. An example is done for you.

> **Topic:** My brother's car accident
> **Controlling idea:** Tragic results
> **Topic sentence:** My brother's car accident had (tragic results) for the entire family.

1. **Topic:** Teaching a child good manners

   Controlling idea: _____

   Topic sentence: _____

   _____

2. **Topic:** Two years in the armed forces

   Controlling idea: _____

   Topic sentence: _____

   _____

3. **Topic:** Making new friends

   Controlling idea: _____

   Topic sentence: _____

   _____

4. **Topic:** The old woman

   Controlling idea: _____

   Topic sentence: _____

   _____

5. **Topic:** Going on a diet

   Controlling idea: _____

   Topic sentence: _____

   _____

Working Together

1. In this chapter, you have written many topic sentences in various exercises. Choose one of your best sentences to put on the board. After several students have written some of their sentences on the board, other students will underline the topics and circle the controlling ideas. If the sentences need improvements, students can write their own versions under the other sentences so the class can make a comparison.

2. Every topic contains numerous possibilities for controlling ideas. Take, for example, the topic of *marriage*. Each student thinks for a moment and jots down one or two controlling ideas that come to mind. Then a class member lists on the blackboard all the different controlling ideas that the members of the class have generated. Your instructor may want the class to use the remainder of the period to write a paragraph by selecting one of these controlling ideas on the topic of *marriage*.

Chapter 11
Working with
Supporting Details

What Is a Supporting Detail?

Def   A **supporting detail** is a piece of evidence used by the writer to make the controlling idea of the topic sentence convincing to the reader.

Once you have constructed your topic sentence with its topic and controlling idea, you are ready to move on to supporting your idea with details. These details will convince your readers that what you are claiming in the topic sentence is believable or reasonable.

As you choose these supporting details, realize that readers do not necessarily have to agree with your point of view. However, your supporting details must be good enough to convince your readers at least to respect your attitude. Your goal is to educate your readers. Try to make them experts on the subject you are writing about. The quality and number of your supporting details will determine how well you do this. If you have enough details, and if your details are specific enough, your readers will feel they have learned something new about the subject. This is always a satisfying experience for writers and readers.

It is also true that specific details tend to stay in readers' minds much longer than general ideas. The statement that over 25 000 males died of cancer in Canada in 1995 is much more effective and memorable than a statement saying only that cancer killed many people.

Finally, specific details make a piece of writing more fun to read. When the reader has concrete objects, particular people, or recognizable places to hang on to, the contents of the writing become a pleasure to read. It is important to notice that longer paragraphs with complicated topics usually contain a large number of supporting details.

The following paragraph, taken from an essay about the richness of North American Native peoples' languages, contains a topic sentence with several good supporting details.

Languages are remarkably adaptable, easily borrowing or coining new words as circumstances change. The horse, unknown when the Spanish landed, soon took on a central role among Native tribes, and words for the horse and its many uses were introduced. One device was to borrow some form of the Spanish word *caballo*. Another was to invent a descriptive term. Native people of eastern New York State used a word meaning "one rides its back"; in the western part of the state, the word for horse means "it hauls out logs." Presumably these were the first uses of horses seen in the two areas. Among the Kwakiutl of British Columbia, a steamboat was "fire on its back moving in the water." To the Tsimshian of the same area, the word for rice was "looking like maggots."

Notice that the topic sentence gives us the topic (language) and the writer's attitude toward the topic (remarkably adaptable). Each of the sentences that follow this topic sentence is a supporting detail that convinces us that the controlling idea is a reasonable attitude. The writer provides more than one example and chooses these examples from more than one group of Native people. This wide range makes the topic sentence more convincing and interesting.

Based on the sample paragraph above, the following example gives the exact topic sentence of the paragraph, then indicates, in the author's words, the supporting details in this paragraph. Be prepared to discuss how each of the supporting sentences supports or explains the controlling idea contained in the topic sentence.

Topic sentence: Languages are remarkably adaptable, easily borrowing or coining new words as circumstances change.

First supporting detail: The word for "horse" was adapted to meet certain situations among Native tribes.

Second supporting detail: Spanish was adapted.

Third supporting detail: A descriptive term was used.

Fourth supporting detail: The word "steamboat" was adapted by the Natives of British Columbia to serve a descriptive purpose.

Fifth supporting detail: Another British Columbia tribe had a descriptive word for "rice."

EXERCISE 1   Finding the Topic Sentence and Supporting Details

For each of the paragraphs below, divide the sentences into topic sentence and supporting details.

1. The time when the darkness that envelops me is most disturbing is the moment when I roll over onto my back and face the ceiling, still encased in the web of drowsiness sleep has woven, and from which it is reluctant to release me. As I become more aware of the sounds around me in the darkness, the ticking of my alarm clock draws my attention, and I look toward it to see what time this morning I have awakened. I am unable to comprehend why I can't locate its familiar face when I know it should be there. It is at this moment that reality crashes in and reminds me, once again, that morning never comes for me anymore. Life

has indeed abandoned me to the night, which is, and always will be, my constant companion. After this moment passes, I reach out into the void toward the sound of the clock. Grasping it and tracing the face that had eluded me moments ago, I sense it forfeit the time to my touch, and thus I broach another day.

Glenn David du Moulin, blind student,
"Five Hours in a Life"

Topic sentence: _____

_____

First supporting detail: _____

_____

Second supporting detail: _____

_____

Third supporting detail: _____

_____

Fourth supporting detail: _____

_____

_____

Fifth supporting detail: _____

_____

_____

2. Then my father and I walked gradually down a long, shabby sort of street, with Silverwoods Ice Cream signs standing on the sidewalk, outside tiny, lighted stores. This is in Tuppertown, an old town on Lake Huron, an old grain port. The street is shaded, in some places, by maple trees whose roots have cracked and heaved the sidewalk and spread out like crocodiles into the bare yards. People are sitting out, men in shirt-sleeves and undershirts and women in aprons — not people we know but if anyone looks ready to nod and say, "Warm night," my father will nod too and say something the same. Children are still playing. I don't know them either because my mother keeps my brother and me in our own yard, saying he is too young to leave it and I have to mind him. I am not so sad to watch their evening games because the gardens themselves are ragged, dissolving. Children, of their own will, draw apart, separate into islands of two or one under the heavy trees, occupying themselves in such solitary ways as I do all day, planting pebbles in the dirt or writing in it with a stick.

From Alice Munro,
"Walker and Brothers Cowboy"

Topic sentence: _____

_____

First supporting detail: _____

_____

Second supporting detail: _____

_____

Third supporting detail: _____

_____

Fourth supporting detail: _____

_____

Fifth supporting detail: _____

_____

Sixth supporting detail: _____

_____

Using Examples as Supporting Details

An **example** is a very specific illustration or piece of evidence that supports a writer's point of view. Examples make general ideas more concrete and therefore easier to comprehend and remember.

When you use examples in your writing, you are convincing your reader that what you are saying is true and worthy of belief. Often, when you use examples to support your ideas, you will find yourself using further examples to help your reader see your first examples more clearly. If you are writing about cars, for instance, you may find yourself using Ford, Dodge, Buick, and Honda to illustrate your points. However, to make your points even more clear, you could find yourself referring to a Ford Tempo, a Dodge Caravan, a Buick Skylark, and a Honda Accord. The more precise your examples, the more clearly your reader will be able to see what you mean, and therefore the more memorable your writing will be.

Examples may be given in more than one way. They may appear as lists of specific items to illustrate a particular point, or they may be written as extended examples.

Extended examples include lengthy descriptions or stories that can be an entire paragraph long.

A good piece of writing is filled with both kinds of examples that work together to create a well-developed, convincing whole. Read the following paragraph from Jesse Birnbaum's "The Perils of Being a Lefty" (*Time*, April 15, 1991). As you read, look for the different kinds of examples that show the extent to which being left-handed is less than desirable.

> Left-handed people are such a sorry lot. Though they are a minority (perhaps 10% of the population) no antidiscrimination laws protect them. They bump elbows with their partners at the dinner table. They are clumsy with scissors and wrenches. In a world designed and dominated by righties, they are condemned to a lifetime of snubs, of fumbling with gadgets and switches and buttons. Possibly because of a stressful birth or because the left side of the brain doesn't know what the right side is doing, they suffer disproportionately from migraine headaches and stuttering. Since lefties also tend to be dyslexic, they are forever going right when they want to go left, transposing digits when they punch up phone numbers, and when writing words, getting their letters all mixed pu.

EXERCISE 1   Finding Examples

Analyze the paragraph from "The Perils of Being a Lefty." What kind(s) of examples can you find in the paragraph?

EXERCISE 2   Finding Examples

Find a newspaper or magazine article on a current topic or other subject that interests you. Examine the article for paragraphs containing lists of examples and paragraphs containing extended examples. How has the writer made the article interesting and memorable through the use of examples?

Avoid Restating the Topic Sentence

One of your most important jobs as you write a paragraph is recognizing the difference between a genuine supporting detail and a simple restatement of the topic sentence.

This paragraph, from Michael Ignatieff's *The Russian Album*, has good supporting details:

> In the family album there is a photograph of my grandmother, Natasha Ignatieff, that dates from the period when she and her family came to live in St. Petersburg in the dark and cluttered apartment two blocks from the Neva river. She is dressed for a formal winter evening, a fox fur draped over her shoulders, Brussels lace on the bodice of her velvet gown, her hair swept back in a tight chignon, and a twelve-strand pearl choker around her stiffly upright neck. She is thin and pale, the cheekbones of her long angular face taking the light, the eyes deep-set and dark. Her expression is guarded, and she seems at odds with the occasion. She was a private soul: in the public

glare, she shrank back. She hated Petersburg society: paying courtesy calls on the wives of Paul's superiors, making curtsies and small talk and all the while feeling she was up on a high wire one step from a fall.

EXERCISE 1 **Distinguishing a Supporting Detail from a Restatement of the Main Idea**

Each of the following topic sentences is followed by four additional sentences. Three of these additional sentences contain acceptable supporting details, but one of the sentences is simply a restatement of the topic sentence. In the space provided, identify each sentence as *SD* for *supporting detail* or *R* for *restatement*.

1. I am surprised at myself when I think how neat I used to be before I started school full-time.

    _____ a. In my closet, I had my clothes arranged in matching outfits with shoes, hats, and even jewellery to go with them.

    _____R_____ b. I always used to take great pride in having all my things in order.

    _____ c. If I opened my desk drawer, compartments of paper clips, erasers, staples, pens, pencils, stamps, and rulers greeted me without one lost penny or safety pin thrown in out of place.

    _____ d. On top of my chest of drawers sat a comb and brush, two oval frames with pictures of my best friends, and that was all.

2. Iceland has a very barren landscape.

    _____ a. One-tenth of the island is covered with ice.

    _____R_____ b. Not one forest with magnificent trees is to be found.

    _____ c. Nature has not been kind to the people of Iceland.

    _____ d. Three-fourths of the island is uninhabitable.

EXERCISE 2 **Distinguishing a Supporting Detail from a Restatement of the Main Idea**

Each of the following topic sentences is followed by four additional sentences. Three of these additional sentences contain acceptable supporting details, but one of the sentences is simply a restatement of the topic sentence. In the space provided, identify each sentence as *SD* for *supporting detail* or *R* for *restatement*.

1. In the last 30 years, the number of people living alone in Canada has increased by 400 percent.

    _____ a. People are living alone because the number of divorces has dramatically increased.

_____   b. Many young people are putting off marriage until they are financially more secure or emotionally ready.

____ ʔ ____   c. More and more Canadians are finding themselves living alone.

_____   d. An increasing percentage of our population is the age group over 65, among whom are many widows and widowers.

2. Writing as Sandra Field and Jocelyn Haley, Jill MacLean makes love pay the bills.

_____   a. Her first book, _To Trust My Love_, was published by Harlequin.

_____   b. Jill received a royalty cheque of about $1800 for her first book.

_____   c. She is the author of 36 full-fledged romance novels.

____ ʔ ____   d. Jill MacLean writes love stories under two pen names.

How Do You Make Supporting Details Specific?

Students often write paragraphs that are made up of only general statements. When you read such paragraphs, you doubt the author's knowledge and you suspect that the point being made may have no basis in fact. Here is one such paragraph that never gets off the ground.

> Doctors are terrible. They cause more problems than they solve. I don't believe most of their treatments are necessary. History is full of the mistakes doctors have made. We don't need all those operations. We should never ingest all those drugs doctors prescribe. We shouldn't allow them to give us all those unnecessary tests. I've heard plenty of stories that prove my point. Doctors' ideas can kill you.

Here is another paragraph on the same topic. This paragraph is much more interesting and convincing because the general statements throughout the essay have been changed to supporting details.

> Evidence shows that "medical progress" has been the cause of tragic consequences and even death for thousands of people. X-ray therapy was thought to help patients with tonsillitis. Now many of these people are found to have developed cancer from these X-rays. Not so long ago, women were kept in bed for several weeks following childbirth. Unfortunately, this cost many women their lives, since they developed fatal blood clots from being kept in bed day after day. One recent study estimates that 30 000 people each year die from the side effects of drugs that were prescribed by doctors. Recently, the Center for Disease Control reported that 25 percent of the tests done by clin-

ical laboratories were done poorly. All this is not to belittle the good done by the medical profession, but to impress on readers that it would be foolish to rely totally on the medical profession to solve all our health problems.

This second paragraph is much more likely to be of real interest. Even if you would like to disprove the author's point, it would be very hard to dismiss these supporting details, which are based on facts and information that can be researched. Because the author sounds reasonable, you can respect him or her even if you have a different position on the topic.

In writing effectively, the ability to go beyond the general statement and get to the accurate pieces of information is what counts. A writer tries to make his or her reader an expert on the subject. Readers should go away excited to share with the next person they meet the surprising information they have just learned. A writer who has a statistic, a quotation, an anecdote, a historical example, or a descriptive detail has the advantage over all other writers, no matter how impressive these writers' styles may be.

Good writing is filled with supporting details that are specific, correct, and appropriate for the subject. Poor writing is filled with generalizations, stereotypes, vagueness, untruths, and even sarcasm and insults.

EXERCISE 1 **Creating Supporting Details**

Below are five topic sentences. Supply three supporting details for each one. Be sure each detail is specific and not general or vague.

1. Your first semester in college can be overwhelming.

    a. _____

    b. _____

    c. _____

2. Clothing is a bad investment of your money.

    a. _____

    b. _____

    c. _____

3. Dr. Kline is an easy teacher.

    a. _____

    b. _____

    c. _____

4. It is difficult to stop eating junk food.

    a. _____

b. _____

c. _____

5. My sister is the sloppiest person I know.

a. _____

b. _____

c. _____

E X E R C I S E 2   Creating Supporting Details

Below are five topic sentences. Supply three supporting details for each one. Be sure each detail is specific and not general or vague.

1. December has become a frantic time at our house.

a. _____

b. _____

c. _____

2. My best friend can often be very immature.

a. _____

b. _____

c. _____

3. Each sport has its own peculiar injuries associated with it.

a. _____

b. _____

c. _____

4. My car is on its "last wheels."

a. _____

b. _____

c. _____

5. Watching too much television has serious effects on family life.

a. _____

b. _____

c. _____

Working Together

1. Divide into groups. Select one of the topic sentences on pages 132–133. Together make a list of as many supporting details or examples as you can. Then each student writes a paragraph selecting details from the list prepared by his or her group.
2. Circulate everyone's answers to the assignment within the group. Be sure to give every member of the group enough time to read through all the papers. Then discuss the various paragraphs that have been written. Even though each paragraph began with the same topic sentence and supporting details, all of the paragraphs have turned out differently. Why?

Chapter 12
Developing Paragraphs: Narration

What Is Narration?

Def

Narration is the oldest and best-known form of verbal communication. It is, quite simply, the telling of a story.

Every culture in the world, past and present, has used narration to provide entertainment as well as information for the people of that culture. Since everyone likes a good story, the many forms of narration, such as novels, short stories, soap operas, and full-length movies, are always popular.

The following narrative paragraph, taken from an essay by Al Purdy titled "The Iron Road," tells the story of Purdy's trip westward in 1937, the height of the Great Depression, when he was looking for work. In this passage, Purdy had been caught illegally riding a freight train by the railway police, and he is imprisoned in a caboose.

> When returned to my prison-on-wheels I felt panicstricken. I was only seventeen, and this was the first time I'd ventured far away from home. I examined the caboose-prison closely, thinking: two years. Why, I'd be nineteen when I got out, an old man! And of course it was hopeless to think of escape. Other prisoners had tried without success, and windows were broken where they'd tried to wrench out the bars. And the door: it was wood, locked on the outside with a padlock, opening inward. It was a very springy door, though. I could squeeze my fingertips between sill and door, one hand at the top and the other a foot below. That gave me hope, blessed hope, for the first time. My six-foot-three body was suspended in air by my hands, doubled up like a coiled spring, and I pulled. Lord, how I pulled! The door bent inward until I could see a couple of daylight inches between door and sill. Then Snap! and screws fell out of the steel hasp outside. I fell flat on my back.

Working with Narration: Using Narration to Make a Point

At one time or another you have met a person who loves to talk on and on without making any real point. This person is likely to tell you everything that happened in one day, including every cough and sideways glance. Your reaction to the seemingly needless and endless supply of details is probably one of fatigue and hope for a quick getaway. This is not narration at its best! A good story is almost always told to make a point: it can make us laugh, it can make us understand, or it can change our attitudes.

When Al Purdy tells the story of his escape from the caboose, he is careful to use only those details that are relevant to his story. For example, the way the door is constructed is important. Had it not been made of wood and springy, he might never have been able to get his fingertips in and force an opening. He might have had to spend two years in prison. Then Purdy would have had a different story to tell.

What is Purdy's point in this paragraph? The excerpt is part of an essay about Purdy's experiences during the Depression, and specifically, in this part, about the dangers of travelling illegally by train during that time, which many thousands of people had to do, illegal and dangerous or not. On its surface, then, the story is merely about a trip, although an unusual one. Being imprisoned in the caboose, however, might be metaphorical: the caboose in which Purdy was imprisoned might represent the life of hopeless despair caused by unemployment that he and thousands of others were imprisoned in, and Purdy's escape was the escape from despair toward the hope that a trip to the West could bring, with its opportunities for a better life.

E X E R C I S E   1   Using Narration to Make a Point

Each of the following examples is the beginning of a topic sentence for a narrative paragraph. Complete each sentence by providing a controlling idea that could be the point for the story.

1. Since my family is so large (or small), I have had to learn to _____

   _____

2. When I couldn't get a job, I realized _____

   _____

3. After going to the movies every Saturday for many years, I discovered _____

   _____

4. When I arrived at the room where my business class was to meet, I found

   _____

5. When my best friend got married, I began to see that _____

   _____

E X E R C I S E   2   Using Narration to Make a Point

Each of the following examples is the beginning of a topic sentence for a narrative paragraph. Complete each sentence by providing a controlling idea that could be the point for the story.

1. When I looked more closely at the man, I realized that _____

_____

2. When the prime minister finished his speech, I concluded that _____

_____

3. By the end of the movie, I decided that _____

_____

4. After I changed the course as well as the teacher, I felt _____

_____

5. When I could not get past the office secretary, I realized that _____

_____

Coherence in Narration: Placing Details in Order of Time Sequence

Ordering details in a paragraph of narration usually follows a time sequence. That is, you tell what happened first, then next, and next, until finally you get to the end of the story. An event could take place in a matter of minutes or over a period of many years.

In the following paragraph, the story takes place in a single day. The six events that made the day a disaster are given in the order in which they happened. Although some stories flash back to the past or forward to the future, most use the natural chronological order of the events.

> My day was a disaster. First, it had snowed during the night, which meant I had to shovel before I could leave for work. I was mad that I hadn't gotten up earlier. Then I had trouble starting my car, and to make matters worse, my daughter wasn't feeling well and said she didn't think she should go to school. When I eventually did arrive at school, I was twenty minutes late. Soon I found out the secretary had forgotten to type the exam I was supposed to give my class that day. I quickly had to make another plan. By three o'clock, I was looking forward to getting my paycheque. Foolish woman! When I went to pick it up, the woman in the office told me that something had gone wrong with the computers. I would not be able to get my cheque until Tuesday. Disappointed, I walked down the hill to the parking lot. There I met my final defeat. In my hurry to park the car in the morning, I had left

my parking lights on. Now my battery was dead. Even an optimist like me had the right to be discouraged!

E X E R C I S E   1   Working for Coherence: Using Details in Order of Time Sequence

Each of the topics below is followed by six supporting details. These supporting details are not listed in any order. Order the events according to time sequence by placing the appropriate number in the space provided.

1. The driving test

_____   She had her last lesson with Mr. Panakos on Saturday morning.

_____   As she ate breakfast Monday morning, Daniela read the driver's manual one more time because she knew it was her last chance to review.

_____   Daniela's driving test was scheduled for Monday morning.

_____   On Sunday afternoon her father gave her some advice on what to be careful of when she took her road test.

_____   As her mother drove her to the motor vehicle bureau, Daniela tried to relax and not think about the test.

_____   The night before her test, Daniela had phone calls from two friends who wished her good luck.

2. Making up my mind

_____   By the time I saw the dean for final approval of the change, I knew I had made the right decision.

_____   When I registered for my new courses for the next semester, I knew that I was doing what I should have done all along.

_____   I spent the summer of my second year thinking about the career I really wanted to follow.

_____   I suppose the experience taught me that you should always make a change in your life after you have thought it through completely.

_____   When I finally did decide to change majors, my friends acted as though I had decided to change my citizenship.

_____   When I told my favourite professor about my change of mind, he was very supportive, even though I had begun my major with him.

E X E R C I S E   2   **Working for Coherence: Using Details in Order of Time Sequence**

Each of the topics below is followed by supporting details. These supporting details are not listed in any order. Order the events according to time sequence by placing the appropriate number in the space provided.

1. From the life of Amelia Earhart, pioneer aviator and writer

_____1_____ Amelia Earhart was born in Atchison, Kansas, in 1897.

_____3_____ Toward the end of World War I, she worked as a nurse's aide.

_____2_____ When she was sixteen, her family moved to St. Paul, Minnesota.

_____5_____ Four years after her history-making flight across the Atlantic, she made her solo flight across that same ocean.

_____4_____ After learning to fly in the early 1920s, she became, in 1928, the first woman to cross the Atlantic in an airplane, although on that trip she was a passenger and not a pilot.

_____6_____ Three years after her solo Atlantic flight, she became the first person to fly from Hawaii to California.

_____7_____ On her last flight, in 1937, she was lost at sea; no trace of her was ever found.

2. From the life of Joseph-Henri-Maurice "Rocket" Richard, hockey player

_____1_____ Maurice Richard, born in Montreal in 1921, became a legend in the National Hockey League.

_____3_____ He collected 32 goals in his first full year of playing for the Montreal Canadiens.

_____2_____ Injuries restricted his scoring in his last two years of amateur competition and his first year in the NHL.

_____7_____ After retiring, Richard was seen occasionally on television endorsing commercial products.

_____4_____ Richard was an outstanding playoff scorer, once scoring five goals in a playoff game against Toronto.

_____5_____ In 1944–45, he scored 50 goals in 50 games, becoming the first hockey player to do so.

_____6_____ His 544-goal total was a record in the NHL when he retired.

Transitions and Time Order

Transitions that use time order help readers get from one part of the text to another.

Here is a passage from Frederick Philip Grove's "A Storm in July," which describes a violent summer storm on the prairies. The transitional words and phrases are printed in boldface.

> **The first day** it had died down towards evening; and we had a quiet night; but **the second morning** it had sprung up again, bringing with it waves of vapor and a suggestion of smoke in the air which grew stronger **as the day advanced**; till **at last** towards noon the wind seemed to blow from a huge conflagration in the south. Down there the big marsh which stretches north of the open prairie was on fire **as it often is**. The speed of the wind was increasing, too, **on this second day**. The leaves strained at their stalks; the small aspens stood vibrating at an angle; the large black poplars huddled their tops together on the north side of their trunks, **while** the wind pulled and snatched at the edges of their green garments. A rag tied to a pole to mark off a neighbouring homestead claim cracked and crackled with the slight changes in the direction of the blast; and in the kitchen-garden behind the house the cucumber vines were lying helpless, belly up, with their foliage ragged and dusty and worn by the sand which even in this country of the northern bush began to blow.

Notice how the time transitions used in this paragraph make the order of events clear. "*The first day* it had died down towards evening" gives the reader the sense that the story of the storm is being told on a daily basis, and that the description actually begins late in the day when the worst of the storm was over for the day and there was a lull toward evening. "*The second morning* it had sprung up again" continues the action into the next day, but this time the wind carried a hint of smoke, which hadn't been there before. The smoke "grew stronger *as the day advanced*," then, "*at last*," it was obvious that the big marsh in the south was on fire, "*as it often is*," which adds to the awesome power of the natural elements, still being described by Grove in a sequential fashion. The storm is still building "*on this second day*," "*while*" the remainder of the paragraph goes on to describe the effects of this storm on the second day to the Grove homestead.

Frederick Philip Grove has used time words and phrases to give us an idea of how long the storm lasted and what other elements in the prairie environment were at work. His use of transitions helps to make his meaning clear.

E X E R C I S E   1   Working with Transitions

Using the transitions given in the list below or using ones you think of yourself, fill in each of the blanks in the following student paragraph. Refer to the transition chart on the inside back cover of this book.

at once	later, later on	after a little while
immediately	now, by now	first, first of all
soon afterward	finally	then
suddenly	in the next moment	next

I arrived at Aunt Lorinda's in the middle of a heat wave. It was 40°C in the shade and very humid. Aunt Lorinda as usual greeted me with the list of activities she had scheduled for the day. ~~Immediately~~ we went to the attic to gather old clothes for the Salvation Army. I nearly passed out up in the attic. Sweat poured down my face. Aunt Lorinda, in her crisp cotton sundress, looked cool and was obviously enjoying herself. "If you see something you want, take it," she said graciously. "It's so nice of you to give me a hand today. You're young and strong and have so much more energy than I." _Next_ her plans included the yard work. I took off my shirt and mowed the lawn while my 80-year-old aunt trimmed hedges and weeded the flower beds. _Then_ it was time to drive into the dusty town and do errands. Luckily, Auntie stayed behind to fix lunch and I was able to duck into an air-conditioned coffee shop for ten minutes' rest before I dropped off the old clothes at the Salvation Army. I wasn't anxious to find out what help I could be to my aunt in the afternoon. I hoped it wouldn't be something like last year when I had to put a new roof on the old shed in the backyard. I could feel the beginning of a painful sunburn.

EXERCISE 2   Working with Transitions

Below is a narrative paragraph from a story by the Russian writer Ivan Turgenev. Make a list of all the transitions that give order to the paragraph.

I went to the right through the bushes. Meantime the night had crept close and grown up like a storm cloud; it seemed as though, with the mists of evening, darkness was rising up on all sides and flowing down from overhead. I had come upon some sort of little, untrodden, overgrown path; I walked along it, gazing intently before me. Soon all was blackness and silence around — only the quail's cry was heard from time to time. Some small nightbird, flitting noiselessly near the ground on its soft wings, almost flapped against me and scurried away in alarm. I came out on the further side of the bushes, and made my way along a field by the hedge. By now I could hardly make out distant objects; the field showed dimly white around; beyond it rose up a sullen darkness, which seemed moving up closer in huge masses every instant. My steps gave a muffled sound in the air, that grew colder and colder. The pale sky began again to grow blue — but it was the blue of night. The tiny stars glimmered and twinkled in it.

_____   _____

_____   _____

_____   _____

Writing the Narrative Paragraph Step by Step

To learn a skill with some degree of ease, it is best to follow a step-by-step approach so that various skills can be worked on one at a time. This will ensure that you are not missing a crucial point or misunderstanding a part of the whole. There are other ways to go about writing an effective paragraph, but here is one logical method you can use to achieve results.

Steps for Writing the Narrative Paragraph

1. Study the given topic, and then plan your topic sentence with its controlling idea.
2. List the events that come to mind when you think about the topic you have chosen.
3. Choose the five or six most important events from your list.
4. Put your final list in order.
5. Write at least one complete sentence for each of the events you have chosen from your list.
6. Write a concluding statement that gives some point to the events of the story.
7. Finally, copy your sentences into standard paragraph form.

EXERCISE 1 **Writing the Narrative Paragraph Step by Step**

The following exercise will guide you through the construction of a narrative paragraph. Start with the suggested topic. Use the seven steps above to help you work through each stage of the writing process. This exercise is done for you.

Topic: Every family has a favourite story they like to tell about one of their members, often something humorous that happened to one of them. There are also crises and tragic moments in the life of every family. Choose a story, funny or tragic, from the life of a family you know.

1. Topic sentence: My family likes to exchange unusual Christmas gifts.
2. Make a list of events.
   a. Mom — same card
   b. Dad — Hawaiian ties
   c. Square inch of moon
   d. Star named
   e. Pets' gifts
   f. No usual gifts

3. Circle the five or six events you believe are the most important for the point of the story.
4. Put your final choices in order by numbering them.
5. Using your final list, write at least one sentence for each event you have chosen.
    a. My mother sends a card to my aunt, and my aunt sends the same card back next year.
    b. My father sends Hawaiian ties to every male member of the family every year.
    c. Last year I received the deed to one square inch of the moon.
    d. This year my sister gave me a certificate saying a star was named after me.
    e. We all make it a habit to exchange only unusual, inexpensive gifts.
6. Write a concluding statement: People may think that my family is unusual when it comes to exchanging Christmas gifts, but we enjoy ourselves.
7. Copy your sentences into standard paragraph form.

   My family likes to exchange unusual Christmas gifts. My mother sends a card to my aunt, and my aunt sends the same card back the next year. My father sends Hawaiian ties to every male member of the family every year. Last year I received the deed to one square inch of the moon. This year my sister gave me a certificate saying a star was named after me. We all make it a habit to exchange only unusual, inexpensive gifts. People may think my family is unusual when it comes to exchanging Christmas gifts, but we enjoy ourselves.

EXERCISE 2 **Writing the Narrative Paragraph Step by Step**

The following exercise will guide you through the construction of a narrative paragraph. Start with the suggested topic. Use the seven steps on page 142 to help you work through each stage of the writing process.

Topic: Recount the plot of a book you have read recently or a movie you have seen within the last few weeks.

1. Topic sentence: _____

   _____

2. Make a list of events.

    a. _____   f. _____
    b. _____   g. _____
    c. _____   h. _____
    d. _____   i. _____
    e. _____   j. _____

3. Circle the five or six events you believe are the most important for the point of the story.
4. Put your choices in order by numbering them.

5. Using your final list, write at least one sentence for each event you have chosen.

   a. _____

   _____

   b. _____

   _____

   c. _____

   _____

   d. _____

   _____

   e. _____

   _____

   f. _____

   _____

   g. _____

   _____

6. Write a concluding statement. _____

   _____

   _____

7. Copy your sentences into standard paragraph form.

   _____

   _____

   _____

   _____

   _____

   _____

   _____

   _____

   _____

   _____

   _____

   _____

On Your Own: Writing Narrative Paragraphs from Model Paragraphs

The Story of How You Faced a New Challenge

ASSIGNMENT 1: Write a paragraph telling the story of a day or part of a day in which you faced an important challenge of some kind. It could have been a challenge you faced in school, at home, or on the job. The following paragraph is an example of such an experience.

Model Paragraph

I hate to be late. So, when I began my new job, I was determined to be on time for my first day. I awoke early, had a leisurely breakfast, and gave myself lots of time to get through the traffic. I entered my new office building and sat down at my new desk a good fifteen minutes before starting time. My boss noticed me, smiled, and came over to my desk. "I'm glad you're early," she said. "In fact, you're a week early. You start *next* Monday."

SUGGESTED TOPICS

1. The day I started a new job
2. The day I began my first term paper
3. The morning of my big job interview
4. Facing a large debt
5. Trying to re-establish a friendship gone sour
6. The day I started driving lessons
7. Coping with a death in the family

The Beginning of a Special Relationship

ASSIGNMENT 2: Write a paragraph telling the story of how you became close to another person. Select one particular moment when the relationship changed from casual friendliness to something deeper and more lasting. Perhaps you shared an experience that brought you together. The following paragraph is taken from Morley Callaghan's short story "One Spring Night."

Model Paragraph

Bob had taken her out a few times when he had felt like having some girl to talk to who knew him and liked him. And tonight he was leaning back good-humoredly, telling her one thing and then another with the wise self-assurance he usually had when with her; but gradually, as he watched her, he found himself talking more slowly, his voice grew serious and much softer, and then finally he leaned across the table toward her as though he had just discovered that her neck was full and soft with her spring coat thrown open, and that her face under her little black straw hat tilted back on her head had a new, eager beauty. Her warm, smiling softness was so close to him that he smiled a bit shyly.

SUGGESTED TOPICS

1. My relationship with a teacher
2. My relationship with a fellow student
3. When I shared an experience with a fellow worker
4. When I made friends with someone older or younger than I am
5. When my relationship with my brother or sister changed
6. The moment when my attitude about a grandparent changed
7. When a stranger became a friend

Paragraph Practice: Narration

The following paragraph, from "I Have the Bar Waitress Blues" by Centennial College student Christine Thomson, uses the narrative approach.

> "Another Saturday night," I mumble quietly, "and I don't know how I got brainwashed into working again. I am going to have to tolerate the usual uninhibited drunks, the muddle of orders, and the harsh working conditions. O Lord, please help me survive the night without any hassles!" Straightening my apron and arming myself with a tray, I push open the doors and enter the "weekender zone."

Imagine the situation that Christine describes. Why do you think she feels as she does? Describe what you think happens next.

Paragraph Opportunity: Narration

In a paragraph, tell the story of a job you once had or now have. Describe a situation you encountered in your job. What happened to you or to someone you worked with?

Working Together

The following personal advertisement appeared in a local newspaper:

> Young man seeks neat, responsible roommate to share off-campus apartment for next academic year. Person must be a non-smoker and respect a vegetarian who cooks at home. Furniture not needed, but CD player would be welcome!

Finding the right roommate in a college or university dormitory, finding the right person with whom to share an apartment, or finding the right long-term companion may be difficult. People's personal habits have a way of causing friction in everyday life. Divide into groups for a brief discussion of the kinds of problems one finds in sharing the same space with another person.

1. Imagine that you must write a paragraph or two in which you provide a character description of yourself for an agency that will match you up with a roommate. As you write, be sure you include information about your hobbies, habits, attitudes, and any other personal characteristics that could make a difference in the kind of person the agency will select for you.
2. Imagine that you must write a paragraph or two in which you provide a character sketch of the person you would like the agency to find for you.

Chapter 13
Developing Paragraphs: Description

What Is Description?

Description is one of the basic building blocks of good writing. When you are able to write an effective description of a person, an object, a place, or even an idea, you are in control of your writing. Good description also makes you able to control what your reader sees and does not see.

The key to writing a good description is the choice of the **specific details** you will use. Specific details make your descriptions real and help your reader remember what you have written. A careful writer always pays special attention to specific details in any piece of writing.

A second important aspect of good description is the use of **sensory images.**

Def

Sensory images are details that relate to your sense of sight, smell, touch, taste, or hearing.

When you use at least some of these five senses in your descriptive writing, your reader will be able to relate directly to what you are saying. Sensory images also help your reader remember what you have written.

A third important aspect of good description is the order in which you place the details you have chosen. The combination of specific details, sensory images, and the order in which you present these details and impressions will help your reader form a **dominant impression** of what you are describing.

The following example of descriptive writing shows all of the elements of a good description. As you read this description of a typical neighbourhood delicatessen, note the specific details and the sensory images the writer uses. After you have read the description, ask yourself what dominant impression the writer wanted us to have of the place.

The delicatessen was a wide store with high ceilings that were a dark brown colour from many years of not being painted. The rough wooden shelves on both sides of the store were filled from floor to ceiling with cans of fruits and vegetables, jars of pickles and olives, and special imported canned fish. A large refrigerator case against one wall was always humming loudly from the effort of keeping milk, cream, and several cases of pop and juice cool at all times. At the end of the store was the main counter with its gleaming white metal scale on top and its cold cuts and freshly made salads inside. Stacked on top of the counter beside the scale today were baskets of fresh rolls and breads that gave off an aroma that contained a mixture of onion, caraway seed, and pumpernickel. Behind the scale was the friendly face of Mr. Rubino, who was in his store seven days a week, fourteen hours or more each day. He was always ready with a smile or a friendly comment, or even a sample piece of cheese or smoked meat as a friendly gesture for his "growing customers," as he referred to us kids in the neighbourhood.

Working with Description: Selecting the Dominant Impression

When you use a number of specific, sensory images as you write a description, you should do more than simply write a series of sentences that deal with a single topic. You should also create a dominant impression in your reader's mind. Each individual sentence that you write is part of a picture that becomes clear when the reader finishes the paragraph.

For example, when you describe a place, the dominant impression you create might be of a place that is warm, friendly, or comfortable; or it could be a place that is formal, elegant, or artistic. When you write a description of a person, your reader could receive the dominant impression of a positive, efficient person who is outgoing and creative, or of a person who appears to be cold, distant, or hostile. All the sentences should support the dominant impression you have chosen.

Here is a list for you to use as a guide as you work through this chapter. Picking a dominant impression is essential in writing the descriptive college paragraph.

Possible Dominant Impressions for Descriptions of Places

crowded	cosy	inviting	cheerful	dazzling
romantic	restful	dreary	drab	uncomfortable
cluttered	ugly	tasteless	unfriendly	gaudy
stuffy	eerie	depressing	spacious	sunny

Possible Dominant Impressions for Descriptions of People

creative	angry	independent	proud	withdrawn
tense	shy	aggressive	generous	sullen
silent	witty	pessimistic	responsible	efficient
snobbish	placid	bumbling	bitter	easygoing

E X E R C I S E   1   **Selecting the Dominant Impression**

Each of the following places could be the topic for a descriptive paragraph. First, the writer must decide on a dominant impression. A dominant impression is noted in the blank to the right. This exercise is done for you.

Topic	Dominant Impression
1. A high school gym on prom night	dazzling
2. Your barber or hairdresser's shop	crowded
3. The room where you are now sitting	drab
4. The grocery store nearest you	spacious
5. A hardware store	cluttered
6. An overcrowded waiting room	stuffy
7. The kitchen in the morning	sunny

E X E R C I S E 2   **Selecting the Dominant Impression**

Each of the following persons could be the topic for a descriptive paragraph. First, the writer must decide on a dominant impression. Fill in each blank to the right of the topic with an appropriate dominant impression. Use the list on page 149 if you need help.

Topic	Dominant Impression
1. An actor or actress being interviewed on television	_____
2. An old woman in a nursing home	_____
3. A librarian	_____
4. A bank clerk on a busy day	_____
5. A farmer	_____
6. A politician running for office	_____
7. A cab driver	_____

Revising Vague Dominant Impressions

Certain words in the English language have become so overused that they no longer have any specific meaning for a reader. Careful writers avoid these words because they are almost useless in descriptive writing. Here is a list of the most common overused words:

good, bad
nice, fine, okay
normal, typical
interesting
beautiful

The following paragraph is an example of the kind of writing that results from the continued use of vague words:

I had a typical day. The weather was nice and my job was interesting. The food for lunch was okay; supper was really good. After supper I saw my girlfriend, who is really beautiful. That's when my day really became fun.

Notice that all of the details in the paragraph are vague. The writer has told us what happened, but we cannot really see any of the details that are mentioned. This is because the writer has made the mistake of using words that have lost much of their meaning. Replacing the vague words in the paragraph above will create an entirely different impression:

> I had an event-filled day that was typical of the type of day I've been enjoying lately. The weather on this summer day was perfect for late June, and the challenge of my job in the health-care field made me feel that this warm and sunny day was made just for me. I had a delicious lunch in a tiny Italian restaurant, and a supper to excite the taste buds at a cosy Greek restaurant that just oozed atmosphere. After supper I met my girlfriend, a person with a warm sense of humour who was a partner in a major law firm down the street from where I worked.

The next group of exercises will give you practice in recognizing and eliminating overused words.

E X E R C I S E 1 **Revising Vague Dominant Impressions**

In each of the spaces provided, change the underlined word to a more specific dominant impression. An example is done for you.

> **Vague:** The tablecloth was beautiful.
> **Revised:** The tablecloth was of white linen with delicate blue embroidery.

1. The sky was beautiful.   _____

2. The water felt nice.   _____

3. Walking along the beach was fun. _____

4. The storm was bad.   _____

5. The parking lot was typical.   _____

6. The main street is interesting. _____

7. The dessert tasted good.   _____

E X E R C I S E 2 **Revising Vague Dominant Impressions**

In each of the spaces provided, change the underlined word to a more specific dominant impression.

1. It was a really nice date.   _____

2. The window display was beautiful. _____

3. The boat ride was fine.   _____

4. The circus was fun.   _____

5. The lemonade was awful.   _____

6. The play was <u>bad</u>.   _____

7. His new suit looked <u>okay</u>.   _____

Working with Description: Sensory Images

One of the basic ways all good writers communicate experiences to their readers is by using sensory impressions. We respond to writing that makes us *see* an object, *hear* a sound, *touch* a surface, *smell* an odour, or *taste* a flavour. When a writer uses one or more of these sensory images in a piece of writing, we tend to pay more attention to what he or she is saying, and we tend to remember the details of what we have read.

For example, if you come across the word *door* in a sentence, you may or may not pay attention to it. However, if the writer tells you it was a *brown wooden* door that was *rough to the touch* and *creaked loudly* when it opened, you would hardly be able to forget it. The door would stay in your mind because the writer used sensory images to make you aware of it.

The following sentences are taken from the description of Mr. Rubino's delicatessen that you read on pages 148–49. Notice how in each sentence the writer uses at least one sensory image to make the details of that sentence remain in our minds. The physical sense the writer is appealing to by the use of one or more sensory images is indicated after the sentence.

1. A large refrigerator case against one wall was always humming loudly from the effort of keeping milk, cream, and several cases of pop and juice cool at all times.

   Physical sense: hearing

2. Stacked on top of the counter . . . were baskets of fresh rolls and breads that gave off an aroma that contained a mixture of onion, caraway seed, and pumpernickel.

   Physical sense: smell

3. He was always ready with . . . a sample piece of cheese or smoked meat as a friendly gesture. . . .

   Physical sense: taste

When you use sensory images in your own writing, you will stimulate your readers' interest, and these images created in their minds will be remembered.

EXERCISE 1   **Recognizing Sensory Images**

The following paragraph contains examples of sensory images. In the spaces following the paragraph, identify the sensory images used by the writer.

Hear it! the crunching smash of twenty-four bottles of beer, all splintering against each other as I misdeal on the packing machine. Smell the stink of warm beer pouring over my clothes, washing over the sour sweat of my body. I can feel the unheard curse as I toss the wet, mangled carton down the rollers for some poor bastard to sort out. And back to the mother-eating machine where the bottles are already starting to pile up on the conveyor belt. The ten second delay bell starts ringing. The jangling vibrations echo in my skull, and the foreman comes running over, screaming incoherently. How the hell can I hear him over the roar of four acres of machinery, and the teeth-jarring rattle of 25 000 bottles, all clinking against each other as they ride down the hundred yards of clanking metal conveyor belts.

From Ian Adams,
Living with Automation in Winnipeg

Sensory Images

Sight: _____

_____

_____

Sound: _____

_____

_____

Smell: _____

_____

_____

E X E R C I S E 2   Recognizing Sensory Images

The following paragraph contains examples of sensory images. In the spaces following the paragraph, identify the sensory images used by the writer.

The temperature in Winkler at 7 p.m. on Thursday, January 20, 1972, is 35 below zero and dropping. The air is frozen into little slivers of glass which pierce the lungs. The light from the full moon reflected in the crystallized air makes the night fluorescent. People scurry through the neon streets beneath small white clouds of congealed breath like balloons in comic strips. Tears run down their cheeks. The cold freezes hands and feet to blocks of wood. It hurts to walk more than a few feet; even the cars scream and groan.

From Heather Robertson,
Sale Night

Sensory Images

Sight: _____

_____

Sound: _____

_____

Touch: _____

_____

E X E R C I S E   1   Creating Sensory Images

Each of the following topic sentences contains an underlined word that names a physical sense. For each topic sentence, write three sentences that give examples of sensory images. The first one is done for you.

1. I knew I was walking past the hospital emergency room from the sounds I could <u>hear</u>.

   Three sentences with sensory images:

   a. The ambulance siren screamed as the vehicle raced into the emergency entrance.
   b. The hospital's public address system constantly paged hospital staff.
   c. People in the waiting room, many in pain, spoke in subdued voices.

2. I can't help stopping in the bakery every Sunday morning because the <u>smells</u> are so good.

   Three sentences with sensory images:

   a. _____

   _____

   b. _____

   _____

   c. _____

   _____

3. The best part of my vacation last year was the <u>sight</u> that greeted me when I got up in the morning.

   Three sentences with sensory images:

   a. _____

   _____

   b. _____

   _____

   c. _____

   _____

E X E R C I S E   2   Creating Sensory Images

Each of the following topic sentences contains an underlined word that names a physical sense. For each topic sentence, write three sentences that give examples of sensory images.

1. It is a luxury to wear clothing made with natural fibres because the <u>feeling</u> is quite different from how polyester makes you feel.

   Three sentences with sensory images:

   a. _____

   _____

   b. _____

   _____

   c. _____

   _____

2. I knew the garbage strike had gone on for a long time when I had to <u>hold my nose</u> walking down some streets.

   Three sentences with sensory images:

   a. _____

   _____

   b. _____

   _____

   c. _____

   _____

Coherence in Description: Putting Details in Space Order

In descriptive paragraphs, the writer often chooses to arrange supporting details according to space. With this method, you place yourself at the scene and then use a logical order such as moving from nearby to farther away, right to left, or top to bottom. Often you move in such a way that you save the most important detail until last in order to achieve the greatest effect.

In the paragraph about the delicatessen on pages 148–49, the writer first describes the ceilings and walls of the store, then proceeds to the shelves and large refrigerator, and ends by describing the main counter of the deli with its owner, Mr. Rubino, standing behind it. The ordering of details has been from the outer limits of the room to the inner area, which is central to the point of this paragraph. A description of a clothes closet might order the details differently. Perhaps the writer would begin with the shoes standing on the floor and finish with the hats and gloves arranged on the top shelf, an arrangement that goes from the ground up.

Here is a paragraph from Thierry Mallet's *Glimpses of the Barren Lands*, a description of his travels through the Canadian Arctic:

> Our camp had been pitched at the foot of a great, bleak, ragged hill, a few feet from the swirling waters of the Kazan River. The two small green tents, pegged down tight with heavy rocks, shivered and rippled under the faint touch of the northern breeze. A thin wisp of smoke rose from the embers of the fire.

Notice that the writer begins with a description of the landscape, then gives a description of the camp, and ends with a picture of the small fire. We are able to follow the writer through the description because there is a logic or plan. No matter which method of space order you choose in organizing details in a descriptive paragraph, be sure the results allow your reader to see the scene in a logical order.

EXERCISE 1 **Working for Coherence: Using Space Order**

Each of the following topic sentences is followed by descriptive sentences that are out of order. Put these descriptive sentences in order by placing the appropriate number in the space provided. The first one is done for you.

1. The old wallet lay on the nightstand.
   (Order the material from the outside to the inside.)

   _____3_____   A clear plastic insert held photos and necessary items such as a driver's licence and credit cards.

   _____5_____   The secret compartment, which could hold extra money for emergencies, was visible when a small flap of leather was turned up.

   _____4_____   Behind the photographs and other papers was a small pocket for postage stamps.

   _____1_____   The rich brown leather of the wallet, worn smooth from years of hard use, faintly showed the owner's name stamped in gold.

   _____2_____   The wallet seemed to double in size when it was opened, and the colour inside was a lighter brown.

2. The young woman was a teen of the eighties.
   (Order the material from top to bottom.)

   _____   She wore an oversized sweater that she had borrowed from her father.

_____ Her shoes were white tennis sneakers.

_____ Her dangling earrings, which were red and green, matched her outfit.

_____ Her short blond hair was clean and feathered attractively.

_____ Her jeans, which were the latest style, had a faint paisley print.

3. My aunt's kitchen is a very orderly place.
   (Order the material from near to far.)

_____ As usual, in the centre of the table sits a vase with a fresh daffodil.

_____ Nearby on the refrigerator, a magnet holds the week's menu.

_____ Sitting at the kitchen table, I am struck by the freshly pressed linen tablecloth.

_____ Looking across the room through the stained-glass doors of her kitchen cupboards, I can see neat rows of dishes, exactly eight each, matching the colours of the tablecloth and wall-paper.

EXERCISE 2 Working for Coherence: Using Space Order

Each of the following topic sentences could be expanded into a fully developed para-graph. In the spaces provided, give appropriate supporting details for the topic sen-tence. Be sure to give your supporting details in a particular order. That is, the details should go from top to bottom, from outside to inside, from close to far, or around the area you are describing. The first example is done for you.

1. The airport terminal was as busy inside as it was outside.
   a. Taxis were constantly dropping people off at the departure level.
   b. The ticket counters of most major airlines resembled a mob scene.
   c. Attendants were labelling passengers' bags as soon as the passengers had their tickets.
   d. Loudspeakers announced a succession of departures to all parts of the globe.
2. The cafeteria is a large and often deserted area of our school.

   a. _____

   _____

   b. _____

   _____

   c. _____

   _____

d. _____

_____

3. The picnic area was shady and inviting.

a. _____

_____

b. _____

_____

c. _____

_____

d. _____

_____

Writing the Descriptive Paragraph Step by Step

To learn a skill with some degree of ease, it is best to follow a step-by-step approach so that various skills can be worked on one at a time. This will ensure that you are not missing a crucial point or misunderstanding a part of the whole. There are other ways to go about writing an effective paragraph, but here is one logical method you can use to achieve results.

Steps for Writing the Descriptive Paragraph

1. Study the given topic, and then plan your topic sentence, especially the dominant impression.
2. List at least ten details that come to mind when you think about the topic.
3. Choose the five or six most important details from your list. Be sure these details support the dominant impression.
4. Put your final list in order.
5. Write at least one complete sentence for each of the details you have chosen from your list.
6. Write a concluding statement that offers some reason for describing this topic.
7. Finally, copy your sentences into standard paragraph form.

EXERCISE 1 **Writing the Descriptive Paragraph Step by Step**

The following exercise will guide you through the construction of a descriptive paragraph. Start with the suggested topic. Use the seven steps to help you work through each stage in the writing process. This exercise is done for you.

Topic: A place you have lived

1. Topic sentence: My home town was a pretty little village in southwestern Ontario.
2. Make a list of possible supporting details.

a. near the lake
b. friendly people
c. well-kept buildings
d. trees
e. Sunday concerts

f. few cars, noise
g. weather
h. local farmers
i. Saturday night

3. Circle the five or six details you believe are the most important for the description.
4. Put your choices in order by numbering them.
5. Using your final list, write at least one sentence for each detail you have chosen.
   a. It was situated near a lake, and the weather was usually moderate.
   b. The people were friendly, and most knew each other.
   c. People's houses were well-kept and reflected people's pride in their town.
   d. There seemed to be trees everywhere you looked.
   e. Sunday concerts in the park were major events.
   f. Very few people in town owned cars, so there wasn't much noise.
6. Write a concluding statement: I still have fond memories of my home town.
7. Copy your sentences into standard paragraph form.

   My home town was a pretty little village in southwestern Ontario. It was situated near a lake, and the weather was usually moderate. The people were friendly, and most knew each other. People's houses were well-kept and reflected people's pride in their town. There seemed to be trees everywhere you looked. Sunday concerts in the park were major events. Very few people in town owned cars, so there wasn't much noise. I still have fond memories of my home town.

E X E R C I S E 2   Writing the Descriptive Paragraph Step by Step

The following exercise will guide you through the construction of a descriptive paragraph. Start with the suggested topic. Use the seven steps to help you work through each stage in the writing process.

Topic: A person you admire

1. Topic sentence: _____

   _____

2. Make a list of possible supporting details.

   a. _____ f. _____
   b. _____ g. _____
   c. _____ h. _____
   d. _____ i. _____
   e. _____ j. _____

3. Circle the five or six details you believe are the most important for the description.
4. Put your choices in order by numbering them.
5. Using your final list, write at least one sentence for each detail you have chosen.

a. _____

_____

b. _____

_____

c. _____

_____

d. _____

_____

e. _____

_____

f. _____

_____

g. _____

_____

6. Write a concluding statement. _____

_____

_____

7. Copy your sentences into standard paragraph form.

_____

_____

_____

_____

_____

_____

_____

_____

_____

_____

_____

_____

_____

_____

On Your Own: Writing Descriptive Paragraphs from Model Paragraphs

A Description of a Person

ASSIGNMENT 1: Describe a person — preferably one you have observed more than once. If you saw this person only once, indicate the details that made him or her stay in your mind. If you choose to describe a person with whom you are familiar, select the most outstanding details that will help your reader have a single, dominant impression. In the model paragraph, from Alistair MacLeod's story "The Lost Salt Gift of Blood," the author describes his mother in Nova Scotia.

Model Paragraph

My mother ran her house as her brothers ran their boats. Everything was clean and spotless and in order. She was tall and dark and powerfully energetic. In later years, she reminded me of the women of Thomas Hardy, particularly Eustacia Vye, in a physical way. She fed and clothed a family of seven children, making all of the meals and most of the clothes. She grew miraculous gardens and magnificent flowers and raised broods of hens and ducks. She would walk miles on berry-picking expeditions and hoist her skirts to dig for clams when the tide was low. She was fourteen years younger than my father, whom she had married when she was twenty-six, and had been a local beauty for a period of ten years. My mother was of the sea as were all of her people, and her horizons were the very literal ones she scanned with her dark and fearless eyes.

SUGGESTED TOPICS

1. A loyal friend
2. An overworked waitress
3. A cab driver
4. A fashion model
5. A gossipy neighbour
6. A street vendor
7. A rude salesperson

A Description of a Time of Day

ASSIGNMENT 2: Write a paragraph in which you describe the sights, sounds, and events of a particular time of day in a place you know well. In the model paragraph that follows, from John Riley's "Growing up in Cleveland," the writer has chosen to describe an especially busy time of day, namely, the morning hours, when activity can be frantic in a household.

Model Paragraph

I remember the turmoil of mornings in our house. My brothers and sisters rushed about upstairs and down trying to get ready for school. Mom would repeatedly tell them to hurry up. Molly would usually scream down from her bedroom, "What am I going to do? I don't have any clean underwear!" Amy, often in tears, sat at the kitchen table still in her pajamas trying to do her math. Paul paced back and forth in front of the mirror angrily combing his unruly hair which stuck up in all directions while Roland threatened to punch him if he didn't find the pen he had borrowed the night before. Mother was stuffing sandwiches into bags while she sighed, "I'm afraid there isn't anything for dessert today." No one heard her. Then came the yelling up the stairs, "You should have left ten minutes ago." One by one, these unwilling victims were packed up and pushed out the door. Mother wasn't safe yet. Somebody always came back frantic and desperate. "My flute, Mom, where's my flute, quick? I'll get killed if I don't have it today." Every crisis apparently meant the difference between life and death. Morning at our house was like watching a troop preparing for battle. When they had finally gone, I was left in complete silence while my mother slumped on a chair at the kitchen table. She paid no attention to me.

SUGGESTED TOPICS

1. A Saturday filled with errands
2. The dinner hour at my house
3. Lunchtime in a cafeteria
4. A midnight raid on the refrigerator
5. Christmas morning
6. TGIF (Thank God It's Friday)
7. Getting ready to go out on a Friday night

Paragraph Practice: Description

The following example is from an essay, "Sunblock," written by a student, Ann Palantzas, Innis College, University of Toronto. In this essay a description is given of an outfit worn by a woman on vacation in Italy. Even though the paragraph begins as a narrative, the descriptive elements are dominant.

"We're leaving tomorrow so don't do anything stupid like fall in love with him," my sister screamed from the shower.

"I only said yes because he would make a great guide. He does live in Venice," I bellowed back as I finished dressing.

I looked in the mirror. I wore what I called the outfit for the modern explorer, suitable for all the adventures of a tourist: a cotton top and skirt and a pair of sneakers. The top had two wide straps, the ends of which scooped down to form an oval neckline. The skirt was gathered at the waist so that it flared, swirling just above my knees when I walked. Blotches of dirt marred my once-white sneakers. I always felt comfortable in this outfit, for it portrayed me exactly as I was: a young traveller able to go where I wanted (the worn sneakers did not give me blisters), see what I wanted (the skirt and a big shawl even allowed my entrance into a mosque), and flirt whenever I wanted (as the strap of the top sometimes fell off my shoulder). But today, before I left, I wore a T-shirt over my top, thinking that my shoulders, already rosy, would burn under the scorching Italian sun. Now I was ready to meet Franco. I stuffed my camera into my purse and yelled goodbye to Sophie.

What do you learn about this woman as she is described? From the details given in the paragraph, attempt to describe her more fully. Can you describe her facial features, her personality? What picture do you have in mind about this tourist?

Paragraph Opportunity: Description

Describe a fellow student as you have observed him or her reading, either in class, in the library, or in some other place. First, describe what the student was wearing, and then describe how he or she held the book or magazine that was being read. Be sure to use such details as the expression on the student's face and whether or not he or she was concentrating on what was being read. Did the student ignore distractions?

Working Together

Aesop is believed to have been a Greek slave of some 2 500 years ago. He wrote over 200 fables which have become part of our literary heritage. Below is one of Aesop's most famous fables, often called "The Story of the Tortoise and the Hare."

A tortoise and a hare disagreed about which one of them was faster, so they decided to settle the dispute by having a race. The hare was so confident of his ability to move swiftly that after running awhile, he decided to take a nap by the side of the road. The tortoise was very aware of his own slow movement, and so he went steadily along the road. He did not stop until he had passed the sleeping hare and so won the race.

Moral: a person who has great natural abilities but who does not make use of them is often beaten by a slow and steady person.

Sometimes a writer's purpose is to teach a lesson. Notice how Aesop points out a moral lesson to his readers. You might enjoy creating a fable of your own with a moral lesson added at the end. Your fable might also use animals, but you could set the action of your fable in a modern town or city. You might discuss with your classmates some of the social or personal concerns that might be the subject of a particular fable. For example, you might want to teach a lesson about human ambition or greed. Your narration might make a very good story to read to the children in your family. What lesson would you like them to learn?

Chapter 14
Developing Paragraphs:
Process

What Is Process?

Process is the method that explains how to do something or that shows how something works. There are two kinds of process writing: **directional** and **informational.**

A process that is directional actually shows you, step by step, how to do something. For example, if you want to show someone how to brew a perfect cup of coffee, you would take the person through each step of the process, from selecting and grinding the coffee beans to pouring the finished product. Instructions on a test, directions on how to get to a wedding reception, or your favourite spaghetti sauce recipe are a few examples of the kinds of process writing you see and use regularly. You can find examples of directional process writing everywhere you look, in newspapers, magazines, and books, as well as on the containers and packages of products you use every day.

On the other hand, *a process that is informational tells you how something is or was done, for the purpose of informing you about the process.* For example, in a history course, it might be important to understand how the process of Confederation joined Upper and Lower Canada. Of course, you would not use this process yourself. The purpose is for information.

The following paragraph, from Mary Finlay's *Communication at Work*, shows the several steps you need to keep in mind when determining the length of an oral presentation.

Ascertain how long your presentation is expected to take. Normally, a speech is delivered at about 150 words a minute. Make sure that your material is adequate for the time allotted. Of course, this does not mean that a ten-minute oral report will be as dense as a 1500-word essay. You will need to build in much more repetition to ensure that you are getting your point across. Rehashing points you have already made in order to fill up your time is a sure-fire way to annoy and frustrate your listeners. Leave time for questions and feedback. If there are none, don't fill in the time by answering the questions nobody asked. This suggests that you are having second thoughts about the organization and planning of your report.

Working with Process: Don't Overlook Any of the Steps

The writer of the process essay is almost always more of an authority on the subject than the person reading the essay. In giving directions or information on how something is to be done or was done, it is possible to leave out a step that you think is so obvious that it is not worth mentioning. The reader, on the other hand, does not necessarily fill in the missing step, as you did. An important part of process writing, therefore, is understanding your reader's level of ability. All of us have been given directions that, at first, seemed very clear. However, when we actually tried to carry out the process, something went wrong. A step in the process was misunderstood or missing. The giver of the information either assumed we would know certain parts of the process or didn't stop to think through the process completely. The important point is that directions must be complete and accurate. Here is one further consideration: if special equipment is required in order to perform the process, the directions must include a clear description of the necessary tools.

E X E R C I S E   1 **Is the Process Complete?**

In each of the following processes, try to determine what important step or steps have been omitted. Try to imagine yourself going through the process using only the information provided.

How to Use the Copying Machine
1. Open the top of the copier.
2. Position the paper you are copying on the glass surface.
3. Set the copier to the kind of copying you are going to do (light, normal, or dark).
4. Check the size of the paper. Most copiers have a setting for two sizes of paper.
5. Put your money into the copier machine.

Missing step or steps: _____

_____

_____

How to Plan a Wedding
1. Make an appointment with the minister or other authority involved, to set a date for the wedding.
2. Discuss plans with both families as to the budget available for the wedding; this will determine the size of the party and where it is to be held.
3. Reserve the banquet hall as much as eight months in advance.
4. Choose members of the wedding party and ask them whether they will be able to participate in the ceremony.

5. Begin to choose the clothing for the wedding party, including your own wedding gown or tuxedo.

6. Enjoy your wedding!

Missing step or steps: _____

_____

_____

EXERCISE 2 Is the Process Complete?

In each of the following processes, try to determine what important step or steps have been omitted. Try to imagine yourself going through the process using only the information provided.

How to Prepare for an Essay Exam

1. Read the chapters well in advance of the test as they are assigned.
2. Take notes in class.
3. If the teacher has not described the test, ask him or her what format the test will take.
4. Get a good night's sleep the night before.
5. Bring any pens or pencils that you might need.
6. Arrive at the classroom a few minutes early in order to get yourself settled and to keep yourself calm.

Missing step or steps: _____

_____

_____

How to Balance Your Chequebook with the Monthly Bank Statement

1. Put your returned cheques in order by number or date.
2. Check them off in your chequebook, making sure the amount of each cheque agrees with each amount listed in your chequebook.
3. Subtract from your chequebook balance any amounts that are automatically deducted from your account (loan payments, for example).
4. Add to your bank statement balance the amounts of deposits you made after the date on the statement.
5. Subtract from the bank statement balance the total number of cheques still outstanding.
6. The balance you get should agree with your chequebook balance.

(Do you see now why so many people cannot balance their chequebooks?)

Missing step or steps: _____

_____

_____

Coherence in Process: Order in Logical Sequence

When you are writing about a process, it is important not only to make sure the steps in the process are complete: you must also make sure they are given in the right sequence. For example, if you are describing the process of cleaning a mixer, it is important to point out that you must first unplug the appliance before you actually remove the blades. The importance of this step is clear when you realize that a person could lose a finger if this part of the process were missing. Improperly written instructions could cause serious injuries or even death.

E X E R C I S E 1   Coherence in Process: Order in Logical Sequence

The following steps describe the process of refinishing a hardwood floor. Number the steps in their proper sequence. This exercise is done for you.

4	Keep sanding until you expose the hardwood.
8	Apply a coat of polyurethane finish.
7	When the sanding is done, clean the floor thoroughly with a vacuum cleaner to remove all the sawdust.
10	Allow the finish to dry for three days before waxing and buffing.
1	Take all furnishings out of the room.
3	Do the initial sanding with coarse sandpaper.
5	The edger and hand sander are used after the machine sanding to get to those hard-to-reach places.
9	Put the second coat of polyurethane finish on the following day, using a brush or a roller.
6	Change to a fine sandpaper for the final sanding.
2	Any nails sticking out from the floor should be either pulled out or set below the surface of the boards before you start the sanding machine.

E X E R C I S E 2   Coherence in Process: Order in Logical Sequence

The following steps describe the processes of setting up a filing system that works. Number the steps in their proper sequence.

_____	When your mind begins to blur, stop filing for that day.
_____	Now label the file folder and slip the piece of paper in.
_____	Gather together all materials to be filed so that they are all in one location.
_____	Alphabetize your file folders and put them away into your file drawer, and you are finished for that session.

_____   Add to these materials a wastebasket, folders, labels, and a pen.

_____   Pick up the next piece of paper and go through the same procedure, the only variation being that this new piece of paper might fit into an existing file, rather than one with a new heading.

_____   Pick up an item from the top of the pile and decide whether this item has value for you. If it does not, throw it away. If it does, go on to the next step.

_____   Finally, to maintain your file once it is established, each time you consult a file folder, riffle through it quickly to pick out and throw away the deadwood.

_____   If the piece of paper is worth saving, ask yourself the question "What is this paper about?"

Transitions for Process

Writers of process, like writers of narration, usually order their material by time sequence. Although it would be tiresome to use "and then" for each new step, a certain number of transitions are necessary for the process to read smoothly and be coherent. Here is a list of transitions frequently used in process writing.

Transitions		
the first step	while you are . . .	the last step
in the beginning	as you are . . .	the final step
to start with	next	finally
to begin with	then	at last
first of all	the second step	eventually
	after you have . . .	

Refer again to the chart of transitional words and phrases on the inside back cover of this book, and to the temporal and spatial (time and space) methods of ordering paragraphs in Chapters 12 and 13.

EXERCISE 1   **Using Transitions to Go from a List to a Paragraph**

Select one of the four processes outlined on pages 165–66. Change this list into a process paragraph that uses enough transitional devices so that the paragraph is coherent and flows smoothly.

EXERCISE 2   **Using Transitions to Go from a List to a Paragraph**

Select one of the four processes outlined on pages 165–66. Change this list into a process paragraph that uses enough transitional devices so that the paragraph is coherent and flows smoothly.

Writing the Process Paragraph Step by Step

To learn a skill with some degree of ease, it is best to follow a step-by-step approach so that various skills can be worked on one at a time. This will ensure that you are not missing a crucial point or misunderstanding a part of the whole. There are other ways to go about writing an effective paragraph, but here is one logical method you can use to achieve results.

Steps for Writing the Process Paragraph

1. Write a topic sentence.
2. List as many steps or stages in the process as you can.
3. Eliminate any irrelevant points; add equipment needed or special circumstances of the process.
4. Put your final list in order.
5. Write at least one complete sentence for each of the steps you have chosen from your list.
6. Write a concluding statement that says something about the results of completing the process.
7. Finally, copy your sentences into standard paragraph form.

E X E R C I S E   1   Writing the Process Paragraph Step by Step

The following exercise will guide you through the construction of a process paragraph. Start with the suggested topic. Use the seven steps to help you work through each stage of the writing process.

Topic: How to burglar-proof your home

The incidence of break-and-enter crimes increases yearly, and many people are concerned about their homes when they are away on vacation. Give advice to a homeowner on how to protect a house against burglary.

1. Topic sentence: _____

   _____

2. Make a list of possible steps.

   a. _____   f. _____

   b. _____   g. _____

   c. _____   h. _____

   d. _____   i. _____

   e. _____   j. _____

3. Circle the five or six steps you believe are the most important to complete the process.

4. Put your final choices in order by numbering them.

5. Using your final list, write at least one sentence for each step you have chosen.

a. _____

_____

b. _____

_____

c. _____

_____

d. _____

_____

e. _____

_____

f. _____

_____

g. _____

_____

6. Write a concluding statement. _____

_____

_____

7. Copy your sentences into standard paragraph form.

EXERCISE 2 **Writing the Process Paragraph Step by Step**

The following exercise will guide you through the construction of a process paragraph. Start with the suggested topic. Use the seven steps to help you work through each stage of the writing process.

Topic: How to manage a budget

Imagine you are the expert who has been hired by a couple to help them sort out their money problems. They bring in a reasonable income, but they are always spending more than they earn.

1. Topic sentence: _____

_____

2. Make a list of possible steps.

a. _____   f. _____

b. _____   g. _____

c. _____   h. _____

d. _____   i. _____

e. _____   j. _____

3. Circle the five or six steps you believe are the most important to complete the process.
4. Put your final choices in order by numbering them.
5. Using your final list, write at least one sentence for each step you have chosen.

a. _____

_____

b. _____

_____

c. _____

_____

d. _____

_____

e. _____

_____

f. _____

_____

g. _____

_____

6. Write a concluding statement. _____

_____

_____

7. Copy your sentences into standard paragraph form.

On Your Own: Writing Process Paragraphs from Model Paragraphs

Directional: How to Accomplish a Physical Task

ASSIGNMENT 1: Write a paragraph in which you describe the process of doing a physical task of some kind, or the process of doing a task in order to accomplish something else. For example, you might have learned how to refinish an old piece of furniture in order to save money, or you might have learned how to drive so that you would be in a better position to get a job. The following paragraph describes how to trace your family tree.

Model Paragraph

Genealogy, or the art of tracing your family history, has become a popular hobby. How far back can you trace your family? To begin the genealogical process, first speak to all members of your family to find out what they know about the family's history. Then, consult whatever birth certificates, marriage licences, and death certificates may be available. If these documents aren't in the family any longer, they may be obtained for a price from the proper authorities if you know where the event took place and the approximate date of the event. You may be able to obtain help from the Church of Jesus Christ of Latter-Day Saints, from parish registers, or from back issues of newspapers. However, once your obvious sources dry up, you may need help from a professional genealogist to continue your search.

SUGGESTED TOPICS

1. How to move from one city to another
2. How to install your own telephone
3. How to install a stereo system
4. How to make homemade ice cream
5. How to prepare a package for mailing
6. How to pack a suitcase
7. How to furnish an apartment inexpensively

Directional: How to Care for Your Health

ASSIGNMENT 2: Write a paragraph in which you give the major steps in some area of caring for your physical or mental health. Concern for health and physical fitness is enjoying great popularity, bringing in big profits to health-related magazines, health clubs, health-food producers, and sports equipment manufacturers. The following paragraph tells us how to get a good night's sleep.

Model Paragraph

The process of getting a good night's sleep depends on several factors. First, the conditions in your bedroom must be correct. Be sure the room temperature is around 18°C and that the room is as quiet as possible. Next, pay attention to your bed and how it is furnished. A firm mattress is best, and wool blankets are better than blankets made of synthetic material. In addition, pillows that are too soft can cause a stiff neck and lead to a poor night's sleep. Also, keep in mind that what and how you eat are part of the process of preparing for bed. Do not go to bed hungry, but do not overeat, either.

Avoid candy bars or cookies; the sugar they contain acts as a stimulant. Finally, do not go to bed until you are sleepy; do something relaxing until you are tired.

SUGGESTED TOPICS

1. How to plan a daily exercise program
2. How to choose a sport that is suitable for you
3. How to live to be 100
4. How to pick a doctor
5. How to make exercise and dieting fun
6. How to stop eating junk food
7. How to deal with depression

Informational: How to Accomplish a Task

ASSIGNMENT 3: Write a paragraph in which you show how an important task is accomplished. The task may be something that is frequently done by humans or that occurs in the world of nature. The following paragraph describes how an insect builds a nest.

Model Paragraph

The insect known as the hunter wasp goes through a regular procedure when it builds a nest. First, it digs a small tunnel into the earth. Then it goes in search of a cicada, a large insect that resembles a cricket. After stinging and paralyzing the cicada, the hunter wasp brings it to the tunnel, lays an egg on the helpless insect, and seals the tunnel. The hunter wasp then leaves. When the egg hatches, the larva uses the cicada as a source of food.

SUGGESTED TOPICS

1. How cheese is made
2. How a school yearbook is produced
3. How people obtain a divorce
4. How Madame Curie discovered radium
5. How the ancient Egyptians built the pyramids
6. How a bill becomes a law
7. How the snowmobile was developed

Directional: How to Write School Assignments

ASSIGNMENT 4: Your writing in school takes many forms. Write a paragraph in which you show the process of writing a specific assignment related to school. The following paragraph, adapted from Donald Murray's *Write to Learn*, shows the several steps you need to follow in the writing of a term paper.

Model Paragraph

Doing a term paper involves both careful research on a topic and a methodical approach to the writing of the material. First, consult the important and up-to-date books and articles related to your subject. Next, find out the style of writing that your instructor wants; also find out details about length, organization, footnoting, and bibliography that will be part of the presentation of your paper. Then write a draft of the paper as quickly as you can, without using notes or bibliography; this will help you see your ideas and how they can be further developed. Before you go any further, review what you have written to see if you have begun to develop a point of view about your subject or an attitude toward your topic. Finally, write a draft of your paper that includes all of the important information about your subject, a draft that includes your footnotes and bibliography.

SUGGESTED TOPICS

1. How to write a book review
2. How to write a résumé
3. How to write a letter of application to a school or for a job
4. How to write a science experiment
5. How to take classroom notes
6. How to write a letter home, asking for money
7. How to write a story for the school newspaper

Working Together

1. If you were the one to advise this person, what would you tell her to do? Explain the process she should follow in order to solve this problem.

   In order to better answer this question, the class could divide into groups to consider the following questions:
   a. Should she confront the man who is harassing her?
   b. Should she go to her supervisor? Should she have told her co-workers about the problem?
   c. Should she share her problem with the man she is dating?
   d. Should she avoid the problem and quit her job?

> **DEAR ABBY**
>
> Dear Abby: I work for a cable television company as a computer operator. Lately, every morning when I sign in on my computer I find suggestive messages from the man I relieve from the night shift.
>
> I am a single mother. I am also dating another man and have no interest in this co-worker. Should I report him to my supervisor? Someone in my office suggested that I file a sexual harassment charge. — *Harassed*

e. How important is evidence for a person in this situation? How and when should she gather documentation for a possible formal action?

f. Does she need a lawyer? Does she need to consider the consequences of a formal action?

2. Sexual harassment is not the only problem workers or students might face. In a brief discussion with your classmates, list some other common complaints workers or students might have. Are there steps that need to be followed in order to successfully resolve all such problems? Following the class discussion, write your own paragraph describing the steps you feel are necessary to deal with such situations.

Chapter 15
Developing Paragraphs: Comparison or Contrast

What Is Comparison or Contrast?

Comparison and contrast are two related methods of explaining subjects.

Def

When we use **comparison**, we emphasize the similarities between two subjects. When we use **contrast**, we emphasize the differences between two subjects.

We sometimes use the word *comparison* to refer to both similarities and differences between people or things, but it is more exact to use *comparison* for similarities and *contrast* for differences. For example, if you were to write about twin sisters you know, and how close they are in appearance and personality, the similarities you would include would make up a comparison. On the other hand, if you wanted to emphasize some important differences between the two sisters, the result of your work would be a contrast.

We use comparison or contrast in a variety of ways every day. We put similar products side by side in the store before we decide to buy one of them; we listen to two politicians on television and think about the differences between their positions before we vote for one of them; and we read college catalogues and talk to our friends before we make a final choice as to which school we should attend.

When we compare two items, we are able to judge which is better. In addition, when we use comparison we are able to see each individual item more clearly. For example, if you were trying to decide whether to buy a desktop computer or a laptop you would find someone who often uses both. This person could compare or contrast the two machines: show you the similarities or the differences. If you decide to buy one or the other, then the comparison or contrast process begins again: finding out the similarities or differences among the many different makes. One must consider price, capability, availability of service, compatibility with other equipment, and amount of memory. Even the wisest shopper would find such a purchase a complicated procedure.

Working with Comparison or Contrast: Choosing the Two-Part Topic

The problem with writing a good comparison or contrast paragraph usually centres on the fact that you now have a two-part topic. This demands very careful attention to the topic sentence. While you must be careful to choose two subjects that have enough in common to make them comparable, you must also not choose two things having so much in common that you cannot possibly handle all the comparable points in one paragraph or even ten paragraphs. For example, a student trying to compare the French word *chaise* with the English word *chair* might be able to come up with only two sentences of material. With only a dictionary to consult, it is unlikely that the student would find enough material for several points of comparison. On the other hand, contrasting Canada with Europe would present such an endless supply of points to compare that the tendency would be to give only general facts that your reader would already know. When the subject is too broad, the writing is often too general. A better two-part topic might be to compare travelling by train in Europe with travelling by train in Canada.

Once you have chosen a two-part topic that you feel is not too limiting and not too broad, you must remember that a good comparison or contrast paragraph should devote an equal or nearly equal amount of space to each of the two parts. If a writer is interested in only one of the topics, the danger is that the paragraph will end up being very one-sided.

Here's an example of a one-sided contrast:

While Canadian trains go to only a few towns, are infrequent, and are often shabby and uncomfortable, the European train is much nicer.

The following example is a better-written contrast that gives attention to both topics:

While Canadian trains go to only a few large cities, run very infrequently, and are often shabby and uncomfortable, European trains go to virtually every small town, are always dependable, and are clean and attractive.

EXERCISE 1   Evaluating the Two-Part Topic

Study the following topics and decide whether each topic is *too broad* for a paragraph, or whether it is *suitable* as a topic for a paragraph of comparison or contrast. Mark your choice in the appropriate space to the right of each topic. The first two are done for you.

Topic	Too Broad	Suitable
1. Australia and England	✓	
2. Indian elephants and African elephants		✓
3. Canadian wine and French wine		

4. Wooden furniture and plastic furniture   _____   _____

5. Wood and plastic   _____   _____

6. Photography and oil painting   _____   _____

E X E R C I S E 2 **Working with Comparison or Contrast**

Each of these suggested comparison or contrast topics is followed by a more specific topic that has not been completed. Complete each of these specific topics by supplying details of your own. Each topic you complete should be one that you could develop as an example of comparison or contrast. The first one is done for you.

1. Compare two friends:

   My friend _____Bill_____ with my friend _____Fred_____

2. Compare two kinds of coats:

   _____ coats with _____ coats

3. Compare two kinds of diets:

   The _____ diet and the _____ diet

4. Compare two kinds of floors:

   _____ floors with _____ floors

5. Compare two kinds of entertainment:

   Watching _____ with looking at _____

6. Compare two kinds of rice:

   _____ rice with _____ rice

7. Compare two places where you can study:

   Studying in the _____ with studying in the _____

Coherence in Comparison or Contrast: Two Approaches to Ordering Material

The first method for ordering material in a paragraph or an essay of comparison or contrast is known as the **point-by-point method**. When you use this method, you compare a point of one topic with a point of the other topic. For example, here is a paragraph in which the writer uses the point-by-point method to compare the difficulties of being a freelance editor with those of working as an editor on staff at a magazine.

Now, of course, I knew that it was going to be as difficult making an income as a freelance editor as it was being an editor on staff at the magazine, if not more so. I would be at home hustling editing contracts via telephone, while everyone else spent their mornings at the office gabbing over endless cups of coffee. I sometimes resented having to work so hard to make a living, while my old colleagues on staff sat in meetings, went to conferences, and attended company luncheons. But I never envied them on their way to work on cold, dark winter mornings. And I wondered how many of them would have gladly switched places with me as I worked outside on my patio in the summer, while they looked longingly out their office windows.

Notice how, after the opening topic sentence, the writer uses half of each sentence to describe a freelance editor's experience and the other half of the same sentence to describe the experience of an editor who works for a magazine. This technique is effective in such a paragraph, and it is most often used in longer pieces of writing in which many points of comparison are made. This method helps the reader keep the comparison or contrast carefully in mind at each point.

The second method for ordering material in a paragraph of comparison or contrast is known as the **block method**. When you use this approach, you present all of the facts and supporting details about your first and second topics. Here, for example, is another version of the paragraph you studied above, but this time it is written according to the block method:

Now, of course, I knew that it was going to be as difficult making an income as a freelance editor as it was being an editor on staff at the magazine, if not more so. I spent my mornings hustling editing contracts on the telephone and I sometimes resented having to work so hard to earn a living. On the other hand, I didn't envy my old colleagues on their way to work on cold, dark winter mornings. They could spend as much time as they wanted to gabbing over coffee and going to meetings, conferences, and company luncheons; but I wonder how many of them would have gladly switched places with me as I worked outside on my patio in the summer?

Notice how the first half of this version presents almost all of the details about the freelance editor, while the second part of the paragraph presents all of the information about the editor on staff. This method is often used in shorter pieces of writing because with a shorter piece it is possible for the reader to keep the blocks of information in mind.

Looking at the above two paragraphs in outline form will help you see the shape of their development.

Point-by-Point Method

Topic sentence: "Now, of course, I knew that it was going to be as difficult making an income as a freelance editor as it was being an editor on staff at the magazine, if not more so.

First point, first topic: "I would be at home hustling editing contracts via telephone . . . "

First point, second topic: " . . . while everyone else spent their mornings at the office gabbing over endless cups of coffee."

Second point, first topic: "I sometimes resented having to work so hard to earn a living . . . "

Second point, second topic: " . . . while my old colleagues on staff sat in meetings, went to conferences, and attended company luncheons."

Third point, first topic: "But I never envied them on their way to work on cold, dark winter mornings."

Third point, second topic: "And I wondered how many of them would have gladly switched places with me as I worked outside on my patio, while they looked longingly out their office windows."

Block Method

Topic sentence: Now, of course, I knew that it was going to be as difficult making an income as a freelance editor as it was being an editor on staff at the magazine, if not more so.

First topic, points one, two, and three:
"I spent my mornings hustling editing contracts on the telephone and I sometimes resented having to work so hard to earn a living. On the other hand, I didn't envy my old colleagues on their way to work on cold, dark, winter mornings."

Second topic, points one, two, and three:
"On the other hand, I didn't envy my old colleagues on their way to work on cold, dark winter mornings. They could spend as much time as they wanted to gabbing over coffee and going to meetings, conferences, and company luncheons; but I wonder how many of them would have gladly switched places with me as I worked outside on my patio in the summer?"

You will want to choose one of these methods before you write a comparison or contrast assignment. Although the block method is most often used in shorter writing assignments, such as a paragraph, you will have the chance to practise the point-by-point method as well.

E X E R C I S E 1   Working for Coherence: Recognizing the Two Approaches to Ordering Material

Each of the following passages is an example of comparison or contrast. Read each paragraph carefully and decide whether the writer has used the point-by-point method or the block method. Indicate your choice in the spaces provided after each example. Also indicate whether the piece emphasizes similarities or differences.

1. Female infants speak sooner, have larger vocabularies, and rarely demonstrate speech defects. (Stuttering, for instance, occurs almost exclusively among boys.) Girls exceed boys in language abilities, and this early linguistic bias often prevails throughout life. Girls read sooner, learn foreign languages more easily, and, as a result, are more likely to enter occupations involving language mastery. Boys, in contrast, show an early visual superiority. They are also clumsier, performing poorly at something like arranging a row of beads, but excel at other activities calling on total body co-ordination. Their attentional mechanisms are also different. A boy will react to an inanimate object as quickly as he will to a person. A male baby will often ignore the mother and babble to a blinking light, fixate on a geometric figure, and, at a later point, manipulate it and attempt to take it apart.

   _____ Point-by-Point   _____ Block

   _____ Similarities   _____ Differences

2. Canadians have always been great inventors, and while some of their inventions have contributed to civilization, others have faded into obscurity. On one hand, Canadians have invented the chain saw, the paint roller, the power mower, Pablum, the zipper, the snowmobile, the Jolly Jumper, and the pop-up carrying handle for beer cases. On the other hand, Canadians have also come up with such ingenious ideas as the cast-iron airship, the reverse cooking stove, a mechanical skirt lifter (to keep women's dresses clean while crossing muddy streets), and a medical patent designed to cure all common ailments with carrots. Whatever else, Canadians are creative!

   _____ Point-by-point   _____ Block

   _____ Similarities   _____ Differences

EXERCISE 2   Using the Point-by-Point and Block Methods

Choose one of the paragraphs from Exercise 1 and rewrite it using the opposite method for comparison or contrast. For instance, if a paragraph uses the point-by-point method, rewrite it using the block method.

EXERCISE 3   Using the Point-by-Point and Block Methods

Use the lists below to write a comparison or contrast paragraph on life in the city compared with life in the suburbs. Review the lists provided and add to them any of your own ideas. Omit any you do not wish to use. Then, selecting either the block method or the point-by-point method, write a comparison or contrast paragraph.

> ***Topic sentence:*** If I could move back to the city from the suburbs, I know I would be happy.

The following points provide details that relate to living in the city and living in the suburbs:

Topic I	**Topic II**
Advantages of the City	**Disadvantages of the Suburbs**
A short ride on the bus or subway gets you to work.	Commuting to work in the city is often long and exhausting.
Less time spent commuting leaves more time to get involved in the community.	More time commuting means less time to get involved in neighbourhood activities.
Variety is more stimulating.	Sameness of people and streets is monotonous.
Families and single people.	Mostly families.
Local shopping for nearly everything.	Mostly highway shopping.
Mingle with people walking in the neighbourhood daily.	Little walking, use cars to go every-where.

Notice that the maker of these lists focussed only on the disadvantages of the suburbs in contrast to the city. No mention, for instance, has been made of crime. You could also present the contrast from the point of view of someone who prefers the suburbs.

Working for Coherence: Using Transitions

A number of words and phrases are useful to keep in mind when writing the comparison or contrast paragraph. Some of them are used in phrases, some in clauses.

Common Transitions

Transitions for Comparison	**Transitions for Contrast**	
similar to	on the contrary	though
similarly	on the other hand	unlike
like	in contrast with	even though
likewise	in spite of	nevertheless
just like	despite	however
just as	instead of	but
furthermore	different from	otherwise
moreover	whereas	except for
equally	while	and yet
again	although	still
also		
too		
so		

Notice the different uses of *like* and *as*:

 TIP   *Like* **is a preposition and is used in the prepositional phrase "like me."**

My sister is just *like* me.

As is a subordinate conjunction and is used in the clause below with a subject and a verb.

My sister sews every evening, *as* does her oldest daughter.

See the chart on the inside back cover of this book for additional transitions.

E X E R C I S E 1   **Using Transitions in Comparisons and Contrasts**

Each of the following examples is made up of two sentences. Read both sentences and decide whether the idea being expressed is one of comparison or contrast. Next, combine the two sentences by using a transition you have chosen from the chart above. Then write your new sentence. You may find you have to reword your new sentence slightly in order to make it grammatically correct. An example is done for you.

Mr. Johnson is a teacher.
His wife is a teacher.

First you decide that the two sentences show a comparison. Then you combine the two by using an appropriate transition:

Mr. Johnson is a teacher just like his wife.
or
Mr. Johnson is a teacher; so is his wife.

1. Dr. Rappole has a reputation for an excellent bedside manner.

   Dr. Singh is very withdrawn and speaks so softly that it is almost impossible to understand what he says.

   Your combined sentence: _____

   _____

   _____

2. In Canada, interest in soccer has become apparent only in recent years.

   Soccer has always been immensely popular in Brazil.

   Your combined sentence: _____

   _____

   _____

3. Robertson Davies's novel *Fifth Business* is part of the Deptford Trilogy.

   The same writer's novel *The Manticore* is also part of the Deptford Trilogy.

   Your combined sentence: _____

   _____

   _____

4. Celène is carefree and fun-loving, with little interest in school.

   Brigitte, Celène's sister, is so studious and hardworking that she is always on the honour roll.

   Your combined sentence: _____

   _____

   _____

5. The apartment had almost no furniture, was badly in need of painting, and felt chilly even though I was wearing a coat.

   The other apartment was attractively furnished, had been freshly painted, and was so warm I had to take off my coat.

   Your combined sentence: _____

   _____

   _____

E X E R C I S E   2   Using Transitions in Comparison and Contrasts

First, identify each of the following examples as comparison or contrast. Then, combine the two sentences by using a transition from the chart on page 182. Finally, write your new sentence.

1. English-speaking Canadians have numbered about 67 percent of the population over the past 30 years.

   The number of French-speaking Canadians declined from 19 percent of the population in the 1960s to 16 percent in the 1980s.

   Your combined sentence: _____

   _____

   _____

2. Canada has never won an Olympic gold medal in men's springboard diving.

   Sylvie Bernier won Canada's first-ever gold medal in women's springboard diving in the 1984 Olympics.

   Your combined sentence: _____

   _____

   _____

3. The French Revolution was directed by the common people.

   The Russian Revolution was directed by an elite group of thinkers.

   Your combined sentence: _____

   _____

   _____

4. Some scientists believe that dinosaurs became extinct because they ran out of food.

Some scientists think that dinosaurs were victims of radiation from a meteor from outer space.

Your combined sentence: _____

_____

_____

5. The University of Toronto is a large urban university that has the resources of a big city as part of its attraction for faculty and students.

Mount Allison University is a small rural university that overlooks the Tantramar marshes of New Brunswick.

Your combined sentence: _____

_____

_____

Writing the Comparison or Contrast Paragraph Step by Step

To learn a skill with some degree of ease, it is best to follow a step-by-step approach so that various skills can be worked on one at a time. This will ensure that you are not missing a crucial point or misunderstanding a part of the whole. There are other ways to go about writing an effective paragraph, but here is one logical method you can use to achieve results.

Steps for Writing the Comparison or Contrast Paragraph

1. Study the given topic, and then plan your topic sentence, especially the dominant impression.
2. List all your ideas for points that could be compared or contrasted.
3. Choose the three or four most important points from your list, and put them in order.
4. Decide whether you want to use the point-by-point method or the block method of organizing your paragraph.
5. Write at least one complete sentence for each of the points you have chosen from your list.
6. Write a concluding statement that summarizes the main points, makes a judgement, or emphasizes what you believe is the most important point.
7. Finally, copy your sentences into standard paragraph form.

EXERCISE 1   **Writing the Comparison or Contrast Paragraph Step by Step**

The following exercise will guide you through the construction of a comparison or contrast paragraph. Start with the suggested topic. Use the seven steps to help you work through each stage of the writing process.

Topic: Compare or contrast going to work with going to college immediately after high school.

1. Topic sentence: _____

   _____

   _____

2. Make a list of possible comparisons or contrasts.

   a. _____   f. _____

   b. _____   g. _____

   c. _____   h. _____

   d. _____   i. _____

   e. _____   j. _____

3. Circle the three or four comparisons or contrasts that you believe are most important, and put them in order.

4. Choose either the point-by-point method or the block method.

5. Using your final list, write at least one sentence for each comparison or contrast you have chosen.

   a. _____

   _____

   b. _____

   _____

   c. _____

   _____

   d. _____

   _____

   e. _____

   _____

   f. _____

   _____

   g. _____

   _____

6. Write a concluding statement. _____

   _____

   _____

7. Copy your sentences into standard paragraph form.

E X E R C I S E   2   **Writing the Comparison or Contrast Paragraph Step by Step**

The following exercise will guide you through the construction of a comparison or contrast paragraph. Start with the suggested topic. Use the seven steps to help you work through each stage of the writing process.

Topic: Compare or contrast the styles of two television personalities (or two public figures often in the news).

1. Topic sentence: _____

   _____

   _____

2. Make a list of possible comparisons or contrasts.

   a. _____   f. _____

   b. _____   g. _____

   c. _____   h. _____

   d. _____   i. _____

   e. _____   j. _____

3. Circle the three or four comparisons or contrasts that you believe are most important, and put them in order.
4. Choose either the point-by-point method or the block method.
5. Using your final list, write at least one sentence for each comparison or contrast you have chosen.

   a. _____

   _____

   b. _____

   _____

   c. _____

   _____

   d. _____

   _____

   e. _____

   _____

   f. _____

   _____

g. _____

_____

6. Write a concluding statement. _____

_____

_____

7. Copy your sentences into standard paragraph form.

On Your Own: Writing Comparison or Contrast Paragraphs from Model Paragraphs

Comparing or Contrasting Two Places

ASSIGNMENT 1: Write a paragraph in which you compare or contrast two places you know, either from personal experience or from your reading. The following paragraph contrasts the East Coast and a major urban centre as they appear to a person who has been to both places.

Model Paragraph

Since I travel East so often, I am usually asked to compare the lifestyles of the East Coast with those of the big city where I live. That's easy. Both places leave a distinct impression, and readers will have to decide for themselves which lifestyle is more desirable. When I was riding a bus between Louisbourg and Sydney, Nova Scotia, an old man waved the bus down, boarded, and handed the driver a large fish to pay for his fare. In the city, exact change is the rule on the bus, and that only in coin of the realm. In St. John's, Newfoundland, I found that some nightclubs and bars remained open until the last customer had left, and that the best time was had when patrons brought their own musical instruments and set up some Down East foot-stompin' music. Back home, you sit, behave yourself, and drink your beer, or out you go. Incidentally, the best pizza I ever had was from a small shop on the St. John's waterfront, with a Volcano pizza from Windsor, Ontario, a close second. The cardboard pizzas from the fast-food joints in Toronto and Montreal don't even rate. On the other hand, my favourite hamburger came from Montreal, and nothing can beat Prince Edward Island for seafood. Do I sound biased toward the East? If you're not from the East, take your next vacation there. You'll see what I mean.

SUGGESTED TOPICS

Compare or contrast two places you have lived in, visited, or read about:

1. Two neighbourhoods
2. Two towns or cities

3. Two vacation spots
4. Two provinces
5. Two countries
6. Two streets
7. Two schools

Comparing or Contrasting Two Cultures

ASSIGNMENT 2: Write a paragraph in which you compare or contrast two cultures, or an aspect of culture that may be observed in two societies. The following paragraph compares grandparents, the father's parents and the mother's parents, and their competition to win the affections of "the little people."

Model Paragraph

I became a grandfather for the first time recently. My daughter had twin girls, and my wife and I were thrilled. Of course, my son-in-law also has parents, and they were just as thrilled, or so they said, even though we felt that *we* were just a little bit more thrilled than they were. We bought baby gifts; they bought baby gifts; however, I think that *we* bought a few more baby gifts than they did. *We* bought a crib for the babies when they came to visit at our house, and they bought a crib for the same reason, although our crib was a teeny bit better than their crib. One of the babies takes after my son-in-law, while the other looks like my daughter, and I think that the one that looks like my daughter is just a bit cuter than the one that looks like my son-in-law. Whatever the case, when the girls grow up, they're going to know that they have grandparents who might fight for their affections, but whom the girls know as grandparents who love them dearly — both sets of grandparents.

SUGGESTED TOPICS

Compare or contrast:

1. Marriage customs in Africa and in Canada
2. Attitudes toward women's roles in Saudi Arabia and in Canada
3. Raising children in Asia with raising them in Canada
4. Urban people with small-town people
5. The reputation of a place with the reality of the place as you found it
6. The culture you live in now with the culture in which your parents were raised
7. Medical care in our society with the medical care of any other society

Comparing or Contrasting a Place Then and Now

ASSIGNMENT 3: Write a paragraph in which you compare or contrast the appearance of a place you knew when you were growing up with the appearance of that same place now. The following paragraph compares a small city as it was some years ago with how it appeared to the writer on a recent visit.

Model Paragraph

As I drove up Swede Hill, I realized that the picture I had had in my mind all these years was largely a romantic one. It was here that my father had boarded, as a young man of eighteen, with a widow who rented rooms in her house. Now the large old wooden frame houses were mostly two-family homes; no single family could afford to heat them in the winter. The porches that had once been beautiful and where people had passed their summer evenings had peeling paint and were in poor condition. No one now stopped to talk; the only sounds to be heard were those of cars whizzing past. The immigrants who had come to this country, worked hard, and put their children through school were now elderly and mostly alone, since their educated children could find no jobs in the small upstate city. From the top of the hill I looked down fondly upon the town built on the hills and noticed that a new and wider highway now went through the town. My father would have liked that; he would not have had to complain about Sunday drivers on Foote Avenue. In the distance I could see the large shopping mall that now had most of the business in the surrounding area and that had forced several local businesses to close. Now the centre of town no longer hummed with activity, as it once had. My town was not the same place I had known, and I could see that changes were taking place that would eventually transform the entire area.

SUGGESTED TOPICS

Compare or contrast a place as it appears now with how it appeared some years ago:

1. A barbershop or beauty salon
2. A friend's home
3. Your elementary school
4. A local bank
5. A downtown shopping area
6. A restaurant or diner
7. An undeveloped place such as an open field or a wooded area

Working Together

1. On the facing page is a typical advertisement from a 1933 *Good Housekeeping* magazine. Read it carefully and then discuss it with your classmates. How many aspects of this advertisement seem out of date by modern standards? In how many ways would a contemporary advertisement for a similar product be different?
2. The 1933 advertisement is followed by a contemporary advertisement for skin products. Write a paragraph in which you contrast the two advertisements. Before you begin to write, be sure to list all the differences you can observe.

As Madonna more stirringly Beautiful than _nine years ago_ .. Lady Diana Manners says

"_I depend entirely on the creams I chose then_"

In 1924

Lady Diana Manners, when she first appeared in "The Miracle"—the most beautiful woman of English aristocracy—said: "Every woman can accomplish loveliness by using Pond's Creams."

Today

Loving audiences are again spellbound by the still beauty, more enchanting than ever, of Lady Diana Manners, now Lady Diana Duff-Cooper, as she plays Madonna in the recent London revival of "The Miracle."

"CONTRARY to common belief, women on the stage seek the simplest methods to care for the skin." Lady Diana Duff-Cooper speaks with disarming British candor.

"After all," she declares, "good care of your skin consists only in cleansing it thoroughly with a pure cream, and _always_ protecting it."

That surprises you. As you look at the exquisite loveliness of Lady Diana's complexion, you imagine that she uses many secret and expensive formulas for beauty.

Uses Just Two Creams

"It was in America, when I first opened in 'The Miracle,' that I discovered Pond's Two Creams. From that time on I have been positively devoted to them.

"I use Pond's Cold Cream _constantly_ (day and night and after exposure) to cleanse my skin thoroughly—and it removes make-up perfectly! Also when one's face feels tired a generous patting of Pond's Cold Cream revives and stimulates it.

"And the Vanishing Cream is a hope fulfilled. It is a glorious foundation for cosmetics. And I never expose my skin in any climate without first smoothing it on. I am always preaching its efficacy."

Lady Diana Manners adds: "Pond's new Face Powder is so exquisite a powder at so moderate a price!"

Lady Diana Manners uses Pond's Cold Cream —"To cleanse the skin thoroughly of all foreign particles after every exposure.

Pond's Famous Creams and New Face Powder

"To remove all traces of cosmetics."

She uses Pond's Vanishing Cream: "Always as a foundation for make-up. It holds powder like nothing else.

"Before every sport and every exposure.

"To smooth chapped and roughened skin.

"Almost every day to keep my hands and arms soft and white."

Titled Englishwomen who use Pond's Creams:
The Marchioness of Carisbrooke
The Lady Louis Mountbatten
The Countess Howe   The Lady Violet Astor
Lady Georgiana Curzon

Send 10¢ (to cover cost of postage and packing) for choice of free samples

POND'S EXTRACT COMPANY, Dept. D

109 Hudson Street . . . . New York City
Please send me (check* choice): _Pond's New Face Powder_ in attractive jar. Light Cream ☐; Rose Cream ☐; Brunette ☐; Naturelle ☐.
OR _Pond's Two Creams, Tissues and Freshener_ ☐.

_Name_____

_Address_____

Copyright, 1933, Pond's Extract Company

Tune in on Pond's Fridays, 9:30 P. M., E. S. T. . . . Leo Reisman and his Orchestra . . . WEAF and NBC Network

Chapter 16
Developing Paragraphs: Definition and Classification

What Is Definition?

You define a term in order to explain its meaning or significance. The starting point for a good definition is to group the word into a larger **category**.

For example, the trout is a kind of fish; a doll is a kind of toy; a shirt is an article of clothing. Here is a dictionary for the word *family*.

> **family** (fam′e -le, fam′le) *n., pl.* **-lies.** *Abbr.* **fam.** 1. The most instinctive, fundamental social or mating group in man and animal, especially the union of man and woman through marriage and their offspring; parents and their children. 2. One's spouse and children. 3. Persons related by blood or marriage; relatives; kinfolk. 4. Lineage; especially, upper-class lineage. 5. All the members of a household; those who share one's domestic home.

To what larger category does the word *family* belong? The family, according to this entry, is a kind of *social group*.

Once the word has been put into a larger class, the reader is ready to understand the **identifying characteristics** that make it different from other members in the class.

What makes a *trout* different from a *bass*, a *doll* different from a *puppet*, a *shirt* different from a *sweater*? Here a definition can give examples. The first dictionary definition of *family* identifies the family as a married man and woman and their children. Four additional meanings provide a suggestion of some variations.

When you write a paragraph or an essay that uses definition, the dictionary entry is only the beginning. In order for your reader to understand a difficult term or idea, you will need to expand this definition into what is called **extended definition**. It is not the function of a dictionary to go into great depth. It can provide only the basic meanings and synonyms.

Extended definition, however, seeks to analyze a concept so that the reader will have a more complete understanding.

For instance, you might include a historical perspective. When or how did the concept begin? How did the term change or evolve over the years, or how do different cultures understand the term? You will become involved in the word's connotations. Extended definition, or **analysis** as it is sometimes called, uses more than one method to arrive at an understanding of a term.

The following paragraph, taken from *Sociology: An Introduction* by John E. Conklin, is the beginning of a chapter on the family. The author's starting point is very similar to the dictionary entry.

> In every society, social norms define a variety of relationships among people, and some of these relationships are socially recognized as family or kinship ties. A *family* is a socially defined set of relationships between at least two people who are related by birth, marriage, or adoption. We can think of a family as including several possible relationships, the most common being between husband and wife, between parents and children, and between people who are related to each other by birth (siblings, for example) or by marriage (a woman and her mother-in-law, perhaps). Family relationships are often defined by custom, such as the relationship between an infant and godparents, or by law, such as the adoption of a child.

The author began this definition by putting the term into a larger **class**. *Family* is one type of social relationship among people. The writer then identifies the people who are members of this group. Family relationships can be formed by marriage, birth, adoption, or custom, as with godparents. The author does not stop here. The extended definition explores the functions of the family, conflicts in the family, the structure of the family, and the special characteristics of the family.

The writer could also have defined *family* by **negation**. That is, he could have described what a family is *not*:

A family is not a corporation.
A family is not a formal school.
A family is not a church.

When a writer defines a concept using negation, the definition should be completed by stating what the subject *is*:

A family is not a corporation, but it is an economic unit of production and consumption.
A family is not a formal school, but it is a major centre for learning.
A family is not a church, but it is where children learn their moral values.

E X E R C I S E   1   Working with Definition: Class

Define each of the following terms by placing it in a larger class. Keep in mind that when you define something by class, you are placing it in a larger category so that the reader can see where it belongs. Use the dictionary if you need help. The first example has been done for you.

Chemistry is *one of the branches of science* that deals with a close study of the natural world.

1. A *tricycle* is _____

2. *Cabbage* is _____

3. *Democracy* is _____

4. *Asbestos* is _____

5. A *piccolo* is _____

6. *Poetry* is _____

7. A *university* is _____

E X E R C I S E   2   Working with Definition: Distinguishing Characteristics

Using the same terms as in Exercise 1, give one or two identifying characteristics that differentiate your term from other terms in the same class. An example is done for you.

Chemistry studies the structure, properties, and reactions of matter.

1. A *tricycle* _____

_____

_____

2. *Cabbage* _____

_____

_____

3. *Democracy* _____

_____

_____

4. *Asbestos* _____

_____

_____

5. A *piccolo* _____

_____

_____

6. *Poetry* _____

_____

_____

7. A *university* _____

_____

_____

_____

E X E R C I S E   3   Working with Definition: Example

Help define each of the following terms by providing one example. Examples always make writing more alive. An example has been done for you.

> ***Term:*** Chemistry
>
> ***Example:*** Chemistry studies an element like hydrogen. This element is the simplest in structure of all the elements, with only one electron and proton; it is colourless, highly flammable, the lightest of all gases, and the most abundant element in the universe.

1. *Patriotism*

_____

_____

_____

2. *Friendship*

_____

_____

_____

3. *Terrorism*

_____

_____

_____

4. A *planet*

_____

_____

_____

5. *Equality*

_____

_____

_____

6. *Greed*

_____

_____

_____

7. A *volcano*

_____

_____

_____

E X E R C I S E 4   Working with Definition: Negation

Define each of the following terms by using negation to construct your definition. Keep in mind that such a definition is not complete until you have also included what the topic is that you are defining.

1. A *disability* is not _____,

   but it is _____.

2. The *perfect car* is not _____,

   but it is _____.

3. *Drugs* are not _____,

   but they are _____.

4. *Freedom* is not _____,

   but it is _____.

5. A *good job* is not _____,

   but it is _____.

6. *Exercise* is not _____ ,

   but it is _____ .

7. A *university* is not _____ ,

   but it is _____ .

Writing a Paragraph Using Definition

Here is a list of topics for possible paragraph assignments. For each topic that you choose to write about, develop a complete paragraph of definition by using one or more of the techniques you have studied — *class, identifying characteristics, example,* and *negation* — as well as any further analysis, historical or cultural, that will help the reader.

TOPICS

1. Photosynthesis
2. Ecology
3. Coma
4. Football
5. Paranoia
6. Courage
7. Algebra

What Is Classification?

Classification is the placing of items into separate categories for the purpose of helping us to think about these items more clearly. This can be extremely useful and even necessary when large numbers of items are being considered.

In order to classify things properly, you must always take the items you are working with and put them into **distinct categories**, making sure that each item belongs in only one category. For example, if you were to classify computers into imported computers, Canadian-made computers, and used computers, this would not be an effective use of classification because an imported computer or a Canadian-made computer could also be a used computer. When you classify, you want each item to belong in only one category.

A classification should also be **complete**. For example, if you were to classify computers into the two categories of new and used, your classification would be complete because any item can be only new or used.

In the following paragraph, the writer classifies different kinds of neighbours:

To me, there are only two kinds of neighbours: those with cats and those without cats. I refuse to get along with cat owners, regardless of how pleasant either the cats or their owners happen to be. I take great exception to having cats on my property, fighting with each other in the middle of the night, dirtying my flower beds, and chasing the birds that come to my feeder. I don't have a great deal to say to neighbours who let their cats out at night to get into my garbage, and when I point out the mess that these cats leave, I'm told, "There's no law against it." As far as those neighbours who don't have cats are concerned — they can borrow my lawn mower any time.

In this paragraph, the writer presents two distinct types of neighbours — cat owners and those who don't own cats. These are the only types that have any significance for the writer. The writer's classification is complete because it covers the entire range of neighbours — there are, in the writer's opinion, no other types of neighbours. This is a useful classification, because many of us have neighbours with cats; perhaps you are that neighbour.

E X E R C I S E   1   **Working with Classification: Finding the Basis for a Classification**

For each of the following topics, pick three different ways that topic could be classified. You may find the following example helpful.

> ***Topic:*** Ways to choose a vacation spot.
> ***Basis for classification:*** By price (first class, medium price, economy), by its special attraction (the beach, the mountains, the desert, etc.), by the accommodations (hotel, motel, cabin, trailer)

1. **Topic:** Cars
   Ways to divide the topic: _____

   _____

2. **Topic:** Houses
   Ways to divide the topic: _____

   _____

3. **Topic:** Neighbourhoods
   Ways to divide the topic: _____

   _____

4. **Topic:** Soft drinks
   Ways to divide the topic: _____

   _____

5. **Topic:** Medicines
   Ways to divide the topic: _____

   _____

6. **Topic:** Snack foods
   Ways to divide the topic: _____

   _____

7. **Topic:** Relatives
   Ways to divide the topic: _____

   _____

E X E R C I S E   2   Working with Classification: Making Distinct Categories

First pick a basis for classifying each of the following topics. Then break it down into distinct categories. Divide the topic into as many distinct categories as you think the classification requires.

Keep in mind that when you divide your topic, each part of your classification must belong to only one category. For example, if you were to classify cars, you would not want to make *sports cars* and *international cars* two of your categories because several kinds of sports cars are also international cars.

1. Clothing stores
   Distinct categories:

   _____

   _____

2. Television commercials
   Distinct categories:

   _____

   _____

3. College sports
   Distinct categories:

   _____

   _____

4. Doctors
   Distinct categories:

   _____

   _____

5. Dances
   Distinct categories:

   _____

   _____

6. Mail
   Distinct categories:

   _____

   _____

7. Music
   Distinct categories:

   _____

   _____

Writing a Paragraph Using Classification

Here is a list of topics for possible paragraph assignments using classification. As you plan your paragraph, keep in mind the following points. Does the classification help to organize the material? Are you sure the classification is complete and that no item could belong to more than one category? Is there some purpose for your classifying the items as you did? (For example, will it help someone make a decision or understand a concept?)

TOPICS

1. Parents
2. Dogs
3. Careers
4. Parties
5. Summer jobs
6. Movies
7. Restaurants

Working Together

Brainstorming can be wonderfully helpful when several people put their heads together! Divide into groups and brainstorm on one of the topics given below. After the members of each group have thought of everything they can, come together as a class and put your classifications on the board. Compare and contrast them. What makes one more successful than another? Can you use each other's material?

Suggested Topics for Brainstorming:

1. Fads
   What is a "fad"? Classify as many different types of fads as you can.

or

2. Friendship
   What is "friendship"? Classify as many different types of friendships as you can.

Your instructor may now ask each student to write his or her own essay using this material.

Chapter 17
Developing Paragraphs: Cause and Effect

What Is Cause and Effect?

People have always looked at the world and asked the questions, "Why did this happen?" or "What are the results of that event?" Ancient societies created beautiful myths and legends to explain the origin of the universe and our place in it, while modern civilization has emphasized scientific methods of observation to find the cause of a disease or to determine why the planet Mars appears to be covered by canals. When we examine the spiritual or physical mysteries of our world, we are trying to discover the connections or links between events. In this chapter, we will refer to connections between events as **causal relationships**.

Causal relationships are part of our daily lives and provide a way of understanding the cause, result, or consequence of a particular event. The search for cause or effect is a bit like detective work. Probing an event is a way of searching for clues to discover what caused an event or what result it will have in the future.

For example, we might ask the question, "Why did the car break down just after it came back from the garage?" as a way of searching for the cause of the car's new problem. Or we might ask, "What will be the side effects of a certain medicine?" in order to determine what effect a particular medicine will have on the body. This search for connections can be complex. Often the logical analysis of a problem reveals more than one possible explanation. Sometimes the best one can do is find possible causes or probable effects. In the exercises that follow, you will be asked to search for causes, effects, and connections that are causal relationships.

PRACTICE Become familiar with the causal relationship by thinking through a few typical situations signalled by the following expressions:

If .... then

1. **If** you _____ , **then** you will

_____ .

The cause, reason .... **the result, consequence, effect**

2. Because I _____ , the result was

that I _____ .

The problem .... **the solution**

3. _____ could be solved

by _____ .

EXERCISE 1 **Finding Causes and Effects in Paragraphs**

Below are two paragraphs about the same topic: headaches. One paragraph considers causes, and the other looks at some of the effects recurring headaches have on people's lives. In each case, list the causal relationships suggested in the paragraph.

1. Cause: Explaining WHY

   Headaches can have several causes. Many people think that the major cause of headache is nervous tension, but there is strong evidence that suggests diet and environment as possible factors. Some people get headaches because they are dependent on caffeine. Other people may be allergic to salt, or they may have low blood sugar. Still other people are allergic to household chemicals including polishes, waxes, bug killers, and paint. If they can manage to avoid these substances, their headaches tend to go away. When a person has recurring headaches, it is worthwhile to look for the underlying cause, especially if the result of that search is freedom from pain.

What causes a headache?

1. _____
2. _____
   a. _____
   b. _____
   c. _____
3. _____
   a. _____
   b. _____
   c. _____
   d. _____

2. Effect: Understanding or predicting RESULTS, CONSEQUENCES, EFFECTS, SOLUTIONS

> Recurring headaches can have several disruptive effects on a person's life. Severe headaches are more than temporary inconveniences. In many cases, these headaches make a person nauseous to the point that he or she must go to bed. Sleep is often interrupted because of the pain. This worsens the physical and emotional state of the sufferer. For those who try to maintain a normal lifestyle, drugs are often relied on to get through the day. Such drugs, of course, can have other negative side effects. Productivity on a job can certainly be reduced, even to the point of regular absences. Finally, perhaps the most distressing aspect of all this is the seemingly unpredictable occurrence of these headaches. The interruption to a person's family life is enormous: cancelling plans at the last minute and straining relationships with friends and family. It is no wonder that many of these people feel discouraged and even depressed.

What are some of the effects of headaches?

1. _____

2. _____

3. _____

4. _____

5. _____

6. _____

7. _____

E X E R C I S E   2   **Separating the Cause from the Effect**

In each sentence, separate the cause, problem, or reason from the effect, solution, or result. Remember, the cause is not necessarily given first.

1. More than half of the mothers with children under one year of age work outside the home, which has resulted in the unprecedented need for day care in this country.

   Cause: _____

   _____

   Effect: _____

2. By 1995, two-thirds of all preschool children will have mothers who work, and four out of five school-age children will have working mothers, facts that will lead to increased strain on our present system of day care.

Cause: _____

_____

Effect: _____

3. In one national survey, over half the working mothers reported that they had either changed jobs or cut back on their hours in order to be more available to their children.

Problem: _____

Solution: _____

4. Many mothers who work do so only when their children are in school, while other mothers work only occasionally during the school year because they feel their children need the supervision of a parent.

Cause: _____

Effect: _____

_____

5. Many mothers experience deep emotional crises as a result of their struggle to meet both the financial obligations of their home and their own emotional needs as parents.

Problem: _____

Result: _____

Working with Cause and Effect: Recognizing Relationships and Connections between Events

> ### Avoid These Common Errors in Logic
>
> 1. Do not confuse coincidence or chronological sequence with evidence.
> 2. Look for underlying causes beneath the obvious ones and for far-reaching effects beyond the ones that first come to mind. Often what appears to be a single cause or a single effect is a much more complex problem.

Here is an example of a possible error in logic:

> Every time I try to write an essay in the evening, I have trouble getting to sleep. Therefore, writing must prevent me from sleeping.

In this case, writing may indeed be a stimulant that prevents the person from sleeping. However, if the person is serious about finding the cause of insomnia, he or she must observe whether any other **factors** may be to blame. For instance, if the person is drinking several cups of coffee while writing each evening, this could be a more likely cause of the person's wakefulness.

E X E R C I S E 1 **Looking for the Causal Relationship**

Study each of the following situations. In each case, if the sequence of events is merely coincidental or chronological, put a *T* for *time* in the space provided. If the relationship is most likely *causal*, put a *C*. Be prepared to explain your answers in class.

_____ 1. Every time I carry my umbrella, it doesn't rain. I am carrying my umbrella today; therefore, it won't rain.

_____ 2. We put the fertilizer on the grass. A week later the grass grew two inches and turned a deeper green.

_____ 3. On Tuesday morning, I walked under a ladder. On Wednesday morning, I walked into my office and was told I had lost my job.

_____ 4. The child was born with a serious kidney condition. Seven days later, the child died.

_____ 5. Tar and nicotine from cigarettes damage the lungs. People who smoke cigarettes increase their chances of dying from lung cancer.

_____ 6. A political scandal was exposed in the city on Friday. On Saturday night, only twenty-four hours later, a power blackout occurred in the city.

_____ 7. Very few tourists came to the island last year. The economy of the island declined last year.

E X E R C I S E 2 **Underlying Causes**

Below are five topics. For each topic, give a possible immediate or direct cause and then give a possible underlying cause. Discuss your answers in class. An example has been done for you.

Causes for a Disease

Immediate or direct cause: contact with a carrier of the disease
Underlying cause: weakened immune system due to poor nutrition

1. Causes for being selected out of several candidates for a position

   Immediate cause: _____

   Underlying cause: _____

2. Causes for immigrants to come to Canada

   Immediate cause: _____

   Underlying cause: _____

3. Causes for an increase in used car sales

Immediate cause: _____

Underlying cause: _____

4. Causes for an unreasonable fear you have

Immediate cause: _____

Underlying cause: _____

5. Causes for a bad habit you have

Immediate cause: _____

Underlying cause: _____

E X E R C I S E   3   **Immediate or Long-Term Effects**

Below are five topics. For each topic give an immediate effect and then give a possible long-term effect. Discuss your answers in class. An example has been done for you.

Possible Effects of Using Credit Cards

Immediate effect: money available on the spot for purchases
Long-term effect: greater cost due to interest payments

1. Effects of horror movies on young children

Immediate effect: _____

Long-term effect: _____

2. Effects of tuition increases in universities

Immediate effect: _____

Long-term effect: _____

3. Effects of increased number of accidents on people's driving habits

Immediate effect: _____

Long-term effect: _____

4. Effects of a microwave oven on how a family lives

Immediate effect: _____

Long-term effect: _____

5. Effects of having a family member with special needs

Immediate effect: _____

Long-term effect: _____

Working for Coherence: Using Transitions

Several transitions and expressions are particularly useful when writing about causes or effects. You will need to feel comfortable using these words and expressions, and you will need to know what punctuation is required.

Common Transitions

Common Transitions for *Cause*:
because
caused by
results from
the reason is that . . . + a complete sentence
since

Common Transitions for *Effect*:
accordingly
as a result, resulted in
consequently
for this reason
so, so that
then, therefore, thus

E X E R C I S E 1 **Using Transitional Words and Expressions of Cause**

Use each of the following words or phrases in a sentence that demonstrates your understanding of its use for expressing *cause* relationships.

1. to be caused by _____

   _____

2. because (of) _____

   _____

3. resulted from _____

   _____

4. the reason is that + complete sentence _____

   _____

5. since _____

   _____

E X E R C I S E 2 **Using Transitional Words and Expressions for Effect**

Use each of the following words or phrases in a complete sentence to demonstrate your understanding of how the word or phrase is used to point to an *effect*.

1. accordingly _____

_____

2. as a result _____

_____

3. results in _____

_____

4. consequently _____

_____

5. for this reason _____

_____

6. so _____

_____

7. therefore _____

_____

Writing the Cause or Effect Paragraph Step by Step

To learn a skill that has so many different aspects, it is best to follow a step-by-step approach, so that one aspect can be worked on at a time. This will ensure that you are not missing a crucial point or misunderstanding a part of the whole. There are other ways to go about writing an effective paragraph, but here is one logical method you can use to achieve results.

Steps for Writing the Cause or Effect Paragraph

1. After you have chosen your topic, plan your topic sentence.
2. Brainstorm by jotting down all possible causes or effects. Ask others for their thoughts. Research if necessary. Consider long-range effects or underlying causes.
3. Choose the three or four best points from your list.
4. Decide on the best order for these points. (From least important to most important is one way to organize them.)
5. Write at least one complete sentence for each of the causes or effects you have chosen from your list.
6. Write a concluding statement.
7. Finally, copy your sentences into standard paragraph form.

E X E R C I S E   1   **Writing the Cause Paragraph Step by Step**

This exercise will guide you through the cause paragraph. Start with the suggested topic. Use the seven steps to help you work through each stage of the writing process.

Topic: Why do many Canadians want to learn to speak French?

1. Topic sentence: _____

_____

2. Make a list of possible causes. (Consider underlying causes.)

   a. _____

   b. _____

   c. _____

   d. _____

   e. _____

3. Cross out any points that may be illogical or merely coincidental.
4. Put your list in order.
5. Using your final list, write at least one sentence for each of the causes you have found.

   a. _____

   _____

   b. _____

   _____

   c. _____

   _____

   d. _____

   _____

6. Write a concluding statement. _____

_____

_____

_____

7. Copy your sentences into standard paragraph form.

EXERCISE 2 **Writing the Effect Paragraph Step by Step**

This exercise will guide you through the effect paragraph. Start with the suggested topic. Use the seven steps to help you work through each stage of the writing process.

Topic: What are the effects of teenagers having part-time jobs after school?

1. Topic sentence: _____

_____

2. Make a list of possible effects. (Consider long-range effects.)

   a. _____

   b. _____

   c. _____

   d. _____

   e. _____

3. Cross out any points that may be illogical, merely coincidental, or the result of only time sequence.
4. Put your list in order.
5. Using your final list, write at least one sentence for each of the effects you have found.

   a. _____

   _____

   b. _____

   _____

   c. _____

   _____

   d. _____

   _____

6. Write a concluding statement. _____

   _____

   _____

   _____

7. Copy your sentences into standard paragraph form.

On Your Own: Writing Cause and Effect Paragraphs from Model Paragraphs

The Causes of a Social Problem

ASSIGNMENT 1 Write a paragraph about the causes of a social problem that is of concern to you. The following paragraph looks at possible reasons for placing an elderly relative in a nursing home.

Model Paragraph

Industrialized societies have developed homes for the elderly who are unable to care for themselves. In spite of much criticism, these homes have a growing percentage of our nation's elderly. Why do some people feel forced into placing parents into a nursing home? The most immediate cause is that following some serious illness, there is often no place for the elderly person to go where he or she can be cared for. In the family of today, it is often the case that both partners work outside the home so no one is home during the day to care for the person. Hiring a nurse to be in the home every day is beyond the budget of nearly every family. Even when a family member can be home to care for the elderly person, the problems can be overwhelming. The older person can be too heavy for one or even two to manage. Bathing, particularly, can be dangerous in these circumstances. In addition, many elderly people have to be watched very carefully because of their medical condition. Many families do not have the proper training to meet these needs. Finally, elderly people who may be senile and difficult can often intrude on a family's life to the point that a caregiver may never be able to leave the house or get a proper night's rest. Perhaps a better system of visiting nursing care could help some families keep their loved ones in their homes longer.

SUGGESTED TOPICS

1. The causes of homelessness
2. The causes of prostitution
3. The causes of teenage runaways
4. The causes of high school drop-outs
5. The causes of divorce
6. The causes of tax cheating
7. The causes of high stress among college students

The Effects of a Substance or Activity on the Human Body

ASSIGNMENT 2 Write a paragraph about what happens to the human body when it uses a substance or engages in some activity. The following model paragraph is from Norman Taylor's *Plant Drugs That Changed the World*.

Model Paragraph

The ordinary cup of coffee, of the usual breakfast strength, contains about one and a half grains of caffeine (100 mg.). That "second cup of coffee" hence means just about three grains of caffeine at one sitting. Its effects upon the nervous system, the increased capacity for thinking, its stimulating effects on circulation and muscular activity, not to speak of its sparking greater fluency — these are attributes of the beverage that few will give up. If it has any dangers, most of us, in ordinary doses, are inclined to ignore them. But there is no doubt that excessive intake of caffeine at one time, say up to seven or eight grains (*i.e.*, 5 or 6 cups), has harmful effects such as restlessness, nervous irritability, insomnia, and muscular tremor. The lethal dose in man is unknown, for there are no records of it. Experimental animals die in convulsions after overdoses and from such studies it is assumed that a fatal dose of caffeine in man may be about 150 grains (*i.e.*, one-half ounce). That would mean about one hundred cups of coffee!

SUGGESTED TOPICS

1. The effects of alcohol on the body
2. The effects of regular exercise
3. The effects of overeating
4. The effects of a strict diet
5. The effects of fasting
6. The effects of drug abuse
7. The effects of sunburn

The Effects of a Community Disaster

ASSIGNMENT 4 Select a community or area disaster that you have personally experienced or heard about. This could include a severe climatic condition or a man-made disaster. Describe the effects it had on you or the people involved. The following model paragraph looks at the causes for the loss of life in the sinking of a supposedly unsinkable ship on its maiden voyage over 80 years ago.

Model Paragraph

One of the most tragic events of the twentieth century was the sinking of the British ship *Titanic* in the Atlantic Ocean on April 15, 1912, with the loss of over 1500 lives. The immediate cause of this terrible loss of life was a large iceberg that tore a three-hundred-foot gash in the side of the ship, flooding five of its watertight compartments. Some believe that the tragedy took place because the crew members did not see the iceberg in time, but others see a chain of different events that contributed to the tragedy. First was the fact that the ship was not carrying enough lifeboats for all of its passengers: it had enough boats for only about half of the people on board. Furthermore, the ship's crew showed a clear lack of caring about the third class or "steerage" passengers, who were left in their cramped quarters below decks with little or no help as the ship went down. It has often been said that this social attitude of helping the wealthy and neglecting the poor was one of the real causes of the loss of life that night. Indeed, some of the lifeboats that were used were not filled to capacity when the rescue ships eventually found them. Finally, the tragedy of the *Titanic* was magnified by the fact that some ships nearby did not have a radio crew on duty and therefore missed the distress signals sent by the *Titanic*. Out of all this, the need to reform safety regulations on passenger ships became obvious.

SUGGESTED TOPICS

1. The effects of a hurricane
2. The effects of a power blackout on a town

3. The effects of a flood or other extensive water damage on a home or community
4. The effects of a long, dark winter or other lengthy bad weather
5. The effects of a bus, train, or taxi strike on a community
6. The effects of a major fire on a downtown block
7. The effects of the loss of small businesses in a community

Working Together

Listen while the following analysis of the causes for the decline of Central America's Mayan culture is read aloud to the class. The class should then divide into groups. Work with your group to list the immediate and the underlying causes for the decline of Mayan civilization. One person from each group will then read the group's complete list of immediate and underlying causes to the class. After a complete listing is agreed upon, make a judgement as to how positive scientists are about the underlying causes of this historical phenomenon.

In the last few years scholars have made great strides in translating the Mayas' previously indecipherable writing system. From the emerging texts and from recent excavations has emerged a new, at times bewildering, picture of the Maya civilization at its peak, from A.D. 250 to 900. Great as their cultural and economic achievements manifestly were, they had anything but a peaceful society.

Indeed, the latest feeling among scholars is that the increasing militarism of Maya society may have undermined the ecological underpinnings of the economy. Some of them speculate that siege warfare concentrated population in urban centres, caused desperate farmers to abandon previously successful practices of diversified agriculture, and led to overexploitation of the forest.

Dr. Arthur A. Demarest, an archaeologist who directs an ambitious Maya dig in Guatemala, has said that the evidence from stone art and texts points to the surprising conclusion that "the Maya were one of the most violent state-level societies in the New World, especially after A.D. 600."

Various writings and artifacts, Dr. Demarest says, indicate continual raiding and warfare between the elites of adjacent city-states and also the practice of ritual bloodletting and human sacrifice. The prestige of ruling dynasties, and hence their power, seemed to depend on their success in battle and the sacrifice of prisoners of war.

Dr. Linda Schele, a Maya scholar, writes in this month's issue of *Natural History* magazine, "We don't know if the early Maya went to war mainly to acquire territory, take booty, control conquered groups for labour, take captives for sacrifice in sanctification rituals, or a combination of these."

Whatever the specific goal, archaeologists think that for centuries the wars were limited to ritualized conflicts between the elite troops of two rulers. The losing ruler was sometimes decapitated with great ceremony, as depicted in Maya art.

PART III

Structuring the College Essay

Chapter 18
Moving from the Paragraph to the Essay

When you learned to write a well-developed paragraph in Part II, you were creating the basic support paragraph for the college essay. An essay is a longer piece of writing, usually five or more paragraphs, in which you can develop a topic in much more depth than you could in a single paragraph. In college, this longer piece of writing is usually called the college essay, although you may also hear it called a composition, theme, or paper. In most schools, such writing is an important part of almost every course, not only the English composition class.

You learned in Part II that the paragraph with its topic sentence and supporting details must have an organization that is both unified and coherent. The college essay must also have these characteristics. Furthermore, since the essay develops a topic at greater length or depth, making all the parts work together becomes an added challenge.

What Kinds of Paragraphs Are in an Essay?

In addition to the support paragraphs that you studied in Part II, the essay has two new kinds of paragraphs.

1. The **introductory paragraph** is the first paragraph of the essay. Its purpose is to be so inviting that the reader will not want to stop reading. In most essays, and in all college essays, this introduction contains a **thesis statement**.
2. **Support paragraphs** (sometimes called body paragraphs) provide the evidence that shows your thesis is valid. A college essay must have at least three well-developed support paragraphs. (You have studied these kinds of paragraphs in Part II.) One paragraph must flow logically into the next. This is accomplished by the careful use of **transitional devices**.
3. The **concluding paragraph** is the last paragraph of the essay. Its purpose is to give the reader a sense of coming to a satisfying ending, a sense that everything has been said that needed to be said.

Before you begin the process of writing your own college essays, this chapter will prepare you to understand and work with these special essay features:

Thesis statement
Introductory paragraph
Transitions between body paragraphs
Concluding paragraph

What Is a Thesis?

 The **thesis** of an essay is a statement of the main idea of that essay.

It states what you are going to explain, defend, or prove about your topic. It is usually placed at the end of the introductory paragraph.

How to Recognize the Thesis Statement

1. The thesis statement is a complete sentence. Students sometimes confuse a title with a thesis. Remember that titles are usually phrases rather than complete sentences.

> *Title:* The Advantages of All-Day Kindergarten
> *Thesis:* Schools should offer parents the option of an all-day kindergarten program for their children, not only for the benefit of the mother who works outside the home but also because of the advantages for the children.

2. The thesis statement presents a viewpoint about the topic that can be defended or shown in your essay.

> *Fact:* Nearly all kindergartens in Canada offer a half day of instruction.
> *Thesis:* Parents know there is more than one reason why most children at five years of age should be in school for only half a day.

P R A C T I C E Read each of the following statements. If you think the statement is a fact, mark it with an *F*. If you think the statement is a thesis, mark it with a *T*.

_____ 1. In Canada, kindergarten is not compulsory.

_____ 2. Children should begin learning to read in kindergarten.

_____ 3. Putting a child into kindergarten before he or she is physically or emotionally ready can have several unfortunate effects on a child.

_____ 4. In some European countries, children do not begin formal schooling until age seven or eight.

E X E R C I S E 1   **Recognizing the Thesis Statement**

In the space provided, identify each of the following as (1) a *title*, (2) a *thesis*, or (3) a *fact* that could be used to support a thesis.

_____ 1. The personal interview is the most important step in the employment process.

_____ 2. Looking for a job

_____ 3. Sixty percent of all jobs are obtained through newspaper advertisements.

_____ 4. The best time to begin a foreign language is in grade school.

_____ 5. The importance of learning a foreign language

_____ 6. In the 1970s, the number of students studying foreign languages declined dramatically.

_____ 7. Most Canadians doing business with Japan do not know a word of Japanese.

E X E R C I S E 2   **Recognizing the Thesis Statement**

In the space provided, identify each of the following as (1) a *title*, (2) a *thesis*, or (3) a *fact* that could be used to support a thesis.

_____ 1. It is estimated that between 5000 and 9000 grizzly bears live in the Yukon.

_____ 2. The survival of grizzly bears in our country should be a top priority.

_____ 3. When bears are young cubs, there are twice as many males as females.

_____ 4. Only about 60 percent of bear cubs survive the first few years of life.

_____ 5. Bears: a precious natural resource

_____ 6. The average life span of a bear today is only five or six years.

_____ 7. The sad plight of the grizzly bear

Writing an Effective Thesis Statement

An effective thesis statement has the following parts:

1. **A topic that is not too broad:** Broad topics must be narrowed down in scope. You can do this by *limiting the topic* (changing the term to cover a smaller

part of the topic) or *qualifying the topic* (adding phrases or words to the general term that will narrow down the topic).

> *Broad topic:* Swimming
> *Limited topic:* Learning to float (Floating is a kind of swimming, more specialized than the term *swimming*.)
> *Qualified topic:* Swimming for health two hours a week (The use of the phrase *for health two hours a week* narrows the topic down considerably. Now the topic concentrates on the fact that the *time* spent swimming and the *reason* for swimming are important parts of the topic.)

There are a number of ways to narrow a topic in order to make it fit into a proper essay length, as well as make it fit your experience and knowledge.

2. **A controlling idea that you can defend:** The controlling idea is what you want to show or prove about your topic; it is your attitude about that topic. Often the word is an adjective such as *beneficial, difficult*, or *maddening*.

> Learning to float at the age of twenty was a *terrifying* experience.

> Swimming two hours a week brought about a *dramatic* change in my health.

3. **An indication of what strategy for development is to be used:** Often you can use words such as the following: *description, steps, stages, comparison, contrast, causes, effects, reasons, advantages, disadvantages, definition, analysis, persuasion.*

Although not all writers include the strategy in the thesis statement, they must always have in mind what major strategy they plan to use to prove their thesis. Professional writers often use more than one strategy to prove the thesis. However, in this book, you are asked to develop your essays by using one major strategy at a time. By working in this way, you can concentrate on understanding and developing the skills needed for each specific strategy.

Study the following thesis statement:

Although a date with the right person is marvellous, going out with a group can have many advantages.

Now look back and check the parts of this thesis statement.

> *General topic:* Going out
> *Qualified topic:* Going out in a group (as opposed to a single date)
> *Controlling idea:* To give the advantages
> *Strategy for development:* Contrast between the single date and the group date

E X E R C I S E   1   Writing the Thesis Statement

Below are three topics. For each one, develop a thesis statement by (1) limiting or qualifying the general topic, (2) choosing a controlling idea (what you want to explain or prove about the topic), and (3) selecting a strategy that you could use to develop that topic. An example is done for you.

General topic: Senior citizens

    a. **Limited or qualified topic:**

    Community services available to the senior citizens in my town

    b. **Controlling idea:**

    To show the great variety of programs

    c. **Strategy for development** (narration, description, process, comparison or contrast, definition, classification, cause and effect):

    Classify the services into major groups.

Thesis statement: The senior citizens of New Glasgow, Nova Scotia, are fortunate to have programs available to help them deal with health, housing, and leisure time.

1. Saskatoon (or another city with which you are familiar)
   a. Limited or qualified topic:

   _____

   b. Controlling idea:

   _____

   c. Strategy for development (narration, description, process, comparison or contrast, definition, classification, cause and effect):

   _____

   Thesis statement:

   _____

   _____

2. Shopping
   a. Limited or qualified topic:

   _____

   b. Controlling idea:

   _____

   c. Strategy for development (narration, description, process, comparison or contrast, definition, classification, cause and effect):

   _____

Thesis statement:

_____

_____

3. The library
   a. Limited or qualified topic:

   _____

   b. Controlling idea:

   _____

   c. Strategy for development (narration, description, process, comparison or con-trast, definition, classification, cause and effect):

   _____

   Thesis statement:

   _____

   _____

EXERCISE 2   Writing the Thesis Statement

Below are three topics. For each one, develop a thesis statement by (1) limiting or qualifying the general topic, (2) choosing a controlling idea (what you want to explain or prove about the topic), and (3) selecting a strategy that you could use to develop that topic. Review the example in Exercise 1.

1. Television
   a. Limited or qualified topic:

   _____

   b. Controlling idea:

   _____

   c. Strategy for development (narration, description, process, comparison or con-trast, definition, classification, cause and effect):

   _____

   Thesis statement:

   _____

   _____

2. Hockey (or another sport)
   a. Limited or qualified topic:

   _____

b. Controlling idea:

_____

c. Strategy for development (narration, description, process, comparison or contrast, definition, classification, cause and effect):

_____

Thesis statement:

_____

_____

3. Math (or another field of study)
   a. Limited or qualified topic:

   _____

   b. Controlling idea:

   _____

   c. Strategy for development (narration, description, process, comparison or contrast, definition, classification, cause and effect):

   _____

Thesis statement:

_____

_____

Ways to Write an Effective Introductory Paragraph

 An **introduction** has one main purpose: to "grab" your readers' interest so that they will keep reading.

There is no one way to write an introduction. However, since many good introductions follow the same common patterns, you will find it helpful to look at a few examples of the more typical patterns to help you write your own introductions.

1. **Begin with a general subject that can be narrowed down to the specific topic of your essay.** Here is an introductory paragraph on astronomy, from *Universe* by W.J. Kaufmann:

   > Speculation about the nature of the universe is one of the most characteristic human endeavours. The study of the stars transcends all boundaries of culture, geography, and politics. The modern science of

astronomy carries an ancient tradition of observation and speculation, using the newest tools of technology and mathematics.

Then comes the specific topic of this paragraph:

In the most literal sense, astronomy is a universal subject — its subject is indeed the universe.

2. **Begin with specifics (a brief anecdote, a specific example or fact) that will broaden into the more general topic of your essay.** Here is the introduction to Miriam Waddington's "The Hallowe'en Party," an essay about a family of Russian Jews settling on a prairie farm just outside of Winnipeg:

The year that I was twelve my father came home one day and announced that he had bought a farm. My sister Helen and I could hardly wait to see the farm which, according to my father, consisted of twenty-six acres in St. Vital, just beyond the outskirts of Winnipeg. There were twenty acres of bush with buildings, and six acres of meadow beside the river. My father had dreamed of such a farm all the years he was shut up in the dark greasy machine shop where he earned his living.

What follows is the topic of the story, a topic that is larger than the idea of merely buying a farm:

Now as I look back, I can understand my father's deep hunger for land.

3. **Give a definition of the concept that will be discussed.** Here is the introduction to "Man, Woman and Child," by Lydia Bailey, an essay about the rising trend toward single motherhood:

They are a new breed of mother — single, self-sufficient, and in their thirties. They have opted for motherhood without marriage. Some call it a return to tribal times when women raised children on their own with the help of other women. Others see it as a dangerous trend, labelling them as "the most narcissistic group of people you will ever see." Regardless of how it's perceived, statistics show that in the past few years the number of single mothers in their thirties has increased dramatically.

4. **Make a startling statement.** Here is an example from Arthur C. Clarke's "We'll Never Conquer Space":

Man will never conquer space. Such a statement may sound ludicrous, now that our rockets are already 100 million miles beyond the moon and the first human travelers are preparing to leave the atmosphere. Yet it expresses a truth which our forefathers knew, one we have forgotten — and our descendants must learn again, in heartbreak and loneliness.

5. **Start with an idea or statement that is a widely held point of view. Then surprise the reader by stating that this idea is false or that you hold a different**

point of view. Here is an example from "A Planet for the Taking," by David Suzuki:

> Canadians live under the remarkable illusion that we are a technologically advanced people. Everything around us denies that assumption. We are, in many ways, a Third World country, selling our natural resources in exchange for the high technology of the industrialized world. Try going through your home and looking at the country of origin of your clothes, electrical appliances, books, car. The rare technological product that does have Canada stamped on it is usually from a branch plant of a multinational company centred in another country.

6. **Start with a familiar quotation or a quotation by a famous person,** as Frank Trippett does in this example from "Getting Dizzy by the Numbers":

> "The very hairs of your head," says Matthew 10:30, "are all numbered." There is little reason to doubt it. Increasingly, everything tends to get numbered one way or another, everything that can be counted, measured, averaged, estimated or quantified. Intelligence is gauged by a quotient, the humidity by a ratio, pollen by its count, and the trends of birth, death, marriage and divorce by rates. In this epoch of runaway demographics, society is as often described and analyzed with statistics as with words. Politics seems more and more a game played with percentages turned up by pollsters, and economics a learned babble of ciphers and indexes that few people can translate and apparently nobody can control. Modern civilization, in sum, has begun to resemble an interminable arithmetic class in which, as Carl Sandburg put it, "numbers fly like pigeons in and out of your head."

7. **Give a number of descriptive images that will lead to the thesis of your essay:**

> The nuclear family is breaking up. Both parents are working and children are left on their own for long periods of time, or are sent to day care centres. Youngsters are learning about life from television and from movies, although the life that they learn about is often far removed from the truth. The incidence of crime is increasing among children because they receive little guidance and even less teaching on the difference between right and wrong. Social, moral, and religious values are declining.

Then comes the thesis of the paragraph:

> These are among the reasons why the fabric of society is decaying.

8. **Ask a question that you intend to answer.** Many essays you read in magazines and newspapers use a question in the introductory paragraph to make the reader curious about the author's viewpoint. Some writing instructors prefer that students do not use this method. Check with your instructor before using this method. Here is an example of such an introduction, from "The Fatal Question," by Vivian Rakoff:

Human beings sustained in a state of technical "life" through complex machinery present to society and medicine a terribly and increasingly familiar dilemma. All the meaning and pleasure of ordinary life are absent and there's no hope of return to a dignified existence. Who has the authority to decide that the time has come to stop the machines?

9. **Use classification to indicate how your topic fits into the larger class to which it belongs, or how your topic can be divided into categories that you are going to discuss.** Here is how Robert Fulford began "How the West Was Lost," an essay on the destruction of Métis and Native societies in the West:

> They may never have seen each other's faces, but the two most famous non-whites in late nineteenth-century Canada — Louis Riel and Big Bear — were linked by history and by the events of the crisis year 1885. They were dissimilar in many ways — Riel a Montreal-educated Métis who travelled widely and was three times elected to the Canadian parliament, Big Bear a Plains Cree, who knew no world beyond the Prairies. But they were also alike: both were mystics and prophets and both were charismatic leaders of peoples doomed by the westward thrust of the Canadian empire.

What *Not* to Say in Your Introduction

1. Avoid telling your reader that you are beginning your essay:

   In this essay I will discuss . . .
   I will talk about . . .
   I am going to prove . . .

2. Don't apologize:

   Although I am not an expert . . .
   In my humble opinion . . .

3. Do not refer to later parts of your essay:

   By the end of this essay, you will agree . . .
   In the next paragraph, you will see . . .

4. Don't use trite expressions. Since they have been so overused, they will lack interest. Using such expressions shows that you have not taken the time to use your own words to express your ideas. Some examples of trite expressions are

   busy as a bee
   you can't tell a book by its cover
   haste makes waste

Using Transitions to Move the Reader from One Idea to the Next

Successful essays help the reader understand the logic of the writer's thinking by using transitional expressions when needed. Usually this occurs when the writer is moving from one point to the next. It can also occur whenever the idea is complicated. The writer may need to summarize the points covered thus far; the writer may need to emphasize a point already made; or the writer may want to repeat an important point. The transition may be a word, a phrase, a sentence, or even a paragraph.

Here are some of the transitional expressions you might use to help the reader make the right connections. Also refer to the chart on the inside back cover of this book and notice what other transitions could be used in the categories indicated below.

1. **To make your points stand out clearly:**

the first reason	second, secondly	finally
first of all	another example	most important
in the first place	even more important	all in all
	also, next	in conclusion
	then	to summarize

2. **To present an example of what has just been said:**

   for example
   for instance

3. **To present the consequence of what has just been said:**

   therefore
   as a result
   then

4. **To make a contrasting point clear:**

   on the other hand
   but
   contrary to current thinking
   however

5. **To admit a point:**

   of course
   granted

6. **To resume your argument after admitting a point:**

   nevertheless
   even so
   nonetheless
   still

7. **To call the reader's attention to your organization:**

Before attempting to answer these questions, let me . . .
In our discussion so far, we have seen that . . .
At this point, it is necessary to . . .
It is beyond the scope of this paper to . . .

A more subtle way to link one idea to another in an essay is to repeat a word or phrase from the preceding sentence.

I have many memories of my childhood in Cuba. These *memories* include the aunts, uncles, grandparents, and friends I had to leave behind.

Sometimes instead of the actual word, a pronoun will take the place of the word.

Like all immigrants, my family and I have had to build a new life from almost nothing. *It* was often difficult, but I believe the struggle made us strong.

E X E R C I S E   1   Finding Transitional Devices

Below are the first three paragraphs of an essay on African art. Circle all the transitional devices or the repeating words that are used to link one sentence to another or one idea to the next. The first paragraph is done for you.

Like language and social organization, art is essential to human life. As embellishment and as creation of objects beyond the requirements of the most basic needs of living, (art) has accompanied man since prehistoric times. Because of its almost unfailing consistency as an element of many societies, (art) may be the response to some biological or psychological need. (Indeed,) it is one of the most constant forms of human behaviour.

However, use of the word *art* is not relevant when we describe African "art" because it is really a European term that at first grew out of Greek philosophy and was later reinforced by European culture. The use of other terms, such as *exotic art, primitive art, art sauvage,* and so on, to delineate differences is just as misleading. Most such terms are pejorative — implying that African art is on a lower cultural level. Levels of culture are irrelevant here, since African and European attitudes toward the creative act are so different. Since there is no term in our language to distinguish between the essential differences in thinking, it is best then to describe standards of African art.

African art attracts because of its powerful emotional content and its beautiful abstract form. Abstract treatment of form describes most often — with bare essentials of line, shape, texture, and pattern — intense energy and sublime spirituality. Hundreds of distinct cultures and languages and many types of people have created over 1000 different styles that defy classification. Each art and craft form has its own history and its own aesthetic content. But there are some common denominators (always with exceptions).

Ways to Write an Effective Concluding Paragraph

A concluding paragraph has one main purpose: to give the reader the sense of reaching a satisfying ending to the topic discussed. Students often feel they have nothing to say at the end. A look at how professional writers frequently end their essays can ease your anxiety about writing an effective conclusion. You have more than one possibility; here are some of the most frequently used patterns for ending an essay.

1. **Come full circle; that is, return to the material in your introduction.** Finish what you started there. Remind the reader of the thesis. Be sure to restate the main idea using different wording. Here is an example from the essay by Vivian Rakoff (pages 227–28).

   > We are involved in an unending process of questioning and adaptation — an adaptation that, with luck, will not fall into a simple-minded rejection of the machine as the work of the devil. It is at least equally valid to see the manufacture of machines and goods as the continuous unfolding of human endowment in a cumulative history. Man the toolmaker is man expressing an ancient and important component of his true nature.

2. **Summarize by repeating the main points.** This example is from the preceding essay on African art.

   > In summary, African art explains the past, describes values and a way of life, helps man relate to supernatural forces, mediates his social relations, expresses emotions, and enhances man's present life as an embellishment denoting pride or status as well as providing entertainment such as with dance and music.

3. **Show the significance of your thesis by making predictions, giving a warning, giving advice, offering a solution, suggesting an alternative, or telling the results.** This example is from the essay by David Suzuki (page 227).

   > But Canadians do value the spiritual importance of nature and want to see it survive for future generations. We also believe in the power of science to sustain a high quality of life. And while the current understanding of science's power is, I believe, misplaced, in fact the leading edges of physics and ecology may provide the insights that can get us off the current track. We need a very profound perceptual shift and soon.

4. **End with an anecdote that illustrates your thesis.** This example is from Robert Fulford's essay on the Métis and Native people (page 228).

   > The criminal trials of the Indians and the Métis in the autumn of 1885 seem, in retrospect, outrageously illogical — the rebels were convicted of treason against an empire that had conscripted them as citizens without consulting them. But the North-West Rebellion also produced a

trial that was merely bizarre. Shortly after the rebellion ended, an article in the Toronto *News* said that Montreal's Sixty-fifth Battalion had conducted itself during the hostilities in a way that was mutinous, reckless, disorderly, and drunken. Officers of the battalion sued, and eventually the editor of the *News* — a notorious enemy of French Canadians and the French language — was summoned to Montreal to stand trial for criminal libel. Convicted and fined $200, he emerged from the courtroom, barely escaped with his life from a howling mob of outraged Montrealers, and went home to be treated to a torchlight parade of 4000 cheering supporters in Toronto. Two years later, fed up with the stresses of daily newspaper work, the editor, Edmund E. Sheppard, founded a new periodical, *Saturday Night*.

What *Not* to Say in Your Conclusion

1. Do not introduce a new point.

   > I will tell you something else . . .
   > Additional information has come to light . . .
   > Let me leave you with a new idea . . .

2. Do not apologize.

   > I'm sorry that I can't end on a more positive note . . .
   > If I had more space . . .
   > I can't be sure of every point . . .

3. Do not end up in the air, leaving the reader feeling unsatisfied. This sometimes happens when the very last sentence is not strong enough.

   > Maybe the problem will never be solved . . .
   > There is no obvious solution . . .
   > We can only hope things will get better . . .

A Note about Titles

Be sure to follow the standard procedure for writing your title.

1. Capitalize all words except articles (*the, a, an*) and prepositions.
2. Do not underline the title or put quotation marks around it.
3. Try to think of a short and catchy phrase (three to six words). Often writers wait until they have written a draft before working on a title. There may be a phrase from the essay that will be perfect. If you still cannot think of a clever title after you have written a draft, choose some key words from your thesis statement.
4. Centre the title at the top of the page, and remember to leave about three centimetres of space between the title and the beginning of the first paragraph.

Working Together

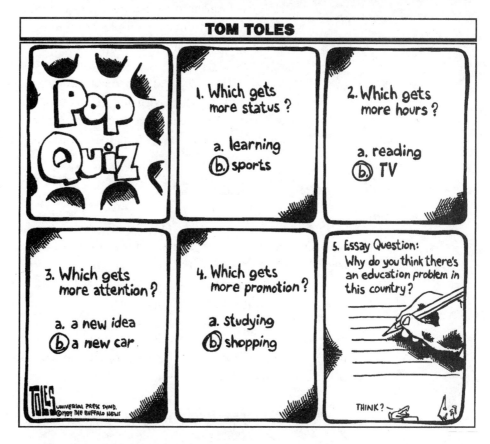

1. The above cartoon uses the technique of a multiple-choice quiz to suggest some of the possible reasons why education in North America is in trouble. As a class or in groups, discuss each of the four areas of concern raised by the cartoonist. Then write a five-paragraph essay (an introductory paragraph, three support paragraphs, and a paragraph of conclusion). Use the information you have learned in this chapter to write a good introduction and conclusion. For your supporting paragraphs, choose three of the four areas of concern shown in the cartoon and make each one the main idea for one of the support paragraphs. Be sure to make use of the ideas generated during the class discussion. Don't be afraid to use the ideas you've heard in the general discussion.

2. Divide into three groups. Each group will study the introductory and concluding paragraphs for each of the following essays:

   "Ancestors — The Genetic Source" (page 309)
   "You're Thinking of Getting a *What*?" (page 312)
   "Electronic Confidants" (page 319)

   Analyze each introduction and conclusion to decide if the author has chosen one of the patterns suggested in this chapter. Can you point to one sentence as the author's thesis statement?

Chapter 19
The Writing Process

What Is the Process for Writing a College Essay?

Writing is a craft. This means that a writer, no matter how experienced or inexperienced, needs to follow a certain process in order to arrive at a successful finished product. Very few writers can "dash off" a masterpiece. We sometimes think that a person is "a born dancer" or "a born writer," but the reality is that the person has worked long hours for many years to achieve his or her level of skill.

Just as no two chefs or carpenters or painters approach their work in the same way, no two writers work in exactly the same way. In spite of this individuality, each writer goes through a surprisingly similar series of steps to reach the finished product.

Steps in the Writing Process

1. Getting the idea for developing a topic.
2. Gathering information (brainstorming, taking notes).
3. Selecting and organizing details.
4. Writing the rough draft.
5. Revising the rough draft (some writers revise their work through many, many drafts before they are satisfied).
6. Writing the second draft.
7. Proofreading.
8. Typing or word processing the final copy.
9. Checking for errors.

Following this process will help you produce your best writing. You will feel more in control, since you will be working on one step at a time and not trying to do everything all at once. Careful preparation before writing and careful revisions after writing always pay off. You will see your initial idea change and develop into something much more detailed and organized than your first thoughts on the topic. Remember that writing, just like the other skills you develop in life, improves when you follow the same process used by those who have already been successful. If you take the time to practise using this process regularly, your writing will improve.

Many students believe that a writer somehow has a magical inspiration that allows him or her to sit down and produce the piece immediately. Although this very seldom happens, you may be lucky enough on occasion to have the exciting experience of being "turned on" to your topic, an experience in which the words flow easily from your pen. At such a time, you will feel how satisfying writing can be, for writing is a route to self-discovery. It is a method of finding within yourself the wealth of untapped ideas and thoughts that are waiting for expression.

Understanding the Writing Process

Choosing the Topic and the Controlling Idea

Usually a writer sits down to write knowing the general topic he or she wants to write about. You might have to write an essay on the political system in Canada for a history class. You might have to write a paper for psychology class on coping with stress. Maybe you are angry about a toxic waste site near your home, and you decide to write a letter to the local newspaper. Perhaps your employer asks you to write a report to describe the ways in which productivity could be increased in your department. In all these cases, the topic is set before you. You do not have to say to yourself, "Now what in the world shall I write about?" Most students prefer to be given a specific topic rather than have no direction at all. Furthermore, if the topic is of interest to you, your writing is much more likely to be interesting to your readers. When you enjoy your work, you will spend more time on it and use more of your inner resources.

Even though you will usually be assigned a particular topic or given a group of topics from which to choose, you will need to spend some time thinking of a possible approach that can make use of your experience or knowledge. In writing, this approach is called the "controlling idea." One of our students, for example, loved to play chess. He admitted to us in his senior year of college that he had tried to use his interest in and knowledge of this hobby to help him complete several of his college assignments. For an assignment in his psychology class, when the teacher asked for a paper titled "Stereotypes — Are They True?" he wrote about the characteristics of people who play chess. For a political science class, this same student discussed the importance of international games, including chess, of course. For a paper in his literature course, he wrote about four writers who used games in their writing to symbolize a struggle for power between two characters. You can see from these examples that this student was able to use his own special interest and knowledge to make his writing interesting for himself and undoubtedly interesting to the teachers who read his papers. Don't ever think that you have nothing to write about!

You should always keep in mind that your goal is to find an angle that will interest whoever is going to read your work. All writers write best about topics that are related to their own experience and knowledge. You cannot hope to interest the reader if the material does not first interest you! This section of the book will guide you in this important step of searching for the approach or controlling idea that will work for you.

A Student Essay in Progress: Getting the Idea for an Essay

A student is asked to write a personal-experience essay about fear or anxiety. She begins by making a list of the possibilities:

Taking tests
Speaking in front of a large group
Going on a date with someone for the first time
Performing on the piano
Walking alone at night
Having an argument with one's parents

Which one should she choose? She goes over the possibilities and discovers that when she comes to the one about the piano, she feels a tightness in her chest. Here is an experience in her life that makes her nervous just to think about it! Furthermore, she has had several experiences performing on the piano that she thinks could make an interesting piece of writing. She feels excited because she realizes that she does indeed have many thoughts and feelings about this traumatic experience in her life.

Gathering Information

Once you have decided on a topic, you still have many choices to make. What will be your main point about the topic? What angle or strategy will you use? You might choose to tell a story, give several examples or anecdotes to prove your point, define and analyze, or compare or contrast. In other words, you can choose from these different strategies the one that best suits your knowledge or experience.

To make these choices, writers usually need to gather some information to find out what they have to work with. If the assignment calls for your own experience, you will not need to conduct outside research — in the library or in interviews, for instance — to get information. In such a case, you can begin with the technique known as **brainstorming**. Writers use brainstorming to discover what they already know and feel about a given topic.

When you brainstorm, you allow your mind to roam freely around the topic, letting one idea lead to another, even if the ideas seem unrelated or irrelevant. You jot down every word and phrase that pops into your mind when you think about your topic.

Sometimes it helps to brainstorm with another person or a group of people. Since this list will be for your own use only, you can jot down single words, phrases, or entire sentences. Your thoughts will be listed in the order in which you originally think of them. The important point about brainstorming is that it helps to stimulate your thinking on the topic, as well as giving you the opportunity to write down your first thoughts on the topic. Once you have some ideas jotted down on paper, you will begin to feel less anxious and perhaps even pleasantly surprised that you have discovered so many possibilities for your essay.

A Student Essay in Progress: Brainstorming the Topic

Topic: Performing on the piano
Approach (or controlling idea): Makes me frightened, anxious, nervous

stage fright	my teacher
strange pianos	lack of self-confidence
parents in the audience	dread of recitals
embarrassed if I make a mistake	being the oldest in the group but not
my shyness	the best
memorizing music	Mrs. Stuart's performance classes
forgetting a chord in the left hand	the performance class last year
hands and legs shaking	playing the sonata
wanting to please my teacher	Leonard's playing
fingers get sweaty	jealous
Leonard always plays better than the	computer programming
rest of us	always late
contest in June,	feel stupid
trills in my piece	Michelle's poor playing
finding time to practise in the spring	some people don't appreciate
	classical music

Selecting and Organizing Details

When you brainstorm, ideas come from your mind in no particular order, and you jot them down as they come. Your next step in the writing process is to give a sense of organization to these ideas. You do this when you place the results of your brainstorming in an order that helps you see a sequence of events, or logical order, for the ideas. This need not be the final order, but it will help you plan an order for your first draft.

As you select and organize the details on your list, do not hesitate to cross out items you know you cannot use. This is an important part of the writing process at this stage. If you are careful in your choice of items, your essay will eventually have more, not less, to offer your reader.

A Student Essay in Progress: Organizing the Material

The student writer strikes out the ideas that do not seem useful and then begins to group the other ideas that she can use. As she works with the words and phrases, she is considering what she should do with all this material. What she realizes is that she could write the essay in many ways: analyze her fears, give several examples of performances and describe her fears, or tell one special story that would reveal how she feels. She chooses the last possibility because she thinks an actual incident will be the most interesting. Furthermore, if she does this, she will have a chance to use many specific details.

She begins to work out an order. Some teachers ask students to make this order into an informal outline. Here is how this student grouped her material:

Introduction
My problems
  shyness
  lacking self-confidence
  older than the others
  not enough time to practise such long pieces
  wanting to do well
  difficulty memorizing
  stage fright
  shaky hands and legs
  cold fingers

Supporting Details
Coming to Mrs. Stuart's performance class
  her personality
  her house
  the other students
My performance
  the difficulty of the sonata trills
  runs shaky, better than I thought
  wanting to please my teacher
Leonard's performance
  his appearance
  his talent

Conclusion
My reaction
  feel stupid
  disappointed
  jealous
  still determined

Notice how some of the ideas on the brainstorming list have been omitted or have changed slightly. Since this essay will primarily use narration, ordering is not as difficult as in some other writing. The student will start by telling her problem, then give the story of one particular performance, and conclude with her reactions to the experience.

Writing the Rough Draft

After you have gone through the brainstorming process and you have organized the material into some kind of order, the time has come to write a rough draft.

A rough draft is just what its name implies: your first attempt to write your essay. The first attempt is "rough" because it will undoubtedly undergo many changes before it is finished: parts may be missing; some paragraphs will probably lack sufficient detail; and some parts may be repetitious or inappropriate. Some sentences are likely to sound awkward and will need to be rewritten later. The experienced writer expects all this and does not worry. All that you should try to accomplish in the rough draft is to let your mind relax and to get down on paper all of your initial ideas. These first ideas will provide the seeds that can be better developed later on.

Armed with a first draft, you will now have something with which to work. No longer is there a blank paper staring you in the face. This accomplishment is a great relief to most writers, but remember, you are not yet finished.

A Student Essay in Progress: The Rough Draft

Performing on the Piano

Sometimes I wonder why I play the piano. It makes me so nervous when I have to play in front of people. I want to do well. But I can never play my best when I'm so nervous. I'm going to tell you about a typical performance I gave last February. On a Saturday afternoon I walked up the long driveway to my piano teachers house. My hands were already shaking and my stomach felt upset. I was not looking forward to this at all. In fact, I had been dreading this moment for over a month. This day would not be the end of my terror. In the Spring I would be playing in a special contest where I would be judged and given a score.

Today, as usual, I felt my piece was not securely memorized. I never had enough time to practise. Although I wanted to please my teacher. I felt funny being nearly the oldest student in her class. I should be the best, I thought.

Now I hoped I wouldn't make a fool of myself in front of the younger kids in my teacher's class, especially that little wizard, Leonard.

He was skinny with big glasses. When he looked at you it seemed to be with a laugh. He was as great at the violin, the computer, and everything else as he was at the piano. At least I could always count on Michelle to mess up her piece. She never practised but it didn't seem to bother her. She always acted as if she was pleased with herself. At least I knew I sounded better than she did.

I was late as usual the class had begun. Mrs. Stuart was pleased to see me and she motioned to me to take a chair near the piano. The house was so nice. Filled with beautiful furniture and things on the shelves and tables.

Mrs. Stuart was kind to everyone, always trying to make us feel like "somebody." There was something about her looks and personality that made everybody who knew her like her. She had dark eyes and brown hair, was not too tall, and never seemed to wear makeup.

Before I knew it, it was my turn. Everyone was watching me.

I said what piece I was going to play and sat down. Starting was always the worst. This piece had hard trills and runs and I was really scared. I counted to ten, took a deep breath, and began.

It went better than I thought. The trills weren't so great, my runs were shaky, but at least I got through it without forgetting any part. What a relief when it was over.

My teacher seemed pleased. She says a few nice words and then moves on to the next student. People were beginning to get tired of sitting. One little girl yawned. Then it was Leonard's turn. He got up and announced that he was going to play the same piece as me. My heart started to beat faster. I was really upset. This little kid was going to play my piece.

You can guess what happened. He played better than me. The teacher praised him to the sky and I ended up feeling like a jerk. Why should I even bother to play piano when there are kids like Leonard?

Revising the Rough Draft

If you have time, put aside your rough draft for a day or two. Then, when you reread it, you will look at it with a fresh mind. In this important revision stage, you should be concerned with how you have organized your ideas into paragraphs. At this point, do not worry about grammar, spelling, and punctuation.

Begin this important revision stage by asking these major questions:

a. Is the essay unified? Do you stick to the topic you have announced? Go through the essay and take out irrelevant material.

b. Do you repeat yourself? Look back over your essay to determine whether or not you have given the same information more than once. Even if you find you have used some different words, you should delete the repetitious material.

c. Does the essay make sense? Can a reader follow your logic or train of thought? (Giving the rough draft to someone else to read will often answer this question for you.) If the essay is confusing to the reader, you must find out where it goes wrong and why. Sometimes when you read your writing out loud, you will hear a strange sentence or feel that one paragraph has leaped to some point that doesn't follow from the sentence before.

d. Are the paragraphs roughly the same length? If you see one sentence presented as a paragraph, you know something is wrong. Usually each paragraph should develop its point by the use of at least five sentences. Check through your essay. Do you need to change the paragraphing? You may need to develop one paragraph more fully, or a one-sentence paragraph may really belong with the paragraph that comes before or with the paragraph that follows.

e. Do you have all the types of paragraphs essential to an essay: the introduction with its thesis, at least three well-developed body paragraphs with transitional devices used to connect ideas, and a concluding paragraph?

f. Can you add more specific details? Most writing teachers agree that nearly every paper they read could be improved by adding more details, more descriptive verbs, and more sensory images to make the writing come alive.

g. Can you add dialogue or a quotation from someone?

h. Could you make the introduction, conclusion, or title more creative?

Here is the same essay. This time marginal comments have been added by the student's writing instructor to aid in revision. No corrections of punctuation, spelling, or grammar have been made yet. At this stage, the student should focus on the organization and content. As the student works with the text, she may correct some of the grammar errors when she rewrites, deletes, or adds material.

A Student Essay in Progress: Revising the Rough Draft

Performing on the Piano

A more creative title?

Student has another idea for an introduction.

Sometimes I wonder why I play the piano. It makes me so nervous when I have to play in front of people. I want to do well. But I can never play my best when I'm so nervous. I'm going to tell you about a typical performance I gave last February. ¶On a Saturday afternoon I walked up the long driveway to my piano teachers house. My hands were already shaking and my stomach felt upset. I was not looking forward to this at all. In fact, I had been dreading this moment for over a month. This day would not be the end of my terror. In the Spring I would be playing in a special contest where I would be judged and given a score.

This is the end of the introduction. Should begin new paragraph.

Paragraph 2 is too short.

Today, as usual, I felt my piece was not securely memorized. I never had enough time to practise. Although I wanted to please my teacher. I felt funny being nearly the oldest student in her class. I should be the best, I thought.

Paragraph 3 is too short. Belongs to paragraph 2.

Now I hoped I wouldn't make a fool of myself in front of the younger kids in my teacher's class, especially that little wizard, Leonard.

Needs to be a new paragraph.

He was skinny with big glasses. When he looked at you it seemed to be with a laugh. He was as great at the violin, the computer, and everything else as he was at the piano. ¶At least I could always count on Michelle to mess up her piece. She never practised but it didn't seem to bother her. She always acted as if she was pleased with herself. At least I knew I sounded better than she did.

Be more specific.

I was late as usual the class had begun. Mrs. Stuart was pleased to see me and she motioned to me to take a chair near the piano. The (house was so nice.) Filled with beautiful furniture and things on the shelves and tables.

Be more specific.

Mrs. Stuart was kind to everyone, always trying to make us feel like "somebody." There was (something) about her looks and personality that made everybody who knew her like her. She had dark eyes and brown hair, was not too tall, and never seemed to wear makeup.

Use a quote here.

Before I knew it, it was my turn. Everyone was watching me. I said what piece I was going to play and sat down. Starting was always the worst. This piece had hard trills and runs and I was really scared. I counted to ten, took a deep breath, and began.

Paragraph too short.
Give more detail.

It went better than I thought. The trills weren't so great, my runs were shaky, but at least I got through it without forgetting any part. What a relief when it was over.

My teacher seemed pleased. She says a few nice words and then moves on to the next student. People were beginning to get tired of sitting. One little girl yawned. Then it was Leonard's turn. He got up and announced that he was going to play the same piece as me. My heart started to beat faster. I was really upset. This little kid was going to play my piece.

Use a quote here.

Slang — not appropriate.
Give more thought to
your reactions.

You can guess what happened. He played better than me. The teacher praised him to the sky and I ended up feeling like a (jerk.) Why should I even bother to play piano when there are kids like Leonard?

Preparing the Final Copy

If you have worked hard in revising the rough draft, you will be delighted with the improvements as you write the final copy.

Feedback is an important aid in each of the final stages of writing an essay. A good way to help yourself see your own work better is to put the writing aside for a few days, if you can. Then read what you have written aloud to someone else, or to yourself if no one is available. You will be very surprised at the number of places in your writing where you will hear a mistake and make a change even as you read.

Checklist for the Final Copy

Use 21.5 cm by 28 cm paper.
Type on one side of the paper only.
Double-space.
Leave approximately 3.5 cm margins on each side of the paper.
Do not hyphenate words at ends of lines unless you consult a dictionary to check how to divide
    the word correctly into syllables.
Centre the title at the top of the first page.
Put your name, the date, and the title of your paper on a separate title page.
If you have more than one page, staple or clip them together so they will not be lost.

A Student Essay in Progress: The Final Copy

Sonata in C Major, Opus 35

Have you ever been to a children's piano recital? The little seven-year-olds walk eagerly up to the piano, play their 30-second piece that is sixteen bars long, feel very pleased with themselves, and walk back to their seats to wait for everyone else to finish. All they are thinking about is the cookies and punch. I, on the other hand, sit pale and still, twisting my hands, dreading the moment when I must take my place at the piano. I must play well. What if I don't play well? What if I make a mess? The thought of forgetting the piece or stumbling through a difficult passage in front of an audience would be so embarrassing. My experience last month at a class recital still makes me shudder.

It was a bleak Saturday afternoon in February. I trudged up the long driveway to my piano teacher's house. My hands were already shaking and my stomach felt upset. I had been dreading this moment all week. I had to perform my contest piece in front of my teacher and fifteen other talented students. Later in the spring I would be performing the same piece for a judge who would give me a score.

Today, as usual, I felt my piece was not securely memorized. I never had enough time to practise. Even though I practised one hour a day, I really needed to spend at least two hours to get the Mozart sonata that I was playing in good shape. To make matters worse, I was the oldest student. This made me feel that I should be the best even though I knew that several of the others had been playing much longer than I had. Now I could only hope I didn't make a fool of myself in front of the younger kids in my teacher's class. They never seemed to make any mistakes when they played, especially that little Leonard.

Leonard was a skinny little kid with a mat of black hair slicked smoothly back against his egg-shaped head. His thick glasses made him look like the stereotype of a brainy kid. When he looked at anyone, it was always with a look of amusement. I guess he knew his grey matter was far superior to whatever was in the rest of our brains! He was as good in computer programming, creative writing, and chemistry as he was at the piano. He had been taking lessons for only three years and was already playing pieces at an advanced level. What's more, I heard his mother complaining once that Leonard didn't spend much time at the piano. The worst part of performing in the same room with Leonard was his age. He was only nine!

Now, a student like Michelle made me feel better about myself. I could always count on her to break down in the middle of her piece. She seldom practised. Nevertheless, she was content to do what she could. At least I knew I sounded better than she sounded.

I entered the large Victorian house through the back door as the sound of a familiar Bach prelude drifted out from the heavy doors of the music room. As usual I was late. I took off my shoes and crept noiselessly into the room, where I slipped into an armchair near the door.

Oh, if only I could sit here and just listen. My eyes wandered across the large room filled with beautiful antique furniture and treasures from around the world. In the far corner stood the black ebony grand piano. How much more beautiful its tone was than the old spinet on which I practised. Children ranging in age from five to twelve sat motionless in the rows of sturdy wooden folding chairs set up across a large Oriental rug.

Mrs. Stuart looked over and smiled, seeming to know how nervous I was. She had tried for years to assure me of my talent, yet I still tended to doubt it — particularly on these occasions. Mrs. Stuart was not your typical overbearing piano instructor. She was kind and always encouraging. She was in her mid-thirties, yet appeared younger. Her face was free of makeup, yet her high cheekbones and large dark eyes seemed not to need it. She radiated a warmth that was felt by all of her students.

As soon as the music ceased, I was jolted back into the reality of my situation. I was next. I approached the piano cautiously, feeling the eyes of the younger children riveted upon me. "Uhm . . . this piece is a Mozart sonata," I murmured quietly. Filled with difficult runs and countless trills, it was the kind of piece that could easily fall apart. Specially when the performer is nervous. I counted to ten in an attempt to calm my nerves, and with one deep breath I began.

To my surprise, I played the first movement smoothly, hardly missing a note. In the second movement I made a small memory slip, but I managed to keep going. The third movement gave me some trouble. My fingers didn't seem to be able to move fast enough for the trills. I had to slow down. I missed two of the hard runs. Finally, I reached the last notes of the sonata, heaved a great sigh of relief, and stood up from the bench.

"Beautiful, Suzanne. I think that was the best I've heard you play this piece. By April you will sound more secure." The reassuring voice of Mrs. Stuart broke the silence and I started to relax. The younger students were beginning to get restless. One girl yawned, and two boys in the back were poking at each other. Then it was Leonard's turn.

Leonard marched up to the piano with the posture of a West Point cadet. In a high, somewhat nasal voice he announced, "This afternoon I will perform the Mozart Sonata in C Major, Opus 35."

My heart started to beat faster. I was disgraced! Leonard was going to play my piece. How could Mrs. Stuart have given us both the same piece?

Of course all of my hopes were shattered as he began to play. The sound of the music took everyone by surprise. I stared at my teacher in disbelief. I could hardly recognize this as the same piece. The evenness of the trills, the beauty of the melody, the flawless technique on the runs — I had to admit the piece was more beautiful than I had imagined. I was thrilled and devastated. The piece was gorgeous, but my performance had been mediocre and I felt discouraged.

So now I ask myself, "What keeps me going back to the piano? How can all this misery be worth it?" It's the thrill and challenge of hearing a beautiful piece and then trying to re-create that beauty myself.

Proofreading

An important step still remains. You must check each sentence to see that the sentence is correct, including grammar, spelling, and punctuation. In the rush to get a paper in on time, this is a step that is often overlooked. If you take each sentence, starting with the last and going sentence by sentence back toward the beginning, you will be able to look at the sentence structure apart from the other aspects of the essay. Taking the time to look over a paper will usually result in your spotting several sentence-level errors. (At this point, you might want to correct errors of grammar, spelling, and punctuation in the first draft of the student essay on pages 239–40.)

Note: In most cases, your teacher will not accept handwritten work, and you will be expected to submit a paper produced on a typewriter or a word processor. Do not forget to proofread your work after it has been typed or printed; even if you have your paper typed for you, you are still responsible for errors. If there are not too many errors, you can make corrections neatly in ink on your typed or printed copy before handing it in.

Working Together

1. Imagine yourself in the following situation: you and your classmates are guidance counsellors in a high school. You have been asked to produce a brochure that will be entitled, "When a Young Person Quits School." This brochure is intended for students who are thinking of dropping out of school. You and the other counsellors meet to brainstorm on the topic.

   Divide into groups. Each group will brainstorm for 15 minutes or so, and then come together again as a class. On the board make a final grouping of the ideas for this topic and discuss.

2. In groups or as a class, construct an outline for the essay on "When a Young Person Quits School" using the information gathered in the brainstorming activity above. Organize the information into main points and supporting details under those main points.

Chapter 20
Writing the Narrative Essay

At one time or another, you have found yourself in a situation where you have been nervous or uncomfortable. Perhaps you were overwhelmed by the rules of a large organization, or perhaps you were intimidated by a person who had authority over you at the time.

The essay you will write in this chapter will be a narrative essay, in which you will tell a story about yourself. Because the experience happened to you, you are the expert on the topic. As you read the model essay in this chapter, and as you study how a narrative essay is constructed, you will be preparing to write your own essay based on your personal experience.

Exploring the Topic

1. From your own observations, how do most students treat people who have a disability?
2. Are there proper facilities for the disabled at your school?
3. If you are not disabled, how do you feel when you have to deal with someone who is? If you are disabled, how do you feel about dealing with someone who isn't?

The following essay originally appeared in the *Niagara Falls Review*. It was written by a nineteen-year-old student at Niagara Falls Collegiate, Ontario, who has had cerebral palsy since birth. The essay won a province-wide competition and is reprinted here from Kerrigan, Matthews, and Webb, *Who's Going to Read This Anyway?*

The Model Essay: Shawn Dalgleish, "I'm Making It"

In March 1970, my older sister Linda ran home from school and raced upstairs to see her new baby brother. The crib was empty. The baby was still at the hospital in an incubator. He had tubes in his arms to feed him and tubes in his nose to help him breathe. The doctors said he was very weak and would probably die. Well, that was me — Shawn Dalgleish! I'm alive and making it!

Something had gone wrong inside my mother even before I was born. No one could have prevented it; it just happened. Somehow, the oxygen supply was cut off. When I was three months old, they took me to Toronto for assessment. I was diagnosed as having Atheroid Cerebral Palsy. This meant that I would have problems with muscle co-ordination, speech, and maybe even learning.

The doctors in Toronto told my mother that she could raise me until I was five or six years old, but then she would have to put me into an institution. I hate that word! My mother was angry and refused to believe the doctors. We have proved those doctors wrong. I have lived with my mother all my life and soon I will live on my own.

My independence means a lot to me. Much of my independence was learned at Lakewood Camp near Port Colborne, which is run by the Easter Seal Society. They have many workshops including archery, swimming, and canoeing. We stayed in cabins but often we slept in tents or under the stars. No matter what kind of problem you had, the counsellors always treated you like someone special.

Just this past summer, I spent three-and-a-half weeks in Toronto with a program called TIPS, which stands for Teen Independence Program. There were kids with different kinds of handicaps. Some of us still write letters to each other. I made a very good friend there named Tiffany and we were together all the time except at night. At TIPS they taught us how to use a stove, a microwave, and a washing machine and dryer. Also, I learned how to get around in a large city on my own. Cleaning my room, making my bed, and cooking for myself when no one is around are all things I don't enjoy doing, but they are a part of life. I'm just happy I can do these things on my own.

The biggest influence in my life has been my mother. She has made me what I am today. When I was little, she carried me everywhere and she taught me how to walk. When I started kindergarten at King George V, I took a taxi to school. My mother carried me out to the cab and the cab driver would carry me into school and set me on my no-speed tricycle. I still take a taxi to high school, but now my mother puts my computer outside on the driveway, goes back into the house, and shuts the door. I just give her a dirty look — especially on cold days. The driver carries my computer into school because I'm afraid I'll drop it.

I take four classes and my friends carry my computer to each class for me. If there is a fire drill, my friends pick me up and throw me over their shoulders. They've had to "rescue" me at least twice this year. I have a peer tutor who helps me with my school work. She does most of the typing for me because I only type about ten words per minute. She also corrects my spelling for me. Lisa treats me just like everyone else. She is more than a peer tutor — she is a friend. Two weeks ago, we went to a dance and the bouncer wasn't going to let us in because he thought I was drunk. Lisa told him to . . . !

It was in Grade 5 that I really realized that I couldn't do everything everyone else could do. My friends at school decided that they were going to sign up for ice hockey. That night I asked my dad if I could play hockey too. My father told me that I wouldn't be able to skate like my friends, because my legs weren't strong enough to hold me up and I wouldn't have the balance to stay on my feet. This was the first time I realized that I was different.

As I grew older I didn't have to worry about having CP until the day when I was thirteen and I went roller-skating. I remember trying my hardest to be just like the other kids. I couldn't do it; I kept falling. I got so frustrated that I ran into the washroom and whipped my skates against the wall and started crying. It didn't seem fair.

One of the reasons why I never worried about being different was that my sisters and mother and father treated me like a regular brother. We would bug each other and fight just like other brothers and sisters. And I knew that they loved me even when I was being a bratty little brother.

I'm now in Grade 12 and I can't wait to graduate next year. I've been working at the Minolta Tower for four years as a coin roller. When I graduate, I want to work for a year, save some money, and travel. Eventually, I would like to go to college and study music or horticulture. I like to have a good time with my friends. I like to joke around with them. But someday I want to be just like Terry Fox or Rick Hansen. I respect them because they both had a handicap but they did something with their lives.

I think that my CP has helped make me a better person. When people make fun of me, I just ignore them. I don't let them hurt me. I never feel sorry for myself; because I have so many friends, I don't need to worry about the people who don't understand.

In spite of my handicap, I've grown up with a full and exciting life. I've come to a major time and I have to choose the path I'm going to follow. I'm confident about the future because I have strengths in place of the ones I'm missing. I'm Shawn Dalgleish. I've made it and I'm still making it.

Analyzing the Writer's Strategies

1. What is the thesis of this narrative essay?
2. Give the main supporting details of the thesis. How do these details reveal the writer's point of view?
3. How is the humour in this story used?
4. What is the dominant mood of the story?
5. What purpose does the conclusion serve in this essay?

Suggested Topics for Writing

Choose one of the following topics and write a narrative essay of at least five paragraphs to develop that topic. The section that follows this list will help you work through the stages of the writing process.

1. My worst classroom experience
2. A parent who would not listen

   3. My first _____
   4. When I tried to convince someone to hire me for a job
   5. My experience with an aggressive salesperson
   6. A day when nothing went right
   7. A mix-up with a friend
   8. Trouble at the office
   9. A day that changed my life
  10. A frustrating experience at a doctor's office
  11. How my nervousness made matters worse
  12. A perfect evening
  13. The day I made a fool of myself
  14. An embarrassing experience
  15. The day I got a job

Writing a Narrative Essay

Choosing the Topic and the Controlling Idea

Using the preceding list of fifteen topics or using ideas of your own, jot down two or three different topics that appeal to you. From this list of possibilities, select the topic that you think would give you the best opportunity for writing. Which one do you feel most strongly about? Which one are you the most expert in? Which one is most likely to interest your readers? Which one is best suited to being developed into a college essay?

    Your next step is to decide what your controlling idea should be. What is the point you want to make about the experience? Was the experience humiliating, absurd, or hilarious?

Gathering Information Using Brainstorming Techniques

Take at least 15 minutes to jot down everything about your topic that comes to mind. If your topic is one that you can easily share, brainstorm with other people who can help you think of additional material, including specific details or additional vocabulary that you will be able to use to give your writing more accuracy, completeness, and depth. If you can, go to the spot where the story you plan to tell in the essay will take place and jot down some details, particularly the sensory images that you have forgotten.

Selecting and Organizing Details

Review your brainstorming list and cross out any ideas that you decide are not appropriate. Prepare to build on the ideas that you find promising. Put these remaining ideas into an order that will serve as your temporary guide. Keep in mind that a narrative essay usually follows a chronological order.

Some instructors may require you to work this material into an outline so you can see which ideas are subsidiary to the main points.

Writing the Rough Draft

At this point in your work, you should not feel that every phrase is set in final form. Many writers feel it is more important to let your mind be relaxed and allow the words to flow freely at this stage, even if you are not following your plan exactly. Sometimes a period of "free writing" can lead you to new ideas, ideas that are better than the ones you had in your brainstorming session. Keep in mind that you are free to add ideas, drop others, or rearrange the order of your details at any point. There are an infinite number of possibilities, so it is natural that you will make changes.

Revising the Rough Draft

As you work on your rough draft, you may work alone, with a group, with a peer tutor, or directly with your instructor. Here are some of the basic questions you should consider at this most important stage of your work:

a. Does the rough draft satisfy the conditions for essay form? Does it have an introductory paragraph, at least three well-developed paragraphs in the body, and a concluding paragraph? Remember that one sentence is not a developed paragraph. (One exception to this rule is when you have dialogue between two people. Then each line of dialogue is written as a separate paragraph.)

b. Is your essay a narration? Does it focus on a single topic rather than on a general situation? Where does the action take place? Can the reader see it? What time of day, week, or year is it?

c. Have you put the details of the essay in a certain time order? Find the expressions that show the time sequence.

d. Can you think of any part of the story that is missing and should be added? Is there any material that is irrelevant and should be omitted?

e. Are there sentences or paragraphs that are repetitious?

f. Find several places where you can substitute better verbs or nouns. Add adjectives to give the reader better sensory images.

g. Find at least three places where you can add details, perhaps even a whole paragraph, that will more fully describe the person or place that is central to your story.

h. Can you think of a better way to begin or end your essay?

i. Show your draft to at least two other readers and ask for suggestions.

Preparing the Final Version

If you have worked hard in revising the rough draft, you will be delighted with the improvements as you write the second draft.

Feedback is an important aid in each of the final stages of writing an essay. A good way to help yourself see your own work more clearly is to put the writing aside for a few days, if you can. Then read what you have written aloud to someone else, or to yourself if no one else is available. You may be surprised at the number of places in your writing where you will hear the need for a change.

Checklist for the Final Copy

Use 21.5 cm by 28 cm paper.

Type on one side of the paper only.

Double-space.

Leave approximately 3.5 cm margins on each side of the paper.

Do not hyphenate words at ends of lines unless you consult a dictionary to check how to divide words correctly into syllables.

Centre the title at the top of the first page.

Put your name, the date, and the title of your paper on a separate title page.

If you have more than one page, staple or clip them together so they will not be lost.

Proofreading

Check your second draft for:

misspellings
fragments or run-ons
incorrect punctuation
consistency of voice and tense
verb problems
agreement
parallel structure

Working Together

1. A parlour game that is amusing is the telling of a story by creating it on the spot. One person begins with a sentence that sets the scene. Then it is continued sentence by sentence as each person takes a turn. Do this for perhaps twenty minutes. Elect one student in charge of putting the sentences on the board. Then discuss the outcome. In what ways is the narrative a success? What are its weaknesses?

2. In this chapter, each student has written a narrative essay. Divide into groups and share the narrative essays in your group. Attach a sheet of paper to each essay in which you critique the essay by answering two questions:

   a. In your opinion, what is one aspect of the essay that you believe is very strong?

   b. In your opinion, what is one aspect of the essay that still needs improvement?

Chapter 21
Writing the Process Essay

It is your sister's birthday. You have bought her a gift that you must first put together. Carefully following the instructions, you try to assemble the item, but something is wrong. It does not work. Either you have not followed the instructions properly, or the instructions themselves are not clear. All of us have found ourselves in this situation at one time or another. It takes careful thought to write about a process. The writer must not assume the reader knows more than he or she is likely to know.

Exploring the Topic

1. Think of a time when you had to put something together, but you were not given adequate directions. What did you do?
2. When people write instructions or give directions, what do they usually neglect to keep in mind?
3. Recall a time when you had to explain a process to someone. You might have had to show someone how to get somewhere, or you might have had to write a detailed description of how you did a science experiment. What was the process? Was it hard to explain? Why or why not?
4. What was your worst experience with trying to follow a process? You could have been trying to work something out yourself, or you could have been trying to follow someone else's directions. How did you overcome your difficulty?

In the following selection from *The Online Student*, the authors provide a guide to communicating via e-mail.

The Model Essay: Randy Reddick and Elliot King, "Creating and Sending an E-Mail Message"

Creating and sending short electronic (e-mail) messages is easy regardless of the computer system you're using. The steps generally will be the same regardless of the system; however, specific commands needed to complete each step will vary from system to system. Currently, even VMS and UNIX have fairly easy-to-use mail programs. You will have to consult with whomever you depend on for e-mail access to learn the exact set of commands to complete the following steps.

To create and send a short e-mail message, first you log onto the computer on which your electronic mailbox is located and then access the specific mail program running there. For example, when you log onto a VMS system, the first thing you see is a "$", which is called the system prompt. At the system prompt, you type the command "mail". This changes your system prompt to the mail prompt, which looks like "MAIL>".

Once you are into your mail program, you will tell the system that you want to send a message. In VMS Mail, which is an older program, you type the command "send". In other mail programs, you can use your mouse to click on the send command.

The computer responds with "To:" and you enter the e-mail address of the person to whom you wish to send mail. After you enter the address, the computer responds with the line "Subject:". After you enter the subject, you begin composing your message. When you compose a message, you will be using a text editor. The text editor probably will not work exactly like your word processor, so, depending on how user friendly it is, you may want to obtain a list of commands from your computer resource person.

Often, text editing in the mail program is awkward. For example, it may be hard to move between lines to correct mistakes. In those cases, you may want to compose longer messages using your word processor and then upload those messages to send them. Once again, the exact process of uploading files from a personal computer to a central computer varies greatly, depending on the exact setup, so you will have to ask someone for a set of instructions on how to do that.

When you finish composing your note, you exit the mail composition utility to send the message to its intended destination. To exit from VMS Mail, you press Ctrl-Z. That is, you hold down the Ctrl key while pressing the Z key. If, after typing your message, you decide that you do not want to send it, you can press Ctrl-C to cancel the message.

If you use a computer running UNIX instead of VMS, when you log onto the computer the system prompt may be "%". Using UNIX Mail, you can send a mail message either from the system prompt or the mail prompt (the prompt you get after you begin running the mail program). From the system prompt "%", you type "mail" and the address of the person to whom you wish to send the message. More commonly, you will first call up the mail program to read your mail and then you will want to send messages. To call up the mail program, type "mail" at the system prompt. This will give you the mail prompt, which in UNIX Mail is "&". You then type "m" and the recipient's address.

In either case, once you have started the send procedure, you will then receive the "Subject:" prompt. After you enter the subject, you hit Return and begin typing the message. If you want to use a text editor to compose the message, you type "~vi" on a blank line. When you are finished composing the message, type "<esc>:wq" to quit the text editor. To send the message, after you have finished writing it hit Return and then type Ctrl-D. If you want to cancel the message before you send it, type "~q" on a separate line.

Sending relatively short e-mail messages is easy, even if you must use software such as the basic UNIX and VMS Mail utilities. Programs such as Pine for UNIX and VMS make it even more efficient. Instead of forcing you to remember commands, Pine provides menus from which you can select what you want to do.

Analyzing the Writers' Strategies

1. What method did the writers use for the introduction?
2. What method did they use for the conclusion?
3. How many steps are there to the process as the writers described it?
4. Where, at each step of the process, do the writers give specific examples to make each part of the process clear?

Suggested Topics for Writing

Choose one or more of the following topics and write a process essay of at least six paragraphs to develop that topic. Use the section that follows this list to help you work through the various stages of the writing process.

1. How to get good grades in college
2. How to do well in a job interview
3. How to plan a budget
4. How to buy a used car
5. How to study for a test
6. How to choose the right college
7. How to redecorate a room
8. How to buy clothes on a limited budget
9. How to find the right place to live
10. How to make new friends

Writing the Process Essay: How to . . .

Thousands of books and articles have been written that promise to help us accomplish some goal in life: how to start a business, how to cook, how to lose weight, how to install a shower, how to assemble a bicycle. In the essay you are about to write, you will have the opportunity to describe how you once went through a process to achieve a goal of some kind.

Choose the Topic and the Controlling Idea

Using the preceding list of suggested topics or using ideas of your own, jot down two or three different topics that appeal to you. From this list of two or three topics, select the topic that you think would give you the best opportunity for writing. Which one do you feel most strongly about? Which one are you the most expert in? Which one is most likely to interest your readers? Which one is best suited to being developed into a college essay?

Your next step is to decide what your controlling idea should be. What is the point you want to make about the process? Is the process tedious, useful, unpredictable, or complicated?

Gathering Information Using Brainstorming Techniques

Take at least 15 minutes to jot down everything about your topic that comes to mind. If your topic is one that you can easily share, brainstorm with other people who can help you think of additional material, including specific details or additional vocabulary that you will be able to use to give your writing more accuracy, completeness, and depth.

Selecting and Organizing Material

Review your brainstorming list and cross out any ideas that you decide are not appropriate. Prepare to build on the ideas that you find promising. Put these remaining ideas into an order that will serve as your temporary guide. Keep in mind that in a process essay it is essential to include *all* the steps in the *correct* order.

Some instructors may require you to work this material into an outline so you can see which ideas are subsidiary to the main points.

Writing the Rough Draft

At this point in your work, you should not feel that every phrase is set in final form. Many writers feel it is more important to let your mind be relaxed and allow the words to flow freely at this stage, even if you are not following your plan exactly. Sometimes a period of "free writing" can lead you to new ideas, ideas that are better than the ones you had in your brainstorming session. Keep in mind that you are free to add ideas, drop others, or rearrange the order of your details at any point. By re-evaluating the logic of your ideas, you will undoubtedly make changes in content and approach.

Revising the Rough Draft

As you work on your rough draft, you may work alone, with a group, with a peer tutor, or directly with your instructor. Here are some of the basic questions you should consider at this most important stage of your work:

a. Does the rough draft satisfy the conditions for essay form? Does it have an introductory paragraph, at least three well-developed paragraphs in the body, and a concluding paragraph? Remember that one sentence is not a developed paragraph.
b. Does this essay show the reader how to do something specific?
c. Are the steps in the process in the correct order?
d. Is any step or important piece of information left out? Is any of the material included irrelevant?
e. Are there sentences or paragraphs that are repetitious?
f. Find several places where you can substitute better verbs or nouns. Add adjectives to give the reader better sensory images.
g. Does the essay flow logically from one idea to the next? Could you improve the essay with better use of transitional devices?
h. Can you think of a better way to begin or end your essay?
i. Show your draft to at least two other readers and ask for suggestions.

Preparing the Final Version

If you have worked hard in revising the rough draft, you will be delighted with the improvements as you write the second draft.

Feedback is an important aid in each of the final stages of writing an essay. A good way to help yourself see your own work better is to put the writing aside for a few days, if you can. Then read what you have written aloud to someone else, or to yourself if no one else is available. You may be surprised at how often you hear the need for a change.

Checklist for the Final Copy

Use 21.5 cm by 28 cm paper.
Type on one side of the paper only.
Double-space.
Leave approximately 3.5 cm margins on each side of the paper.
Do not hyphenate words at ends of lines unless you consult a dictionary to check how to divide words correctly into syllables.
Centre the title at the top of the first page.
Put your name, the date, and the title of your paper on a separate title page.
If you have more than one page, staple or clip them together so they will not be lost.

Proofreading

Check your second draft for:

misspellings
fragments or run-ons
incorrect punctuation
consistency of voice and tense
verb problems
agreement
parallel structure

Working Together

1. The class as a whole discusses and lists some of the current problems on their particular campus today. Then the class divides into groups of three or four, each group choosing one of the problems identified. After discussion, each group draws up a list of steps that need to be taken in order to improve the situation.

2. Each group chooses a secretary. The group uses the list to create sentences that will go into a letter to be sent to the appropriate college official suggesting the process that could be followed to solve the problem. The secretary will write the finished letter. Be sure there is an introductory paragraph that presents the problem and a conclusion that thanks the official for his or her attention.

Chapter 22
Writing the Comparison
or Contrast Essay

Computer technology is advancing so rapidly that scientists are already discussing the possibility of creating what they call "artificial intelligence," a computer that will be able to duplicate the thinking processes of the human mind. In fact, scientists in this country and abroad are now actively designing such a computer. In the following sections, you'll explore this topic further while learning more about writing the comparison or contrast essay.

Exploring the Topic

1. What are some of the jobs that computers can already do better and faster than human beings can?
2. What are some of the jobs you have to do now that you would like a computer to do for you? How many of these jobs do you think a computer will take over in your lifetime?
3. Do you think a computer could ever be programmed to be as creative as the human mind?
4. In your opinion, are there any dangers in the advanced computer technology we see all around us today?

In the following selection from his book *Please Explain*, science writer Isaac Asimov compares the workings of the modern computer and the workings of the human mind.

The Model Essay: Isaac Asimov, "The Difference Between a Brain and a Computer"

The difference between a brain and a computer can be expressed in a single word: complexity.

The large mammalian brain is the most complicated thing, for its size, known to us. The human brain weighs three pounds, but in that three pounds are ten billion neurons and a hundred billion smaller cells. These many billions of cells are interconnected in a vastly complicated network that we can't begin to unravel as yet.

Even the most complicated computer man has yet built can't compare in intricacy with the brain. Computer switches and components number in the thousands rather than in the billions. What's more, the computer switch is just an on-off device, whereas the brain cell is itself possessed of a tremendously complex inner structure.

Can a computer think? That depends on what you mean by "think." If solving a mathematical problem is "thinking," then a computer can "think" and do so much faster than a man. Of course, most mathematical problems can be solved quite mechanically by repeating certain straightforward processes over and over again. Even the simple computers of today can be geared for that.

It is frequently said that computers solve problems only because they are "programmed" to do so. They can only do what men have them do. One must remember that human beings also can only do what they are "programmed" to do. Our genes "program" us the instant the fertilized ovum is formed, and our potentialities are limited by that "program."

Our "program" is so much more enormously complex, though, that we might like to define "thinking" in terms of the creativity that goes into writing a great play or composing a great symphony, in conceiving a brilliant scientific theory or a profound ethical judgment. In that sense, computers certainly can't think and neither can most humans.

Surely, though, if a computer can be made complex enough, it can be as creative as we. If it could be made as complex as a human brain, it could be the equivalent of a human brain and do whatever a human brain can do.

To suppose anything else is to suppose that there is more to the human brain than the matter that composes it. The brain is made up of cells in a certain arrangement and the cells are made up of atoms and molecules in certain arrangements. If anything else is there, no signs of it have ever been detected. To duplicate the material complexity of the brain is therefore to duplicate everything about it.

But how long will it take to build a computer complex enough to duplicate the human brain? Perhaps not as long as some think. Long before we approach a computer as complex as our brain, we will perhaps build a computer that is at least complex enough to design another computer more complex than itself. This more complex computer could design one still more complex and so on and so on and so on.

In other words, once we pass a certain critical point, the computers take over and there is a "complexity explosion." In a very short time thereafter, computers may exist that not only duplicate the human brain — but far surpass it.

Then what? Well, mankind is not doing a very good job of running the earth right now. Maybe, when the time comes, we ought to step gracefully aside and hand over the job to someone who can do it better. And if we don't step aside, perhaps Supercomputer will simply move in and push us aside.

Analyzing the Writer's Strategies

1. An essay of comparison usually emphasizes the similarities between two subjects, while an essay of contrast usually emphasizes the differences. With this in mind, is the essay you have just read an essay of comparison or contrast? Why?
2. Does the writer use the point-by-point method or the block method in writing this essay?
3. Does the writer provide an equal number of details that relate to both computers and the human brain?
4. Specifically, how does the writer demonstrate the complexity of a computer and the complexity of the human brain?

Suggested Topics for Writing

Compare or contrast:

1. High school classes with college classes
2. Shopping in a mall with shopping in a downtown area
3. Two movies (the acting, the cinematography, the quality of the story)
4. A friend from your childhood with a present friend
5. Two similar items you have owned (e.g., cars, bicycles, radios)
6. Two stores that sell the same kind of merchandise
7. Two vacation spots
8. Two apartments or houses where you have lived
9. Watching television with reading a book
10. Cooking dinner at home with eating out

Writing the Comparison or Contrast Essay

Every time you go to the grocery store or look in your closet to decide what to wear, you are involved in making comparisons or contrasts. When you have to make a big decision in life, usually the problem involves weighing the advantages and disadvantages of one choice against the advantages and disadvantages of another choice. Should you go to college or get a job? Should you get married now or wait another year? Should you tell that person how upset you are by what he or she did? In all cases, you must compare the two choices to see which seems to be the better one. Making a decision is not easy, just as writing a good comparison or contrast essay is not easy. You have to consider two topics rather than one.

Choosing the Topic and Controlling Idea

Using the preceding list of topics or using ideas of your own, jot down two or three different topics that appeal to you. From these two or three topics, select the topic that you think would give you the best opportunity for writing. Which one do you feel most strongly about? Which one are you the most expert in? Which one is most likely to interest your readers? Which one is best suited to being developed into a college essay?

Your next step is to decide what your controlling idea should be. What is the point you want to make about the comparison or contrast? Is your conclusion that one is better than the other?

Gathering Information Using Brainstorming Techniques

Take at least 15 minutes to jot down everything about your topic that comes to mind. If your topic is one that you can easily share, brainstorm with other people who can help you think of additional material, including specific details or additional vocabulary that you will be able to use to give your writing more accuracy, completeness, and depth.

Selecting and Organizing Material

Review your brainstorming list and cross out any ideas that you decide are not appropriate. Prepare to build on the ideas that you find promising. Put these remaining ideas into an order that will serve as your temporary guide. Remember that in a comparison or contrast essay, the order is important because it helps the reader to keep the points in mind.

Writing the Rough Draft

At this point in your work, you should not feel that every phrase is set in final form. Many writers feel it is more important to let your mind be relaxed and allow the words to flow freely at this stage, even if you are not following your plan exactly. Sometimes a period of "free writing" can lead you to new ideas, ideas that are better than the ones you had in your brainstorming session. Keep in mind that you are free to add ideas, drop others, or rearrange the order of your details at any point. By re-evaluating the logic of your ideas, you will undoubtedly make changes in content and approach.

Revising the Rough Draft

As you work on your rough draft, you may work alone, with a group, with a peer tutor, or directly with your instructor. Here are some of the basic questions you should consider at this most important stage of your work:

a. Does the rough draft satisfy the conditions for essay form? Does it have an introductory paragraph, at least three well-developed paragraphs in the body, and a concluding paragraph? Remember that one sentence is not a developed paragraph.

b. Did you use the point-by-point method or the block method?

c. What is the point of your comparison or contrast?

d. Is any important comparison or contrast left out? Is any of the material included irrelevant?

e. Are there sentences or paragraphs that are repetitious?

f. Find several places where you can substitute better verbs or nouns. Add adjectives to give the reader better sensory images.

g. Does the essay flow logically from one idea to the next? Could you improve the essay with better use of transitional devices?

h. Can you think of a better way to begin or end your essay?

i. Show your draft to at least two other readers and ask for suggestions.

Preparing the Final Version

If you have worked hard at revising the rough draft, you will be delighted with the improvements as you write the second draft.

Feedback is an important aid in each of the final stages of writing an essay. A good way to help yourself see your own work better is to put the writing aside for a few days, if you can. Then read what you have written aloud to someone else, or to yourself if no one else is available. You may be surprised at the number of places in your writing where you will hear a mistake and, indeed, make a change even as you read.

Checklist for the Final Copy

Use 21.5 cm by 28 cm paper.

Type on one side of the paper only.

Double-space.

Leave approximately 3.5 cm margins on each side of the paper.

Do not hyphenate words at ends of lines unless you consult a dictionary to check how to divide words correctly into syllables.

Centre the title at the top of the first page.

Put your name, the date, and the title of your paper on a separate title page.

If you have more than one page, staple or clip them together so they will not be lost.

Proofreading

Check your second draft for:

misspellings

fragments or run-ons

incorrect punctuation

consistency of voice and tense

verb problems
agreement
parallel structure

Working Together

The selection that follows was written by Sun-Kyung Yi, a freelance author who has written for a number of newspapers, and who has published articles dealing with the problems of the Korean community in Toronto. A person in the class should read the selection out loud while the rest of the students make a list of the areas being contrasted. Following the reading, the areas that have been contrasted, along with specific examples, are listed on the chalkboard. With these general areas in mind, the class considers other cultural communities that are found in Canada to see what information class members can contribute, and selects two communities to focus on. Working together in small groups, see what further information you can find in the library. Then work individually to write an essay of comparison or contrast about these two cultures.

An Immigrant's Split Personality

I am Korean-Canadian. But the hyphen often snaps in two, obliging me to choose to act as either a Korean or a Canadian, depending on where I am and who I'm with. After 16 years of living in Canada, I discovered that it's very difficult to be both at any given time or place.

When I was younger, toying with the idea of entertaining two separate identities was a real treat, like a secret game for which no one knew the rules but me.

I was known as Angela to the outside world, and as Sun-Kyung at home. I ate bologna sandwiches in the school lunch room and rice and kimchee for dinner. I chatted about teen idols and giggled with my girlfriends during my classes, and ambitiously practiced piano and studied in the evenings, planning to become a doctor when I grew up. I waved hellos and goodbyes to my teachers, but bowed to my parents' friends visiting our home.

I could also look straight in the eyes of my teachers and friends and talk frankly with them instead of staring at my feet with my mouth shut when Koreans talked to me.

Going outside the home meant I was able to relax from the constraints of my cultural conditioning, until I walked back in the door and had to return to being an obedient and submissive daughter.

The game soon ended when I realized that it had become a way of life, that I couldn't change the rules without disappointing my parents and questioning all the cultural implications and consequences that came with being a hyphenated Canadian.

Many have tried to convince me that I am a Canadian, like all other immigrants in the country, but those same people also ask me which country I came from with great curiosity, following with questions about the type of food I ate and the language I spoke. It's difficult to feel a sense of belonging and acceptance when you are regarded as "one of them." "Those Koreans, they work hard. . . . You must be fantastic at math and science." (No.) "Do your parents own a corner store?" (No.)

Koreans and Canadians just can't seem to merge into "us" and "we."

Some people advised me that I should just take the best of both worlds and disregard the rest. That's ideal, but unrealistic when my old culture demands a complete conformity with very little room to manoeuvre for new and different ideas.

After a lifetime of practice, I thought I could change faces and become Korean on demand with grace and perfection. But working with a small Korean company in Toronto proved me wrong. I quickly became estranged from my own people.

My parents were ecstatic at the thought of their daughter finally finding her roots and having a working opportunity to speak my native tongue and absorb the culture. For me, it was the most painful and frustrating $2\frac{1}{2}$ months of my life.

When the president of the company boasted that he "operated little Korea," he meant it literally. A Canadianized Korean was not tolerated. I looked like a Korean, therefore I had to talk, act, and think like one, too. Being accepted meant a total surrender to ancient codes of behaviour rooted in Confucian thought, while leaving the "Canadian" part of me out in the parking lot with my '86 Buick.

In the first few days at work, I was bombarded with inquiries about my marital status. When I told them I was single, they spent the following days trying to match me up with available bachelors in the company and the community.

I was expected to accept my inferior position as a woman and had to behave accordingly. It was not a place to practice my feminist views, or be an individual without being condemned. Little Korea is a place for men (who filled all the senior positions) and women don't dare to speak up or disagree with their male counterparts.

The president (all employees bow to him and call him Mr. President) asked me to act more like a lady and smile. I was openly scorned by a senior employee because I spoke more fluent English than Korean. The cook in the kitchen shook her head in disbelief upon discovering that my cooking skills were limited to boiling a package of instant noodles. "You want a good husband, learn to cook," she advised me.

In less than a week I became an outsider because I refused to conform and blindly nod my head in agreement to what my elders (which happened to be everybody else in the company) said. A month later, I was demoted because "members of the workplace and the Korean community" had complained that I just wasn't "Korean enough," and I had "too much power for a single woman." My father suggested that "when in Rome do as the Romans." But that's exactly what I was doing. I am in Canada so I was freely acting like a Canadian, and it cost me my job.

My father also said, "It doesn't matter how Canadian you think you are, just look in the mirror and it'll tell you who you *really* are." But what he didn't realize is that an immigrant has to embrace the new culture to enjoy and benefit from what it has to offer. Of course, I will always be Korean by virtue of my appearance and early conditioning, but I am also happily Canadian and want to take full advantage of all that such citizenship confers.

But for now I remain slightly distant from both cultures, accepted fully by neither. The hyphenated Canadian personifies the ideal of multiculturalism, but unless the host culture and the immigrant cultures can find ways to merge their distinct identities, sharing the best of both, this cultural schizophrenia will continue.

Chapter 23
Writing Persuasively

What Is Persuasion?

So far, your purpose in various writing assignments in this text has been to describe, narrate, or explain by using various strategies for development. Still another purpose in writing is to persuade.

Persuasion is an attempt to change the reader's present viewpoint, or at least to convince him or her that your viewpoint is a valid one.

Every time you write a paper for a course, you are trying to persuade your teacher that what you are presenting is the correct view of the subject matter. You might want to show that Canadian airlines are among the safest in the world, or that the crime novel is becoming Canada's favourite form of fiction. As you approach such types of assignments, you need to be aware of each part of the persuasion process so that you will be able to use it effectively in your own writing.

You could view all writing as persuasion, since one of the writer's main goals is always to get the reader to see, think, and believe in a certain way. However, **formal persuasion** follows certain guidelines. If you have ever been a member of a debating team, you have spent a good deal of time studying this special form. How to recognize techniques of persuasion and use them in your own writing is the subject of this chapter.

Guide to Writing the Persuasive Essay

1. **State a clear thesis.** Use words such as *must, ought,* or *should.*

   We should not ban all handguns.
   Canada must reform its prison system.
   All provinces should have the same legal drinking age.

2. **Use examples.** Well-chosen examples are the heart of any essay. Without them, the writing will be flat, lifeless, and unconvincing. Providing a good

example for each of your main points will help make a much stronger argument. Examples help your reader *see* what you are talking about.

3. **Use opinions from recognized authorities to support your points.** One of the oldest methods of supporting an argument is to use one or more authorities to support your particular position. People will usually believe what well-known experts claim. You should use carefully chosen experts to help make your position on a topic more persuasive. However, be sure that your authority is someone who is respected in the area you are discussing. For example, if you are arguing that we must end the nuclear arms race, your argument will be stronger if you quote a respected scientist who can accurately predict the consequences of a nuclear war. A famous movie star giving the same information might be more glamorous and get more attention, but he or she would not be as great an authority as the scientist.

4. **Answer your critics in advance.** When you point out, beforehand, what your opposition is likely to say in answer to your argument, you will be writing from a position of strength. You are letting your reader know that there is another side to the argument you are making. By pointing out this other side and then answering its objections in advance, you are strengthening your own position.

5. **Point out the results.** Help your reader see what will happen if your argument is (or is not) believed or acted upon as you think it should be. You should be specific and rational when you point out results, making sure that you avoid exaggerations of any kind. For example, if you are arguing against the possession of handguns, it would be an exaggeration to say that everyone is going to be murdered if the opposition's point of view is listened to instead of your position.

The following essay is about physical abuse against women. As you read the essay, look for the major parts of an effective argument: strong thesis, carefully chosen examples, quotations from authorities, answers to the opposition, and predictions. Can you find any weaknesses in the argument?

The Model Essay: Emil Sher, "There Is No Excuse for Physical Abuse"

Last week, Kirby Inwood was given 30 days in jail for assaulting his baby son Misha, and a suspended sentence for assaulting his wife, Tatyana Sidorova. He also received three years' probation.

The storm of publicity surrounding the lengthy trial has left in its wake serious concerns about violence against women and the way the issue is treated by the justice system. But still standing after the storm, with barely a scratch, are men's unshakeable attitudes toward women.

Judge Gordon Hachborn ordered Mr. Inwood to take psychiatric treatment for alcoholism and for his chronic violent tendencies toward women. For those men who have given thought to the issue, it's easy and comforting to portray Mr. Inwood as aberrant, one of the boys who's just a little more wild than most.

That's small comfort to women. In Canada, one in every 10 women who are either married or in a marital-type relationship is assaulted by her husband or partner. The difference between Mr. Inwood and other violent men must seem academic to a woman with a hand around her throat.

But for all our differences, Mr. Inwood and all other men, myself included, are members of the same fraternity. Initiation is painless. The benefits are enormous. Women, we quickly learn, are here to serve all our needs. If we want sexual gratification, we know whom to call. If we need to be nurtured emotionally, we know whom to lean on. If there's a ring around our collar, we know whom to blame.

"I just don't know how much I can take physically before my health breaks," Mr. Inwood stated at the thought of a protracted trial, unaware of his ironic choice of words. Had he lived in England in the nineteenth century, he would have had an easier time of it. Under English law it was legal for a husband to beat his wife, provided the instrument was "a rod not thicker than his thumb."

The laws have changed, but the spirit continues. "Under my thumb," The Rolling Stones' Mick Jagger sang in the song of the same name, "is the squirming dog who's just had her day."

He can hardly be blamed for the abuse of women that occurs in teen relationships, but his lyrics are part of a larger message that is so readily accepted. It's difficult to imagine Mick Jagger singing about the black or the Jew who once pushed him around but is now under his thumb.

They may be just lyrics, but words are an essential part of the artillery men carry in their assault against women. Verbal abuse takes it own toll and leaves a different type of scar. Some men hurl verbal arrows dipped in venom. Most of us use more subtle weapons: there are ten times as many words for a sexually promiscuous female as for a similarly inclined male. Just spend a few minutes in the proverbial locker room.

When defence lawyer Edward Greenspan raised the issue of Ms. Sidorova's past relationships, you could hear the words to a favourite rallying cry of men: she was a loose woman who got what she deserved. So once again it's the woman's fault. It's another version of the song belted out by men who rape: I was provoked. When will men realize that the cuts, welts, and bruises that cover a battered woman's body are not self-inflicted?

From schoolyards to boardrooms, we are taught that might — physical, political, financial — makes right. And we need not fear the consequences. Any man we would have to face — a police officer, lawyer, or judge — would almost certainly share our patronizing attitude toward women.

A man's home, we'd all agree, is his castle. The moat around it ensures that no outsiders interfere with such family concerns as keeping a woman in her place.

In the book *No Safe Place: Violence Against Women and Children* (The Women's Press), a lawyer speaks of our court system and notes that those who sit on the bench might, in fact, hold the very same attitudes as other men who regard women as "second-class citizens, the purveyors of family dishar-mony and their problems probably lie in the fact that they are just not ade-quate wives, mothers and women."

Thirty days in jail will not change Mr. Inwood's attitude toward women. Psychiatric treatment may help him. But the institutions that allow him to beat women will remain intact.

It is these economic, political and religious institutions that shape men's attitudes and give tacit approval to the way they behave.

The Kirby Inwood assault trial should not be seen in isolation. Assault must become a "men's issue." Men have a lot to answer for, and must begin to question the assumptions that allow violence against women to happen in the first place. If we don't, little Misha will grow up in a world no different from his father's.

Analyzing the Writer's Strategies

Because Emil Sher's essay deals with a controversial topic, many people may take exception to some of the points he makes. However, the writer combines the results of his own experience, his observations, and his reports of facts to con-vince us that we should take a stand against the physical abuse of women.

The writer first gains our attention by referring to the Kirby Inwood trial in 1988, and uses this trial as a central theme throughout the essay. He summarizes the trial by stating that we should have serious concerns about the social mecha-nisms that appear tacitly to approve of, or at least allow, violence in the family.

Sher then shifts to a broader perspective, delineating male myths about women, before moving to a historical overview of the problem, and ends this sec-tion with a discussion of the image of women conveyed in modern song lyrics. Combined with this is an overtone of moral outrage at traditional attitudes toward women and their role in society. Even more incredible, to the author, is the attitude conveyed by the Western judicial system toward women. To give cre-dence to his position, Sher quotes from a book written by a lawyer, who com-ments on the lax attitude of the judicial system toward those who abuse women.

Finally, having made his point clear and having offered a mixture of clearly labelled fact and opinion to support his position, the author concludes by saying that "assault must become a 'men's issue.' Men have a lot to answer for, and must begin to question the assumptions that allow violence against women to happen in the first place."

After reading this essay, do you see any weaknesses or oversights in Sher's logic?

EXERCISE 1   **Using Research Material to Write the Persuasive Essay**

Below are several pieces of information on the controversial topic of pollution. Use this information as the basis for your own essay on the topic. You may choose to rely on as many facts as you want, or you may adapt the opinions to agree with your own way of thinking. As you study the list, try to decide in which of your paragraphs you would use each of the facts or opinions you have been given.

1. We are polluting our environment at an alarming rate.
2. Governments and industries appear to be doing little to reduce pollution levels in the environment.
3. One government scientist criticized most levels of pollution judged acceptable in Canada as "usually far too high."
4. The garbage glut has produced a frantic search for dumpsites.
5. Metro Toronto dumps 5000 t of garbage daily and is running out of dump space.
6. Hazardous chemicals are still entering the Niagara River from the American side.
7. In 1989, the tanker *Exxon Valdez* ran aground in Prince William Sound near Alaska, spewing massive amounts of oil into the water.
8. Ozone is created when other pollutants, such as those from automobile exhausts, interact with the air in the sun's heat.
9. In its natural state, 15 to 25 km above the earth, ozone protects us from the sun's ultraviolet rays.

The following essay is about euthanasia. As you read the essay, look for the major parts of an effective argument: strong thesis, carefully chosen examples, quotations from authorities, answers to the opposition, and predictions. Can you find any weaknesses in the argument?

Howard Caplan is a medical doctor who specializes in geriatrics, the branch of medicine that deals with the care of older people. He is also the medical director of three nursing homes in Los Angeles, California.

As you read Dr. Caplan's essay, look for all of the elements of an effective argument. Where does the writer give his thesis statement? Where are his major examples? At what point does he use authorities to support his point of view? In addition, look for the paragraphs where he answers those who do not agree with him, and be sure to find that section of the essay where he predicts the future of euthanasia. As you read the essay, do you see any weaknesses in the writer's argument?

The Model Essay: Dr. Howard Caplan, "It's Time We Helped Patients Die"

For three years, the husband of one of my elderly patients watched helplessly as she deteriorated. She'd burst an aneurysm and later had an astrocytoma removed from her brain. Early in the ordeal, realizing that she'd never recover from a vegetative state, he'd pleaded with me to pull her nasogastric tube.

I'd refused, citing the policy of the convalescent hospital. I told him I could do it only if he got a court order. But he couldn't bring himself to start such proceedings, although the months dragged by with no signs of improvements in his wife's condition. He grieved as her skin broke down and she developed terrible bedsores. She had to have several courses of antibiotics to treat the infections in them, as well as in her bladder, which had an indwelling catheter.

Finally I got a call from a lawyer who said he'd been retained by the family to force me to comply with the husband's wishes.

"I'm on your side," I assured him. "But you'll have to get that court order just the same."

I went on to suggest — though none too hopefully — that we ask the court to do more than just let the patient starve to death. "If the judge will agree to let her die slowly, why won't he admit that he wants death to happen? Let's ask for permission to give her an injection and end her life in a truly humane manner."

The lawyer had no answer except to say, "Aw, come on, Doc — that's euthanasia!"

Frankly, I'd have been surprised at any other reaction. Although most states have enacted living-will laws in the past decade, none has yet taken the next logical step — legalizing euthanasia. But I believe it's time they did. Ten years of practice in geriatrics have convinced me that a proper death is a humane death, either in your sleep or being *put* to sleep.

I see appropriate patients every day in the extended-care facilities at which I practice. About 50 of the 350 people under my care have already ended their biographical lives. They've reached the stage in life at which there's no more learning, communicating, or experiencing pleasure. They're now simply existing in what is left of their biological lives.

Most of these patients are the elderly demented. A typical case is that of a woman in her 80s or 90s, who speaks only in gibberish and doesn't recognize her family. She has forgotten how to eat, so she has a feeding tube coming from her nose. She is incontinent, so she has an indwelling catheter. She can no longer walk, so she is tied into a wheelchair. She's easily agitated, so she gets daily doses of a major tranquilizer. Why shouldn't I, with the concurrence of her family and an independent medical panel, be allowed to quickly and painlessly end her suffering?

I think of another patient, a woman in her 50s, with end-stage multiple sclerosis, unable to move a muscle except for her eyeballs and her tongue. And younger patients: I have on my census a man in his early 40s, left an aphasic triplegic by a motorcycle accident when he was 19. For nearly a quarter of a century, while most of us were working, raising children, travelling, reading, and otherwise going about our lives, he's been vegetating. His biographical life ended with that crash. He can't articulate — only make sounds to convey that he's hungry or wet. If he were to become acutely ill, I would prefer not to try saving him. I'd want to let pneumonia end it for him.

Of my remaining 300 patients, there are perhaps 50 to 100 borderline functional people who are nearing the end of their biographical lives and — were euthanasia legal — would probably tell me: "I'm ready to go. My bags are packed. Help me."

Anyone who's had front-line responsibility for the elderly has been asked if there wasn't "something you can give me" to end life. Such requests are made by patients who clearly see the inevitability of their deterioration and dread having to suffer through it. For these people, there is no more pleasure, let alone joy — merely misery. They want out.

What is their fate? Chances are they'll be referred for psychiatric consultation on the grounds that they must be seriously depressed. The psychiatrist, usually decades younger than the patient, does indeed diagnose depression and recommends an antidepressant.

But if such patients lived in the Netherlands, odds are they'd get assistance in obtaining a release from the slow dying process to which our modern technology condemns them. While euthanasia is not yet legal there, it's openly practiced. On a segment of the CBS show "60 Minutes" not long ago, I heard a Dutch anesthesiologist describe how doctors in his country help 5000 terminal patients slip away peacefully each year. Isn't that a promising indication of how well euthanasia would work in this country?

I realize that there are those who vigorously oppose the idea. And there are moral issues to confront — how much suffering is too much, the one-in-several-million chance that a person given no hope of improving will beat the odds. But it's time for society to seriously reconsider whether it is immoral to take the life of someone whose existence is nothing but irreversible suffering. Euthanasia ought to be treated the same way the abortion issue has been treated: People who believe it a sin to take a life even for merciful reasons would not be forced to do so. What I'm pleading for is that doctors and their patients at least have the choice.

I doubt that we'll get congressional action on such an emotionally charged issue during my lifetime. Action may have to come at the state level. Ideally, legislatures should permit each hospital and each nursing home to have a panel that would approve candidates for euthanasia. Or it might be more practical to have one panel serve several hospitals and nursing homes in a geographic area. Made up of one or two physicians and a lawyer or judge, plus the attending doctor, the panel would assess the attending's findings and recommendations, the patient's wishes, and those of the immediate family. This would ensure that getting a heart-stopping injection was truly in the patient's best interests, and that there was no ulterior motive — for example, trying to hasten an insurance payout. Needless to say, members of the board would be protected by law from liability claims.

Then, if the patient had made it known while of sound mind that under certain circumstances he wanted a deadly substance administered, the process would be easy for everyone. But in most cases, it would be up to the attending to raise the question of euthanasia with the patient's relatives.

I'd start with those who've been part of the patient's recent life. If there are relatives who haven't seen the patient for years, it really shouldn't be any of their business. For instance, I'd try involving a son who's just kept in touch by phone. I'd say to him, "If you really want to stop this from happening, then you'd better come out here to see firsthand what's going on."

However, if he said, "Well, I can't really get away, Doctor, but I violently disagree," my answer would be, "Well, not violently enough. Everyone here can see what shape your mother's in. We're quite sure what she'd want if she could tell us, and we're going to help her."

Before any of this can happen, though, there's going to have to be widespread public education. The media will have to do a better job of discussing the issues than it has with living wills. Among my patients who are nearing death, there aren't more than a half-dozen with living wills attached to their charts. Patients' families often haven't even heard of them, and even when large institutions encourage families to get these things taken care of while the patient is still alert, it's hardly ever done.

Not knowing about living wills, unaware of no-code options, many families plunge their loved ones — and themselves — into unwanted misery. How many rapidly deteriorating patients are rushed from a nursing home to a hospital to be intubated, simply because that's the facility's rigid policy? How many families impoverish themselves to keep alive someone who's unaware of himself and his surroundings?

Every day in my professional life, I encounter illogical, irrational, and inhumane regulations that prevent me, and those with whom I work, from doing what we know in our souls to be the right thing. Before high technology, much of this debate was irrelevant. There was little we could do, for example, when a patient arrested. And what we could do rarely worked.

But times have changed. Now we have decisions to make. It helps to understand that many of the elderly infirm have accepted the inevitability — and, indeed, the desirability — of death. We who are younger must not mistake this philosophical position for depression. We need to understand the natural acceptance of death when life has lost its meaning.

About 28 percent of our huge Medicare budget is spent providing care during the last year of life. Far too little of that money goes to ensure that dying patients' last months are pain-free and comfortable. Far too much is wasted on heroic, pain-inducing measures that can make no difference. It's time to turn that ratio around — and to fight for the right to provide the ultimate assistance to patients who know their own fight to prolong life is a losing one.

Analyzing the Writer's Strategies

Because Dr. Caplan deals with a very sensitive subject, many people might find his position to be dangerous and even frightening. Even before we examine his essay, the title of the piece and the writer's medical background gain our attention. When a doctor writes on matters of life and death, we tend to pay more attention than we ordinarily might; the fact that Dr. Caplan works so closely with older people tends to give his views even more authority. For example, the facts and figures he gives go a long way toward strengthening his point of view. In addition, the writer uses both his own experience and his knowledge of practices in other countries to convince us that his stand on this controversial topic is the correct one.

The writer's position is also supported by the fact that he is so precise when he deals with the law; almost from the beginning, Dr. Caplan is seen as a careful and caring professional. We notice, too, that he points out what happens when the present system operates, and he gives practical suggestions that would help put his own system into operation. Finally, we see that he pays attention to the other side's arguments and then answers those arguments.

Dr. Caplan's persuasive essay is carefully written and complete; it has all of the parts needed for a good persuasive essay. After you have studied the essay, can you find any weaknesses in the writer's presentation?

E X E R C I S E 1   Using Research Material to Write the Persuasive Essay

Below are several pieces of information on the controversial topic of mercy killing. Who should make the life-and-death decisions in such matters? Use this information as the basis for your own essay on the topic. You may choose to rely on as many facts as you want, or you may adapt the opinions to agree with your own way of thinking. As you study the list, try to decide in which of your paragraphs you would use each of the facts or opinions you have been given.

1. Nearly 4000 Canadians commit suicide every year.
2. The idea of suicide has been rejected by society for many centuries.
3. Some societies discourage suicide by enacting strict laws against it.
4. Mercy killing is an act of charity when there is no hope that the sick person will ever enjoy a healthy life.
5. In the famous Karen Anne Quinlan case, when Karen's life-support system was turned off, she lived for nearly ten more years.
6. As our technical ability to extend life increases, the pressure on us to make life-and-death decisions will also increase.
7. "Suicide," the German poet Goethe said, "is an incident in human life which, however much disputed and discussed, demands the sympathy of every man, and in every age must be dealt with anew."
8. In 1962, Corinne van de Put was born without arms and with deformed feet. Eight days after she was born, her mother killed her.
9. If we had laws that encouraged mercy killing, we would not have the lives of such people as Helen Keller to show the world what handicapped people can do.
10. The general reaction to mercy killing will change as people realize that life should not always go on no matter what the cost may be.
11. The Canadian Medical Association does not support mercy killing.
12. The worst tragedy in life is to live without dignity.
13. People often make "living wills" stating that they should be allowed to die naturally.
14. Years ago, people seldom spoke openly about suicide; now there are organizations that openly advocate it.
15. A very common form of mercy killing occurs when parents and doctors agree not to give disabled newborn children needed medical attention, eventually causing their deaths.

16. All life has dignity and mercy killing threatens that dignity.
17. Society pressures its members to look "normal," and mercy killing legalizes the rejection of the "abnormal."

E X E R C I S E   2   Writing the Persuasive Essay

Choose one of the following ten topics and write an essay of at least five paragraphs. Use the five points discussed on pages 267–68 as a guide for your writing.

1. Write a strong thesis statement.
2. Provide examples for each of your reasons.
3. Use at least one authority to support your thesis.
4. Admit that others have a different point of view.
5. Indicate the results or your predictions in the conclusion.

Essay Topics: Argue for or against one of these issues.

1. Capital punishment
2. Censorship of books or movies
3. Funding cuts to education
4. Continuation of the space program
5. Gambling casinos
6. Stricter immigration laws
7. Prayer in the public schools
8. Single-parent adoption
9. Abortion
10. Tax exemptions for religious organizations

Working Together

This essay, by Carol Marsel of the University of Victoria, is a persuasive essay intended to convince the reader of the need for environmental awareness.

Environmentalism

Our environment includes land, sea, and air, and all things that inhabit them. With the growing populations of the earth, the balance of our ecological system is becoming more and more difficult to maintain. It is this fragile balance of nature I am concerned with, and would like to discuss.

Nature consists of plants and animals, and their relationships with people. Plants and animals, when free from interference by people, seem to have a well-balanced interdependence. Animals that graze on plants fertilize the soil with their waste products, as well as their bodies, when they die. In a sense, they feed one another. In this manner, both survive and contribute to each's life cycle. Too little plant life will result in too little food for the animals, which, in turn, results in fewer animals surviving and, eventually, less stress on plants. This then allows the plants to replenish their numbers and once again become abundant.

Natural disasters and diseases account for significant upsets in the ecosystem. Such infestations by pine bark beetles and spruce budworms can take a tremendous toll on trees. Forest fires can alter the habitat so greatly that it takes several decades for growth to resume. These occurrences are part of nature and contribute to the way in which our environment is balanced or unbalanced.

The more complex component of the ecological system is the human race, and there are three ways in which it interacts with nature. The first is people living. We need air to breathe, food to eat, clothing to wear, and shelter to keep us warm. These are necessities. Other activities, such as driving cars, may be desirable, but not essential. Just to maintain our biological functions is complex. We must find ways to dispose of garbage and sewage. Environmentalists are exploring the ways in which we can do this, without harming the components of nature. Disposing of garbage in large cities, such as Vancouver, poses a difficult problem. Because of the tremendous amount of waste accumulated, its citizens must find alternate areas in which to place its garbage. Many citizens of Cache Creek are not at all pleased that their town has been chosen as a dumping site for Vancouver's garbage. Vancouver long ago ran out of places to bury its waste. Burning of most garbage is no longer acceptable, because we are now discovering that harmful chemicals and other pollutants are often released into the atmosphere.

Sewage disposal is also becoming more difficult. Just recently, Victoria's newspaper was filled with pre-election promises by political candidates who vowed to look into better sewage treatment systems. Raw sewage being pumped out to sea, which is current practice in many ports like Victoria, has contributed to an upset in the balance of the oceanic ecosystem. In addition to the harmful effects the raw sewage has on aquatic life, the temperature of the ocean has been affected, and the inclusion of various chemicals and nutrients has altered the living conditions on the ocean floor.

The second way in which people interact with the environment is in how we earn our living. To have money to buy the things we need to survive, we eke out our livelihood by performing a variety of tasks. When we thoughtlessly perform our jobs, disregarding the environment around us, we often change drastically, or even destroy, elements in nature. A logger who clear-cuts large tracts of land, leaving it barren, can damage the area so that the soil may be irreversibly depleted, leaving it vulnerable to erosion. Valuable nutrients are carried away, leaving the soil unable to support plant life. Devoid of plants, the area does not attract animals which may carry seeds in their excrement. The cycle continues until the land will no longer support plants or animals. People who practise these same irresponsible habits in mining harm the ecosystem in much the same way. Thousands of hectares of land are gouged away, leaving gaping holes and mounds of unproductive rock. Environmentalists focus their attention on problems such as these.

Factories and industrial firms are often not aware of, or not concerned with, the disposal of their wastes. Some are buried. Some are stockpiled, waiting for a better place to be stored. More often than not, we find that harmful toxins have escaped into the soil from these storage systems. Many production methods in factories result in the release of harmful air pollutants, which have contributed to the breakdown of our protective ozone layer and effected a "green-house," or warming tendency. This heating of the earth will have a great impact on ports and shorelines as some of the ice caps melt and the oceans rise. The warming alone will alter the growing season of crops, like apples, for example, which need a short cold spell at the end of their growth to produce crisp, red fruit. Concern about these changes is environmentalism.

The third manner in which people co-exist with nature is what we do for recreation. We hike, ski, bike, and ride through the woods. In carrying out our activities, we do not always consider the needs of nature. We ride our snow machines over the dens of sleeping bears, often disturbing their hibernation, sometimes causing premature birth of cubs or aborted fetuses. We build ski tows and sky trains high into the realm of birds who are unused to the noise and intrusion. We thoughtlessly drive our all-terrain vehicles through previously inaccessible destinations, to disturb and disrupt the quietude of elk, deer, and grizzly bear. Examining how we play is also environmentalism.

There is nothing that does not contribute to the balance of our ecological system. Nothing we do is not involved with the way the world turns. What we eat, where we sleep, how we play, and how we work, all contribute to the operation of our planet. Eating, playing, and working in greater and greater numbers affects the earth more quickly, and in greater ways, but all we do, in some small way, touches our environment. If there are too many of us, and we breathe too much air, the system will cease to support us. If we grow too much of one crop, we deplete the soil of one set of nutrients, eventually affecting all other growing systems. If we release too much of one chemical, from our factories, into the air, we upset the balance in the atmosphere. There is nothing that we do, nothing that we eat or breathe, that does not contribute to the state of our planet, and therefore the need for environmentalism.

The class should divide into groups and read the essay looking for the following points:

1. Does the thesis statement reveal the author's position on the subject she is going to write about?
2. How does the author reinforce her thesis statement?
3. Does the author use any authorities to reinforce her position?
4. Are any objections to the author's position pointed out and dealt with in the essay?
5. Does the author convince you that her position on the matter of environmentalism is the right one? Why or why not?

Chapter 24
Writing under Pressure

How to Write Well under Pressure

Most people prefer to do their writing when they have the time to develop their subject, but it often happens that you do not have the chance to write and revise as you would like. Sometimes you have to write under pressure. For example, you may be given a last-minute assignment that must be done right away, or what is even more likely, you have to produce an in-class written examination for a course you are taking.

No matter what the circumstances are, you want to be able to do the best writing you can with the time you are given. For example, if you are given an essay question for a final examination in a course, your first step should *not* be to begin writing. Instead, you should take a few moments to analyze the question you have been given. What does the question require you to do? Is there more than one part to the question? Does the professor want you to *define* a term or *compare* two historical figures or *narrate* the story of your search for the right part-time job? Furthermore, how many points is the question worth? How much time do you have to spend on the question?

Study the following sample essay question to determine exactly what is being asked for:

Describe the rise of the feminist movement in the 1960s in Canada. Be specific.

If this were one of five short essay questions on a final examination, the following answer would probably be adequate.

The late 1960s saw, in Canada as throughout the Western world, the emergence of a new women's movement. This new feminism rejected all limits to the equality of women's rights and showed that equality in daily life could not be obtained through simple legal, political, or institutional modifications. Discovering that "sisterhood is powerful," women from Vancouver to Halifax began forming groups. The Vancouver Women's Caucus was organized in 1968. The Montreal Women's Liberation Movement was founded in 1969, and the Front de libération des femmes du Québec published a feminist manifesto in 1970. At first, some were consciousness-raising groups, but others quickly turned to concrete action, providing abortion services, health centres, militant theatre, day care, shelters for battered women, and rape crisis centres, and they began agitating for equal pay. By the end of the 1960s, Canada had begun to adjust to the rebirth of a major social movement.

Strategies for Answering Timed In-class Essay Questions

1. Read the question again. How many points is it worth? Decide how much time you should spend answering it.
2. What is the method of development asked for?
3. From key words in the question, compose your thesis statement.
4. Answer the question using several specific details (include names and dates of important facts).
5. Check the question again to be sure all parts of the question have been answered. (A question can have more than one part.)

Frequently Used Terms in Essay Questions

There are five popular methods of developing an answer to an essay question: definition, comparison or contrast, narration, summary, and discussion. The following terms used in essay questions will tell you which method the instructor is asking for.

Define: A definition is the precise meaning of a word or term. When you define something in an essay, you usually write an *extended definition*, in which you select an appropriate example or examples to illustrate the meaning of a term.

Compare or Contrast: When you *compare* two items, you point out the similarities between them. When you *contrast* two items, you point out the differences. Sometimes you may find yourself using both comparison and contrast in an essay.

Narrate: To *narrate* is to tell a story by carefully using a sequence of events. The events are usually (but not always) given in chronological order.

Summarize: When you *summarize*, you supply the main ideas of a longer piece of writing. A summary, as described in the *Harbrace College Handbook*, is a concise restatement, shorter than the source. When you summarize or paraphrase, avoid not only copying the actual words but also imitating the writer's style or sentence structure. Restate in your own words what has been stated previously.

Discuss: This is a general term that encourages you to analyze a subject at length. Inviting students to *discuss* some aspect of a topic is a widely used method of asking examination questions.

Of course, answering an essay question correctly depends largely on the work you have done preparing for the test. To study for an essay exam, you should try to anticipate questions the teacher is likely to ask. Then prepare the information you need to have in order to answer these questions. Unlike the multiple-choice or true/false test, the essay examination requires you to have absorbed the material so well that you can give it back in your own words.

EXERCISE 1   Methods of Development

Each of the following college essay questions deals with the topic of computers. Use the preceding list of frequently used terms to help you decide which method of development is being called for in each case.

1. Tell the story of the first time you encountered a computer. Did you first see a computer at school, at work, or in a friend's home? What was your reaction to this new technology? What did you learn about computers at this first encounter?

   Method of development: _____

2. Point out the similarities and differences between computer use in the home and at school. In how many ways are these uses similar? In how many ways are they different?

   Method of development: _____

3. Analyze the present role of computers in society.

   Method of development: _____

4. List and explain the uses of computers in school, at work, and at home.

   Method of development: _____

5. Write a condensed account of the history of computers, from the time they were invented up to the present day.

   Method of development: _____

EXERCISE 2   Methods of Development/Parts of a Question

Each of the following is an example of an essay question. In the spaces provided after each question indicate (a) what method of development (definition, comparison or contrast, narration, summary, or discussion) is being called for, and (b) how many parts there are to the question. This indicates how many parts there will be in your answer. The first question is done for you.

1. What does the term *sociology* mean? Include in your answer at least four different meanings the term *sociology* has had since this area of study began.

   Method of development: definition

   How many parts to the question: four

2. Compare the reasons Canada entered the Korean War with the reasons it
   entered World War II.

   Method of development: _____

   How many parts to the question: _____

   _____

3. Trace the history of our knowledge of the planet Jupiter from the time it was first
   discovered until the present day. Include in your answer at least one nineteenth-
   century discovery and three of the most recent discoveries that have been made
   about Jupiter through the use of crewless space vehicles sent near that planet.

   Method of development: _____

   How many parts to the question: _____

   _____

4. Contrast baseball and soccer.

   Method of development: _____

   How many parts to the question: _____

   _____

5. Explain the three effects of high temperatures on space vehicles as they re-enter
   the earth's atmosphere.

   Method of development: _____

   How many parts to the question: _____

   _____

6. What was the complete process of building the transcontinental railway? Include
   in your answer six different aspects of the construction, from laying the rails
   across the Canadian Shield to the effects of the Riel Rebellion.

   Method of development: _____

   How many parts to the question: _____

   _____

7. Trace the history of the English language from its beginnings to the present day.
   Divide the history of the language into at least three different parts, using Old
   English, Middle English, and Modern English as your main divisions.

Method of development: _____

How many parts to the question: _____

_____

8. Discuss the events that led up to World War I. Be sure to include both the political and social problems of the time that directly and indirectly led to the war.

Method of development: _____

How many parts to the question: _____

_____

9. Summarize the four theories that have been proposed as to why dinosaurs became extinct 65 million years ago.

Method of development: _____

How many parts to the question: _____

_____

10. Define the term *monarchy* and discuss the relevance or irrelevance of this form of government in today's world.

Method of development: _____

How many parts to the question: _____

_____

Using the Thesis Statement in Essay Questions

One of the most effective ways to begin an essay answer is to write a thesis statement. Your thesis statement should include the important parts of the question and should also give a clear indication of the approach you intend to take in your answer. Writing your opening sentence in this way gives you a real advantage: as your professor begins to read your work, it is clear *what* you are going to write about and *how* you are going to treat your subject.

For example, suppose you were going to write an essay on the following topic:

A woman prime minister could handle the demands of the most stressful job in the country.

An effective way to begin would be to write the following thesis sentence:

I agree that a woman prime minister could handle the demands of the most stressful job in the country.

The reader would then know that this was the topic you had chosen and would also know how you intended to approach this topic.

E X E R C I S E   3   **Writing Thesis Statements**

Rewrite each of the following essay questions in thesis statement form. Read each question carefully and underline the important words or phrases in it. Then decide on the approach you would take in answering that question. An example has been done for you.

> ***Essay question:*** How does one learn another language?
>
> ***Thesis statement:*** The process of learning another language is complicated but usually follows four distinct stages.

1. Essay question: Discuss the effects of raising the legal driving age to eighteen.

   Thesis statement: _____

   _____

   _____

2. Essay question: What are the effects of TV violence on children?

   Thesis statement: _____

   _____

   _____

3. Essay question: What is the value of being able to speak two languages in Canada?

   Thesis statement: _____

   _____

   _____

4. Essay question: What are three reasons why schools should spend less time on optional subjects and more time on the basics such as English and mathematics?

   Thesis statement: _____

   _____

   _____

5. Essay question: Is it harmful or beneficial to adopt a child from one culture and raise that child in another culture?

   Thesis statement: _____

   _____

   _____

6. Essay question: What factors should a college consider when judging the merits of a particular student for admission?

Thesis statement: _____

_____

_____

7. Essay question: In what ways can the government prevent people from smoking in public?

   Thesis statement: _____

   _____

   _____

8. Essay question: Trace the various methods by which people can overcome boredom.

   Thesis statement: _____

   _____

   _____

9. Essay question: Discuss the quotation "One picture is worth a thousand words."

   Thesis statement: _____

   _____

   _____

10. Essay question: Are some forms of advertising harmful, and if so, should harmful advertising be banned?

    Thesis statement: _____

    _____

    _____

Working Together

The following passage on the consequences of the shift of human society from nomadic to agricultural is taken from *Biology*, by Helena Curtis:

> Whatever its causes, the change to agriculture had profound consequences. Populations were no longer nomadic. Thus they could store food not only in silos and granaries, but in the form of domesticated animals. In addition to food stores, other possessions could be accumulated to an extent far beyond that previously possible. Even land could be owned and accumulated and passed on by inheritance. Thus the world became divided into semipermanent groups of haves and have-nots, as it is today.

Because the efforts of a few could produce enough food for everyone, the communities became diversified. People became tradesmen, artisans, bankers, scholars, poets, all the rich mixture of which a modern community is composed. And these people could live much more densely than ever before. For hunting and food-gathering economies, 2 square miles, on the average, are required to provide enough for one family to eat.

One immediate and direct consequence of the agricultural revolution was an increase in populations. A striking characteristic of hunting groups is that they vigorously limit their numbers. A woman on the move cannot carry more than one infant along with her household baggage, minimal though that may be. When simple means of birth control — often just abstention — are not effective, she resorts to abortion or, more probably, infanticide. In addition, there is a high natural mortality, particularly among the very young, the very old, the ill, the disabled, and women at childbirth. As a result, populations dependent on hunting tend to remain small.

1. After you have studied the selection, construct an essay question that a professor in a biology or anthropology course could ask as part of a mid-term or final examination. At the same time, your present instructor could also make up a question based on the selection. When everyone has finished, your instructor could read his or her question first. Is it the question you had expected? How many students in the class came close to the instructor's choice of question?

2. After the instructor's question and the student's questions have been discussed, use the following checklist to analyze each question.
   a. Does the question seem to be fair?
      (Some questions might be too vague or too general to really be a test of what the student has learned.)
   b. How many parts does the question have?
   c. Does the question call for a specific method of development (for example, definition and analysis)?
   d. What are the key terms that should be used in the answer?
   e. What would be an effective opening sentence for the answer?

PART IV

Readings

Good Manners

Carol Shields

1   The stern, peremptory social arbiter, Georgia Willow, has been overseeing Canadian manners for thirty-five years. She did it in Montreal during the tricky fifties and she did it in the unsettled sixties. In the seventies she operated underground, so to speak, from a converted Rosedale garage, tutoring the shy wives of Japanese executives and diplomats. In the eighties she came into her own; manners were rediscovered, particularly in the West where Mrs. Willow has relocated.

2   Promptly at three-thirty each Tuesday and Thursday, neatly dressed in a well-pressed navy Evan-Picone slub silk suit, cream blouse, and muted scarf, Georgia Willow meets her small class in the reception area of the MacDonald Hotel and ushers them into the long, airy tearoom — called, for some reason, Gophers — where a ceremonial spread has been ordered.

3   Food and drink almost always accompany Mrs. Willow's lectures. It is purely a matter of simulation since, wherever half a dozen people gather, there is sure to be a tray of sandwiches to trip them up. According to Mrs. Willow, food and food implements are responsible for fifty per cent of social unease. The classic olive pit question. The persisting problem of forks, cocktail picks, and coffee spoons. The more recent cherry-tomato dilemma. Potato skins, eat them or leave them? Saucers, the lack of. The challenge of the lobster. The table napkin quandary. Removing parsley from between the teeth. On and on.

4   There are also sessions devoted to hand-shaking, door-opening and rules regarding the wearing and nonwearing of gloves. And a concluding series of seminars on the all-important *langue de la politesse*, starting with the discourse of gesture, and moving on quickly to the correct phrase for the right moment, delivered with spiritual amplitude or imprecation or possibly something in between. Appropriateness is all, says Georgia Willow.

5   Our *doyenne* of good manners takes these problems one by one. She demonstrates and describes and explains the acceptable alternatives. She's excellent on fine points, she respects fine points. But always it's the philosophy *behind* good manners that she emphasizes.

6   Never forget, she tells her audience, what manners are *for*. Manners are the lubricant that eases our passage through life. Manners are the means by which we deflect evil. Manners are the first-aid kit we carry out on to the battlefield. Manners are the ceremonial silver tongs with which we help ourselves to life's most alluring moments.

7   She says these things to a circle of puzzled faces. Some of those present take notes, others yawn; all find it difficult to deal with Mrs. Willow's more exuberant abstractions. As a sensitive person, she understands this perfectly well; she sympathizes and, if she were less well-mannered, would illustrate her philosophy with personal anecdotes culled from her own experience. Like everyone else's, her life has been filled with success and failure, with ardor and the lack of ardor, but she

is not one of those who spends her time unpicking the past, blaming and project-ing and drawing ill-bred conclusions or dragging out pieces of bloodied vision or shame. She keeps her lips sealed about personal matters and advises her clients to do the same. Nevertheless, certain of her experiences refuse to dissolve. They're still on center stage, so to speak, frozen tableaux waiting behind a thickish curtain.

8   Only very occasionally do they press their way forward and demand to be heard. She is ten years old. It is an hour before dusk on a summer evening. The motionless violet air has the same density and permanence as a word she keeps trip-ping over in story books, usually on the last page, the word *forever*. She intuitively, happily, believes at this moment that she will be locked forever into the simplicity of the blurred summer night, forever throwing a rubber ball against the forever side of her house and disturbing her mother with the sound of childish chanting. It is impossible for her to know that the adult world will someday, and soon, carry her away, reject her thesis on the *Chanson de Roland* and the particular kind of dated beauty her features possess; that she will be the protagonist of an extremely unpleasant divorce case and, in the end, be forced to abandon a studio apartment on the twenty-fourth floor of an apartment building in a city two thousand miles from the site of this small wooden house; that she will feel in her sixtieth year as tired and worn down as the sagging board fence surrounding the house where she lives as a child, a fence that simultaneously protects and taunts her ten-year-old self.

9   On the other side of the fence is old Mr. Manfred, sharpening his lawn-mower. She puts down her ball and watches him cautiously, his round back, his chin full of gray teeth, the cloud of white hair resting so lazily on top of his head, and the wayward, unquenchable dullness of his eyes. Twice in the past he has offered her peppermints, and twice, mindful of her mother's warnings, she has refused. "No, thank you," she said each time. But it had been painful for her, saying no. She had felt no answering sense of virtue, only the hope that he might offer again.

10   Tonight Mr. Manfred walks over to the fence and tells her he has a secret. He whispers it into her ear. This secret has a devious shape: grotesque flapping ears and a loose drooling mouth. Mr. Manfred's words seem ghosted by the scent of the oil can he holds in his right hand. In his left hand, in the folds of his cotton work pants, he grasps a tube of pink snouty dampish flesh. What he whispers is formlessly narrative and involves the familiar daylight objects of underwear and fingers and the reward of peppermint candy.

11   But then he draws back suddenly as though stung by a wasp. The oil can rolls and rolls and rolls on the ground. He knows, and Georgia, aged ten, knows that something inadmissible has been said, something that cannot be withdrawn. Or can it? A dangerous proposition has been placed in her hand. It burns and shines. She wants to hand it back quickly, get rid of it somehow, but etiquette demands that she first translate it into something bearable.

12   The only other language she knows is incomprehension, and luckily she's been taught the apt phrase. "I beg your pardon?" she says to Mr. Manfred. Her face does a courteous twist, enterprising, meek, placatory, and masked with power, allowing Mr. Manfred time to sink back into the lavender twilight of the uncut grass. "I'm afraid I didn't quite hear. . . ."

[. . .]

13   Later, twenty-three years old, she is on a train, the Super Continental, traveling eastward. She has a window seat, and sunlight gathers around the crown of her hair. She knows how she must look, with her thin clever mouth and F. Scott Fitzgerald eyes.

14   "I can't resist introducing myself," a man says.

15   "Pardon?" She is clearly flustered. He has a beautiful face, carved cheeks, crisp gray hair curling at the forehead.

16   "The book," he points. "The book you're reading. It looks very interesting."

17   "Ah," she says.

18   Two days later they are in bed together, a hotel room, and she reflects on the fact that she has not finished the book, that she doesn't care if she ever does, for how can a book about love compare with what she now knows.

19   "I'm sorry," he says then. "I hadn't realized I was the first."

20   "Oh, but you're not," she cries.

21   This curious lie can only be accounted for by a wish to keep his love. But it turns out she has never had it, not for one minute, not love as she imagines it.

22   "I should have made things clear to you at once," he says. How was he to know she would mistake a random disruption for lasting attachment? He is decent enough to feel ashamed. He only wanted. He never intended. He has no business. If only she.

23   She seems to hear cloth ripping behind her eyes. The syntax of culpability — he's drowning in it, and trying to drown her too. She watches him closely, and the sight of his touching, disloyal mouth restores her composure. Courtesy demands that she rescue him and save herself at the same time. This isn't shrewdness talking, this is good manners, and there is nothing more economical, she believes, than the language of good manners. It costs nothing, it's portable, easy to handle, malleable, yet pre-formed. Two words are all that are required, and she pronounces them slippingly, like musical notes. "Forgive me," she says.

24   There. It's said. Was that so hard?

25   There is a certain thing we must all have, as Georgia Willow has learned in the course of her long life. We may be bankrupt, enfeebled, ill or depraved, but we must have our good stories, our moments of vividness. We keep our door closed, yes, and move among our scratched furniture, old photographs, calendars and keys, ticket stubs, pencil ends and lacquered trays, but in the end we'll wither away unless we have a little human attention.

26   But no one seems to want to give it away these days, not to Georgia Willow. It seems she is obliged to ask even for the unpunctual treats of human warmth. A certain amount of joyless groping is required and even then it's hard to get enough. It is especially painful for someone who, after all, is a personage in her country. She has her pride, her reputation — and a scattering of small bruise-colored spots on the back of her long thin hands. It makes you shudder to think what she must have to do, what she has to say, how she is obliged to open her mouth and say *please.*

27   Please is a mean word. A word in leg irons. She doesn't say it often. Her pleases and thank-yous are performed in soft-focus, as they like to say in the cinema world. It has nothing to do with love, but you can imagine how it is for her, having to ask and then having to be grateful. It's too bad. Good manners had such a happy childhood, but then things got complicated. The weave of complication has brought Georgia Willow up against those she would not care to meet again, not in broad daylight anyway, and others who have extracted far more than poor Mr. Manfred at the garden fence ever dreamed of. Good manners are not always nice, not nice at all, although Mrs. Willow has a way of banishing the hard outlines of time and place, and of course she would never think of naming names. Discretion is one of her tenets. She does a special Monday afternoon series on discretion in which she enjoins others to avoid personal inquiries and pointed judgments.

28   "Courtesy," concludes Georgia Willow, "is like the golden coin in the princess's silk purse. Every time it's spent worthily, another appears in its place."

29   Almost everyone agrees with her. However much they look into her eyes and think she is uttering mere niceties, they are sworn to that ultimate courtesy which is to believe what people want us to believe. And thus, when Mrs. Willow bids them good afternoon, they courteously rise to their feet. "Good afternoon," they smile back, shaking hands carefully, and postponing their slow, rhythmic applause and the smashing of the teacups.

Questions for Discussion or Writing

1. What are the characteristics of the narrative that are found in this story?

2. What is the thesis of this narrative? Is it an implied thesis or a stated thesis?

3. How does the author use description to help the reader share the author's experiences? Give examples.

4. How does the author's use of sentence variety create emphasis and clarity?

5. Is the conclusion to this story satisfactory? Why or why not?

*   *   *   *   *

As It Was in the Beginning

Pauline Johnson

1   They account for it by the fact that I am a Redskin, but I am something else, too — I am a woman.

2   I remember the first time I saw him. He came up the trail with some Hudson's Bay trappers, and they stopped at the door of my father's tepee. He seemed even

then, fourteen years ago, an old man; his hair seemed just as thin and white, his hands just as trembling and fleshless as they were a month since, when I saw him for what I pray his God is the last time.

3   My father sat in the tepee, polishing buffalo horns and smoking; my mother, wrapped in her blanket, crouched over her quill-work, on the buffalo-skin at his side; I was lounging at the doorway, idling, watching, as I always watched, the thin, distant line of sky and prairie, wondering, as I always wondered, what lay beyond it. Then he came, this gentle old man with his white hair and thin, pale face. He wore a long black coat, which I now know was the sign of his office, and he carried a black leather-covered book, which, in all the years I have known him, I have never seen him without.

4   The trappers explained to my father who he was, the Great Teacher, the heart's Medicine Man, the "Blackcoat" we had heard of, who brought peace where there was war, and the magic of whose black book brought greater things than all the Happy Hunting Grounds of our ancestors.

5   He told us many things that day, for he could speak the Cree tongue, and my father listened, and listened, and when at last they left us, my father said for him to come and sit within the tepee again.

6   He came, all the time he came, and my father welcomed him, but my mother always sat in silence at work with the quills; my mother never liked the Great "Blackcoat."

7   His stories fascinated me. I used to listen intently to the tale of the strange new place he called "heaven," of the gold crown, of the white dress, of the great music; and then he would tell of that other strange place — hell. My father and I hated it; we feared it, we dreamt of it, we trembled at it. Oh, if the "Blackcoat" would only cease to talk of it! Now I know he saw the effect upon us, and he used it as a whip to lash us into his new religion, but even then my mother must have known, for each time he left the tepee she would watch him going slowly away across the prairie; then when he disappeared in the far horizon she would laugh scornfully, and say:

8   "If the white man made this Blackcoat's hell, let him go to it. It is for the man who found it first. No hell for Indians, just Happy Hunting Grounds. Blackcoat can't scare me."

9   And then, after weeks had passed, one day as he stood at the tepee door he laid his white, old hand on my head and said to my father: "Give me this little girl, chief. Let me take her to the mission school; let me keep her, and teach her of the great God and His eternal heaven. She will grow to be a noble woman, and return perhaps to bring her people to the Christ."

10   My mother's eyes snapped. "No," she said. It was the first word she ever spoke to the "Blackcoat." My father sat and smoked. At the end of a half-hour he said:

11   "I am an old man, Blackcoat. I shall not leave the God of my fathers. I like not your strange God's ways — all of them. I like not His two new places for me when I am dead. Take the child, Blackcoat, and save her from hell."

[. . .]

12   The first grief of my life was when we reached the mission. They took my buck-skin dress off, saying I was now a little Christian girl and must dress like all the white people at the mission. Oh, how I hated that stiff new calico dress and those leather shoes! But, as little as I was, I said nothing, only thought of the time when I should be grown, and do as my mother did, and wear the buckskins and the blanket.

13   My next serious grief was when I began to speak the English, that they forbade me to use any Cree words whatsoever. The rule of the school was that any child heard using its native tongue must get a slight punishment. I never understood it, I cannot understand it now, why the use of my dear Cree tongue could be a matter for correction or an action deserving punishment.

14   She was strict, the matron of the school, but only justly so, for she had a heart and a face like her brother's, the "Blackcoat." I had long since ceased to call him that. The trappers at the post called him "St. Paul," because, they told me, of his self-sacrificing life, his kindly deeds, his rarely beautiful old face; so I, too, called him "St. Paul," though oftener "Father Paul," though he never liked the latter title, for he was a Protestant. But as I was his pet, his darling of the whole school, he let me speak of him as I would, knowing it was but my heart speaking in love. His sister was a widow, and mother to a laughing yellow-haired little boy of about my age, who was my constant playmate and who taught me much of English in his own childish way. I used to be fond of this child, just as I was fond of his mother and of his uncle, my "Father Paul," but as my girlhood passed away, as womanhood came upon me, I got strangely wearied of them all; I longed, oh, God, how I longed for the old wild life! It came with my womanhood, with my years.

15   What mattered it to me now that they had taught me all their ways? — their tricks of dress, their reading, their writing, their books. What mattered it that "Father Paul" loved me, that the traders at the post called me pretty, that I was a pet of all, from the factor to the poorest trapper in the service? I wanted my own people, my own old life, my blood called out for it, but they always said I must not return to my father's tepee. I heard them talk amongst themselves of keeping me away from pagan influences; they told each other that if I returned to the prairies, the tepees, I would degenerate, slip back to paganism, as other girls had done; marry, perhaps, with a pagan — and all their years of labor and teaching would be lost.

16   I said nothing, but I waited, And then one night the feeling overcame me. I was in the Hudson's Bay store when an Indian came in from the north with a large pack of buckskin. As they unrolled it a dash of its insinuating odor filled the store. I went over and leaned above the skins a second, then buried my face in them, swallowing, drinking the fragrance of them, that went to my head like wine. Oh, the wild wonder of that wood-smoked tan, the subtlety of it, the untamed smell of it! I drank it into my lungs, my innermost being was saturated with it, till my mind reeled and my heart seemed twisted with a physical agony. My childhood recollections rushed upon me, devoured me. I left the store in a strange, calm frenzy, and going rapidly to the mission house I confronted my

Father Paul and demanded to be allowed to go "home," if only for a day. He received the request with the same refusal and the same gentle sigh that I had too often been greeted with, but *this* time the desire, the smoke-tan, the heart-ache, never lessened.

17   Night after night I would steal away by myself and go to the border of the village to watch the sun set in the foothills, to gaze at the far line of sky and prairie, to long and long for my father's lodge. And Laurence — always Laurence — my fair-haired, laughing, child playmate, would come calling and calling for me: "Esther, where are you? We miss you: come in, Esther, come in with me." And if I did not turn at once to him and follow, he would come and place his strong hands on my shoulders and laugh into my eyes and say, "Truant, truant, Esther; can't *we* make you happy?"

18   My old child playmate had vanished years ago. He was a tall, slender young man now, handsome as a young chief, but with laughing blue eyes, and always those yellow curls about his temples. He was my solace in my half-exile, my comrade, my brother, until one night it was, "Esther, Esther, can't *I* make you happy?"

19   I did not answer him; only looked out across the plains and thought of the tepees. He came close, close. He locked his arms about me, and with my face pressed up to his throat he stood silent. I felt the blood from my heart sweep to my very finger-tips. I loved him. Oh God, how I loved him! In a wild, blind instant it all came, just because he held me so and was whispering brokenly, "Don't leave me, don't leave me, Esther; *my* Esther, my child-love, my playmate, my girl-comrade, my little Cree sweetheart, will you go away to your people, or stay, stay for me, for my arms, as I have you now?"

20   No more, no more the tepees; no more the wild stretch of prairie, the intoxicating fragrance of the smoke-tanned buckskin; no more the bed of buffalo hide, the soft, silent moccasin; no more the dark faces of my people, the dulcet cadence of the sweet Cree tongue — only this man, this fair, proud, tender man who held me in his arms, in his heart. My soul prayed to his great white God, in that moment, that He let me have only this.

[. . .]

21   It was twilight when we re-entered the mission gate. We were both excited, feverish. Father Paul was reading evening papers in the large room beyond the hallway; his soft, saint-like voice stole beyond the doors, like a benediction upon us. I went noiselessly upstairs to my own room and sat there undisturbed for hours.

22   The clock downstairs struck one, startling me from my dreams of happiness, and at the same moment a flash of light attracted me. My room was in an angle of the building, and my window looked almost directly down into those of Father Paul's study, into which at that instant he was entering, carrying a lamp. "Why, Laurence," I heard him exclaim, "what are you doing here? I thought, my boy, you were in bed hours ago."

23   "No, uncle, not in bed, but in dreamland," replied Laurence, arising from the window, where evidently he, too, had spent the night hours as I had done.

24   Father Paul fumbled about for a moment, found his large black book, which for once he seemed to have got separated from, and was turning to leave, when the curious circumstance of Laurence being there at so unusual an hour seemed to strike him anew. "Better go to sleep, my son," he said simply, then added curiously, "Has anything occurred to keep you up?"

25   Then Laurence spoke: "No, uncle, only — only, I'm happy, that's all."

26   Father Paul stood irresolute: Then: "It is —?"

27   "Esther," said Laurence quietly, but he was at the old man's side, his hand was on the bent old shoulder, his eyes proud and appealing.

28   Father Paul set the lamp on the table, but, as usual, one hand held that black book, the great text of his life. His face was paler than I had ever seen it — graver.

29   "Tell of it," he requested.

30   I leaned far out of my window and watched them both. I listened with my very heart, for Laurence was telling him of me, of his love, of the new-found joy of that night.

31   "You have said nothing of marriage to her?" asked Father Paul.

32   "Well — no; but she surely understands that —"

33   "Did you speak of *marriage*?" repeated Father Paul, with a harsh ring in his voice that was new to me.

34   "No, uncle, but —"

35   "Very well, then; very well."

36   There was a brief silence. Laurence stood staring at the old man as though he were a stranger; he watched him push a large chair up to the table, slowly seat himself; then mechanically following his movements, he dropped onto a lounge. The old man's head bent low, but his eyes were bright and strangely fascinating. He began:

37   "Laurence, my boy, your future is the dearest thing to me of all earthly interests. Why, you *can't* marry this girl — no, no, sit, sit until I have finished," he added, with raised voice, as Laurence sprang up, remonstrating. "I have long since decided that you marry well; for instance, the Hudson Bay factor's daughter."

38   Laurence broke into a fresh, rollicking laugh, "What, uncle," he said, "little Ida McIntosh? Marry that little yellow-haired fluff ball, that kitten, that pretty little dolly?"

39   "Stop," said Father Paul. Then, with a low, soft persuasiveness, "She is *white*, Laurence."

40   My lover startled. "Why, uncle, what do you mean?" he faltered.

41   "Only this, my son: poor Esther comes of uncertain blood; would it do for you — the missionary's nephew, and adopted son, you might say — to marry the daughter of a pagan Indian? Her mother is hopelessly uncivilized; her father has a dash of French somewhere — half-breed, you know, my boy, half-breed." Then, with still lower tone and half-shut, crafty eyes, he added: "The blood is a bad, bad mixture, *you* know that; you know, too, that I am very fond of the girl, poor dear Esther. I have tried to separate her from evil pagan influences; she is the daughter of the Church; I want her to have no other parent; but you never can tell what lurks in *a caged animal that has once been wild*. My whole heart is with

the Indian people, my son; my whole heart, my whole life, has been devoted to bringing them to Christ, *but it is a different thing to marry with one of them.*"

42   His small old eyes were riveted on Laurence like a hawk's on a rat. My heart lay like ice in my bosom.

43   Laurence, speechless and white, stared at him breathlessly.

44   "Go away somewhere," the old man was urging, "to Winnipeg, Toronto, Montreal; forget her, then come back to Ida McIntosh. A union of the Church and the Hudson's Bay will mean great things, and may ultimately result in my life's ambition, the civilization of this entire tribe, that we have worked so long to bring to God."

45   I listened, sitting like one frozen. Could those words have been uttered by my venerable teacher, by him whom I revered as I would one of the saints in his own black book? Ah, there was no mistaking it. My white father, my life-long friend who pretended to love me, to care for my happiness, was urging the man I worshipped to forget me, to marry with the factor's daughter — because of what? Of my red skin; my good, old, honest pagan mother; my confiding French-Indian father. In a second all the care, the hollow love he had given me since my childhood, were as things that never existed. I hated that old mission priest as I hated his white man's hell. I hated his long, white hair; I hated his thin, white hands; I hated his body, his soul, his voice, his black book — oh, how I hated the very atmosphere of him!

46   Laurence sat motionless, his face buried in his hands, but the old man continued: "No, no; not the child of that pagan mother; you can't trust her, my son. What would you do with a wife who might any day break from you to return to her prairies and her buckskins? *You can't trust her.*" His eyes grew smaller, more glittering, more fascinating then, and leaning with an odd, secret sort of movement towards Laurence, he almost whispered. "Think of her silent ways, her noiseless step; the girl glides about like an apparition; her quick fingers, her wild longings — I don't know why, but with all my fondness for her, she reminds me sometimes of a strange — *snake.*

47   Laurence shuddered, lifted his face, and said hoarsely: "You're right, uncle; perhaps I'd better not; I'll go away, I'll forget her, and then — well, then — yes, you are right, it *is* a different thing to marry one of them." The old man arose. His feeble fingers still clasped his black book; his soft white hair clung about his forehead like that of an Apostle; his eyes lost their peering, crafty expression; his bent shoulders resumed the dignity of a minister of the living God; he was the picture of what the traders called him — "St. Paul."

48   "Good-night, son," he said.

49   "Good-night, uncle, and thank you for bringing me to myself."

50   They were the last words I ever heard uttered by either that old arch-fiend or his weak, miserable kinsman. Father Paul turned and left the room. I watched his withered hand — the hand I had so often felt resting on my head in holy benediction — clasp the doorknob, turn it slowly then, with bowed head and his pale face rapt in thought, he left the room — left it with the mad venom of my hate pursuing him like the very Evil One he taught me of.

51   What were his years of kindness and care now? What did I care for his God, his heaven, his hell? He had robbed me of my native faith, of my parents, of my people, of this last, this life of love that would have made a great, good woman of me. God! How I hated him!

52   I crept to the closet in my dark little room. I felt for a bundle I had not looked at for years — yes, it was there, the buckskin dress I had worn as a little child when they brought me to the mission. I tucked it under my arm and descended the stairs noiselessly. I would look into the study and speak good-bye to Laurence; then I would —

53   I pushed open the door. He was lying on the couch where a short time previously he had sat, white and speechless, listening to Father Paul. I moved towards him softly. God in heaven, he was already asleep. As I bent over him the fullness of his perfect beauty impressed me for the first time; his slender form, his curving mouth that almost laughed even in sleep, his fair, tossed hair, his smooth, strong-pulsing throat. God! How I loved him!

54   Then there arose the picture of the factor's daughter. I hated her. I hated her baby face, her yellow hair, her whitish skin. "She shall not marry him," my soul said. "I will kill him first — kill his beautiful body, his lying, false heart." Something in my heart seemed to speak; it said over and over again, "Kill him, kill him; she will never have him then. Kill him. It will break Father Paul's heart and blight his life. He has killed the best of you, of your womanhood; kill *his* best, his pride, his hope — his sister's son, his nephew Laurence." But how? How?

55   What had that terrible old man said I was like? A *strange snake*. A snake? The idea wound itself about me like the very coils of a serpent. What was this in the beaded bag of my buckskin dress? this little thing rolled in tan that my mother had given me at parting with the words, "Don't touch much, but sometime maybe you want it!" Oh! I knew well enough what it was — a small flint arrow-head dipped in the venom of some *strange snake*.

56   I knelt beside him and laid my hot lips on his hand. I worshipped him, oh, how, how I worshipped him! Then again the vision of *her* baby face, *her* yellow hair — I scratched his wrist twice with the arrow-tip. A single drop of red blood oozed up; he stirred. I turned the lamp down and slipped out of the room — out of the house.

[. . .]

57   I dreamt nightly of the horrors of the white man's hell. Why did they teach me of it, only to fling me into it?

58   Last night as I crouched beside my mother on the buffalo-hide, Dan Henderson, the trapper, came in to smoke with my father. He said old Father Paul was bowed with grief, that with my disappearance I was suspected, but that there was no proof. Was it not merely a snake bite?

59   They account for it by the fact that I am a Redskin.

60   They seem to have forgotten I am a woman.

Questions for Discussion or Writing

1. What are some of the conflicts between Natives and non-Native societies that are pointed out in this story?

2. How is description used to illustrate the author's point of view?

3. Who is the intended audience of this story?

4. What is the significance of the title of this story?

5. What techniques of description are used in this story?

* * * * *

Modern Opinion: A Hot-air Balloon That's Lost Ballast

Rick Salutin

1   Consider this self-therapy. For a long time I've been obsessed by a kind of media I think of as freestanding opinion: views and judgments expressed with no reasons given, usually in arts coverage. Take a brief review from The Sunday Sun of the film *Strange Days*. "Begins as a brilliant if cynical satire. . . . But the film spins out of control, goes nutzoid, believes its own hype and turns rancid and stupid. . . ." It doesn't tell *why* the writer thinks this. It's just a set of views, so there's nothing you can base your opinion of the opinion on. If it was a real estate ad, you'd have to say, Sorry, but could you tell me something about the *house*. It's typical of what I've come to think of as our Age of Unreason. No explanations, arguments or examples are required: just conclusions. But maybe I'm seeing this kind of writing too negatively. Maybe seeking reasons for opinions is as quaint today as expecting poetry to scan. Maybe it's a, gulp, trend.

2   I say this because you see it edging into spaces where it previously wasn't. Last spring in his column, Globe and Mail editor-in-chief William Thorsell called Toronto's new Metro Hall "an embarrassing post-modern office-building confection tarted up with public-interest doo-dads," in contrast to old City Hall, which is "a handsome and wholly integrated expression of civic virtue." Now I read almost everything Thorsell writes, not because I agree; I rarely do. But because he *always gives his reasons* so you can argue back — except this time. That absence takes the fun out of public discourse; it gives you no evidence to refute, so all you can do is spit more opinions; "It is *not* integrated," etc. The most you get is equal time, but not a sense of give-and-take.

3   Is it spreading? Take a recent Globe piece by Michael Valpy in which he *stated* that CBC TV's local Toronto news stinks compared to the private stations — with no examples. Yet I'd just watched our CTV outlet lead its supper hour with the news that Regis and Kathie Lee had broadcast their show that day from

Niagara Falls. Both these cases concern culture, and maybe it's an area pundits feel doesn't need the kind of evidence required when you talk economic and social issues. Or maybe it's the thin edge of a wedge.

4   If this thing — opinions without reasons — *is* spreading, let me suggest three possible, uh, reasons:

5   1. The end of the Cold War. I'm glad it's over, but at least back then there was debate between different points of view. Since then, it's been as though only one set of ideas — right-wing, neocon, etc. — can explain reality. "Some ideas are just not worth discussing," columnist Andrew Coyne once wrote. With a world view this cocky you don't have to argue your points, you just state them. So, in David Warren's review in Saturday Night of John Ralston Saul's recent books, Warren doesn't so much review Saul as disdain him. When he quotes something ("The early Socrates is a populist; the later an elitist"), he labels it a "gob-stopper," period. You should at least have to explain your contempt: A philosophical tradition running from Harold Laski in the 1920s to I.F. Stone in the 1980s views Socrates as Saul does. This kind of neocon arrogance can slop over from economic or political questions into general attitude.

6   2. Shopping *über alles*. With citizens largely reduced to consumers in our era, shopping becomes the universal model for human activity. So in arts and culture, you no longer search for beauty or truth, what you want is value for money: not crits, but *tips*. This then extends to other areas; the question is only: what are people buying (into) this season?

7   3. Individualism. The notion of individualism in our time doesn't so much elevate heroic individuals as it atomizes everybody, like shoppers lost in a mall. No one connects. So why bother making arguments for people to ponder; we're all too isolated. Just state a preference; others can take it or leave it. This sounds akin to the old cultural relativism, which argued there are no universal values. But that usually applied to groups: primitive peoples see things differently from civilized societies. The new relativism is totally individualized: *chacun à son* shopping cart.

8   I'd like to close optimistically with a case of someone I'd say has already transcended the old mode but replaced it with a new genre: my colleague John Haslett Cuff, who writes on TV in these pages. It would be wrong to see what Cuff does as traditional criticism or reviewing, even if he anachronistically uses those terms; a kind of internal lag is common among trailbreakers. When he "reviews" something, mostly he just reacts. If you ask for a reason, he reacts again. *thirtysomething* was a "milestone" because it was "wonderfully written, superbly acted and uncannily accurate." In other words: I liked this because I liked that because I liked that. What he's really doing is issuing reports on himself. Take last Friday. "Oh no, not another bleak, bleeding-heart portrait. . . . I thought, settling down to watch [*Dangerous Offender*]. . . . But [the show] soon won me over." This isn't a review; it's The Cuff Channel. You tune in each day to see him react to what crosses his screen. Nor is it "personal" journalism — where the writer includes some experiences he had doing the story. With Cuff, you don't have to care about what he's covering, you just have to be interested in *him*. I sus-

pect reading Cuff on the Mideast peace process would be the same experience as reading him on the new sitcoms. Some writers can't interest you no matter how much of themselves they expose. Cuff does, though to tell the truth, I haven't figured out the reason! Yet people I know say they find him compulsively readable, and that includes me.

9   Maybe with the old, well-argued criticism fading, we can at least hope for something exuberant to replace it. Recently, writing on a TVO documentary, Cuff invoked his father, whose "credo" was "Don't complain, don't explain and never show pain." Aha! I thought, is this — "don't explain" — the source of his "reviewing" style? And if it is, is Cuff aware he's revealing it? And if he isn't, is that one source of the fascination in his writing? I could multiply examples, but hell, just turn the page.

10   And yes, I feel better now.

Questions for Discussion or Writing

1. Who is Salutin's audience?

2. What is the author's thesis? Is it stated or implied? At what point in the article does the thesis appear?

3. What are the arguments outlined in this article?

4. What might counter-arguments be to those suggested in Question 3?

5. Is the first paragraph effective? Why or why not?

*   *   *   *   *

Life in the Stopwatch Lane

Amy Willard Cross

1   If time is money, the rates have skyrocketed and you probably can't afford it. North Americans are suffering a dramatic time shortage since demand greatly exceeds supply. In fact, a recent survey revealed that people lost about 10 hours of leisure per week between 1973 and 1987. Maybe you were too busy to notice.

2   Losing that leisure leaves a piddling 16.6 hours to do whatever you want, free of work, dish-washing or car-pooling. In television time, that equals a season of 13 *thirtysomething* episodes, plus $3\frac{1}{2}$ reruns. Hardly enough time to write an autobiography or carry on an affair.

4   How has replacing free time with more billable hours affected society? It has created a new demographic group: the Busy Class — who usurped the Leisure Class. Easy to recognize, members of the Busy Class constantly cry to anyone

listening, "I'm *soooooo* busy." So busy they can't call their mother or find change for a panhandler. Masters of doing two things at once, they eke the most out of time. They dictate while driving, talk while calculating, entertain guests while nursing, watch the news while pumping iron. Even business melts into socializing — people earn their daily bread while they break it.

4   In fact, the Busies must make lots of bread to maintain themselves in the standard of busy-ness to which they've become accustomed. To do that, they need special, expensive stuff. Stuff like call waiting, which lets them talk to two people at once. Stuff like two-faced watches, so they can do business in two time zones at once. Neither frenzied executives nor hurried housewives dare leave the house without their "book" — leather-bound appointment calendars thick as bestsellers. Forget hi-fi's or racing cars, the new talismans of overachievers also work: coffee-makers that brew by alarm; remote-controlled ignitions; or car faxes. Yet, despite all these time-efficient devices, few people have time to spare.

5   That scarcity has changed how we measure time. Now it's being scientifically dissected into smaller and smaller pieces. Thanks to digital clocks, we know when it's 5:30 (and calculate we'll be home in three hours, eight minutes). These days lawyers can reason in $\frac{1}{10}$th of an hour increments; they bill every six minutes. This to-the-minute precision proves time's escalating value.

6   Time was, before the advent of car phones and digital clocks, we scheduled two kinds of time: time off and work hours. Not any more. Just as the Inuit label the infinite varieties of snow, the Busy Class has identified myriad subtleties of free time and named them. Here are some textbook examples of the new faces of time:

7   *Quality time.* For those working against the clock, the quality of time spent with loved ones supposedly compensates for quantity. This handy concept absolves guilt as quickly as rosary counting. So careerist couples dine à deux once a fortnight. Parents bond by reading kids a story after nanny fed and bathed them. When pressed for time, nobody wastes it by fighting about bad breath or unmade beds. People who spend quality time with each other view their relationships through rose-coloured glasses. And knowing they've created perfect personal lives lets the Busy Class work even harder — guilt-free.

8   *Travel time.* With an allowance of 16.6 hours of fun, the Busy Class watches time expenditures carefully. Just like businesses do while making bids, normal people calculate travel time for leisure activities. If two tram rides away, a friendly squash game loses out. One time-efficient woman even formulated a mathematical theorem: fun per mile quotient. Before accepting any social invitation, she adds up travel costs, figures out the time spent laughing, drinking and eating. If the latter exceeds the former, she accepts. It doesn't matter who asks.

9   *Downtime.* Borrowed from the world of heavy equipment and sleek computers, downtime is a professional-sounding word meaning the damn thing broke, wait around until it's fixed. Translated into real life, downtime counts as neither work nor play, but a maddening no-man's land where nothing happens! Like lining up for the ski-lift, or commuting without a car phone, or waiting a while for the mechanic's diagnosis. Beware: people who keep track of their downtime probably indulge in less than 16 hours of leisure.

10   *Family time.* In addition to 60-hour weeks, aerobics and dinner parties, some people make time for their children. When asked to brunch, a young couple will reply, "We're sorry but that's our family time." A variant of quality time, it's Sunday afternoon between lunch and the Disney Hour when nannies frequent Filipino restaurants. In an effort to entertain their children without exposure to sex and violence, the family attends craft fairs, animated matinees or tree-tapping demonstrations. There, they converge with masses of family units spending time alone with the kids. After a noisy, sticky afternoon, parents gladly punch the clock come Monday.

11   *Quiet time.* Overwhelmed by their schedules, some people try to recapture the magic of childhood when they watched clouds for hours on end. Sophisticated grown-ups have rediscovered the quiet time of kindergarten days. They unplug the phone (not the answering machine), clutch a book and try not to think about work. But without teachers to enforce it, quiet doesn't last. The clock ticks too loudly. As a computer fanatic said, after being entertained at 16 megahertz, sitting still to watch a sunset pales by comparison.

12   As it continues to increase in value, time will surely divide into even smaller units. And people will share only the tiniest amounts with each other. Hey, brother, can you spare a minute? Got a second? A nanosecond?

Questions for Discussion or Writing

1. What is being classified in this essay? Give examples.

2. What is the tone of Cross's essay?

3. Do you agree with the author's classification? Does your concept of time agree with the author's opinions? Why or why not?

4. What is the author's thesis? How is this thesis developed throughout the essay?

5. How does Cross conclude the essay? Do you agree with her conclusion? Why or why not?

*   *   *   *   *

A Bowl of Red

Joe Fiorito

1   Chili is the perfect NAFTA food. It was invented in the USA with Mexican ingredients and it throws enough heat to keep a Canadian warm in the winter. It's also cheap, which is an important consideration now that so few of us have jobs.

2   But no one makes chili any more. You hardly ever see it on a restaurant menu, and the only time you see it on TV is during the first ten seconds of some antacid commercial. I hate that. Spicy food doesn't cause heartburn, bad cooking does.

3   If you want chili, you have to make it at home. There are two schools of thought on how to proceed. The main one you're familiar with. Brown some meat, add some onions and green peppers, some tomatoes, beans, cumin and chili powder. This is the usual way.

4   There is another way, recommended by chili-Jesuits who make their chili with meat and chilis, and nothing else. The meat is beef, browned on its own fat. The seasoning is a mix of dried and powdered chilis. There are no tomatoes added. Beans, if you want 'em, are on the side. I've made it both ways. I like it both ways.

5   I do have some advice.

6   Don't use hamburger. Don't pay for someone else to cut your meat. Don't pay for fat and water. Buy the toughest-looking lump of beef you can find. It'll be cheaper than hamburger and it will taste better. Cut it up yourself; cubes if you prefer, or strips, which is how I like it. You think that kind of meat's too tough? Come on. Chili melts the hardest hearts, slow cooking softens the toughest beef.

7   Also, if you're going to use beans, use real beans. Canned ones are mushy, they cost ten times what dry beans cost and they don't taste as good. Be a cowperson and try pinto beans. Or be trendy and use black beans. You can even mix things up — use a combination of red kidney beans and white cannellini beans. Just remember to soak them overnight, and to cook them before you add them to your pot of chili.

8   Secret ingredients? Some people add beer or mustard to a pot of chili. Some people even add celery salt, although I've no idea why. Chili's not a subtle dish, with a dash of this, a splash of that, and a tiny bit of something else.

9   However (you knew there'd be a however!), if you see any of those dried ancho chilis, the ones that are dusty and black and look like chunks of bakelite plastic after a nuclear meltdown, buy them. Take one and crumble it up. Pour boiling water over it and let it steep for a bit while you're browning the meat. Throw the ancho chili and a cup of the soaking liquid into the pot. However you make your chili, adding an ancho will improve it. Anchos are ineffably smoky, with a taste as complex as good chocolate.

10   Serve your chili plain, or with some raw chopped onion or a little grated cheddar on top. No sour cream. That would be effete.

11   I like a bowl of chili once a month, but for some reason the smell of it makes me sad. The last time I made some, we went out while the pot simmered and when we came back the house was warm and filled with the smell of chili and meat and beans. I thought my heart was breaking. And I've no idea why. I'm not sure I want to know. But I will say this. When you make chili, make a big pot. You want leftovers. Chili, like a broken heart, improves with age.

Questions for Discussion or Writing

1. What is the process described by Fiorito in this essay?

2. State the steps in Fiorito's process. Do these steps clearly explain the process? Why or why not?

3. What is the intended readership for this essay?

4. Select some examples of humour in this essay. How is humour used to enhance the thesis of the essay?

5. Do you find the conclusion to this essay effective? Why or why not?

*   *   *   *   *

The Other Family

Himani Bannerji

1   When the little girl came home it was already getting dark. The winter twilight had transformed the sheer blue sky of the day into the colour of steel, on which were etched a few stars, the bare winter trees and the dark wedges of the house tops. A few lit windows cast a faint glow on the snow outside. The mother stood at her window and watched the little hooded figure walking toward the house. The child looked like a shadow, her blue coat blended into the shadows of the evening. This child, her own, how small and insubstantial she seemed, and how alone, walking home through a pavement covered with ice and snow! It felt unreal. So different was this childhood from her own, so far away from the sun, the trees and the peopled streets of her own country! What did I do, she thought, I took her away from her own people and her own language, and now here she comes walking alone, through an alien street in a country named Canada.

2   As she contemplated the solitary, moving figure, her own solitude rushed over her like a tide. She had drifted away from a world that she had lived in and understood, and now she stood here at the same distance from her home as from the homes which she glimpsed while walking past the sparkling clean windows of the sandblasted houses. And now the door bell rang, and here was her daughter scraping the snow off her boots on the door mat.

3   Dinner time was a good time. A time of warmth, of putting hot, steaming food onto the table. A time to chat about the important things of the day, a time to show each other what they had acquired. Sometimes, however, her mother would be absent-minded, worried perhaps about work, unsettled perhaps by letters that had arrived from home, scraping her feelings into a state of rawness.

This was such an evening. She had served herself and her child, started a conversation about their two cats and fallen into a silence after a few minutes.

4   "You aren't listening to me, Mother."

5   The complaining voice got through to her, and she looked at the indignant face demanding attention from the other side of the table. She gathered herself together.

6   "So what did he do, when you gave him dried food?"

7   "Oh, I don't quite remember, I think he scratched the ground near his bowl and left."

8   The child laughed.

9   "That was smart of him! So why don't we buy tinned food for them?"

10   "Maybe we should," she said, and tried to change the topic.

11   "So what did you do in your school today?"

12   "Oh, we drew pictures like we do every day. We never study anything — not like you said you did in your school. We drew a family — our family. Want to see it?"

13   "Sure, and let's go to the living room, OK? This is messy." Scraping of chairs and the lighting of the lamps in the other room. They both made a rush for the most comfortable chair, both reached it at the same time and made a compromise.

14   "How about you sit in my lap? No? OK, sit next to me then and we will squeeze in somehow."

15   There was a remarkable resemblance between the two faces, except that the face of the child had a greater intensity, given by the wide open eyes. She was fine boned, and had black hair framing her face. Right now she was struggling with the contents of her satchel, apparently trying to feel her way to the paintings.

16   "Here it is," she said, producing a piece of paper. "Here's the family!"

17   The mother looked at the picture for a long time. She was very still. Her face had set into an expression of anger and sadness. She was trying very hard not to cry. She didn't want to frighten the child, and yet what she saw made her feel distant from her daughter, as though she was looking at her through the reverse end of a telescope. She couldn't speak at all. The little girl too sat very still, a little recoiled from the body of her mother, as though expecting a blow. Her hands were clenched into fists, but finally it was she who broke the silence.

18   "What happened?" she said. "Don't you like it?"

19   "Listen," said the mother, "this is not your family. I, you and your father are dark-skinned, dark-haired. I don't have a blond wig hidden in my closet, my eyes are black, not blue, and your father's beard is black, not red, and you, do you have a white skin, a button nose with freckles, blue eyes and blond hair tied into a pony tail? You said you drew our family. This is not it, is it?"

20   The child was now feeling distinctly cornered. At first she was startled and frightened by her mother's response, but now she was prepared to be defiant. She had the greatest authority behind her, and she now summoned it to her help.

21   "I drew it from a book," she said, "all our books have this same picture of the family. You can go and see it for yourself. And everyone else drew it too. You can ask our teacher tomorrow. She liked it, so there!"

22   The little girl was clutching at her last straw.

23   "But you? Where are you in this picture?" demanded her mother, by now thoroughly aroused. "Where are we? Is this the family you would like to have? Don't you want us anymore? You want to be a *mem-sahib*, a white girl?"

24   But even as she lashed out these questions the mother regretted them. She could see that she made no sense to the child. She could feel the unfairness of it all. She was sorry that she was putting such a heavy burden on such young shoulders.

25   "First I bring her here," she thought, "and then I try to make her feel guilty for wanting to be the same as the others." But something had taken hold of her this evening. Panic at the thought of losing her child, despair and guilt galvanized her into speech she regretted, and she looked with anger at her only child, who it seemed wanted to be white, who had rejected her dark mother. Someday this child would be ashamed of her, she thought, someday would move out into the world of those others. Someday they would be enemies. Confusing thoughts ran through her head like images on an uncontrollable television screen, in the chaos of which she heard her ultimate justification flung at her by her daughter — they wanted me to draw the family, didn't they? "They" wanted "her" to draw "the family". The way her daughter pronounced the words "they" or "the family" indicated that she knew what she was talking about. The simple pronoun "they" definitely stood for authority, for that uncontrollable yet organized world immediately outside, of which the school was the ultimate expression. It surrounded their own private space. "They" had power, "they" could crush little people like her anytime "they" wanted to, and in "their" world that was the picture of the family. Whether her mother liked it or not, whether she looked like the little girl in it or not, made not one jot of difference. That was, yes, that was the right picture. As these thoughts passed through her mind, her anger ebbed away. Abandoning her fury and distance, the mother bowed her head at the image of this family and burst into sobs.

26   "What will happen to you?" she said. "What did I do to you?"

27   She cried a great deal and said many incoherent things. The little girl was patient, quietly absorbing her mother's change of mood. She had a thoughtful look on her face, and bit her nails from time to time. She did not protest any more, but nor did she cry. After a while her mother took her to bed and tucked her in, and sat in the kitchen with the fearful vision of her daughter always outside of the window of the blond family, never the centre of her own life, always rejecting herself, and her life transformed into a gigantic peep show. She wept very bitterly because she had caused this destruction, and because she had hated her child in her own fear of rejection, and because she had sowed guilt into her mind.

28   When her mother went to bed and closed the door, the child, who had been waiting for long, left the bed. She crossed the corridor on her tiptoes, past the row of shoes, the silent gathering of the overcoats and the mirror with the wavy surface, and went into the washroom. Behind the door was another mirror, of full length, and clear. Deliberately and slowly the child took off the top of her pyjamas and surveyed herself with grave scrutiny. She saw the brownness of her skin, the wide, staring, dark eyes, the black hair now tousled from the pillows, the scar on her nose and the brownish pink of her mouth. She stood a while lost in this act of contemplation, until the sound of soft padded feet neared the door, and a

whiskered face peeped in. She stooped and picked up the cat and walked back to her own room.

[. . .]

29   It was snowing again, and little elves with bright coloured coats and snow in their boots had reappeared in the classroom. When finally the coats were hung under pegs with names and boots neatly stowed away, the little girl approached her teacher. She had her painting from the day before in her hand.

30   "I have brought it back," she said.

31   "Why?" asked her teacher, "don't you like it any more?"

32   The little girl was looking around very intently.

33   "It's not finished yet," she said. "The books I looked at didn't have something. Can I finish it now?"

34   "Go ahead," said the teacher, moving on to get the colours from the cupboard.

35   The little girl was looking at the classroom. It was full of children of all colours, of all kinds of shapes of noses and of different colours of hair. She sat on the floor, placed the incomplete picture on a big piece of newspaper and started to paint. She worked long at it — and with great concentration. Finally it was finished. She went back to her teacher.

36   "It's finished now," she said, "I drew the rest."

37   The teacher reached out for the picture and spread it neatly on a desk. There they were, the blond family arranged in a semicircle with a dip in the middle, but next to them, arranged alike, stood another group — a man, a woman, and a child, but they were dark-skinned, dark-haired, the woman wore clothes from her own country, and the little girl in the middle had a scar on her nose.

38   "Do you like it?"

39   "Who are they?" asked the teacher, though she should have known. But the little girl didn't mind answering this question one bit.

40   "It's the other family," she said.

Questions for Discussion or Writing

1. Does Bannerji use comparison, contrast, or a combination of both in this story? Explain.

2. Does the author use the block method or the point-by-point method in this story? Explain.

3. What are some of the things being compared or contrasted?

4. Does the author make effective use of transitions in this story? Give three examples of transitions.

5. What is the author's thesis? Does the conclusion effectively summarize the author's thesis?

Ancestors — The Genetic Source

David Suzuki

1   My genes can be traced in a direct line to Japan. I am a pure-blooded member of the Japanese race. And whenever I go there, I am always astonished to see the power of that biological connection. In subways in Tokyo, I catch familiar glimpses of the eyes, hairline or smile of my Japanese relatives. Yet when those same people open their mouths to communicate, the vast cultural gulf that separates them from me becomes obvious: English is my language, Shakespeare is my literature, British history is what I learned and Beethoven is my music.

2   For those who believe that in people, just as in animals, genes are the primary determinant of behaviour, a look at second- and third-generation immigrants to Canada gives powerful evidence to the contrary. The overriding influence is environmental. We make a great mistake by associating the inheritance of physical characteristics with far more complex traits of human personality and behaviour.

3   Each time I visit Japan, I am reminded of how Canadian I am and how little the racial connection matters. I first visited Japan in 1968 to attend the International Congress of Genetics in Tokyo. For the first time in my life, I was surrounded by people who all looked like me. While sitting in a train and looking at the reflections in the window, I found that it was hard to pick out my own image in the crowd. I had grown up in a Caucasian society in which I was a minority member. My whole sense of self had developed with that perspective of looking different. All my life I had wanted large eyes and brown hair so I could be like everyone else. Yet on that train, where I did fit in, I didn't like it.

4   On this first visit to Japan I had asked my grandparents to contact relatives and let them know I was coming. I was the first in the Suzuki clan in Canada to visit them. The closest relative on my father's side was my grandmother's younger brother, and we arranged to meet in a seaside resort near his home. He came to my hotel room with two of his daughters. None of them spoke any English, while my Japanese was so primitive as to be useless. In typical Japanese fashion, they showered me with gifts, the most important being a package of what looked like wood carved in the shape of bananas! I had no idea what it was. (Later I learned the package contained dried tuna fish from which slivers are shaved off to flavour soup. This is considered a highly prized gift.) We sat in stiff silence and embarrassment, each of us struggling to dredge up a common word or two to break the quiet. It was excruciating! My great uncle later wrote my grandmother to tell her how painful it had been to sit with her grandson and yet be unable to communicate a word.

5   To people in Japan, all non-Japanese — black, white or yellow — are *gaijin* or foreigners. While *gaijin* is not derogatory, I find that its use is harsh because I sense doors clanging shut on me when I'm called one. The Japanese do have a hell of a time with me because I look like them and can say in perfect Japanese, "I'm a foreigner and I can't speak Japanese." Their reactions are usually complete

incomprehension followed by a sputtering, "What do you mean? You're speaking Japanese." And finally a pejorative, "Oh, a *gaijin*!"

6   Once when my wife, Tara, who is English, and I went to Japan we asked a man at the travel bureau at the airport to book a *ryokan* — a traditional Japanese inn — for us in Tokyo. He found one and booked it for "*Suzuki-san*" and off we went. When we arrived at the inn and I entered the foyer, the owner was confused by my terrible Japanese. When Tara entered, the shock was obvious in his face. Because of my name, they had expected a "real" Japanese. Instead, I was a *gaijin* and the owner told us he wouldn't take us. I was furious and we stomped off to a phone booth where I called the agent at the airport. He was astonished and came all the way into town to plead our case with the innkeeper. But the innkeeper stood firm and denied us a room. Apparently he had accepted *gaijin* in the past with terrible consequences.

7   As an example of the problem, Japanese always take their shoes off when entering a *ryokan* because the straw mats (*tatami*) are quickly frayed. To a Japanese, clomping into a room with shoes on would be comparable to someone entering our homes and spitting on the floor. Similarly, the *ofuro*, or traditional tub, has hot clean water that all bathers use. So one must first enter the bathroom, wash carefully and rinse off *before* entering the tub. Time in the *ofuro* is for relaxing and soaking. Again, Westerners who lather up in the tub are committing a terrible desecration.

8   To many Canadians today, the word "Jap" seems like a natural abbreviation for Japanese. Certainly for newspaper headlines it would seem to make sense. So people are often shocked to see me bristle when they have used the word Jap innocently. To Japanese-Canadians, Jap or Nip (from "*Nippon*") were epithets used generously during the pre-war and war years. They conjure up all of the hatred and bigotry of those times. While a person using the term today may be unaware of its past use, every Japanese-Canadian remembers.

9   The thin thread of Japanese culture that does link me to Japan was spun out of the poverty and desperation of my ancestors. My grandparents came to a Canadian province openly hostile to their strange appearance and different ways. There were severe restrictions on how much and where they could buy property. Their children, who were born and raised in Canada, couldn't vote until 1948 and encountered many barriers to professional training and property ownership. Asians, regardless of birthplace, were third-class citizens. That is the reality of the Japanese-Canadian experience and the historical cultural legacy that came down to the third and fourth generations — to me and my children.

10   The first Japanese immigrants came to Canada to make their fortunes so they could return to Japan as people of wealth. The vast majority was uneducated and impoverished. But in the century spanning my grandparents' births and the present, Japan has leapt from an agrarian society to a technological and economic giant.

11   Now, the Japanese I meet in Japan or as recent immigrants to Canada come with far different cultural roots. Present-day Japanese are highly educated, upper-middle class and proud of their heritage. In Canada they encounter respect, envy

and curiosity in sharp contrast to the hostility and bigotry met by my grand-parents.

12   Japanese immigrants to North America have names that signify the number of generations in the new land (or just as significantly, that count the generational distance *away* from Japan). My grandparents are *Issei*, meaning the first genera-tion in Canada. Most *Issei* never learned more than a rudimentary knowledge of English. *Nisei*, like my parents, are the second generation here and the first native-born group. While growing up they first spoke Japanese in the home and then learned English from playmates and teachers. Before the Second World War, many *Issei* sent their children to be educated in Japan. When they returned to Canada, they were called *Kika-nisei* (or *Kibei* in the United States). Most have remained bilingual, but many of the younger *Nisei* now speak Japanese with difficulty because English is their native tongue. My sisters and I are *Sansei* (third genera-tion); our children are *Yonsei*. These generations, and especially *Yonsei*, are grow-ing up in homes where English is the only spoken language, so they are far more likely to speak school-taught French as their second language than Japanese.

13   Most *Sansei*, like me, do not speak Japanese. To us, the *Issei* are mysteries. They came from a cultural tradition that is a hundred years old. Unlike people in present-day Japan, the *Issei* clung tightly to the culture they remembered and froze that culture into a static museum piece like a relic of the past. Not being able to speak each other's language, *Issei* and *Sansei* were cut off from each other. My parents dutifully visited my grandparents and we children would be trotted out to be lectured at or displayed. These visits were excruciating, because we chil-dren didn't understand the old culture, and didn't have the slightest interest — we were Canadians.

14   My father's mother died in 1978 at the age of ninety-one. She was the last of the *Issei* in our family. The final months of her life, after a left-hemisphere stroke, were spent in that terrible twilight — crippled, still aware, but unable to communi-cate. She lived the terminal months of her life, comprehending but mute, in a ward with Caucasian strangers. For over thirty years I had listened to her psychologically blackmailing my father by warning him of her imminent death. Yet in the end, she hung on long after there was reason to. When she died, I was astonished at my own reaction, a great sense of sadness and regret at the cleavage of my last link with the source of my genes. I had never been able to ask what made her and others of her generation come to Canada, what they felt when they arrived, what their hopes and dreams had been, and whether it was worth it. And I wanted to thank her, to show her that I was grateful that, through them, I was born a Canadian.

Questions for Discussion or Writing

1. What is the definition being discussed in this essay?

2. Suggest two or more rhetorical devices used by Suzuki to reinforce his thesis.

3. What elements of comparison and contrast are found in this essay?

4. What are some of the examples used by Suzuki to reinforce his thesis?

5. Is the conclusion to this essay appropriate and effective? Why or why not?

*   *   *   *   *

You're Thinking of Getting a *What*?

John Gray

1   Nothing evokes that superior shudder, that anal-retentive cluck of civilized disapproval, quite like a tattoo.

2   Find out for yourself: in casual conversation with a relative or colleague mention casually, as though an afterthought, "By the way, I'm thinking of acquiring a tattoo."

3   After the pause you will hear something like "What are you thinking of doing *that* for?", murmured with the inflection of "Why would you want to pull out all your teeth?"

4   Now switch to a neutral topic — a recent movie or the price of real estate. Note the lingering chill in the basement of the conversation, a vaguely sectarian distance, as though you had just declared yourself a Scientologist.

5   To complete the experiment you will need a point of comparison, a control. Try this:

6   Under similar circumstances, turn to a family member or business associate and declare, "I'm thinking of having a surgeon slice the pouches from under my eyes," or "I want to have bags of silicone sewn into my breasts."

7   Quite another response: concern about your self-esteem, perhaps; or reassurance as to the state of your pouches or bustline; be yourself, beauty only skin deep, etc. Even when laced with contempt (vanity, vanity), the reaction will not vibrate with that hum of theological alarm that accompanied the subject of tattooing.

8   While having animal tissue injected into one's lips with a needle the size of a bug sprayer, or artificial hairs poked into one's skull may not receive enthusiastic applause, these urges are treated as symptoms of a mild psychological crisis, endearing evidence of a vulnerable, insecure nature.

9   A tattoo, however, is a threat.

10   Unlike cosmetic-surgery enthusiasts, tattooees seek not to conform to a conventional standard of beauty, but to distance themselves from the rest of us, to join an alien opposition.

11   People either have tattoos or they do not. A tattoo does not win friends among the untattooed majority. A tattoo is no way to get ahead.

12   ## A Dirty Business

Tattooing has always emitted an unsavory aura in Western culture — a whiff of the criminal, the carnival sharp, the fallen woman, and the unhygienic lover.

13   "Tattooed Thracians are not well-born," sniffed Herodotus, the father of history, in the fifth century B.C. (According to Plutarch, Thracian women acquired tattoos as a souvenir of Orpheus, whom they tore to pieces in a fit of pique over his homosexual preferences.)

14   "Well-born" indeed! Today, tattoos are a common fetish of the shave-and-puncture subculture, to go with the radiation-victim haircuts and multiple rings of surgical steel in nostrils and nipples — visual codes, no doubt, for unseemly sexual enthusiasms.

15   According to the media, tattooing is about to go permanently mainstream. Don't believe it. Rumours of imminent respectability have been chasing the tattoo for a century. When respectable people acquire tattoos, and they do, it's not because the practice has become respectable, it's because the recipient wishes inwardly to be *not* respectable, seeking out acts of private outrage that won't adversely affect the career path.

16   It doesn't matter what the tattoo is — a dedication ("I Love Mom"), a motto ("Death Before Dishonor"), a vow ("Property of Vito"), a warning ("Fuck Off"), a death symbol, predatory or mythical animal, flower, patriotic gesture, cartoon character, pinup girl, automotive logo, or primitive tribal scrawl. It's not the subject but the *fact* of a tattoo that contains its stigma and appeal. The tattooee has chosen to have an image indelibly stamped on his or her hide for no apparent reason other than a desire to be different.

17   What's wrong with the rest of us? Who do they think they are?

18   For a quasi-medical practice that entails injecting a foreign substance into a wound, the tattoo parlor is a breathtakingly unregulated industry. Although the city health inspector may call now and then to update the crumbling certificate on the wall, only the tattooist's personal ethic prompts him or her to maintain sanitary premises, wear surgical gloves, use new needles, and learn the medical effects of the various pigments. (It is not unknown for amateurs and semiprofessional "bootleggers" to use house paint!)

19   Given the Darwinian, *laissez-faire* nature of the craft, it's a testament to human probity that there exist any standards at all: that most tattooists turn away clients who are drunk, stoned, warped, or underage; refuse to mark "public skin" (above the neck or below the waist); and usually refuse racist slogans, Nazi emblems, ill-advised vows, and obscenities. Such restraints are voluntary, however, and like most discretionary industrial standards of safety and cleanliness, apt to slip during an economic downturn.

20   In addition to medical qualms, there is every reason to fret about aesthetic standards, for nothing publicly or professionally identifies the impeccable craftsman or incompetent scratcher. Tattooists earn no degrees or fellowships; no magazine critics review their work. For the buyer there is no trial period, no guarantee, no five-year warranty on parts or labor.

21   Not that the average patron is fussy. Statistically, the majority of tattoos result from a momentary, possibly drunken, impulse (although the desire may have been present for some time), and tattoo parlors are chosen primarily on the basis of geographical convenience. As a rule, more thought goes into the purchase of a stereo than a tattoo.

With predictable results. Face it — most tattoos look dreadful. A few years after application, these ill-considered icons of crude personal symbolism have

22 blurred into dirty blobs of ink with hairs growing from them, as meaningful and attractive as a large strawberry mole.

Oh, What the Hell

23 Despite these obvious drawbacks, approximately ten percent of the adult population choose to have themselves marked for life.

24 Why would they do that?

25 It's inadequate, though tempting, to dismiss them as mildly insane. Although psychiatrists usually view tattoos as symptoms of mental trouble, inmates of mental institutions have fewer tattoos than do the outside population. (On the other hand, it has been said that the three traits common to psychopathic serial killers is that they are male and white and they possess a tattoo.)

26 While it is no great challenge to understand why a person would not acquire a tattoo, the reasons why people *do* are interesting, contradictory, and elusive.

27 Like other persistent cultural practices just outside publicly acknowledged art, such as circuses, soap operas, and rock and roll, tattooing draws from deep wells in the collective and subjective consciousness. A cultural weed growing without encouragement, it is nourished by primitive needs. To frighten off an attacking enemy. To invoke magic or borrow power from another being. To ward off evil. To attract good fortune. To draw attention and sexual respect by means of exaggerated plumage. To declare oneself different from, or part of, a tribe. To make permanent a decision or rite of passage. Tattooing is a complex act — social, sexual, mystical, and cosmetic.

28 The one fact about a tattoo that never varies is its permanence. There's no such thing as a temporary tattoo. Yes, tattoos can indeed be erased, but the resulting patch of scar tissue is as conspicuous as the mark it replaced.

29 People receive a tattoo *because* of its permanence. All tattoos represent a desire for a reality that endures despite our wrinkling skin and mutating identities. All tattoos, ugly or beautiful, Jesus Christ or Tweety Bird, represent the same urge: to transcend.

30 Subconsciously, in an absurd, naïve, slapstick fashion, people who receive tattoos are searching for God.

31 Think about it: a prominent 1930s tattooist named Jack Redcloud displayed a large bust of Jesus, complete with bleeding crown of thorns, *upon his bald head.*

Questions for Discussion or Writing

1. Does this essay focus on causes or effects? Explain.

2. State some of the causes mentioned in this essay, and their effects.

3. What is Gray's thesis? Is it stated or implied? Does the organization of the essay reflect this thesis?

4. Who is Gray's intended audience?

5. Is the use of humour effective in this essay? How does the title prepare the reader for the use of humour in the essay?

*   *   *   *   *

Recollections of Jacques Plante

Rick Boulton

1   Jacques Plante was hockey's great innovator. He was an honors student of the game, had a brilliant grasp of its dynamics and revolutionized two aspects of goal-keeping: he pioneered the use of the face mask and popularized leaving the net to play stray pucks (when attacking teams fired the puck around the end boards, Plante whirled to intercept it behind his net; today, of course, the play has become standard goal-keeping procedure). In his 24 years as a pro (he retired for good in 1975) Plante became an authority on the habits and traits of opposing forwards. Between games he brooded over his game, fretted about how to polish and improve it. In many aspects of hockey he was ahead of his time.

2   In the early 1960s, for instance, Plante said that hockey players were under-coached. He wasn't referring to the kids in the peewees — he meant the pros. He asked how one man could know all there is to know about offence, defence, back-checking, passing, playing left wing, playing right defence, playing goal. He advocated a specialist goal-keeping coach and said that NHL coaches should appoint assistants, as they do in baseball and football, to specialize in specific skills. That, of course, is becoming the trend today: Philadelphia's Fred Shero now has three assistants: Mike Nykoluk to coach the forwards, Barry Ashbee to coach the defence, Marcel Pelletier to coach the goalies. And Johnny Bower now serves as the Maple Leaf goal-keeping coach as well as assistant to Coach Red Kelley.

3   Like any pioneer, Plante endured the criticism that he was unorthodox without cause. He was the first goalie to develop hand signals to warn defencemen about an impending icing call. Because he developed a free-wheeling and now widely copied style of net-minding in which he not only ventured behind his goal but as far out as his own blue line, it was said by some that he played to the crowd. Even today, you can still find people who remember him as a showboat for flashing his hands over his head in an extravagant victory sign the moment the game ended. But by and large the fans loved him — and he usually had the last laugh. After playing in a game at Madison Square Garden in New York, Plante said the nets weren't the right size. People laughed. Then officials measured the nets and found that he was right.

4   He always complained about his asthma, a chronic ailment that led him to switch from defence to goal-tending when he was six years old and playing hockey in Shawinigan, Que. His reaction to Toronto was so severe that he could cope only by flying in just before the game and flying out right after it. No one, then, was more startled than Plante when he was traded to Toronto for the 1970–71 season. Reminded that Plante found Toronto's lakeside climate bothersome, Leaf General Manager Jim Gregory took the precaution of installing him in an apartment in the city's less-polluted north end (Willowdale). In his days with Montreal, he was allowed to stay at the Westbury Hotel, next door to the Gardens, because he swore he was allergic to the Royal York Hotel, where the rest of the Canadiens stayed.

5   Plante was different. He used to knit to relieve tension, he was an avid reader of historical biographies (Lenin, Stalin, Churchill), a competent landscape painter in oils and so dedicated a cook that he never set foot in a Toronto restaurant while he was a Maple Leaf. He didn't smoke or drink. On the road he roomed alone. In ten years with the Montreal Canadiens, on uncountable trips to New York, he never once toured the town. If age slowed his reflexes in the last few years of his career (he played until he was 46) his experience more than compensated for it. He was very shrewd. For example, he worked out a deal with the Leafs so that while he played for the team — 1970–71 to 1973 — he didn't receive a cent in salary; the Leafs are to pay him his salary beginning in 1981.

6   If Plante does not rank as the number one goal-keeper of all time, it is only because statistics aren't everything. No one had better statistics. His lifetime goals-against average was 2.37 in 837 regular-season NHL games. The Canadiens' Bill Durnan, who retired in 1950, compiled a lifetime goals-against average of 2.35, but he played only a little more than seven NHL seasons. Plante had 82 regular-season shutouts, a number surpassed by Terry Sawchuk's 103 and Glenn Hall's 84, but he still holds the record, 14, for the most shutouts in the Stanley Cup playoffs. He won the Vezina Trophy a record seven times, five consecutive years with Montreal beginning in 1956. In 1962, as well as winning the Vezina, his sixth, he won the Hart Trophy as the league's most valuable player — the last goalkeeper to do so. In 1969, playing with the St. Louis Blues, he shared a Vezina (his seventh) with Glenn Hall. He was named to the league's first all-star team four times and the second team four times. He was on six Stanley Cup winning teams, all of them in Montreal.

7   Plante's 10 years with the Canadiens did not end happily. Although he played brilliantly, his Montreal bosses never became accustomed to his eccentricities. His habit of wandering away from the net gave Coach Toe Blake ulcers, and many fans happily anticipated the day when Plante would get caught out of position by an opposing forward (in fact, according to Andy O'Brien's lively book, *The Jacques Plante Story*, Plante was only caught outside his crease six times in his pro career). As strange as it seems, Plante says today that he could never be sure of his job in Montreal; among other things there was some adverse reaction to his introduction of the mask in 1959. His nose had been broken by a shot and cut for seven stitches. Blake had previously opposed his requests that he be allowed

to wear his practice mask in the games, but with his nose broken he reached for his mask and walked past Blake wearing it. Blake did not object, and when the Canadiens won the game — they were playing the Rangers in New York — he let the incident pass. Plante had made goal-tending history.

8   Plante infuriated Blake in other ways. One memorable night he declined to take part in the pregame warm-up on grounds of asthma. Blake was furious. "How can you run a team if you're never sure your goalie is going to play?" he asked. Years later, Plante's often noisy ideas on the subject of the two-goalie system helped introduce the concept to the point where it is standard procedure today. Once again, he was ahead of his time.

9   Plante's unpredictable health bothered Montreal management. Privately, they called him a hypochondriac and noted that he didn't suffer from asthma from the time he was 14 until he joined the Canadiens at age 24. Even when he suffered injuries that were visible on X-rays, Blake was suspicious.

10   At the end of the 1963 season the Canadiens traded Plante to the New York Rangers. In New York, he developed knee trouble, made mistakes in goal, and his goals-against average climbed. Ranger management began talking about his "phantom knee." Finally, Coach Red Sullivan exploded, and Plante found himself playing with Baltimore of the American Hockey League. Eventually he had knee surgery, proving that the Rangers had been wrong in believing that the pain in his knee was in fact a pain in his head. But he quit hockey in 1965, a retirement that would last three years. One of his most distinguished achievements — and happiest memories — occurred during those years when he went into goal, cold, to play for the Junior Canadiens against the touring Russian national team, beating them 2–1 in Montreal.

11   When he came out of retirement in 1968, Plante was 39 years old. Playing for St. Louis he reconfirmed his belief in himself, the money was good and, combining with Glenn Hall, he played well. From St. Louis he came to the Leafs, where he tutored Bernie Parent. In 1973 the Leafs traded him to Boston. He helped the Bruins finish the season, winning seven of eight games and taking over third place from the Rangers, but he was a flop in the playoffs. He admitted his nerves were gone. Soon after, he announced he was heading for the World Hockey Association, where he managed, coached and played until his retirement in 1975.

12   Typically, his last days in the NHL were shrouded in controversy: the Bruins somehow failed to send him his share of the playoff money, and he had to ask NHL President Clarence Campbell to collect. He never did get his equipment back from the Bruins, who claimed it was lost. Plante believed the Bruins were mad at him for jumping to the WHA with a year left on his contract. Playing in the WHA, he developed stomach pains that team doctors could never diagnose.

13   But the most interesting thing about Plante was not his pains but his ideas. For instance, he said that players should talk on the ice — he said he wanted to be told if an opposing player was behind the net — and he himself talked all the time, shouting instructions to his defencemen or warning them when an opposing checker was coming at them from the blind side. If a teammate had the puck behind his net, Plante often indicated to which side he should pass the puck to

ensure that it would clear the zone. And as for his roaming tactics, he admitted he sometimes made mistakes, either by anticipating incorrectly the flow of the play or by getting in the way of his defencemen, but he did not leave the goal until he was sure he could get back. He could afford to wander because he was a superior skater.

14   Indeed, Plante was technically almost a perfect goal-keeper, a stand-up goalie as opposed to a flopper. He had a mathematician's grasp of angles. He knew, in relation to his position between the goalposts, exactly where he was at all times. His mind was a computer bank of opposition plays and shooting characteristics. He was almost impossible to fool. When his playing days were over he admitted that he even studied which players used black tape on their sticks and which used white; the puck was easier to see if the player had white tape on his stick, he said.

15   Plante was dedicated in practice, went to bed faithfully at 9:30 p.m., covered 30 miles a day on the stationary bicycle, watched his weight, what he ate, the temperature of the fruit juices he drank. He was especially careful of how and when he used his eyes. A goal-tender's biggest problems, he used to explain, are his eyes and his nerves. To relax he'd read, cook lasagna, knit undershirts, play bridge. He'd leave a stack of records playing while he slept, placing the loudest, liveliest records at the top of the stack so he'd wake up progressively.

16   As a Maple Leaf, Plante spent most of his spare time answering mail. According to Leaf publicist Stan Obodiac, he received more mail than any player in the team's history, averaging 200 letters a day. Partly, it was a reflection of his personal popularity, and partly it was the result of a television appearance he once made on Hockey Night in Canada in which he mentioned he had prepared a tip sheet for young goal-tenders. It contained 15 pointers, such as, "On a breakaway do not rush toward your opponent. Wait for him at the edge of your goal crease." Or, "Sur un échappe, ne fonce pas vers ton adversaire. . . ." Plante's tip-sheets, mimeographed at the Gardens on Gardens' stationery, often included personal notes to the boys (and sometimes girls) who had special questions. He answered every fan letter.

Questions for Discussion or Writing

1. Which details support Boulton's evaluation of Plante as "an honors student of the game"?

2. How are statistics used in this essay to illustrate the author's thesis?

3. Give an example of the author's purpose in writing this essay.

4. Is the opening paragraph effective in capturing the reader's attention and clearly introducing the topic of the essay?

5. How does Boulton call upon the experiences of other people to illustrate the thesis of the essay?

Electronic Confidants

Tony Leighton

1   Like most things about the Internet, e-mail has become common currency to a small elite but remains a curiosity to most other people. Yet if my own recent experiences with it are any measure, more of us will be e-mailing soon, and it will enrich our lives and embed itself in our culture like the telegraph and telephone did before it.

2   E-mail will be increasingly important because it is fast, convenient and friendly, and can be duplicated effortlessly — an e-mail message can be sent to as many people as you like, as long as you have their Internet addresses (mybrother@compunet.ca). At an inspired moment, without a stamp or an envelope, you can dash off a quick note and e-mail it to your best friend in Vancouver, your dad in Florida, and a geographically inconvenient university pal working at the Asian Development Bank in Manila. If they check their electronic "mailboxes," they can be reading your words in less than an hour and reply just as fast.

3   I have been irretrievably sold on the merits of e-mail since the autumn of 1994 when I joined electronic hands with six others in an informal e-mail conference we named "Doomed To Collide" (a Kurt Vonnegut reference) or, as it came to be known, "DTC." When we started, I was acquainted with three of the members, Tom in Guelph, Ont. (where I live), Stephen in Vancouver and Keith in Toronto. I had never met Tonya (Toronto), David (also Toronto) or Jack (Brougham, Ont.).

4   The set-up was simple: anyone of us at any time would write something and send it to the others. It could be a thought, an observation, a feeling, complaint, story, whatever. Those who chose to respond might build on the first message, or send new thoughts and stories. Every day, I'd open my "mailbox" and find anywhere from one to a half-dozen DTC messages waiting.

5   DTC was utterly free-form. Tom, the unofficial master-of-cybermonies, recently e-mailed me a list of topics we touched: sustainability, economics, ecology, community values, population, pop culture, justice and injustice, corporations, under-30/over-30, reinvention/deconstruction, Springsteen, Cobain, Elvis, life and death, the failure of capitalism, the failure of communism, the Chinese, half-empty glasses, 1955, autophysiological altruism, NGOs, hitting the wall, fleshy-pinky things, taking on TV, spirituality, informed optimism, suburbs, appropriate scale, Newt and Bill, raising kids, leaving marriages, lentil soup and whether or not we are poised at the edge of a New Dawn or Dark Age.

6   But where DTC truly cemented us, and proved its value as a medium with a soul, was when it got emotional. And it did. Affectionate sign-offs were the beginning. "It's midnight. I'm tired. This has been good. I love you all." And, "I don't know what I'd do without you folks tonight." I'll always remember the one from Tonya, an energized young woman in her 20s, who told us, after a long and impassioned e-mail about craving more spirituality in her life, that she was looking forward to waking up to buckwheat pancakes and fresh-squeezed orange juice, but not before turning in with "the man who makes my eyes sparkle."

7   As the winter wore on, big-world issues gave way more frequently to personal vignettes that touched us all. Keith, in his 30s, had never met his biological father because his mother had left England (and the marriage) before Keith was born. He'd always meant to seek out his dad. Suddenly, it was too late. "My dad died yesterday," came the words across our screens. "I never met him."

8   Stephen changed jobs and moved to another city. Keith was traumatically transferred from a job he loved. David's crowded agenda was burning him out. Jack's partner had a health scare. There were as many highs as lows. At two o'clock one morning, Tom, pleasantly inebriated, sat down at his computer before going to bed and wrote sentimentally about stumbling home through the winter streets of Guelph after making music and drinking wine with good friends. He had a great desire to share this minor epiphany with the rest of us, his "virtual" companions, as if we were in the room with him.

9   We offered each other solace, ideas, advice, perspective, good humour and good company. We also berated each other, and on occasion, emotions ran over the top. Twice that I recall, e-mail revealed its limitations when, through messages too harsh or too sloppy, offence was taken that could only be repaired in the flesh. One day, Tom drove to Toronto to clear up some e-mail-inflamed hostilities with Keith, one of his best friends. Another day, I walked down the street with my tail between my legs to apologize to Tom, one of my best friends.

10   E-mail deepened our friendships. We became more intimate through correspondence, in the same way prolific letter writers of times past maintained intensely personal relationships over long distances, often never meeting in person.

11   DTC was both an experience and a place, and, like many things in cyberspace, is best described in doublespeak: a place with no terrain, a tight community loosely bound, an open enclosure, a club-house without walls or roof. Keith, who credits DTC with getting him through a difficult winter, compares it to "a tree fort where people come swinging in on vines, just to see who's hanging out, have a chat, a song, a look out at the sunset." It was an accessible antidote to the dissonance of our lives, a circle of friends.

[. . .]

12   We finally did meet in person. Last April, all of us but Stephen (who was roundly and repeatedly "flamed" for his absence), plus our various partners, converged at a cottage on Skelton Lake near Huntsville, Ont. It was oddly wonderful to meet people we already knew. A printout of our entire e-mail conference was plunked down on a table like a trophy. It was thicker than the Manhattan phone book. We had some laughs. We walked in the woods. We broached a few Important Issues, but there was more interest in food and repose than debate. We were content simply to tie the corporeal to the ethereal, the faces to the names.

13   And then it stopped. DTC dried up after that weekend. It was as if the wires had been cut.

14   There was speculation that by meeting in person we had killed the mystique and hence the conference. But I suspect it was the weather. DTC was an indoor

affair, a way to pass long winter nights, a sort of electronic quilt under which seven people hunkered for seven months to trade secrets and stay warm. Warm weather killed the need for it.

15   But now as another winter begins, with the stowing of bicycles and paddles and the waning of the light, I anticipate soon the first flickers of the next round. Having tasted the pleasures of electronic group communion, I suspect none of us will want to be without it for long.

Questions for Discussion or Writing

1. What elements of the narrative or the descriptive essay appear in this article?

2. What is the author's thesis?

3. How is this thesis developed throughout the article?

4. What elements of argument or persuasion can be found in Leighton's article? Do these elements serve to convince the reader of the author's point of view?

5. Is the article topical? In what ways?

PART V

Appendices

Appendix A
Parts of Speech

Words can be divided into eight categories called **parts of speech**. Understanding these categories will help you work with language, especially when it comes to revising your own writing.

1. A **noun** is a word that names persons, places, or things.

Common Nouns	Proper Nouns
officer	Michael Johnson
station	Union Station
magazine	*Canadian Geographic*

   Nouns are said to be **concrete** if they name things you can see or touch.

   window
   paper
   river

   Nouns are said to be **abstract** if they name things you cannot see or touch. These words can be concepts, ideas, or qualities.

   meditation
   honesty
   carelessness

   To test for a noun, it may help to ask these questions:

   - Can I make the word plural? (Most nouns have a plural form.)
   - Can I put the article *the* in front of the word?
   - Is the word used as the subject or object of the sentence?

2. A **pronoun** is a word that takes the place of a noun. Just like a noun, it is used as the subject or object of a sentence. Pronouns can be divided into several classes. Here are some of them:

Pronouns

Note: Personal pronouns have three forms depending on how they are used in a sentence: as subject, object, or possessive.

Singular	Subjective	Objective	Possessive
1st person	I	me	my (mine)
2nd person	you	you	your (yours)
	he	him	his (his)
	she	her	her (hers)
3rd person	it	it	its (its)

Plural			
1st person	we	us	our (ours)
2nd person	you	you	your (yours)
3rd person	they	them	their (theirs)

Relative Pronouns	Demonstrative Pronouns	Indefinite Pronouns
who, whom, whose	this	all, both, each, one
which	that	nothing, nobody, no one
that	these	anything, anybody, anyone
what	those	something, somebody, someone
whoever, whichever		everything, everybody, everyone

3. An **adjective** is a word that modifies a noun or pronoun. Adjectives usually come before the nouns they modify, but they can also come after the verb.

> The *unusual* package was placed on my desk.
> The package felt *cold*.

4. A **verb** is a word that tells what a subject is doing as well as the time (past, present, or future) of that action. Verbs can be divided into three classes:

Action Verbs

> The athlete *runs* ten kilometres every morning.
> (The action takes place in the present.)

> The crowd *cheered* for the oldest runner.
> (The action takes place in the past.)

Linking Verbs

A linking verb joins the subject of a sentence to one or more words that describe or identify the subject.

> He *was* a dancer in his twenties.
> She *seemed* disappointed with her job.

Common Linking Verbs

be (am, is, are, was, were, have been)	become	look
act	feel	seem
appear	grow	taste

Helping Verbs (also called "auxiliaries")
A helping verb is any verb used before the main verb.

It could show the tense of the verb:

It *will* rain tomorrow.
(Shows future tense.)

It could show the passive voice:

The new civic centre *has been* finished.

It could give a special meaning to the verb:

Anne Murray *may be* singing there tonight.

Common Helping Verbs
can, could
may, might, must
shall, should
will, would
forms of the irregular verbs *be, have,* and *do*

5. An **adverb** is a word that modifies a verb, an adjective, or another adverb. It often ends in *-ly*, but a better test is to ask yourself if the word answers the question how, when, or where.

The student walked *happily* into the classroom.

- The adverb *happily* answers the question "How?"
- It ends in *-ly*, and it modifies the verb *walked*.

It will be *very* cold tomorrow.

- The adverb *very* answers the question "How?"
- It modifies the adjective *cold*.

Winter has come *too* early.

- The adverb *too* answers the question "How?"
- It modifies the adverb *early*.

Here are some adverbs to look out for:

Adverbs of Frequency	Adverbs of Degree	
often	even	quite
never	extremely	surely
sometimes	just	too
seldom	more	very
always	much	
ever	only	

6. A **preposition** is a word used to relate a noun or pronoun to some other word in the sentence. The preposition with its noun or pronoun is called a prepositional phrase.

> The letter is *from* my father.
> The envelope is addressed *to* my sister.

Read through the following list of prepositions several times so that you will be able to recognize them. Your instructor may ask you to memorize them.

Common Prepositions			
about	below	in	since
above	beneath	inside	through
across	beside	into	to
after	between	like	toward
against	beyond	near	under
along	by	of	until
among	down	off	up
around	during	on	upon
at	except	outside	with
before	for	over	within
behind	from	past	without

7. A **conjunction** is a word that joins or connects other words, phrases, or clauses.

Connecting two words:

> Sooner *or* later, you will have to pay.

Connecting two phrases:

> The story was on the radio *and* in the newspaper.

Connecting two clauses:

> Dinner was late *because* I had to work overtime at the office.

Conjunctions		
Co-ordinating Conjunctions	**Subordinating Conjunctions**	
and	after	provided that
but	although	since
or	as, as if, as though	unless
nor	because	until
for (meaning "because")	before	when, whenever
yet	how	where, wherever
so	if, even if	while

(continued)

(continued)

Correlative Conjunctions	**Adverbial Conjunctions** (also known as "conjunctive adverbs")	
either . . . or	To add an idea:	furthermore
neither . . . nor		moreover
both . . . and		likewise
not only . . . but also	To contrast:	however
		nevertheless
	To show results:	consequently
		therefore
	To show an alternative:	otherwise

8. An **interjection** is a word that expresses a strong feeling and is not connected grammatically to any other part of the sentence.

> *Oh*, I forgot my keys.
> *Well*, that means I'll have to sit here all day.

Since one word can function differently or have different forms or meanings, you must often study the context in which the word is found to be sure of its part of speech.

> The parent makes sacrifices *for* the good of the children.

In this sentence, *for* is a preposition.

> The parent sacrifices, *for* the child needed a good education.

In this sentence, *for* is a conjunction meaning "because."

Appendix B
Distinguishing between Words That Are Often Confused

Words That Sound Alike: Group I

it's   contraction of "it is"
its   possessive

> *Example:*
> It's a nice day today.
> The bush has all of its new buds.

they're   contraction of "they are"
their   possessive
there   at that place

> *Example:*
> They're a happy couple.
> This antique is their prized possession.
> I'll meet you over there, behind the store.

who's   contraction of "who is"
whose   possessive

> *Example:*
> Who's going for pizza?
> Whose garbage can is blocking the driveway?

you're   contraction of "you are"
your   possessive

> *Example:*
> You're my best friend.
> Take your gift to the party.

allowed (*verb*)   permitted
aloud (*adv.*)   out loud

Example:
The boy was finally allowed to stay up late.
Her question was stated aloud for all to hear.

altar (*noun*)   an elevated place or table for religious rites
alter (*verb*)   to change or adjust

Example:
The altar was decorated for the church service.
If you alter the plans, they won't work out.

aural (*adj.*)   having to do with the ear or hearing
oral (*adj.*)   having to do with the mouth or speech

Example:
I have poor aural skills because I won't listen.
The history of the First Nations is kept alive through their oral traditions.

brake (*verb*)   to stop
     (*noun*)   a device used for slowing or stopping
break (*verb*)   to smash, crack, or come apart

Example:
Apply the brake when you want to stop.
You'll have to break the lock to get in.

capital (*adj.*)   chief; major; fatal
       (*noun*)   leading city; money
capitol (*noun*)   a building in which a U.S. state legislature assembles

Example:
Ottawa is the capital of Canada.
The capitol building for the legislature is in Washington.

chord (*noun*)   three or more musical tones sounded together; harmony
cord (*noun*)   a small rope of twisted strands; any ropelike structure; a unit of cut fuel wood

Example:
Many guitar chords are easy to play.
A strong cord is needed to tie the bundle together.

close (*verb*)   to shut
clothes (*noun*)   garments
cloth (*noun*)   fabric; a piece of material

Example:
Close the door and keep the cold out.
T-shirts are our favourite type of summer clothes.
His coat was made of cloth, not leather.

coarse (*adj.*)   rough; not fine; common or of inferior quality
course (*noun*)   direction or path of something moving; part of a meal; a school subject

Example:
Coarse sandpaper is used to make a rough finish.
One course I'm taking this year is English grammar.

complement (*noun*)   something that completes or makes up a whole
            (*verb*)   to complete; to supplement, enhance
compliment (*noun*)   an expression of praise
            (*verb*)   to give praise

Example:
A blue blazer complements grey slacks.
Good work deserves a compliment.

fair (*adj.*)   unbiased; light colour; free of clouds; promising; lovely
       (*noun*)   an exhibition; regional event; market
fare (*noun*)   a charge for transportation; food
       (*verb*)   get along; do

Example:
A pink sunset means a fair day will follow.
The train fare is increasing yearly.

flour (*noun*)   the powder produced by grinding a grain
flower (*noun*)   a blossom of a plant
        (*verb*)   to blossom

Example:
Wheat flour is used to make bread.
Tulips flower in early spring.

for (*prep.*)   directed to; in the amount of; on behalf of; to the extent of
      (*conj.*)   because
four (*noun, adj.*)   number

forty: Notice that this number is spelled differently from *four, fourteen,* or *twenty-four.*

fore (*noun, adj.*)   situated near the front

Example:
This gift is for you.
There are four people in attendance.
His ideas came to the fore at work.

forth (*adv.*)   onward in time, place, or order
fourth (*noun, adj.*)   number

Example:
Go forth from this place.
She is fourth in line for tickets.

forward (*verb*)   to send on to another address
     (*adj.*)   bold; progressive
     (*adv.*)   moving toward the front
foreword (*noun*) introduction to a book; preface

Example:
Move forward so you can hear the speaker.
The foreword to a book is sometimes called the preface.

grate (*verb*)   to shred; to annoy or irritate
   (*noun*)   a metal grill

grateful (*adj.*)   appreciative

great (*adj.*)   large; significant; excellent; powerful; skilful; first-rate

Example:
Her negative attitude grates on my nerves.
Winning the prize was a great achievement.

knew (*verb*) past tense of *know*
new (adj.)   not old

Example:
The student knew the correct answer.
His new car is this year's model.

know (*verb*) to understand
no (*adv.*)   a negative response
  (*adj.*)   not any; not one

Example:
You would know the work if you'd study.
Having no money means that you are poor.

Words That Sound Alike: Group II

Here is a second set of words often confused because they sound alike.

pain (*noun*)   suffering
pane (*noun*)   a panel of glass

> *Example:*
> A cut finger can cause a lot of pain.
> Windows contain panes of glass.

passed (*verb*)   the past tense of *to pass* — to move ahead
past (*noun*)   time before the present
  (*prep.*)   beyond
  (*adj.*)   no longer current

> *Example:*
> I passed the exam and moved to the next grade.
> I was past the exit before I noticed that I had missed it.

patience (*noun*)   calm endurance; tolerant understanding
patients (*noun*)   persons under medical treatment

> *Example:*
> Waiting for someone usually takes patience.
> Patients in hospitals often are very ill.

peace (*noun*)   absence of war, calm
piece (*noun*)   a portion, a part

> *Example:*
> Peace came when the war was over.
> His piece of cake was huge.

plain (*adj.*)   simple; ordinary; unattractive; clear
  (*noun*)   a flat, treeless land region
plane (*noun*)   an aircraft; a flat, level surface; a carpenter's tool for levelling
    wood; a level of development

> *Example:*
> The flat plain stretched for miles without a tree.
> I used a plane to make the wood smooth.

presence (*noun*)   the state of being present; a person's manner
presents (*noun*)   gifts
  (*verb*)   (third person singular) to introduce; to give a gift

Example:

The presence of the teacher kept the students quiet.

Presents are given on birthdays.

principal (*adj.*)   most important; chief; main

         (*noun*)   the head of a school; a sum of money

principle (*noun*)   rule or standard

Example:

The principal rule is the most important guideline.

There are principles of conduct to be followed at school.

rain (*noun, verb*)   water falling to earth in drops

reign (*noun, verb*)   a period of rule for a king or queen

rein (*noun*)   a strap attached to a bridle, used to control a horse

Example:

A good rain will soak the crops.

The monarch's reign extended for many years.

To control a horse, learn how to use the reins.

raise (*verb*)   to move upward; to awaken; to increase; to collect

      (*noun*)   an increase in salary

rays (*noun*)   thin lines or beams of radiation

raze (*verb*)   to tear down or demolish

Example:

A raise in pay often rewards good work.

The sun's rays contain harmful radiation.

The old building was razed to the ground.

sight (*noun*)   the ability to see; a view

site (*noun*)   the plot of land where something is located; the place of an event

cite (*verb*)   to quote as an authority or example

Example:

Some people with perfect sight don't see clearly.

The opera house's site is between two theatres.

I can cite my grammar text as my authority.

stair (*noun*)   one of a flight of steps

stare (*noun, verb*)   a fixed gaze; to look at insistently

Example:

Each stair climbed brings you farther up the steps.

A steady gaze can be considered a stare.

stake (*noun*) a post sharpened at one end to drive into the ground; a financial share

(*verb*) to attach or support; to set limits with a stake

steak (*noun*) a slice of meat, usually beef

Example:
My stake in the profits amounted to a quarter share.
I like my steak well done and thick.

stationary (*adj.*) standing still
stationery (*noun*) writing paper and envelopes

Example:
Anything that is stationary does not move.
Stationery can be written upon.

to (*prep.*) in a direction toward
to (+ *verb*) the infinitive form of a verb
too (*adv.*) also; excessively; very
two (*noun*) number

Example:
Go to school.
To see is to believe.
I, too, am going to the party.
Two is one more than one.

vain (*adj.*) conceited; unsuccessful
vane (*noun*) a plate of wood or metal, often in the shape of a rooster, that pivots to indicate the direction of the wind; the weblike part of a feather
vein (*noun*) a blood vessel; the branching framework of a leaf; an occurrence of an ore; a strip of colour; a streak; a transient attitude

Example:
A vain person spends a lot of time in front of a mirror.
The vane on the roof tells the wind direction.
Veins in your body contain blood.

waist (*noun*) the middle portion of a body, garment, or object
waste (*verb*) to use thoughtlessly or carelessly
(*noun*) objects discarded as useless

Example:
A belt around your waist holds your pants up.
Excess packaging contains much waste.

wait (*verb*)   to remain inactive
weight (*noun*)   the measure of the heaviness of an object

Example:
Remain here and wait for my arrival.
My weight goes up every time I eat.

weather (*noun*)   atmospheric conditions
whether (*conj.*)   if it is the case that

Example:
The weather report calls for rain.
She will go whether I go or not.

ware (*noun*)   an article of commerce
wear (*verb*)   to have on
   (*noun*)   deterioration as a result of use
where (*adv.*)   at or in what place

Example:
You can sell your wares at the flea market.
What clothes will you wear?
He asked where the museum could be found.

whole (*adj.*)   complete
hole (*noun*)   an opening

Example:
A pie is whole before it is sliced and served.
Holes in the road need to be filled in.

wood (*noun*)   the tough substance made from trees
would (*verb*)   past tense of *will*

Example:
Most paper is made from wood fibre.
He would go, he said, if he could find a ride.

write (*verb*)   to form letters and words; to compose
right (*adj.*)   conforming to justice, law, or morality; correct; toward a conservative political point of view
   (*noun*)   that which is just, morally good, legal, or proper; a direction; a political group whose policies are conservative
   (*adv.*)   directly; well; completely; immediately
rite (*noun*)   a traditional, solemn, and often religious ceremony

Example:
Write a letter to your aunt.
You should legally do what is right.
Last rites were said over the dying person.

yoke (*noun*)   a harness fastening two or more animals together; a form of bondage
yolk (*noun*)   the yellow of an egg

Example:
Animals in a team are joined by a yoke.
Some diners like their eggs cooked without the yolks broken.

Words That Sound or Look Almost Alike

Some words are often confused with other words that sound or look almost the same. Learning to spell these words correctly involves a careful study of pronunciations along with meanings.

	Pronunciation	**Meaning**
accept	*a* as in *pat*	*verb:* to receive; to admit; to regard as true or right
except	the first *e* as in *pet*	*prep.:* other than; but; only

Example:
I accepted the parcel from the courier.
Everyone was there except the two of us.

	Pronunciation	**Meaning**
access	*a* as in *pat*	*verb:* a means of approaching; the right to enter or make use of
excess	the first *e* as in *pet*	*noun:* a quantity or amount beyond what is required

Example:
Access to the files will provide you with information.
Overeating is an unnecessary excess.

	Pronunciation	**Meaning**
advice	Pronounce *-ice* like the word *ice*.	*noun:* opinion as to what should be done about a problem
advise	Pronounce *-ise* like the word *eyes*.	*verb:* to suggest; to counsel

Example:
My best advice is to accept the offer.
I advise you to do what is right.

affect	*a* as in *about*	*verb:* to influence
effect	the first *e* as the *i*	*noun:* result
	in *pit*	*verb:* to bring about a result

Example:

I can affect his decision with my advice.

The effect of the rain was to cancel the game.

allusion	*a* as in *about*	*noun:* an indirect reference
illusion	the first *i* as in *pit*	*noun:* a mistaken concept or belief

Example:

An allusion was made to my great intelligence.

It is an illusion to think you will get rich without working.

breath	*ea* as the *e* in *pet*	*noun:* the air that is inhaled or exhaled in breathing
breathe	the *ea* as the *e* in *be*	*verb:* to inhale and exhale air

Example:

You can see your breath on the window on a cold day.

Breathe deeply and inhale the clean country air.

clothes	*o* as the *oe* in *toe*	*noun:* garments; wearing apparel
cloths	*o* as the *aw* in *paw*	*noun:* pieces of fabric

Example:

The clothes you are wearing are fashionable.

Pieces of cloth can be torn from the fabric to make rags.

conscience	kŏn′ shəns (two syllables)	*noun:* recognition of right and wrong
conscientious	kŏn shē en′ shəs (four syllables)	*adj.:* careful; thorough
conscious	kŏn′ shəs (two syllables)	*adj.:* awake; aware of one's own existence

Example:

My conscience told me to do the right thing.

I conscientiously performed my duty to the best of my ability.

She was conscious of the fact that he was behind her.

costume	*o* as in *pot*, *u* as the *u* in you	*noun:* a special style of dress for a particular occasion
custom	*u* as in *cut*, *o* as in *gallop*	*noun:* a common tradition

Example:
The costume he wore reflected his Native heritage.
It is our custom to wash our hands before eating.

council		*noun:* a group that governs
counsel	*ou* as in *out*	*verb:* to give advice
		noun: a lawyer; advice
consul	*o* as in *pot*	*noun:* a governmental official in the foreign service

Example:
The town council passed a by-law.
Good counsel is advice well received.
Canada has a consul in many foreign countries.

desert	di zurt′	*verb:* to abandon
	i as in *pit*	
	dez′ ert	*noun:* barren land
	the first *e* as in *pet*	
dessert	di zurt′	*noun:* last part of a meal, often a sweet
	i as in *pit*	

Example:
The desert is usually a hot, arid place.
Our family usually eats dessert following dinner.

diner	*i* as the *ie* in *pie*	*noun:* a person eating dinner; a restaurant with a long counter and booths
dinner	*i* as in *pit*	*noun:* chief meal of the day

Example:
A diner is a place where meals are served.
Dinner is usually eaten in the early evening.

emigrate	*e as in pet*	*verb:* to go out of a country
emigrant		*noun:* someone who leaves a country to settle in another country
immigrate	the first *i as in pit*	*verb:* to come into a country
immigrant		*noun:* someone who enters a country to settle there

Example:
Many people decided to emigrate from Ireland during the famine.
Immigrants to our country bring valuable skills.

farther	*a* as in *father*	*adj., adv.:* greater physical or measurable distance
further	*u* as in *urge*	*adj., adv.:* greater mental distance; more distant in time or degree; additional

Example:
Montreal is farther than Toronto from Windsor.
We drew further apart in our approach to the problem.

local	lo′ kəl *a* as in *about*	*adj.:* relating or peculiar to a place
locale	lo kal′ *a* as in *pat*	*noun:* a place, scene, or setting, as of a novel

Example:
Everyone here goes to the local school on the next block.
Our town was the locale for a movie.

moral	mor′ al Pronounce the *a* as in *about*; the accent is on the first syllable.	*adj.:* a sense of right and wrong *noun:* the lesson of a story, fable, or event
morale	mo ral′ Pronounce the *a* as in *pat*; the accent is on the second syllable.	*noun:* the attitude or spirit of a person or group of people

Example:
The moral of the story taught us never to cheat.
Their morale was shown by their enthusiasm for their jobs.

personal	per′ son al Accent is on the first syllable.	*adj.:* pertaining to a particular person
personnel	per son nel′ Accent is on the third syllable.	*noun:* the people employed by an organization; an administrative division of an organization concerned with the employees

Example:
The matter is a personal one between him and me.
Most of the plant's personnel were laid off.

| **precede** | Pronounce the first *e* as the *i* in *pit*. | *verb:* to come before |
| **proceed** | Pronounce the *o* as the *oe* in *toe*. | *verb:* to continue |

Example:
You go first and precede me down the hall.
Proceed with the story you started yesterday.

quiet	qui′ et *i* as the *ie* in *pie*, *e* as in *pet*	*adj.:* silence
quit	*i* as in *pit*	*verb:* to give up; to stop
quite	*i* as the *ie* in *pie*; the *e* is silent	*adv.:* somewhat; completely; truly

Example:
It was a quiet night when no sound could be heard.
Quit what you are doing and start something else.
It is quite true that I am guilty.

| **receipt** | Pronounce the first *e* as the *i* in *pit*, *ei* as in the *e* in *be*; the *p* is silent. | *noun, verb:* a bill marked as paid; the act of receiving something |
| **recipe** | Pronounce the first *e* as in *pet*, the *i* like the *a* in *about*, the final *e* as in *be*. | *noun:* a formula for preparing a mixture, especially in cooking |

Example:
The receipt for the dinner was marked "paid."
The recipe calls for more chocolate in the cookies.

| **special** | spe cial | *adj.:* exceptional; distinctive |
| **especially** | Notice the extra syllable at the beginning. | *adv.:* particularly |

Example:
She was a special person, one of a kind.
It is especially important to file an income tax return.

| **than** | *a* as in *pat* | *conj.:* used to make a comparison |
| **then** | *e* as in *pet* | *adv.:* at that time; in that case |

Example:

She is smarter than me.

It was then that I made up my mind.

thorough	the first *o* as the *u* in *urge, ou* as the *oe* in *toe*	*adj.:* all that is needed; fully done
though	*ou* as the *oe* in *toe*	*conj.:* despite the fact
thought	*ou* as the *aw* in *paw*	*verb:* past tense of *to think*
through	*ou* as the *oo* in *boot*	*prep.:* preposition used to indicate entrance at one side and exit from the other; finished
threw	sounds like *through*	*verb:* past tense of *to throw*

- *Thru* is only an informal spelling for the word *through*.

Example:

The thorough investigation found a hidden clue.

It's not true, though, that I told a lie.

He thought of the answer before he spoke.

Go through that exit to get outside.

He threw the ball as far as he could.

Words That Sound or Look Almost Alike: *sit/set; rise/raise; lie/lay*

These six verbs are among the most troublesome in English because each is similar in sound, spelling, and meaning to another verb. Since they are all irregular verbs, students must be careful to learn to spell the principal parts correctly. The key to learning how to use the verbs *sit, rise,* and *lie* is to remember that these are actions the subject can do without any help; no other person or thing has to be included in the sentence. When you use the verbs *set, raise,* and *lay* in a sentence, the actions of these verbs are done to other persons or objects; these persons or things have to be included directly in the sentence. For example, when you use the verb *to sit,* all you need is a subject and a form of the verb:

I sit.

However, when you use the verb *to set,* you need a subject, a form of the verb, and an object. For example:

I set the glass on the table.

The subject *I* and the verb *set* are followed by the object *glass,* which is what the subject set on the table.

sit: to take a sitting position *never* takes an object	*set:* to place something into position *always* takes an object

Present: I *sit.*	I *set the glass* down.
Present participle: I *am sitting.*	I *am setting the glass* down.
Past: I *sat.*	I *set the glass* down.
Past participle: I *have sat.*	I *have set the glass* down.

rise: to stand up; to move upward
    never takes an object

raise: to make something move up or grow *always* takes an object

Present: I *rise.*	I *raise the flag.*
Present participle: The sun *is rising.*	I *am raising the flag.*
Past: He *rose* at eight o'clock.	I *raised the flag.*
Past participle: I have risen early today.	I *have raised the flag.*

The verbs *lie* and *lay* are easily confused because two of their principal parts have the same spelling. It takes concentration to learn to use these two verbs correctly.

lie: to recline
    never takes an object

lay: to put
    always takes an object

Present: I *lie* down.	I *lay the pen* down.
Present participle: I *am lying* down.	I *am laying the pen* down.
Past: Yesterday I *lay* down.	I *laid the pen* down.
Past participle: I *have lain* down.	I *have laid the pen* down.

- The verb *lie* can also be a regular verb meaning "to tell an untruth." The principal parts of this verb are *lie, lying, lied, has lied.*

Words That Sound or Look Almost Alike:
choose/chose; lose/loose; lead/led; die/dye

These verbs are often misspelled because there is confusion about how to spell the vowel sounds of the verbs. Study the spelling of the principal parts below.

Present	Present Participle	Past	Past Participle
choose	choosing	chose	has chosen
lose	losing	lost	has lost
lead	leading	led	has led
die	dying	died	has died

- *Loose* is an adjective meaning "not tightly fitted." Remember, it rhymes with *goose.*
- *Lead* can also be a noun meaning a bluish-grey metal. Remember, it rhymes with *head.*
- *Dye* is another verb meaning "to colour." Its principal parts are *dye, dyeing, dyed,* has *dyed.*

Words That Sound or Look Almost Alike: *use/used; suppose/supposed*

To use means *to bring or put into service; to make use of.*

> ***Present:*** I usually *use* my brother's bike to get to school.
> ***Past:*** Yesterday I *used* my father's car.

Used to means *to have as a custom* or *regular practice* in the past.

> I *used to* take the bus downtown, but now I get a ride with my neighbour.

A form of *to be* + *used to* means *to be familiar with* or *accustomed to.*

> I am not *used to* walking to school.

To suppose means *to guess.*

> ***Present:*** I *suppose* he is trying.
> ***Past:*** I *supposed* he was trying.

A form of *to be* + *supposed to* means *ought to* or *should.*

> Waiters *are supposed to* be courteous.

Many people have difficulty knowing when to choose *used* and *supposed* in their writing because in speaking, the final *d* is often not clearly heard.

> ***Incorrect:*** I am *suppose to* be in school today.
> ***Correct:*** I am *supposed to* be in school today.

Appendix C
Solving Spelling Problems

Learning to Spell Commonly Mispronounced Words

Several common English words are often mispronounced or pronounced in such a way that the result is incorrect spelling. Below are sixty common words that are often misspelled. As you study them, be careful to spell each of the underlined syllables correctly.

I.   Common Omission of Vowels

    1. Do not omit the underlined syllable with the *a*:

accident<u>a</u>lly	liter<u>a</u>ture
basic<u>a</u>lly	mini<u>a</u>ture
bound<u>a</u>ry	sep<u>a</u>rate
extr<u>a</u>ordinary	temper<u>a</u>ment
incident<u>a</u>lly	tempe<u>ra</u>ture

    2. Do not omit the underlined syllable with the *e*:

consid<u>e</u>rable	math<u>e</u>matics
diff<u>e</u>rence	num<u>e</u>rous
fun<u>e</u>ral	scen<u>e</u>ry
int<u>e</u>resting	

However, notice the following words in which the *e* should be omitted:

disaster	*becomes*	disastrous
enter	*becomes*	ent<u>r</u>ance
hinder	*becomes*	hind<u>r</u>ance
hunger	*becomes*	hun<u>gr</u>y
launder	*becomes*	laun<u>dr</u>y
monster	*becomes*	monstrous
remember	*becomes*	remem<u>br</u>ance

    3. Do not omit the underlined syllable with the *i*:

asp<u>i</u>rin	fam<u>i</u>ly	sim<u>i</u>lar

4. Do not omit the underlined syllable with the *o*:

chocolate   humorous
environment   laboratory
favourite   sophomore

5. Do not omit the underlined syllable with the *u*:

luxury
accuracy

6. Do not omit the underlined syllable with the *y*:

studying

II. Omission of Consonants

1. *b*
probably

2. *c*
arctic

3. *d*
candidate
handkerchief
handsome
supposed to
used to

4. *g*
recognize

5. *n*
government

6. *r*
February
library
surprise

7. *t*
authentic
identical
identity
partner
promptly
quantity

III. Common Addition of a Syllable

Do not add unnecessary syllables (i.e., athelete):

athlete
athletic

IV. Common Transposition of Letters

Do not transpose the underlined letters:

tragedy   persuade
perform   prefer

E X E R C I S E   **Words Commonly Mispronounced**

Circle the correct spelling for each of the following words.

1. separate   seprate   seperate
2. probably   probaly   probly

3. ardic	arctic	artic
4. suprise	saprize	surprise
5. tragedy	tradgedy	trajedy
6. quantity	quantidy	quanity
7. litrature	literature	literture
8. hungery	hungary	hungry
9. handsome	hansome	handsom
10. favourite	faverite	favrite

Learning to Spell *ie* and *ei* Words

Use this rhyme to help you remember how to spell most *ie* and *ei* words:

i before *e*
except after *c*
or when sounded like *a*
as in *neighbour* or *weigh*.

i before *e*

The majority of all the *ie* and *ei* words use *ie*.

believe
chief
friend
shriek
yield

except after *c*

ceiling
conceit
conceive
receipt
receive

or when sounded like *a*

beige
eight
reins
sleigh
vein

Once you have learned the rhyme, concentrate on learning the following groups of words that are the exceptions to this rhyme.

caffeine	leisure	ancient
codeine	seizure	conscience
protein	seize	efficient
		sufficient

neither	counterfeit
either	Fahrenheit
	foreign
sheik	height
stein	
their	
weird	

EXERCISE

ie and *ei* Words

Choose the correct combination of *ie* or *ei* for the following words.

1. sl_____gh
2. bel_____ve
3. s_____ge
4. v_____l
5. l_____sure

6. dec_____t
7. n_____ce
8. w_____ght
9. prot_____n
10. anc_____nt

Forming the Plurals of Nouns

Almost all nouns can be made plural by simply adding *-s* to the singular form:

girl	*becomes*	girls
dinner	*becomes*	dinners

However, each of the following groups of words has its own special rule for forming the plural.

1. **Words ending in -*y*:**
   In words ending in -*y* preceded by a *consonant*, change the *y* to *i* and add *es*.

la*dy*	*becomes*	lad*ies*
ceremo*ny*	*becomes*	ceremon*ies*

   Words ending in -*y* preceded by a *vowel* form their plurals in the regular way, by just adding -*s*.

d*ay*	*becomes*	days
monk*ey*	*becomes*	monkeys
vall*ey*	*becomes*	valleys

2. **Words ending in -*o*:**
   Most words ending in -*o* preceded by a consonant add -*es* to form the plural.

he*ro*	*becomes*	hero*es*
pota*to*	*becomes*	potato*es*
ec*ho*	*becomes*	echo*es*

However, musical terms or names of musical instruments add only -*s*.

piano	*becomes*	pianos
solo	*becomes*	solos
soprano	*becomes*	sopranos

Words ending in -*o* preceded by a *vowel* add -*s*.

pat*io*	*becomes*	patios
rad*io*	*becomes*	radios
rod*eo*	*becomes*	rodeos

Some words ending in -*o* may form their plural with -*s* or -*es*.

memento	*becomes*	mementos	*or*	mementoes
pinto	*becomes*	pintos	*or*	pintoes
zero	*becomes*	zeros	*or*	zeroes

If you are uncertain about the plural ending of a word ending in -*o*, it is best to use the dictionary. The dictionary gives all the endings of irregular plurals. If no plural form is given, you know the word will form its plural in the regular way, by adding only -*s*.

3. **Words ending in -*ch*, -*sh*, -*s*, -*x*, and -*z*:**
   For words ending in -*ch*, -*sh*, -*s*, -*x*, and -*z*, add -*es*.

   witch*es*
   dish*es*
   dress*es*
   tax*es*
   buzz*es*

4. **Words ending in -*fe* or -*f*:**
   Some words ending in -*fe* or -*f* change the *f* to *v* and add -*es*. You can hear the change from the *f* sound to the *v* sound in the plural.

wi*fe*	*becomes*	wi*ves*
lea*f*	*becomes*	lea*ves*

   Other words ending in -*f* or -*ef* keep the *f* and just add -*s*.

sheri*ff*	*becomes*	sheriffs
belie*f*	*becomes*	beliefs

   Again, you can hear that the *f* sound is kept in the plural. Some words can form their plural either way. If so, the dictionary will give the preferred way first.

5. **Foreign words:**
   Some words borrowed from other languages keep the plurals from those languages to form the plural in English.

alg*a*	*becomes*	alg*ae*
alumn*a*	*becomes*	alumn*ae*
alumn*us*	*becomes*	alumn*i*
cris*is*	*becomes*	cris*es*
phenomen*on*	*becomes*	phenomen*a*

6. **Compound nouns:**
Compound nouns make their plurals by putting the -*s* on the end of the main word.

brother-in-law	*becomes*	brother*s*-in-law
passer-by	*becomes*	passer*s*-by

7. **Irregular plurals:**
Some nouns in English have irregular plurals.

Singular	**Plural**
child	children
deer	deer
foot	feet
goose	geese
man, woman	men, women
moose	moose
mouse	mice
ox	oxen
sheep	sheep
tooth	teeth

E X E R C I S E

Forming the Plurals of Nouns

Using the rules you have learned, make the following words plural.

1. puppy   _____

2. mother-in-law   _____

3. tooth   _____

4. cameo   _____

5. phenomenon   _____

6. loaf   _____

7. match   _____

8. mix   _____

9. enemy   _____

10. bag   _____

Prefixes and Suffixes

Like everything else in this world, words had to begin somewhere. Many English words come from (had their *roots* in) other languages; others were created to describe something new. For example, modern English has many roots in Old English, ancient Greek, and Latin. For example:

Roots and Derivatives

Old English

akr	a field, acre
haelan	to heal, health
foda	food, fodder
war	defence, war

Latin

audio	to hear, audience
clarus	clear, clarify
dignus	dignity, worth
nomen	name

Greek

angelos	angel
gramma	a letter
kosmos	the world
logos	word

Prefixes and suffixes can be added to the roots of words to alter the meaning of the words or to create new words with new meanings. A *prefix* is a word or part of a word placed before the root of a word, and a *suffix* is placed after the root. As is the case with root words, the English language derives many of its prefixes and suffixes from Latin and Greek. For example:

Some Latin Prefixes

ante	=	before
contra	=	against
extra	=	beyond
in	=	in, into
non	=	not
post	=	after
pro	=	before
super	=	above

Some Greek Prefixes

ampli	=	on both sides
anti	=	opposite
auto	=	self
hemi	=	half
hyper	=	over, above
mono	=	alone, single
para	=	beside
pro	=	before

Some Latin Suffixes

-ary	belonging to
-ess	feminine of
-et, ette	denoting diminution
-ty	quality, state, condition

Some Greek Suffixes

-ic	pertaining to
-ism	act, state, condition
-ist	a doer

Some examples of English words with prefixes and suffixes added include

pro + claim	=	proclaim
anti + biotic	=	antibiotic
in + dispensable	=	indispensable

hemi   + sphere = hemisphere
benefit   + ary   = beneficiary
host   + ess   = hostess
communist + ism   = communism

Adding prefixes and suffixes may change the spelling of the former roots. This occurs most frequently when suffixes are added to words. Consult the basic spelling rules on the following pages when prefixes and suffixes are parts of words.

Should the Final Consonant Be Doubled?

The answer to the question of whether a final consonant should be doubled involves the most complicated spelling rule. However, the rule is well worth learning because once you know it, you will suddenly be able to spell thousands of words correctly.

In order to understand the rule, remember first the difference between vowels (a, e, i, o, u, and sometimes y) and consonants (all the other letters in the alphabet). The problem in spelling occurs when you want to add an ending that begins with a vowel, such as *-ed, -er, -est,* or *-ing*. Sometimes a word will double the last letter before adding an ending:

trap + ing = trapping   The fur traders spent their time tra*pp*ing animals.

Sometimes the word will *not* double the last letter before adding the ending:

turn + er = turner   He dropped the pancake tur*n*er.

How do you know when to double the final consonant?

Rule for Doubling One-Syllable Words

Double the final consonant of a one-syllable word when adding an ending that begins with a vowel only if the last three letters of the word are a consonant-vowel-consonant combination.

Since *rap* in the word *trap* is a consonant-vowel-consonant combination, this one-syllable word will double the final consonant when adding an ending beginning with a vowel. Since the last three letters *urn* in the word *turn* are a vowel-consonant-consonant combination, this one-syllable word does not double the final consonant when adding an ending beginning with a vowel.

For each of the following one-syllable words, determine whether or not the word will double the final consonant when adding an ending beginning with a vowel.

PRACTICE

One-Syllable Word	Consonant-Vowel-Consonant Combination?	Double?	Add -ing Ending
drag	yes	yes	dragging
drain	no	no	draining
slip			
crack			
broil			
win			

Note: In words with *qu* like *quit* or *quiz*, think of the *qu* as a consonant. (The *u* does have a consonant *w* sound.) *quit* + ing = qui*tt*ing.

Rule for Doubling Words of More than One Syllable

For words of more than one syllable, the rule adds one more condition: if the first syllable is accented in the newly formed word, you do not double the final consonant.

pre fer′ + ed = pre ferred′

but

pre fer′ + ence = pref′ er ence
(The accent has changed to the first syllable.)

Try these two-syllable words:

con *trol′* + ing   =   _____

fe′ *ver* + ish   =   _____

For each of the following words of more than one syllable, determine whether or not the word will double the final consonant when adding an ending beginning with a vowel.

com *pel′* + ed   =   _____

dif′ *fer* + ence =   _____

be *gin′* + ing   =   _____

EXERCISE

Doubling the Final Consonant When Adding Endings That Begin with Vowels

Decide whether or not to double the final consonant when adding the endings to the following words.

	Word	Ending		New Word
1.	bit	+ en	=	_____
2.	oc cur′	+ ence	=	_____
3.	wa′ ver	+ ing	=	_____
4.	pre fer′	+ ed	=	_____
5.	pre′ fer	+ ence	=	_____
6.	thin	+ er	=	_____
7.	trans fer′	+ ed	=	_____
8.	sail	+ ing	=	_____
9.	ex cel′	+ ent	=	_____
10.	o mit′	+ ed	=	_____

Words Ending in *-y*

1. When a *y* at the end of a word is preceded by a consonant, change *y* to *i* and add the ending.

car*ry*	+ er	=	carr*ier*
mer*ry*	+ ment	=	merr*iment*
fun*ny*	+ er	=	_____
bu*sy*	+ ness	=	_____
va*ry*	+ es	=	_____

Exceptions: Do not change the *y* to *i* if the ending starts with an *i*. In English we seldom have two *i*'s together.

stu*dy*	+ ing	=	stud*ying* (not studiing)
rea*dy*	+ ing	=	_____

Some long words drop the *y* when adding the ending. You can hear that the *y* syllable is missing when you pronounce the word correctly.

milita*ry*	+ ism	=	militar*ism*
accompa*ny*	+ ist	=	_____

2. When *y* at the end of a word is preceded by a vowel, do *not* change the *y* when adding the ending. Simply add the ending.

sur*vey*	+ s	=	surv*eys*
enj*oy*	+ ment	=	_____

E X E R C I S E   **Adding Endings to Words That End in -y**

Add endings to the following words, being sure to change the *y* to *i* whenever necessary.

Word	Ending		New Word
1. key	+ s	=	_____
2. lonely	+ ness	=	_____
3. cry	+ ing	=	_____
4. cry	+ s	=	_____
5. pray	+ er	=	_____
6. cray	+ fish	=	_____
7. monkey	+ ing	=	_____
8. beauty	+ ful	=	_____
9. theory	+ es	=	_____
10. ceremony	+ al	=	_____

Is It One Word or Two?

There is often confusion about whether certain word combinations should be joined together to form compound words. Study the following groups of words to avoid this common confusion.

These words are always written as one word:

another	everything	playroom
bathroom	grandmother	schoolteacher
bedroom	nearby	southeast, northwest, etc.
bookkeeper	nevertheless	workplace
cannot	newspaper	yourself
downstairs		

These words are always written as two words:

a lot	high school
all right	living room
dining room	no one
good night	

These words are written as one or two words depending on their use:

all ready (*pronoun and adj.*)	completely prepared
already (*adv.*)	previously; before

all together (*pronoun and adj.*)	in a group
altogether (*adv.*)	completely
all ways (*adj. and noun*)	every road or path
always (*adverb*)	on every occasion
any one (*adj. and pronoun*)	one person or thing in a specific group
anyone (*indef. pronoun*)	any person at all
every one (*adj. and pronoun*)	every person or thing in a specific group
everyone (*indef. pronoun*)	all of the people
may be (*verb*)	might be
maybe (*adv.*)	perhaps

E X E R C I S E

One Word or Two?

Fill in the blank in each of the following sentences by choosing the correct word or words to complete that sentence.

1. The blue rug looks beautiful in the white _____.
(bed room, bedroom)

2. The room is usually occupied by _____ , but she is not here right now. (grandmother, grand mother)

3. She has _____ left for a winter vacation.
(all ready, already)

4. Last night we all called her and _____ we sang "Happy Birthday" over the phone. (all together, altogether)

5. We _____ remember her birthday, no matter where we are.
(all ways, always)

6. _____ likes to be remembered on special days, particularly a birthday.
(Every one, Everyone)

7. Next year, _____ all the members of the family will be able to
(may be, maybe)
celebrate her birthday with us.

8. If she _____ come to us, we will drive up and surprise her.
(cannot, can not)

9. Most families have members who do not live _____.
(near by, nearby)

10. _____ , we can keep in touch by letter, phone, or visits.
(Never the less, Nevertheless)

Spelling 200 Tough Words

Word List 1: Silent Letters

b	**h**	**p**	**w**
clim*b*	ex*h*ibit	*p*neumonia	ans*w*er
crum*b*	r*h*etoric	*p*sychology	
de*b*t	r*h*ythm		
dou*b*t	sc*h*ool	**s**	
su*b*tle		aisle	
	l	deb*r*is	
c	*col*onel	island	
indi*c*t			
	n	**t**	
d	autum*n*	depo*t*	
knowle*d*ge	colum*n*	lis*t*en	
We*d*nesday	condem*n*	mor*t*gage	

Word List 2: Double Letters

a*cc*identa*ll*y	exa*gg*erate	questio*nn*aire
a*cc*o*mm*odate	fina*ll*y	reco*mm*end
acro*ss*	guarant*ee*	su*cc*eed
add*r*ess	ne*c*e*ss*ary	su*cc*e*ss*
a*nn*ual	o*cc*asiona*ll*y	su*gg*est
a*pp*arently	omi*ss*ion	su*mm*arize
a*rr*angement	posse*ss*ion	tomo*rr*ow
co*mm*i*tt*ee	prefe*rr*ed	wri*tt*en *but* wri*t*ing
emba*rr*a*ss*		

Word List 3: *-able* or *-ible*

-able
Usually, when you begin with a complete word, the ending is *-able*.

acceptable
agreeable

- These words keep the *e* when adding the ending:

peaceable   manageable
noticeable   knowledgeable

- These words drop the *e* when adding the ending:

conceivable   dispensable
desirable   imaginable

-ible

Usually, if you start with a root that is not a word, the ending is *-ible*.

audible	illegible	possible
compatible	incredible	sensible
eligible	permissible	susceptible
feasible	plausible	tangible

Word List 4: *de-* or *di-*

de-	**di-**
decide	dilemma
decision	dilute
delinquent	discipline
descend	discuss
describe	disease
despair	disguise
despicable	dispense
despise	dispute
despite	dissent
despondent	divide
destructive	divine
develop	division
device	

Word List 5: the *-er* Sound

Most words ending with the *-er* sound are spelled with *-er*, as in the words *prisoner*, *customer*, and *hunger*. Words that are exceptions to this should be learned carefully.

-ar

beggar	dollar	polar
burglar	grammar	similar
calendar	pillar	vulgar
collar		

-or

actor	emperor	professor
author	governor	sailor
bachelor	motor	scissors
doctor		

-our	**-re**	**-ur**	**-yr**
humour	centre	murmur	martyr
labour	litre		
neighbour	theatre		

Word List 6: *-ance* or *-ence*

Most words with the *-ence* sound at the end are spelled *-ence*. Here are a few examples:

audience   intelligence
correspondence   licence (noun)
excellence   presence
existence   reference

Learn these exceptions:

-ance
allowance   nuisance
ambulance   observance
appearance   resistance
assistance   significance
attendance   tolerance
balance
dominance   **-ense**
guidance   license (verb)
ignorance
                   -eance
                   vengeance

Word List 7: Problems with *s*, *c*, *z*, *x*, and *k*

absence   criticize   medicine
alcohol   ecstasy   muscle
analyze/analyse   emphasize   prejudice
auxiliary   especially   recede
awkward   exceed   sincerely
biscuit   exercise   supersede
complexion   fascinate   vacillate
concede   magazine   vicious
consensus

Word List 8: Twenty-four Demons

acquire   courageous   occurred
argument   extremely   occurrence
benefit   frightening   privilege
cafeteria   grateful   ridiculous
category   inoculate   secretary
cemetery   lightning   truly
conquer   ninety   until
corroborate   ninth   village

Appendix D
Capitalization

Many students are often confused or careless about the use of capital letters. Sometimes they capitalize words without thinking, or they capitalize "important" words without really understanding what makes them important enough to deserve a capital letter. The question of when to capitalize words becomes easier to answer when you study the following rules and carefully apply them to your own writing.

Ten Basic Rules for Capitalization

1. Capitalize the first word of every sentence.
2. Capitalize the names of specific things and places.

Specific buildings:

I went to the Jamestown Post Office.

but

I went to the post office.

Specific streets, cities, states, countries:

She lives on Elam Avenue.

but

She lives on the same street as my mum and dad.

Specific organizations:

He collected money for the Canadian Cancer Society.

but

Janice joined more than one club at the school.

Specific institutions:

The loan is from the Royal Bank of Canada.

but

The loan is from one of the banks in town.

Specific bodies of water:

My uncle fishes every summer on Lake Winnipeg.

but

My uncle spends every summer at the lake.

3. Capitalize days of the week, months of the year, and holidays. Do *not* capitalize the names of seasons.

The second Monday in October is Thanksgiving Day.

but

I cannot wait until spring.

4. Capitalize the names of all languages, nationalities, races, religions, deities, and sacred terms.

My friend who is Ethiopian speaks very little English.
The *Koran* is the sacred book of Islam.

5. Capitalize the first word, the last word, and every important word in a title. Do *not* capitalize articles, prepositions, or short connecting words in the title.

World of One is a novel by Charles Templeton.
Her favourite short story is "We Have to Sit Opposite" by Ethel Wilson.

6. Capitalize the first word of a direct quotation.

The teacher said, "You have been chosen for the part."

but

"You have been chosen," she said, "for the part."

Note: for is not capitalized because it is not the beginning of the sentence in quotation marks.

7. Capitalize historical events, periods, and documents.

The Rebellion of 1837
The Great Depression
The Charter of Rights and Freedoms

8. Capitalize the words *north*, *south*, *east*, and *west* when they are used as places rather than as directions.

He comes from the East.

but

The farm is about 40 kilometres west of Weyburn.

9. Capitalize people's names.

Proper names:

George Hendrickson

Professional titles when they are used with the person's proper name:

Judge Samuelson	*but*	the judge
Professor Shapiro	*but*	the professor

Term for a relative (like *mother, sister, nephew, uncle*) when it is used in the place of the proper name:

I told Grandfather I would meet him later.

- Notice that terms for relatives are not capitalized if a pronoun, article, or adjective is used with the name.

I told my grandfather I would meet him later.

10. Capitalize brand names.

Band-Aid
Kleenex

In this case, *Band-Aid* and *Kleenex* are product names and therefore are proper nouns.

EXERCISE   **Capitalization**

Capitalize wherever necessary.

1. The italian student got a job in the school cafeteria.
2. Our train ride through the canadian rockies was fabulous.
3. The author often made references in his writing to names from the bible.
4. A student at the university of alberta was chosen for the national award.
5. My uncle's children always have a party on halloween.
6. I met the president of bell canada last friday at a convention in winnipeg, manitoba.
7. The cobalt 60 cancer therapy unit was invented by a canadian, dr. donald green.
8. My niece said, "why don't you consider moving farther south if you hate the winter so much?"
9. The canadian auto workers voted not to go on strike over the new contract.
10. A very popular radio program in the west is called "a prairie home companion."

Appendix E
Irregular Verbs

Principal Parts of Irregular Verbs

Simple Form	Past Form	Past Participle
1. Principal parts are the same.		
beat	beat	beat or beaten
bet	bet	bet
burst	burst	burst
cast	cast	cast
cost	cost	cost
cut	cut	cut
fit	fit	fit
hit	hit	hit
hurt	hurt	hurt
let	let	let
put	put	put
quit	quit	quit
read	*read	*read
rid	rid	rid
set	set	set
shut	shut	shut
split	split	split
spread	spread	spread
wet	wet	wet
2. The past form and past participle are the same.		
bend	bent	bent
lend	lent	lent
send	sent	sent
spend	spent	spent
build	built	built

*Pronunciation changes.

Simple Form	Past Form	Past Participle
creep	crept	crept
feel	felt	felt
keep	kept	kept
sleep	slept	slept
sweep	swept	swept
deal	dealt	dealt
mean	meant	meant
leave	left	left
bleed	bled	bled
feed	fed	fed
flee	fled	fled
lead	led	led
speed	sped	sped
cling	clung	clung
dig	dug	dug
spin	spun	spun
stick	stuck	stuck
sting	stung	stung
strike	struck	struck
swing	swung	swung
wring	wrung	wrung
win	won	won
lay (to put)	laid	laid
pay	paid	paid
say	said	said
sell	sold	sold
tell	told	told
bind	bound	bound
find	found	found
grind	ground	ground
wind	wound	wound
bring	brought	brought
buy	bought	bought
fight	fought	fought
find	found	found
think	thought	thought
seek	sought	sought
teach	taught	taught
catch	caught	caught

Simple Form	Past Form	Past Participle
have	had	had
sit	sat	sat
hear	heard	heard
hold	held	held
shoot	shot	shot
stand	stood	stood

3. All forms are different

draw	drew	drawn
fall	fell	fallen
shake	shook	shaken
take	took	taken
bear	bore	borne
swear	swore	sworn
tear	tore	torn
wear	wore	worn
blow	blew	blown
fly	flew	flown
grow	grew	grown
know	knew	known
throw	threw	thrown
begin	began	begun
drink	drank	drunk
ring	rang	rung
shrink	shrank	shrunk
sink	sank	sunk
sing	sang	sung
spring	sprang	sprung
swim	swam	swum
bite	bit	bitten (or bit)
hide	hid	hidden (or hid)
drive	drove	driven
ride	rode	ridden
stride	strode	stridden
rise	rose	risen
write	wrote	written
dive	dove	dived
break	broke	broken
freeze	froze	frozen
speak	spoke	spoken

Simple Form	Past Form	Past Participle
steal	stole	stolen
weave	wove	woven
get	got	gotten
forget	forgot	forgotten
choose	chose	chosen
give	gave	given
forgive	forgave	forgiven
forbid	forbade	forbidden
do	did	done
eat	ate	eaten
go	went	gone
lie (to recline)	lay	lain
see	saw	seen

E X E R C I S E

Irregular Verbs

Supply the past form or the past participle for each verb in parentheses.

1. We _____ four trout in the stream.
   (to catch)

2. The burglar _____ up the fire escape.
   (to creep)

3. The audience _____ when the singer attempted the high notes.
   (to flee)

4. The pipe _____ yesterday; we are waiting for a plumber.
   (to burst)

5. He has _____ aimlessly around the city for several hours.
   (to ride)

6. The firefighters _____ down the ladder.
   (to slide)

7. The elevator _____ quickly to the tenth floor.
   (to rise)

8. She had _____ her job before the baby was born.
   (to quit)

9. The pond was _____ enough for ice-skating.
   (to freeze)

10. He had washed and _____ out all his clothes in the bathtub.
    (to wring)

Appendix F
Proofreading and Revising

Proofreading and revising your work is the final stage before typing, word processing, or composing the final copy of your work. Of course, you'll need to check your final copy for typos and other mistakes you may have made, but the proofreading stage is the stage at which you should pick up most, if not all, of your errors.

Proofreading and revising is a boring job: No one likes to look for mistakes, but it's better to correct the mistakes at this stage than to have your instructor find mistakes and downgrade your work accordingly.

Too many writers finish their first draft and then start rereading to catch mistakes. The idea is to get the proofreading process over with as soon as possible. If the writer misses a few little mistakes, who's going to notice? But proofreading involves much more than rereading and hoping some mistakes jump out. It involves a well-planned approach to finding mistakes and to discovering better ways of writing.

What you need first is a quiet place and a block of time which will allow you to complete the task in one sitting. You need to examine especially carefully those areas of spelling, grammar, or composition in which you know you have weaknesses, and you need someone to read your material and offer a second opinion on the quality of your work when you've completed your proofreading and revising. But most of all, you need to follow a system. When you've finished the first draft of your work, set it aside for a day or two. Then read through the whole thing, making notes, corrections, or additions based on the following scheme. This scheme, and the checklist on p. 369, are adapted from *The Reluctant Writer* by Roger Mann and John Roberts.

1. Check the macrocomposition: the content and the overall arrangement of ideas.
2. Check the microcomposition: the flow of thought, the sentence structure, the wording, grammar, and usage.
3. Check the spelling.
4. Check the punctuation.
5. Check the manuscript form.

Macrocomposition

Checklist

1. Have you provided enough background explanation at the outset for the reader to
   a. recognize the context;
   b. understand what follows;
   c. want to read further?
2. Do the ideas introduced in the beginning connect logically to a continuous line of thought that moves sensibly from introduction to discussion, and ends in a conclusion? Are appropriate connecting words used?
3. Are the thoughts packaged in small chunks of information that the audience is capable of following? Will the sequence of ideas convince and enlighten the reader?
4. Is the information sufficient to do the job it is intended to do (are there any gaps)? Is all of the discussion relevant to the subject and the purpose?
5. Is the point of view toward the reader consistent throughout the text?
6. Are the time sequences logical and consistent? Check verbs for uniformity of tense and mood.
7. Is the wording concise, and are physical references precise and concrete? If you are dealing with ideas and concepts, are they adequately explained and illustrated? Is the wording geared to the presumed reading level of the reader?
8. Is the tone appropriate to the situation, the purpose, and the reader? Is it consistent throughout the text?
9. Does the conclusion fulfil the intended purpose? At the end, will the reader understand the message, agree with what you have said, and be motivated to act?

Microcomposition

Checklist

Check your sentences for *grammar:*

1. Is every sentence grammatically complete, with no sentence fragments?
2. In sentences with two or more independent clauses, are the clauses grammatically parallel, and either connected by co-ordinate conjunctions or separated by semicolons, with no run-ons or comma splices?
3. Are subordinate clauses and verb phrases clearly related to the words they modify, with no dangling verbals or misplaced modifiers?
4. Are the elements of each sentence consistent in grammar and in thought:

- Do subjects agree with verbs?
- Do pronouns agree with their antecedents and with each other in person and in number?
- Is it clear which nouns the pronouns stand in for?
- Are the verb tenses consistent?
- If you have used lists, are the elements of the list grammatically parallel?
- Is the word order appropriate and unconfusing?

Check your sentences for *style:*

1. Are the beginnings of your sentences varied — do some start with the subject, some with introductory phrases or clauses, and a select few with reversed word order?
2. Have you varied the clause structure of your sentences — some simple, some compound, some complex, some compound–complex?
3. Have you mixed your sentence lengths effectively — long sentences to convey information and establish a rhythm, short sentences to get important points across?

Check your *wording and usage:*

1. Have you used vocabulary suitable to the reader and the situation?
2. Are your nouns concrete, tangible, and specific?
3. Are your verbs active in positive situations, passive in negative situations?
4. Have you used adjectives and adverbs selectively and sparingly? Can you replace any adjective–noun or adverb–verb combinations with single, carefully selected nouns or verbs?
5. Could you explain the reason for your choice of every word and its placement in the sentence?
6. Have you used any words that you are not entirely sure about — the spelling, the meaning, or the way the words should be used?
7. Have you used any clichés? If so, can you justify using them? If not, can you think of original expressions to replace them?
8. Have you used any idiomatic expressions? If so, are you sure you have used them correctly and appropriately?
9. Have you used jargon, such as technical terms or acronyms? Are you sure the reader will understand these terms?

Check your *punctuation:*

1. Have you used periods at the ends of sentences and after abbreviations?
2. Do question marks indicate the ends of interrogative sentences?
3. Have you used exclamation marks to emphasize especially important points or statements? (Do not overuse this device!)
4. Have you used quotation marks properly — for all direct speech, direct quotations from sources, and titles of short works?

5. Have you used, but not overused, commas to pace the reader's understanding of the text, to separate internal parts of your sentences, and to clarify potentially ambiguous word combinations?
6. Have you used semicolons to separate parts of a sentence that are grammatically distinct, or to separate items in a complex list?
7. Have you used dashes and colons correctly?

Check your *spelling, capitalization*, and *apostrophes*:

1. Have you checked the words you traditionally have trouble with?
2. Have you checked *ie* combinations, spelling changes caused by suffixes, and consonants that must be doubled or not?
3. Have you used capital letters properly — for titles, names, places, months, countries, etc.?
4. Have you used apostrophes correctly — for possessive nouns and indefinite pronouns, or for shortened forms of words?

Check your *manuscript form:*

1. Has all your source material been suitably acknowledged and documented?
2. Have you used the proper format conventions for the form you are writing — memo, letter, report, essay?

Appendix G
Answer Key to Selected Practices and Exercises

PART I: DEVELOPING THE COMPLETE SENTENCE

Chapter 1: Finding Subjects and Verbs in Simple Sentences

Finding the Subject of a Sentence

EXERCISE 1 (P. 7)
1. The <u>train</u> stopped.
2. <u>Steven Laye</u> had arrived!
3. <u>He</u> was afraid.
4. <u>Everything</u> looked so strange.
5. The fearful <u>man</u> held his bag tightly.
6. The <u>tunnel</u> led up to the street.
7. <u>Buses</u> and <u>cars</u> choked the avenues.

EXERCISE 2 (P. 7)
1. The <u>road</u> twisted and turned.
2. A young <u>boy</u> hurried along briskly.
3. <u>He</u> carried an important message.
4. A red-winged <u>blackbird</u> flew overhead.
5. Dark <u>clouds</u> and a sudden <u>wind</u> encouraged him to hurry faster.
6. His <u>family</u> would be elated.
7. <u>Someone</u> was working in the yard.

Finding Hidden Subjects

EXERCISE 1 (P. 11)
1. (<u>You</u>) look ~~at a map of South America.~~
2. Where is the ancient <u>city</u> ~~of Chan Chan?~~
3. Here ~~on the coastal desert of northern Peru~~ stand the <u>remains</u> ~~of this city of the kings.~~
4. <u>Chan Chan</u>, ~~once the fabulously wealthy centre of the Chimor,~~ is situated ~~in one of the driest, bleakest regions in the world.~~

5. <u>It</u> was the largest pre-Columbian city ~~in South America.~~
6. ~~In the ruins of this city,~~ <u>scientists</u> have found fragments to piece together the mystery ~~of the past.~~
7. How could this <u>civilization</u> have survived this hostile environment and become so advanced?

Finding Action Verbs

EXERCISE 1 (P. 13)
1. Some <u>people</u> (collect) very strange objects.
2. One <u>man</u> (saves) the fortunes ~~from fortune cookies.~~
3. A <u>group</u> ~~in Alberta~~ often (meets) to discuss their spark plug collections.
4. <u>People</u> ~~in Brandon~~ (gather) many types ~~of barbed wire.~~
5. <u>Collectors</u> (take) pride ~~in the possession of unusual items.~~
6. A <u>collection</u>, ~~like odd rocks or unique automobiles,~~ (gives) a person some individuality.
7. <u>Collections</u> (keep) us happy ~~from childhood to old age.~~

EXERCISE 2 (P. 13)
1. Traditional <u>Chinese medicine</u> (harnesses) ancient healing techniques ~~in the practice of "gigong."~~
2. <u>Masters</u> ~~of this Chinese practice~~ (claim) the ability to cure many diseases.
3. The <u>master</u> (projects) a mysterious force ~~into his students.~~
4. The <u>hands</u> ~~of the Chinese gigong practitioner~~ (pound) ~~at the air above a patient.~~
5. Many <u>patients</u> (respond) ~~to this invisible force.~~
6. Some <u>patients</u> (sway) their bodies ~~with the power of the force.~~

7. Some doctors (conduct) research ~~in China in hopes of finding the secrets of this ancient art.~~

Chapter Review Exercises
Finding Subjects and Verbs in Simple Sentences

EXERCISE 1 (P. 16)

1. Mother and Dad always (blame) me ~~for any trouble with my sister.~~
2. My sister, ~~the most popular girl in her class,~~ (is) two years older than I.
3. Yesterday, ~~for instance,~~ she (was trying on) her new graduation dress.
4. Helpfully, I (took out) her new shoes and purse ~~for her.~~
5. Margaret instantly (became) furious ~~with me.~~
6. I (was) only (sharing) Margaret's excitement ~~about her new clothes.~~

Chapter 2: Correcting the Fragment in Simple Sentences

Practise Putting a Conversation into Complete Sentences (p. 20)

1. You are early again.
2. I want to get a front-row seat.
3. Is your homework done yet?
4. It is nearly finished.
5. Do you think the professor will give us a quiz today?
6. I certainly hope not.
7. It looks like rain today.
8. It had better not rain. I haven't got a bag for these new books.
9. Are you going to the game on Saturday?
10. I will probably go.

Understanding Fragments

EXERCISE 1 (P. 21)

1. a. subject 2. b. verb 3. c. both subject and verb 4. b. verb 5. b. verb 6. a. subject 7. d. contains subject and verb, but lacks complete thought

Making Fragments into Sentences

EXERCISE 2 (P. 22)

Answers will vary. These are sample answers.
1. The otter returned to the river.
2. A bird on the oak branch sang.
3. The river flowed between the island and the mainland.
4. The hawk in a soaring motion flew into the sky.
5. The fishing boats on the lake glided over the water.
6. The loon dropped like a stone into the water.
7. The fisherman put the net away.

Identifying Phrases

EXERCISE 1 (P. 24)

1. infinitive 2. infinitive 3. prepositional 4. prepositional 5. noun 6. noun 7. prepositional

EXERCISE 2 (P. 25)

1. prepositional 2. infinitive 3. prepositional 4. noun 5. verb 6. prepositional 7. infinitive 8. verb 9. infinitive 10. prepositional

Correcting the Fragment That Contains a Participle

EXERCISE 1 (P. 26)

Answers will vary. These are sample answers.
1. a. He is moving out of the house.
   b. He moves out of the house.
   c. Moving out of the house, he left his stereo behind.
   d. Moving out of the house is the thing to do.
2. a. He is talking on the telephone.
   b. He talks on the telephone.
   c. Talking on the telephone, he didn't hear the robbers.
   d. Talking on the telephone is time consuming.
3. a. She is driving the car down Highway 60.
   b. She drives the car down Highway 60.
   c. Driving the car down Highway 60, she had a flat tire.
   d. Driving the car down Highway 60 is pleasant.

Recognizing the Fragment

EXERCISE 2 (P. 28)

1. complete 2. fragment 3. fragment 4. fragment 5. complete 6. fragment 7. complete 8. fragment 9. fragment 10. fragment

Chapter 3: Combining Sentences Using Co-ordination

Use a Comma Plus a Co-ordinating Conjunction

PRACTICE (P. 32)

1. The audience was packed (, for) this was a man with an international reputation.
2. He could have told about all his successes (, but) instead he spoke about his disappointments.

3. His <u>words</u> <u>were</u> electric ⟨ , so ⟩ the <u>crowd</u> <u>was</u> attentive.
4. <u>I</u> <u>should have brought</u> a tape recorder ⟨ , or ⟩ at least <u>I</u> <u>should have taken</u> notes.

Combining Sentences Using Co-ordinating Conjunctions

EXERCISE 1 (P. 33)
Answers will vary. These are sample answers.
1. contrast
   but
2. reason
   for
3. result
   so
4. add
   and
5. reason
   for
6. contrast
   but
7. reason
   for

Use a Semicolon, an Adverbial Conjunction, and a Comma

PRACTICE (P. 37)
1. The <u>restaurant</u> <u>is</u> always too crowded on Saturdays ⟨ ; nevertheless, ⟩ it <u>serves</u> the best food in town.
2. The <u>land</u> <u>was</u> not for sale ⟨ ; however, ⟩ the <u>house</u> <u>could be rented</u>.
3. The <u>lawsuit</u> <u>cost</u> the company several million dollars ⟨ ; consequently, ⟩ the <u>company</u> <u>went</u> out of business a short time later.
4. The <u>doctor</u> <u>told</u> him to lose weight ⟨ ; furthermore, ⟩ she <u>insisted</u> he also stop smoking.

Combining Sentences Using Adverbial Conjunctions

EXERCISE 1 (P. 37)
Answers will vary. These are sample answers.
1. Most people prefer to write with a pen or pencil; however, the computer is quickly becoming anothe favourite writing tool.
2. Computers provide a powerful way to create and store pieces of writing; furthermore, they will become even more important in the future.
3. Computers have already revolutionized today's offices; consequently, no modern business can afford to be without them.

4. The prices of many computers are coming down these days; accordingly, more and more people se that owning a computer is a real possibility.
5. Some children know more about computers than many adults; moreover, some children are teaching adults how to operate computers.
6. Professional writers have become enthusiastic about the use of computers; nonetheless, there are still some writers who will use only a ballpoint pen.
7. We have many technological aids for writing; nevertheless, let us not forget that the source for all our ideas is the human brain.

Chapter 4: Combining Sentences Using Subordination

Use a Subordinating Conjunction to Create a Complex Sentence

PRACTICE (P. 46)
1. a. Since the librarian took constant coffee breaks, the boss fired him.
   b. The boss fired the librarian, since he took constant coffee breaks.
2. a. After he won the wrestling match, he went out to celebrate.
   b. He went out to celebrate after he won the wrestling match.
3. a. When Halyna returned from Europe this spring, the family was excited.
   b. The family was excited when Halyna returned from Europe this spring.

Recognizing Dependent and Independent Clauses

EXERCISE 1 (P. 46)
1. DC   2. DC   3. IC   4. DC   5. IC   6. DC   7. DC

EXERCISE 2 (P. 47)
1. DC   2. IC   3. DC   4. IC   5. IC   6. DC   7. DC

Combining Sentences Using Subordination

EXERCISE 2 (P. 48)
Answers will vary. These are sample answers.
1. While he was eating breakfast, the results of the election came over the radio.
2. The town council voted against the plan because they believed the project was too expensive.
3. I will see my teacher tonight, since she is speaking at the university this evening.

4. Even though not one person in the department was promoted last year, the worker hoped for a promotion

5. Because the worker hoped for a promotion, he made sure all his work was done accurately and on time.

Use a Relative Pronoun to Create a Complex Sentence

PRACTICE (P. 50)

1. The chemistry lab that I attend is two hours long.

2. The student assistant who is standing by the door is very knowledgeable.

3. The equipment that was purchased last year will make possible some important new research.

How Do You Punctuate a Clause with a Relative Pronoun?

PRACTICE (P. 51)

1. Canada's first census, which was taken in 1667, showed 3215 non-Native inhabitants in 668 families.

2. Most of these families were French Canadians who lived near the St. Lawrence River.

3. By the time of Confederation, the population of the country had risen to 3 463 000, which was an increase of 1077 percent over 200 years.

4. If the population, which is about 30 000 000 persons in Canada now, increases by a similar percentage, we'll have a population of 280 200 000 by the year 2167.

5. Where, do you think, will we put everyone who will live in Canada then?

Combining Sentences Using Relative Pronouns

EXERCISE 1 (P. 51)

Answers will vary. These are sample answers.

1. The prime minister, who was an intelligent man, asked his advisers for help.

2. His advisers, whose interests were the same as their leader's, met with him on Parliament Hill.

3. Even the leader of the opposition, whom people respected, appeared visibly alarmed.

4. The meeting that had been scheduled began at two o'clock.

5. Every idea that was put forward was examined in great detail.

6. One adviser who was present was completely opposed to the plan.

7. Finally the group agreed on a plan of action that was acceptable to all.

Chapter Review Exercises
Combining Sentences Using Co-ordination and Subordination

EXERCISE 2 (P. 54)

It is evening, and I am afraid. The sun's rays are weak. That red crucible, sunk in the clouds, is only a dim reflection of itself, but it is not a source of light or life. The plains stretch far into the distance behind me. The human dwellings, the villages and cities, are far away, hidden by the rising mist and fog from the swamps. Only reeds rustle in the wind and waterbirds cry disconsolately there. Beside me, the little grassy glade where I stan in, is a forest — ghana, swapada, shankula — dense and full of dangerous beasts of prey. The overhanging fo liage has the appearance of clouds that hold and nourish a damp darkness. The giant trunks of the trees have grown so close together that the forest becomes both a prison and a fort. No foot paths are visible because the undergrowth denies the possibility of making an inroad.

Chapter 5: Correcting the Run-on

Revising Run-ons

EXERCISE 1 (P. 57)

Answers will vary. These are sample answers.

1. *Simple:* Intelligence tests for children are not always useful. They are a basic tool for measurement in most schools.

   Compound: Intelligence tests for children are not always useful, but they are a basic tool for measurement in most schools.

   Intelligence tests for children are not always useful; however, they are a basic tool for measurement in most schools.

   Complex: Although intelligence tests for children are not always useful, they are a basic tool for measurement in most schools.

2. *Simple:* Many people are opposed to gambling in all its forms. They will not even buy a lottery ticket.

   Compound: Many people are opposed to gambling in all its forms, so they will not even buy a lottery ticket.

   Many people are opposed to gambling in all its forms; indeed, they will not even buy a lottery ticket.

   Complex: Since many people are opposed to gambling in all its forms, they will not even buy a lottery ticket.

3. *Simple:* Public transportation is the major problem facing many of our cities. Little is being done to change the situation.

   Compound: Public transportation is the major problem facing many of our cities, but little is being done to change the situation.

   Public transportation is the major problem facing many of our cities; however, little is being done to change the situation.

   Complex: Although public transportation is the major problem facing many of our cities, little being done to change the situation.

4. *Simple:* Travel is a great luxury. One needs time and money.

   Compound: Travel is a great luxury, for one needs time and money.

   Travel is a great luxury; one needs time and money.

   Complex: Travel is a great luxury because one needs time and money.

5. *Simple:* The need for a proper diet is important in any health program.

   All the junk food on the grocery shelves makes it hard to be consistent.

   Compound: The need for a proper diet is important in any health program, yet all the junk food on the grocery shelves makes it hard to be consistent.

   The need for a proper diet is important in any health program; however, all the junk food on the grocery shelves makes it hard to be consistent.

   Complex: Even though the need for a proper diet is important in any health program, all the junk food on the grocery shelves makes it hard to b consistent.

EXERCISE 2 (P. 59)

Answers will vary. These are sample answers.

1. *Simple:* The airline has begun its new route to the islands. Everyone is looking forward to flying there.

   Compound: The airline has begun its new route to the islands, so everyone is looking forward to flying there.

   The airline has begun its new route to the islands; consequently, everyone is looking forward to flying there.

   Complex: Ever since the airline began its new route to the islands, everyone has been looking forward to flying there.

2. *Simple:* The movie begins at nine o'clock. Let's have dinner before the show.

   Compound: The movie begins at nine o'clock, so let's have dinner before the show.

   The movie begins at nine o'clock; therefore, let's have dinner before the show.

   Complex: Since the movie begins at nine o'clock, let's have dinner before the show.

3. *Simple:* The studio audience screamed at the contestant. They wanted her to try for the big prize.

   Compound: The studio audience screamed at the contestant, for they wanted her to try for the big prize.

   The studio audience screamed at the contestant; they wanted her to try for the big prize.

   Complex: The studio audience screamed at the contestant because they wanted her to try for the big prize.

4. *Simple:* The baby covered his eyes. He thought he could disappear that way.

   Compound: The baby covered his eyes, for he thought he could disappear that way.

   The baby covered his eyes; he thought he could disappear that way.

   Complex: The baby covered his eyes because he thought he could disappear that way.

5. *Simple:* The waitress smiled. She told us the specials of the day.

   Compound: The waitress smiled, and she told us the specials of the day.

   The waitress smiled; she also told us the specials of the day.

   Complex: The waitress smiled as she told us the specials of the day.

Chapter 6: Making Sentence Parts Work Together

Subject–Verb Agreement within the Sentence

PRACTICE 1 (P. 64)
1. barks 2. wakes 3. become 4. deserve 5. throw

PRACTICE 2 (P. 66)
1. doesn't 2. were 3. doesn't 4. Were 5. doesn't

Making the Subject and Verb Agree

EXERCISE 1 (PP. 66)
1. price, has 2. decision, requires 3. She, doesn't
4. elevator operator or security guard, sees 5. committee, agrees 6. Potato chips and soda, are 7. One, is

Making Pronouns and Antecedents Agree

EXERCISE 1 (P. 72)

Answers will vary. These are sample answers.

1. The father mailed his son's high school yearbook to him.
2. No one wants his or her income reduced.
3. When a company fails to update its equipment, it often pays a price in the long run.
4. Women today have many more options open to them than ever before.
5. Everybody knows his or her own strengths best.
6. All of the workers anticipate their summer vacation.
7. If the campers want to eat quickly, they should help themselves.

Parallel Structure: Making a Series of Words, Phrases, or Clauses Balance within the Sentence

PRACTICE (P. 74)

1. dirty
2. sewing her own clothes
3. willingly explain material more than once

Revising Sentences for Parallel Structure

EXERCISE 1 (P. 74)

Answers will vary. These are sample answers.

1. Winter in Edmonton is very windy and <u>bitterly cold</u>.
2. I would prefer <u>fixing an old car</u> to watching television.
3. George is a helpful neighbour, a loyal friend, and a <u>dedicated father</u>.
4. The apartment is crowded and <u>dark</u>.
5. The dancer is slender and <u>graceful</u>.
6. The nursery was cheerful and <u>sunny</u>.
7. My friend loves to play chess, to read science fiction, and <u>to work out at the gym</u>.

EXERCISE 2 (P. 75)

Answers will vary. These are sample answers.

1. The dog had to choose between jumping over the fence or <u>digging a hole underneath it</u>.
2. She disliked going to the beach, hiking in the woods, and <u>going on picnics</u>.
3. As I looked down the city street, I could see the soft lights from restaurant windows, I could hear the mellow sounds of a nightclub band, and <u>I could sense the carefree moods of people walking by</u>.
4. The singers have been on several road tours, have recorded for two record companies, and <u>have expressed a desire to make a movie someday</u>.

5. They would rather order a pizza than <u>eat their sister's cooking</u>.
6. I explained to the teacher that my car had broken down, my books had been stolen, and <u>my assignment pad had been left at home</u>.
7. That night the prisoner was sick, discouraged, and <u>lonely</u>.

Revising Misplaced or Dangling Modifiers

EXERCISE 1 (P. 77)

Answers will vary. These are sample answers.

1. Wearing his tuxedo, Victor fed the dog.
2. While we were visiting Vancouver Aquarium, the killer whales entertained us.
3. Hoping to see the news, we had turned on the television set and were all ready by seven o'clock.
4. A woodpecker that had been considered extinct was found in Cuba.
5. After running over the hill, I noticed that the farm was visible in the valley below.
6. The truck, which was broken down on the highway, caused a traffic jam for kilometres.
7. I saw three spiders hanging from the ceiling in my bedroom.

Chapter 7: Solving More Problems with Verbs

Correcting Unnecessary Shifts in Verb Tense

EXERCISE 1 (P. 86)

Answers will vary. These are sample answers.

1. After I complete that writing course, I will take the required history course.
2. In the beginning of the movie, the action was slow; by the end, I was sitting on the edge of my seat.
3. The textbook gives the rules for writing a bibliography, but it doesn't explain how to do footnotes.
4. While working on her report in the library, my best friend lost her note cards and came to me for help.
5. The encyclopedia gave several pages of information about astronomy, but it didn't give anything about black holes.
6. The invitation requested that Juan be at the ceremony and that he attend the banquet as well.
7. This is an exciting book, but it has too many characters.

EXERCISE 2 (P. 86)

Doctor Norman Bethune **grew** up in Gravenhurst, Ontario. He was educated in Toronto and **served** as a stretcher bearer in World War I. He contracted tuberculosis and thereafter **devoted** himself to helping other victims of the disease when he **practised** surgery in Montreal. He also **invented** or redesigned twelve medical and surgical instruments. Bethune travelled to Russia in 1935, joined the Communist Party, and **went** to Spain in 1936, where he organized the first mobile blood transfusion service during the Spanish Civil War. Afte returning to Canada, he shortly left for overseas again, this time to China, where he helped the Chinese Communists in their fight against Japan. "Spain and China," he **wrote**, "are part of the same battle." While there, he contracted an infection and died. Mao's essay "In Memory of Norman Bethune," prescribed reading during China's Cultural Revolution, urges all Communists to low Bethune's example of selfless dedication to others. Bethune is the best-known Canadian to the Chinese, and many Chinese visit his Canadian birthplace.

What Is the Sequence of Tenses?

PRACTICE (P. 88)

1. have stopped   2. would have   3. will buy   4. had never been   5. liked   6. will soon be   7. is

Chapter Review Exercises
Solving Problems with Verbs

EXERCISE 1 (P. 92)

1. He ought not to drive so fast.
2. It is essential that Krista go to class tonight.
3. I wish I were a senior.
4. She sang for a huge crowd Saturday night.
5. I was shaken up by the accident *or* The accident shook me up.
6. The students studied the books.
7. My father asked me last night to help him build a deck.

Chapter 8: Punctuating Sentences Correctly

The Eight Basic Uses of the Comma

PRACTICE 1 (P. 95)

1. Problems with the water supply of Canada, the United States, Europe, and other parts of the wo are growing.
2. Water is colourless, tasteless, odourless, and free of calories.
3. You will use on an average day 90 L of water for flushing, 120 L for bathing and washing clothes, and 95 L for other uses.

4. It took 450 L of water to create the eggs you ate for breakfast, 13 250 L for the steak you might eat for dinner, and over 200 000 L to produce the steel used to make your car.
5. By 1970, the English–Wabigoon river system, which runs through Grassy Narrows, Ontario, had become polluted with mercury.

PRACTICE 2 (P. 95)

1. The most overused bodies of water are our rivers, but they continue to serve us daily.
2. Canadian cities often developed next to rivers, and industries followed soon after in the same locations.
3. The people of the industrial age can try to clean the water they use, or they can watch pollution take over.
4. The Great Lakes are showing signs of renewal, yet the struggle against pollution there must continue.
5. Most people have not been educated about the dangerous state of our water supply, nor are all members of Parliament fully aware of the problem.

PRACTICE 3 (P. 96)

1. To many people from Canada, the plans to supply more water to the United States seem unnecessary
2. However, people in the western United States know that they have no future without a good water supply.
3. In 1935, the federal government initiated irrigation schemes on the Canadian prairies.
4. Of the total, 1.4 percent of Canadian farmland was irrigated by 1981.
5. Learning from the past, modern farmers are trying to co-operate with nature.

PRACTICE 4 (P. 97)

1. Natural disasters, I believe, have not been historically significant.
2. They have, however, significantly affected the lives of many Canadians.
3. Canada's worst coal-mine disaster, at Hillcrest, Alberta, occurred on June 19, 1914.
4. In Springhill, Nova Scotia, furthermore, 424 persons were killed in the mines between 1881 and 1969.
5. Avalanches, storms, and floods, which are natural disasters, have also made their marks on the face of our country.

PRACTICE 5 (P. 98)

1. Dear, your tea is ready now.
2. I wonder, Samir, if the game has been cancelled.
3. Dad, could I borrow $5?
4. I insist, sir, on speaking with the manager.
5. Ayesha, is that you?

PRACTICE 6 (P. 98)

1. 4 876 454
2. 87 602
3. 156 439 600
4. 187 000
5. 10 000 000 000 000

PRACTICE 7 (P. 98)

1. "I won't," he insisted, "be a part of your scheme."
2. He mumbled, "I won't incriminate myself."
3. "I was told," the defendant explained, "to answer every question."
4. "This court," the judge announced, "will be adjourned."
5. "The jury," said Al Tarvin of *The Star*, "was hand-picked."

PRACTICE 8 (P. 99)

1. Kicking, the child was carried off to bed.
2. To John, Ben Wicks is the funniest cartoonist.
3. When you can, come and visit us.
4. Whoever that is, is going to be surprised.
5. Skin cancer seldom kills, doctors say.

Using the Comma Correctly

EXERCISE 1 (P. 99)

1. no commas
2. One breeding ground for these penguins, tiny Dassen Island, is northwest of Cape Town
3. Today, fewer than 60 000 penguins can be found breeding on this island.
4. At one time, seabirds that stole the penguins' eggs were the only threat to the funny-looking birds.
5. Human egg collectors, not to mention animals that simply take the eggs, have constantly reduced the penguin population.
6. However, the worst threat to the penguins is oil pollution.
7. If a passing tanker spills oil, many penguins can die.

EXERCISE 2 (P. 99)

1. The Commonwealth Games were first held in Hamilton, Ontario, in 1930.
2. The first games, known as the British Empire Games, attracted 400 competitors from eleven countries.
3. By 1978, during the Commonwealth Games in Edmonton, nearly 1500 athletes from 41 countries competed.
4. Canada has been a leading supporter of these games, which are held every four years.

5. Memorable performances, feats by both Canadian and non-Canadian athletes, have become a benchmark of the games.
6. In Edmonton, Canadian athletes won 45 gold, 31 silver, and 33 bronze medals in 1978.
7. Next to the Olympics, the Commonwealth Games are one of the world's best international competitions.

Using the Apostrophe

EXERCISE 1 (P. 101)

1. sun's   2. dress's   3. feet's   4. Antony and Maria's
5. nobody's   6. his   7. 1700's or 1700s   8. That's
9. boys'   10. book's

EXERCISE 2 (P. 102)

1. ice's   2. geese's   3. Ann's and Chris's   4. someone's   5. hers   6. two's   7. can't

Quotation Marks

PRACTICE 1 (P. 103)

1. "The Hot House" is one of the stories contained in Rosemary Sullivan's *More Stories by Canadian Women*.
2. Nellie McClung said, "I'll never believe I'm dead until I see it in the papers."
3. no quotation marks
4. "Punk" is a particular form of rock music.
5. She read the article "Whiz Kids" in *The Review*.

The Semicolon

PRACTICE 2 (P. 104)

1. One of the best ways to remember a vacation is to take numerous photos; one of the best ways to recall the contents of a book is to take notes.
2. The problem of street crime must be solved; otherwise, the number of vigilantes will increase.
3. The committee was made up of Kevin Corey, a writer; Anita Lightburn, a professor; and T.P. O'Connor, a politician.
4. The bank president was very cordial; however, he would not approve the loan.
5. Robots are being used in the factories of Japan; eventually they will be common in this country as well.

The Colon

PRACTICE 3 (P. 105)

1. Three Canadian-born comedians have become well known in the United States: John Candy, Aykroyd, and Catherine O'Hara.

2. The official has one major flaw in his personality: greed.

3. no colons

4. The college offers four courses in English literature: Romantic Poetry, Shakespeare's Plays, The British Short Story, and The Modern Novel.

5. Arriving at 6:15 in the morning, Marlene brought me a sausage and cheese pizza, soda, and a litre of ice cream.

The Dash and Parentheses

PRACTICE 4 (P. 106)

1. Herbert Simon is — and I don't think this is an exaggeration — a genius.

2. George Eliot (her real name was Mary Ann Evans) wrote *Silas Marner.*

3. You should — in fact I insist — see a doctor.

4. Unemployment brings with it a number of other problems (see the study by Brody, 1982)

5. Mass media (television, radio, movies, magazines, and newspapers) are able to transmit information over a wide range and to a large number of people.

Other Marks of Punctuation

EXERCISE 1 (P. 106)

1. To measure crime, sociologists have used three different techniques: official statistics, victimization surveys, and self-report studies.

2. "David" is one of the best-loved poems of Earle Birney.

3. The lake this summer has one major disadvantage for swimmers: weeds.

4. Farley Mowat has written numerous books for adults; however, he also writes very popular boo for children.

5. Tuberculosis (also known as consumption) has been nearly eliminated by medical science.

6. The Victorian Period (1837–1901) saw a rapid expansion in industry.

7. He promised me — I know he promised — that he would come to my graduation.

EXERCISE 2 (P. 106)

1. Many young people have two feelings about science and technology: awe and fear.

2. Mr. Doyle, the realtor; Mrs. Tong, the bank officer; and Ivan Petroff, the lawyer, are the three people to help work out the real estate transaction.

3. The book was entitled *English Literature: The Victorian Age.*

4. "I decided to walk to school," she said, "because the bus fare has been raised again."

5. She brought a bathing suit, towel, sunglasses, and several books to the beach. (no colon after *brought*)

6. The conference — I believe it is scheduled for sometime in January — will focus on the development of a new curriculum.

7. The complex lab experiment has these two major problems: too many difficult calculations and too many variables.

Chapter 9: Part I Review

There is more than one way to correct the fragments and run-ons in the rest of the exercises in this part. T following answers are possible.

Editing Sentences for Errors

EXERCISE 1 (P. 109)

1. Gypsies now are living in many countries of the world.

2. The international community of scientists agrees that these Gypsies originally came from India thousands of years ago.

3. After the original Gypsies left India, they went to Persia; there they divided into groups.

4. One branch of Gypsies went west to Europe, while the other group decided to go east.

5. C

6. C

7. Today, Gypsy families may be found from Canada to Chile, living much as their ancestors did thousands of years ago.

EXERCISE 3 (P. 111)

1. The laser beam, a miracle of modern science, already has many practical uses in today's world.

2. Laser beams are narrow, highly concentrated beams of light that burn brighter than the light of the sun.

3. Scientists have found many possible military uses for the laser, but they are hoping these can be converted into constructive uses.

4. C

5. The possibility of making a laser was first described in 1958, and two years later in California, the first laser beam was created.

6. Since they are so precise, laser beams are used in medicine to help make a specific diagnosis and to perform operations such as repairing delicate retinas and removing cancerous tumours.

7. The future uses of the laser seem endless, and it is up to us whether we want to use this invention for war or for peaceful purposes.

PART II: MASTERING THE PARAGRAPH

Chapter 10: Working with Topic Sentences and Controlling Ideas

Finding the Topic Sentence of a Paragraph

EXERCISE 1 (P. 119)

1. The air shaft was a horrible invention.
2. Anything can happen at a county agricultural fair.

EXERCISE 2 (P. 119)

1. The Canadian game of hockey was born during long northern winters uncluttered by things to do.
2. The brain is one of the most remarkable organs, a part of the body that we have only begun to investigate.

Finding the Topic in the Topic Sentence

EXERCISE 1 (P. 120)

1. Remodelling an old house   2. College work   3. A well-made suit   4. Growing up near a museum   5. My favourite room in the house   6. A student who goes to school full-time and also works part-time   7. One of the disadvantages of skiing

EXERCISE 2 (P. 120)

1. basement   2. Pierre Trudeau   3. an identical twin   4. rail transportation   5. the change that had come over my friend   6. current tax laws   7. *Reader's Digest*

Finding the Controlling Idea

EXERCISE 1 (P. 121)

1. T: vigorous exercise CI: reduces stress   2. T: St. John's and Corner Brook CI: differ   3. T: television violence CI: causes aggressive behaviour in children   4. T: athletic scholarships available to women CI: increasing   5. T: caffeine CI: adverse effects   6. T: Madame Benoit CI: amusing personality   7. T: training a parakeet to talk CI: takes great patience

EXERCISE 2 (P. 122)

1. T: piano lessons CI: disaster   2. T: training of Japanese police CI: different   3. T: Olympic champion CI: characteristics   4. T: unethical financial dealings CI: negative impact   5. T: bicycle ride along the coast CI: breathtaking   6. T: grocery store CI: where people waste money   7. T: being an only child CI: not bad

Chapter 11: Working with Supporting Details

Distinguishing a Supporting Detail from a Restatement of the Main Idea

EXERCISE 1 (P. 130)

1. a. SD   b. R   c. SD   d. SD
2. a. SD   b. SD   c. R   d. SD

Chapter 12: Developing Paragraphs: Narration

Working for Coherence: Using Details in Order of Time Sequence

EXERCISE 1 (P. 138)

1. 2, 5, 1, 3, 6, 4
2. 4, 5, 1, 6, 2, 3

EXERCISE 2 (P. 139)

1. 1, 3, 2, 5, 4, 6, 7
2. 1, 3, 2, 7, 4, 5, 6

Chapter 13: Developing Paragraphs: Description

Recognizing Sensory Images

EXERCISE 1 (P. 152)

Paragraph by Ian Adams

Sight: bottles of beer splintering against each other; wet, mangled cartons, bottles piling up on the conveyor; fore man running; four acres of machinery; conveyor belts

Sound: crunching smash, bell ringing, jangling vibrations, foreman screaming, roar of machinery, teeth-jarring rattle, clinking bottles, clanking metal conveyor belts

Smell: stink of warm beer, sour sweat of my body

EXERCISE 2 (P. 153)

Paragraph by Heather Robertson

Sight: air frozen into little slivers of glass, light from the full moon reflected in the crystallized air, people scurrying, white clouds of breath, congealed breath like balloons in comic strips, tears running down cheeks

Touch: the cold freezes hands and feet to blocks of wood, it hurts to walk more than a few feet

Working for Coherence: Using Space Order

EXERCISE 1 (P. 156)
2. 3, 5, 2, 1, 4
3. 2, 3, 1, 4

Chapter 14: Developing Paragraphs: Process

Coherence in Process: Order in Logical Sequence

EXERCISE 2 (P. 167)
7, 5, 1, 8, 2, 6, 3, 9, 4

Chapter 15: Developing Paragraphs: Comparison or Contrast

Evaluating the Two-Part Topic

EXERCISE 1 (P. 177)
Answers could vary depending on the purpose of the paragraph.
3. too broad   4. suitable   5. too broad   6. too broad

Working for Coherence: Recognizing the Two Approaches to Ordering Material

EXERCISE 1 (P. 180)
1. block; differences   2. block; differences

Chapter 17: Developing Paragraphs: Cause and Effect

Finding Causes and Effects in Paragraphs

EXERCISE 1 (P. 204)
Cause: 1. nervous tension
　　　　2. diet
　　　　　　a. dependency on caffeine
　　　　　　b. allergy to salt
　　　　　　c. low blood sugar
　　　　3. environment (allergy to household chemicals)
　　　　　　a. polishes
　　　　　　b. waxes
　　　　　　c. bug killers
　　　　　　d. paint
Effect: 1. cause nausea
　　　　2. interrupt sleep
　　　　3. adversely affect physical and emotional state

4. taking drugs could have negative side effects
5. can reduce productivity at work, to the point of regular absences
6. interrupt family life
7. make people discouraged and even depressed

Looking for the Causal Relationship

EXERCISE 1 (P. 207)
1. T   2. C   3. T   4. C   5. C   6. T   7. C

PART III: STRUCTURING THE COLLEGE ESSAY

Chapter 18: Moving from the Paragraph to the Essay

How to Recognize the Thesis Statement

PRACTICE (P. 220)
1. F   2. T   3. T   4. F

Recognizing the Thesis Statement

EXERCISE 1 (P. 221)
1. thesis   2. title   3. fact   4. thesis   5. title   6. fact
7. fact

EXERCISE 2 (P. 221)
1. fact   2. thesis   3. fact   4. fact   5. title   6. fact
7. title

Finding Transitional Devices

EXERCISE 1 (P. 230)
(However), use of the word (art) is not relevant when we describe African "art" because it is really a European term that at first grew out of Greek philosophy and was later reinforced by European culture. The use of other (terms,) such as *exotic* (art), *primitive* (art), (art) *sauvage*, and so on, to delineate differences is just as misleading. Most such (terms) are pejorative — art is on a lower cultural level. (Levels) of culture are irrelevant here, since African and European attitudes toward the creative act are so different. (Since) there is no term in our language to distinguish between the essential differences in thinking, it is best (then) to describe standards of African art.

(African art) attracts because of its powerful emotional content and its beautiful abstract form. (Abstract) treatment of (form) describes most often — with bare essentials of line, shape, texture, and pattern — intense energy and sublime spirituality. Hundreds of distinct cultures and languages and many types of people have created over 1000 different styles that defy classification. Each art and craft (form) has its own history and its own aesthetic content. (But) there are some common denominators (always with exceptions).

Chapter 24: Writing under Pressure

Methods of Development

EXERCISE 1 (P. 281)

1. narration   2. comparison or contrast   3. discussion
4. definition   5. summary

APPENDICES

Appendix C: Solving Spelling Problems

Words Commonly Mispronounced

EXERCISE (P. 347)

1. separate	6. quantity
2. probably	7. literature
3. arctic	8. hungry
4. surprise	9. handsome
5. tragedy	10. favourite

_ie_ and _ei_ Words

EXERCISE (P. 349)

1. sleigh	6. deceit
2. believe	7. niece
3. siege	8. weight
4. veil	9. protein
5. leisure	10. ancient

Forming the Plurals of Nouns

EXERCISE (P. 351)

1. puppies	6. loaves
2. mothers-in-law	7. matches
3. teeth	8. mixes
4. cameos	9. enemies
5. phenomena	10. bags

Should the Final Consonant be Doubled?

PRACTICE (P. 354)

slip: yes, yes, slipping; _crack:_ no, no, cracking; _broil:_ no, no, broiling; _win:_ yes, yes, winning;

control: controlling; _fever:_ feverish; _compel:_ compelled; _differ:_ difference; _begin:_ beginning

Doubling the Final Consonant When Adding Endings That Begin With Vowels

EXERCISE (P. 354)

1. bitten	6. thinner
2. occurrence	7. transferred
3. wavering	8. sailing
4. preferred	9. excellent
5. preference	10. omitted

Adding Endings to Words Ending in -_y_

EXERCISE (P. 356)

1. keys	4. cries
2. loneliness	5. prayer
3. crying	6. crayfish
7. monkeying	9. theories
8. beautiful	10. ceremonial

One Word or Two?

EXERCISE (P. 357)

1. bedroom	6. Everyone
2. grandmother	7. maybe
3. already	8. cannot
4. all together	9. nearby
5. always	10. Nevertheless

Appendix D. Capitalization

Capitalization

EXERCISE (P. 363)

1. Italian   2. Canadian Rockies   3. Bible   4. University of Alberta   5. Halloween   6. Bell Canada, Friday, Winnipeg, Manitoba   7. Cobalt 60, Canadian, Dr. Donald Green   8. Why   9. Canadian Auto Workers   10. West, "A Prairie Home Companion"

Appendix E: Irregular Verbs

Irregular Verbs

EXERCISE (PP. 367)

1. caught	6. slid
2. crept	7. rose
3. fled	8. quit
4. burst	9. frozen
5. ridden	10. wrung

Credits

Pp. 299–301, Rick Salutin, "Modern Opinion: A Hot-air Balloon That's Lost Ballast," *The Globe and Mail*, October 11, 1996. Reprinted by permission of the author.

Pp. 301–303, Amy Willard Cross, "Life in the Stopwatch Lane," *The Globe and Mail*, July 5, 1990, p. A18. Reprinted by permission of the author.

Pp. 303–304, Joe Fiorito, "A Bowl of Red," from *Comfort Me with Apples* (Montreal: Nuage Editions, 1994), pp. 65–66. Copyright © 1994 Joe Fiorito. Reprinted by permission of Nuage Editions.

Pp. 305–308, Himani Bannerji, "The Other Family." Reprinted by permission of the author.

Pp. 309–11, David Suzuki, "Ancestors — The Genetic Source," from *Metamorphosis*. Copyright © 1989 by David Suzuki. Reprinted by permission of the author.

Pp. 312–14, John Gray, "You're Thinking of Getting a *What?*" from *I Love Mom: An Irreverent History of the Tattoo*. Reprinted by permission of Key Porter Books Limited.

Pp. 315–18, Rick Boulton, "Recollections of Jacques Plante." This article first appeared in *Maple Leaf Magazine*, the official game-day program of the Toronto Maple Leafs Hockey Club. Boulton served as editor from 1976 to 1982. Reprinted by permission of the author.

Pp. 319–21, Tony Leighton, "Electronic Confidants," *Canadian Geographic*, November/December 1955, pp. 64–66. Reprinted with the author's permission.

Index

Reader Reply Card

We are interested in your reaction to *The Canadian Writer's Workplace*, Third Edition. With your comments, we can improve this book in future editions. Please help us by completing this questionnaire.

1. What was your reason for using this book?

   ☐ university course   ☐ college course
   ☐ continuing education course   ☐ personal interest
   ☐ other (specify)

2. If you are a student, please identify your school and the course in which you used this book.

3. Which chapters or parts of this book did you use? Which did you omit?

4. Did you find the additional readings at the end of the book useful? Why or why not?

5. Which reading(s) did you like best? Which did you like least?

6. What did you like best about this book?

7. What did you like least about this book?

8. Please identify any topics you think should be added to future editions.

9. Please add any comments or suggestions.

10. May we contact you for further information?

   Name: _____

   Address: _____

   _____

   Phone: _____

(fold here and tape shut)

- -

MAIL ➤ **POSTE**

Canada Post Corporation / Société canadienne des postes

Postage paid
If mailed in Canada

Port payé
si posté au Canada

Business Reply

Réponse d'affaires

0116870**399**   **01**

0116870399-M8Z4X6-BR01

Larry Gillevet
Director of Product Development
HARCOURT BRACE & COMPANY, CANADA
55 HORNER AVENUE
TORONTO, ONTARIO
M8Z 9Z9